Ben le Vay's

ECCENTRIC

LONDON

a Practical Guide to a Curious City

Bradt Travel Guides Ltd, UK
The Globe Pequot Press Inc, USA

Bradt

London Elvis impersonator: Bloomsbury Suede Shoes, All Shook Upminster and Return to Sydenham? (CH)

A Harry Potter spell gone wrong? Pavement performers at London Bridge make a startling sight – and notice the baby! (AC)

Portobello Road has a fabulous antique market, and it's not tricky to work out what this avid collector hoards (DR)

ECCENTRIC LONDONERS

Has London got a good selection of characters? Yes, just the odd one or two!

Beards, perms, umbrellas – the Europride Parade is deeply eccentric (CH

Strange Fruit is a performing-arts company whose exhibitions include people swaying on 4-metre-high poles (as here in Docklands) or emerging from illuminated orbs: wacky, but brilliant (SF)

Just a tick, mate: you'll never need a watch if this chap's in the vicinity (MK)

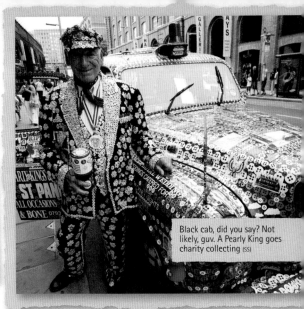

Black cab, did you say? Not likely, guv. A Pearly King goes charity collecting (SS)

Eccentric collector Maurice Collins wears a 19th-century hat-measurer on his head and holds a pair of Victorian skates, surrounded by his collection of over 1,000 bizarre antique gadgets (PAI)

Well, stone me! Are you a statue or a street performer, petal? (SS)

The human peacock: Notting Hill Carnival parades wonderfully wacky way-over-the-top costumes (SS)

FRYING PAN ALLEY, E.I.

Some say this name derives from ironmongers hanging frying pans outside their shops as a means of attracting business. Theories on a postcard, please (JR)

SIGNS OF SERIOUS ECCENTRICITY

Keep your eyes peeled going around London, and you'll never stop marvelling at deeply strange sights.

This tattoo studio in Camden welcomes punters in with 'evil from the needle' (CH)

BY ORDER
NATIONAL HIGHWAYS AGENCY
THIS WALL IS A DESIGNATED
GRAFFITI AREA

PLEASE TAKE YOUR LITTER HOME
EC. REF. URBA 23/368

Celebrated urban artist Banksy likes to try the councils' patience: in this case, by creating a designated graffiti area

Some imaginative graffiti on the wall of a Camden carwash (CH)

Funky footwear covers the roof of this shop in Camden (CH)

Wired-up or is it weird-up London? The larger-than-life giant socket on the electricity sub station at Ganton Street, Soho (SS)

The surreal sculpture *Out of Order* by David Mach sits in Old London Road, Kingston. It's what you feel like doing when the umpteenth phone box has swallowed your 30p for no service... (BL)

Have I got noose for you: the ornament outside the The Prospect of Whitby pub is a sobering reminder of where some customers took their last drop (JG)

A legendary Fleet Street pub, the Cheshire Chees was purportedly the 'local' of Dr Johnson, creato of the first English dictionary (DG)

BARMY BOOZERS

There's no such thing as a normal London pub. You just have to stand there and drink it all in.

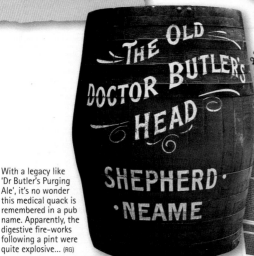

With a legacy like 'Dr Butler's Purging Ale', it's no wonder this medical quack is remembered in a pub name. Apparently, the digestive fire-works following a pint were quite explosive... (RG)

The namesake of Dirty Dick's, Bishopsgate, spent his life in broken-hearted squalor after the death of his bride-to-be. It inspir Dickens (JR)

Blooming marvellous: The Churchill Arms in Kensington goes a bit nuts with the flower displays (DG)

Ben le Vay's

ECCENTRIC

LONDON

a Practical Guide to a Curious City

Bradt

Third edition published April 2012
First published 2002
Bradt Travel Guides Ltd
IDC House, The Vale, Chalfont St Peter, Bucks SL9 9RZ, England
www.bradtguides.com
Published in the USA by The Globe Pequot Press Inc,
PO Box 480, Guilford, Connecticut 06437-0480

ISBN: 978 1 84162 394 8

British Library Cataloguing in Publication Data
A catalogue record for this book is available from the British Library

Photographs
Robin Brittain, twitter.com/robinbrittain (RB); Alison Cousin (AC); Dreamstime.
com: Chris Dorney (CD/D), Elena Rostunova (ER/D); Robert Gale (RG); Johnny
Grimes (JG); Deborah Guber (DG); Cath Harries (CH); iStockPhoto.com: abbesses
(a/iS); Mark Kerrison (MK); Benedict le Vay (BL); Press Association Images (PAI);
James Rice (JR); Deborah Ripley (DR); Nigel Rudyard (NR); Shutterstock.com:
dutourdumonde (d/S), Neil Lang (NL/S); Strange Fruit (SF); SuperStock (SS);
Wikimedia Commons: Andrew Dunn (AD/WC)

Illustrations
Cover artwork and in-text silhouettes Neil Gower (*www.neilgower.com*)
In-text cartoons Rowan Barnes-Murphy (*www.rowanbarnes-murphy.com*)

Maps
David McCutcheon (*www.dvdmaps.co.uk*) based on source material from Trialzoom Ltd

Typeset from the author's disc by D & N Publishing, Baydon, Wiltshire
Production managed by Jellyfish Print Solutions; printed in India

ACKNOWLEDGEMENTS

Dr David le Vay, Hugh Dawson, Jeff Shaw, Jim Garrod, Bill Smith, Flavia Gapper, Jenni Marsh, Ailsa Leslie, Ernie McLaughlin, Sue Barnes, Felix le Vay, Martin le Vay, James Levy, Richard Griffin, Kelvin Wynne and many, many other Londoners. Plus the editors and typesetter who tried to keep up with the many changes, and the ever-creative designers and illustrators. The mistakes, however, are all mine!

DEDICATION

For my father, David le Vay, who died while the first edition of this book was being finished. Typically, he'd done a deal whereby I'd buy his last book and he promised to buy this one. I should have known. Meanwhile he knocked off a radio play and another book about a medieval monk at the age of 86. That was the calibre of the man. But at least I can now reveal he's the angry surgeon quoted in the Earl's Court section.

CONTENTS

Key to maps

Key to map symbols

★ START	Start of walk		🏺	Museum/art gallery
←	Walk direction		🏰	Historic castle/fortification
🚉	Train station		✝	Church/cathedral
⊖	Underground station		☾	Mosque
Ⓓ	Docklands Light Railway (DLR)		✚	Hospital
	Market		🛈	Statue/monument
	Park/garden		𝒊	Tourist information
✕	Restaurant		✉	Post office
🍺	Pub		►	Golf course
🎭	Theatre		🅿	Parking
wc	Public toilets		🧘	Buddhist temple

INTRODUCTION

THE GREATEST CITY IN THE WORLD

London is the greatest big city in the world,
and Londoners need reminding of this even if visitors don't:

- Greatest for theatre, with the National and the Royal Shakespeare Company (RSC), the Globe, the thriving commercial West End, the massive widespread fringe and pub theatre scenes: 159 theatres putting on more plays than anywhere on earth.
- Greatest for nightlife and food (every kind and quality imaginable on the planet in 8,500 restaurants), 59 Michelin stars, hundreds of wonderful pubs and bars.
- Greatest for diversity and tolerance, with more living religions and languages than any other city on the planet.
- Greatest for art, museums and galleries, many of them free or little known (and listed later in this guide), while others such as the British Museum, Dulwich, Greenwich, British Library, Somerset House, etc, have been recently reinvigorated with vast investments of billions of pounds. There is also the dynamic and exciting Tate Modern (already by far the world's most popular modern art museum with 5.2 million visitors in its first year) plus the constantly newly creative artists such as graffiti king Banksy.
- Greatest for the mix in architecture: from the soaring majesty of Westminster Abbey and the unbelievable antiquity of Westminster Hall to the maverick office blocks such as the Gherkin and the Shard; from the low-rise gangland shabbiness of east and 'sarf' London to the white stately stucco and pillars and massive brick mansion blocks of the middle, north and west; from charming ancient villages subsumed within the metropolis to superb Nash terraces with more elegant curves than Nigella Lawson.

- Greatest for layer upon layer of fascinating history in its mellowed, ancient architecture and unique set of churches.
- Greatest for newspapers, with more and better papers every day than anywhere else on the planet.
- Greatest for fashion (so that even Paris shops for couturiers here).
- Greatest for cabbies and their 'knowledge' of its reassuringly absurd medieval street plan.
- Greatest for ceremonials – not a boring president, but a real king or queen in a real palace with real guards in bearskin hats (but with modern sub-machine guns) parading outside; Gurkhas from the high Himalayas, with their lethal kukri knives; Aussies in bush hats and rifles; or Highlanders in kilts, with daggers in their socks. The world's greatest royal coronations, funerals and weddings, and the unending soap opera that real royalty affords.
- Greatest for classical music, with its unequalled set of orchestras, wonderful concert halls, and incomparable Proms concerts, as well as for rock and pop music and the stars they produce.
- Greatest for shopping, with 29,000 shops where people spend £62 billion a year (more than anywhere else on earth, and more than LA, Milan, Rome, Madrid and Berlin combined).
- Greatest for innovative thought, with 22 universities – two in the world top ten, dozens of other colleges and 400,000 students.
- Greatest for liberty and freedom of speech, with its unarmed police, Speakers' Corner, and Her Majesty's Loyal Opposition.
- Greatest for architectural curiosities and – oddly – for the 'village' charm it somehow maintains within its urban sprawl, giving at its best, and for the lucky few, the most pleasant suburbia on the planet.
- Greatest for transport, with the world's biggest yet clearest Tube network, its renowned double-decker buses, and brilliant Boris bikes.
- Greatest for its wonderful open spaces, from the unmatchable jewel-in-the-crown royal parks – including the fabulous Richmond Park and Wimbledon Common – to the unique London squares.

But is it greatest for eccentricities and oddities, quirks and queries? This book provides the answer.

...AND THE DRAWBACKS

I had to utter that gushing but deserved paean of praise not only for visitors but for Londoners, who take the place for granted; but yes, I admit London has its downside. It's very expensive if you don't earn London wages; the litter; the graffiti; the inability of the authorities to match up the homeless with the ludicrously priced empty properties (they could have three houses each at the last count); the pickpockets on the Tube; the rudest shop and catering staff this side of Hong Kong (well, not *all* of them!).

But in many of those great claims London just cannot be rivalled. London by the early 21st century had undergone another cultural renaissance that nobody predicted. It is far more deeply rooted than the much-vaunted Swinging Sixties era when London was said by some to lead the fashion world. That was a thin, gimmicky-but-colourful veneer consisting of Carnaby Street and the King's Road, mini skirts and Mini cars; the bulk of the city, however, was still poor, grey, strait-laced, sexually repressed, artistically stunted, culinarily deprived, architecturally appalling and struggling to recover from the grim, rationed decades of the 1940s and 1950s.

Today, the city's rebirth in terms of food, art, architecture, etc, isn't limited to totally isolated efforts such as the Festival Hall (a fifties attempt to keep culture alive amidst the bombsites) but goes root and branch right across the capital and its population.

And what a changing population! It is the most linguistically diverse city in the world, a polyglot cornucopia of languages and dialects. A recent survey showed that 307 languages were spoken in the city's school playgrounds, with about 100,000 children speaking one of south Asia's four main languages; but up there in the top 30 were Akan (Ashanti) at 6,000 children, Farsi (Persian) at 3,300, and Tagalog (Filipino) at 1,600. Perhaps the loneliest kids in the playground were those who spoke Mbum (it's from Cameroon, I'm told) – there were only two of them – and the only Pidgin speaker, poor thing.

Against this bubbling background it's perhaps harder to spot an individual eccentric because there's so much diversity. Being odd or different isn't unusual, as you'll soon find if you watch people. Unusual *is* usual in London.

ECCENTRICS AHOY

Indeed, from time to time an obviously eccentric Londoner hoves into view. For example, when Jeff Smith, 60, from Muswell Hill tried to drive two sheep across Tower Bridge not long ago, City police stopped him. Then he explained that, as a Freeman of the City of London, he had that right. After checking he wasn't pulling the wool over their eyes, Mr Smith, Clover and Little Man were allowed across by the police. And if you want to drive geese and swine through Dulwich, you will find fixed charges for each sheep or goat.

A constant stream of eccentric explorers sets out from London. In 2001, Jim Shekhdar from Northwood rowed to Australia having spent an astonishing nine months and a day rowing from South America right across the world's biggest ocean. Actually, he didn't row the whole way because he was tossed out in the surf as he arrived. Had he lost his sense of humour? 'I always knew that damned boat wanted to reach Australia before me,' he said as he waded ashore after it. Why did he do it? 'I had to lose some weight.'

Nor is it just all eccentric *old* Londoners. In 2011, an utterly amazing lad called George Atkinson, from Surbiton, southwest London became at just 16 the youngest person in the world to scale the highest mountains in every continent by reaching the top of Everest.

He had started the Seven Summits challenge at age 11 by scaling Kilimanjaro in Tanzania. He followed this with Russia's Elbrus in 2007 and Indonesia's Carstensz Pyramid and Argentina's Aconcagua in 2008. Then it was on to Mount McKinley in Alaska and Mount Vinson in Antarctica.

After doing all that by 16, presumably George will have to look for other planets' mountains.

Eccentricity goes to the top in London society, too. This colours such mundane acts as answering the telephone, as can be demonstrated by the surprisingly complementary tales told by two people about their well-known fathers. One was Tim Healey, son of Denis, later Lord Healey. Apparently, when Denis lived at No 11 Downing Street as Chancellor of the Exchequer, replete with the full panoply of state, red boxes and civil servants, Denis would sometimes answer the phone, 'Aro? Chinese laundly?' Equally, sitting in exactly the same Radio 4 studio with me some months later, novelist Sophie Parkin was discussing her family's eccentric parents. 'My father always answers the phone: "Toad of Toad Hall". He thinks he *is* Toad. He always wears green and has a car that goes "parp, parp" in the same way.'

There are countless examples: there's a crusty old admiral who perfected the very difficult art of sailing backwards down the Thames and persuaded others to do the same annually for a race; and there's a man who drives round in a motorised four-poster bed.

Even the so-called great and good can eccentrically deflate themselves – literally in some cases. Poet Sir Stephen Spender's diary records how one night, thinking himself to be alone, he broke wind after the opera ('It was much louder after five hours of Wagner than I had dreamed possible') causing a group of unseen bystanders in the dark to cheer wildly. He wrote: 'I saw how an incident like this divides people into two categories – those who would laugh and those who would be shocked.' In this book we are in the laughing category.

Talking about humour, or attempts at it, I offer my apologies to those who don't enjoy awful puns and wisecracks. I'm encouraged as I write this book by the occasional bursts of laughter from those reading already completed chapters, but I realise it won't be to everybody's taste.

All I can say is that in buying this book you have shown that you don't want one of those soulless, written-by-committee guidebooks which say 'This is the Tower of London and this is how you get there', but something which gives you more, and tells you something you didn't already know.

I was born in London, have studied and worked and lived all over it for half a century, so I can bring a personal involvement to many places and events. It should bring the real subject – the greatest city in the world and the people who live here – more vividly to life.

SQUALOR & ELEGANCE CHEEK BY JOWL: SHARP DIVISIONS

London fascinates both in how little it changes – the Roman street plan of the City survives, overlaid with those medieval complexities that were not ironed out in the hurried rebuilding that took place after the Great Fire of 1666, despite several grand plans for boring American-style grid patterns being proposed for London's streets – and how much it changes.

In the latter case, consider the now rather posh and respectable area around the Tate Gallery, Millbank. The huge and gloomy Millbank Penitentiary loomed over this area until it was demolished in 1890. A tunnel under the road, still marked by a special bollard, is where the miserable convicts were led *down under* from the penitentiary to the waiting ships for transportation to Australia. That vast land is hence still known as 'Down Under' (see page 196). Between here and Westminster was 'the Devil's Acre', a teeming, disease-infested warren of brothels, opium dens and gambling haunts, and a no-go area for the authorities. Ironically, it was like this because of the sanctuary rules associated with Westminster Abbey. Before that Millbank was where the wind and water mills of Westminster Abbey turned in rural isolation, interrupted only by the horse ferry that gave its name to Horseferry Road. Then again, it is hard to imagine anything more respectable than this rather pompous area today. So the area has transformed itself totally at least twice.

But the geography of London as well as the history is subject to surprisingly sudden shifts. The refreshing thing about wandering about London is how the character of the place can change utterly within 100 yards. Time and time again when researching this book that has surprised me.

Just a few yards from snootiest Mayfair or bookish Fitzrovia one finds oneself diving into Soho sleaze: a quiet Bloomsbury Square full of intellectuals is only a few paces from teeming streets with staggering drunks and hurrying messengers; while the shopaholic bustle of Kensington High Street's designer-label junkies and poseurs soon gives way to leafy Georgian peace and splendour to the south, and in the north to fascinating bystreets.

This, of course, is nothing new. A fascinating book, the *History of London in Maps*, includes Booth's 1889 Poverty Map. This mapped London by social class, by colour-coding the sides of the streets, and thus divided the capital into classes ranging from 'Upper-middle class and Upper classes. Wealthy' (a nice cheerful yellow) down through six classes including 'Poor. 18s to 21s a week for a moderate family' (blue), 'Very poor, casual. Chronic want' (dark blue) to 'Lowest class. Vicious, semi-criminal' (a gloomy black). It's quite amazing today that anyone should categorise people's wealth and morals like this, although of course many people categorise others to some degree. Whole streets, written off as 'Vicious, semi-criminal', would probably sue today.

Yet to a Victorian world this made sense. People were, on the whole, set in their classes, and the rich were the poor's 'betters', while the poor were either the deserving poor, and worth using as servants, or they were criminals. Many Victorians believed you could spot the criminal classes by the shape of their heads. I remember a hymn at school which included a line about social order being ordained by God: 'The rich man in his castle, the poor man at his gate, God made them high and lowly, and ordered their estate.'

What's totally fascinating about those old maps is how one end of a street can be one class, while the other end can be five classes above or below it. This was no coincidence.

The rookeries: crime on a Dickensian scale

Another factor in London's astonishing social blend was the existence of the 'rookeries', great, steaming, slum warrens of theft, alcoholism, gambling, prostitution, insanitary diseases, orphans, poverty – the world that Dickens captures pretty realistically, historians agree, in *Oliver Twist*.

The inhabitants of the early 19th-century rookeries, where police dared not penetrate for fear of being beaten senseless by lawless lowlife, and which surrounded London, needed to be near well-to-do respectable districts, or areas in which the rich indulged their pleasures and vices, to have something to prey on. This parasitical relationship explains why, historically, there were sudden shifts in the social standing of neighbouring areas, differences that are still echoed on the ground today.

The Victorian spirit of social campaigning, which found a voice in organisations such as the Temperance Society and the Salvation Army, pops up in another map in the *History of London in Maps*, which showed pubs as red dots. 'A modern plague of London, a scarlet fever!' the reformers cried. Pubs were so thick on the ground in Soho that the dots merged into a red mass. Predictably, they are far more common in poor areas (1,059 in Whitechapel and Stepney alone) than rich ones (about 25 in Mayfair), and that's still the case. We have not, it seems, much escaped our social history. You can still make a crime map pretty easily by making a pub map.

Covent Garden, however, is an example of an area whose character has changed radically over time. When it was built in the early 17th century, it was home to many titled families and was the very epitome of elegance. Yet, less than a century later, the constant process of the rich moving westwards – away from London's pollution and towards fresh air and the court at Kensington – left Covent Garden as the main centre of prostitution and drunkenness.

Yet the late 20th century saw the Royal Opera House completely refurbished, bringing back the so-called great and the good, with the market banished to Nine Elms on the other side of the river, and the lovely 17th-century buildings being converted for shopping, drinking and the entertainment of the international leisured classes. Re-enter the pickpockets…

LONDON'S WEIRD POLITICS

This city is odd that it has two mayors. The one with the grander title and pompous ceremonial is unimportant, frankly – the Lord Mayor of London. Splendid chap, or chappess, no doubt, but only in charge of the City, being the financial district, and then only in a minor way (akin to the mayor of Lambeth). But with lots of eccentric old ceremonies (including employing the City Remembrancer to remember some things and forget others). The other one, the Mayor of London, has some real power and is in charge of billions of pounds and resides in the 'Glass Testicle' (Londoners' nickname for new City Hall next to Tower Bridge).

Nearly all the candidates for this mayoralty, some may feel, are on an eastbound District Line train. That is, they are halfway to Barking: which is fine by me, as that makes them eccentric in one way or another.

Consider the short record of the Mayoralty of London, a recent invention. What other capital city, when given three official party candidates for the important position of mayor in 2000, would instead vote for a man with no party and, frankly, a pretty mixed track record? I mean, of course, amiable, nasal, newt-fancying Ken Livingstone, once known as 'Red Ken' when he led the late unlamented Greater London Council (abolished for being too loony lefty).

Later, after Ken passed his 'best before' date, Londoners chose Alexander Boris de Pfeffel Johnson, known as Boris Johnson or Bojo. Tousle-haired, calling himself a 'one-man melting pot' for being Christian-Muslim-Jewish in heritage, descended from two English kings, apparently a bumbling scruff but in fact intensely clever (or maybe it's a double bluff!), he got away with stuff that no other politician would dream of trying: quoting Latin at ignorant tabloid reporters, having a love life worthy of Brian Rix (allegedly), marrying two glamorous women who sound like Leyland car models: Allegra and Marina.

The tabloids gleefully attached his name to anything he was responsible for: Boris bikes, Boris island (the possible new airport); Borismasters (the replacement Routemaster buses). He was just hilarious.

Whoever is mayor by the time you read this, it will be some nuttier-than-a-fruitcake larger-than-life character. That's how London likes them.

Meanwhile London continues its own way, bustling with interest and reinvention, teeming with ideas, stuffed with more odd nooks and crannies than one person can ever see, while in the midst of it all, Old Father Thames keeps rolling along, continuously carrying all our yesterdays down towards the sea – 2,000 amazing years of London history. What a city!

GETTING ABOUT

Although there are maps with the walks in this book, you'll need to refer to a Tube map and ideally for further exploration buy a good street guide, the *A–Z* being the best. Or equivalent phone apps.

Public transport costs in London are on first sight truly, madly, deeply unreasonable. They preach at us to get out of our cars then wallop us heavily for doing so. It seems you can't win.

But you can! From a visitor's point of view, there are mitigating factors and ways to beat the system. It's not all bad news.

SAVING NUMBER ONE: WALK MORE Visitors tend to see London as isolated pockets of land around Tube stations instead of a real city. It's quicker to walk from Trafalgar Square to Big Ben than catch the Tube, and more interesting. So consult a real map as well as a Tube map when planning your journey; your destination may be only an interesting stroll away with better views than a Tube tunnel wall.

SAVING NUMBER TWO: OFF-PEAK TRAVELCARDS These are paper go-as-you-like tickets sold for the relevant zones (concentric areas – Central London is Zone 1, Highgate is so far out it is Zone 3, for example), including red buses, ordinary trains, trams, DLR and scheduled riverboat services as well as Tubes (but not Heathrow Express). They save you a packet, as well as umpteen times queueing up when you could have just waltzed straight through.

SAVING NUMBER THREE: OYSTER CARDS These are prepaid plastic smart cards which you load up with money then make huge savings and avoid having to buy any more tickets. The other good news is that if you do lots of journeys in a day the total is capped to the cost of what a Travelcard would have been. The bad news is that you have to buy one for a small fee in the first place to load up (you can do this from overseas in advance at *www.tfl.gov.uk* and at stations here, or on Eurostar trains and some planes *en route* to London). Also note that you MUST touch in (swipe over the yellow reader) at the start AND finish of journeys (except on the bus, when it is just once), otherwise you will be charged the maximum fare and this won't be allowed within the daily ceiling.
REMEMBER: *You really are being ripped off if you just pay the cash single fare all the time.*

FROM OUTSIDE LONDON If you are staying outside London, you can get your Travelcard incorporated in your return mainline train ticket to London, saving a lot of time and money. Again, not valid on trains arriving in the capital before 10am Monday–Friday. If you travel in the morning rush, you will have to pay around double the single fare for a return and suffer serious crowding.

BORIS BIKES Officially the Barclays bike hire scheme, these turquoise bikes are a brilliant way of getting around what is, after all, mostly a flat river basin. You can pick them up at docking stations all over town and leave them at other ones near your destination. You can book online, by phone or just pick one up with a credit card (see instructions on the stand). I cycle to work every day and recommend it, though can't guarantee safety. Wear a helmet, bright clothes, get off and push your bike across complex junctions and don't *ever* go inside (to the left of) vans, trucks and buses waiting at junctions, as this seems to be the biggest cause of fatalities.
☎ 0845 026 3630. 🖳 www.tfl.co.uk

Part One

ECCENTRIC LONDONERS AND THEIR ODD PURSUITS

N Bradt

WEMBLEY

STRATFORD

HACKNEY

ISLINGTON

CAMDEN

HAMPSTEAD

WILLESDEN

ACTON

EALING

PADDINGTON

BETHNAL GREEN

ISLE OF DOGS

River Thames

GREENWICH

LEWISHAM

PECKHAM

CAMBERWELL

BERMONDSEY

CITY

WESTMINSTER

KNIGHTSBRIDGE

CHELSEA

LAMBETH

BRIXTON

CLAPHAM

STREATHAM

BATTERSEA

FULHAM

WANDSWORTH

PUTNEY

WIMBLEDON

CHISWICK

RICHMOND

BRENTFORD

River Thames

TWICKENHAM

HOUNSLOW

WHITECHAPEL WALK page 276

GREENWICH WALK page 308

DULWICH WALK page 295

FLEET ST & SMITHFIELD WALK page 230

SOUTHWARK WALK page 265

SOHO WALK page 252

KENSINGTON WALK page 342

HAMMERSMITH WALK page 326

2km

0

A13

A102

A11

A10

A1

A41

A404

A40

M4

A4

A316

A3

A24

A23

A21

A205

A20

A2

THE ECCENTRIC YEAR

Week by week, the strangest customs of London and its region unfold, only a few of them behind locked doors. Here is your guide to when and where to find the bizarre and inexplicable, plus a reminder for visitors of some rather familiar rituals that Londoners will know and love but, perhaps, have never quite got round to joining in. As events and venues can change over the years, you should check with tourist information centres before making long journeys. Events not open to the public are included because they are unique, fascinating or otherwise eccentric and have stories well worth relating.

JANUARY

MUDATHON 200-yard dash in often icy conditions through waist-deep oozing mud, at Blackwater River, east of London at Maldon, Essex. Often delayed to around Easter – it's them tides. When you hear that you have to gaffer tape your shoes on, you realise how awful this is. *1 January.*

NEW YEAR'S DAY PARADE 10,000 performers pretend it isn't midwinter and parade through the West End. All 32 London boroughs vie with each other for the best effort; American marching bands join in. *1 January.*

CHINESE NEW YEAR Warm-up in Soho's Chinatown, around Gerrard Street, off Leicester Square. Processions with dragon-dancing and firecrackers.

Actual event not usually till about 13 February. Trouble is, an hour or two later, you feel like another one... *Mid-January onwards.*

ROYALIST ARMY ON THE MARCH 17th-century types march in Cavalier outfits from St James's Palace to Banqueting House, Whitehall, only 360 years too late to stop Charles I having his head chopped off there. Prayers are said at the spot. *30 January or last Sunday.*

FEBRUARY

SOHO PANCAKE DAY RACE In Carnaby Street – long known for celebrated tossers – and various venues around the capital. Mardi Gras in other Christian countries means fat Tuesday, in the sense that certain foods had to be used up in a feast before the Lenten fast. Shrove Tuesday means 'blessed' or 'shriven' Tuesday, when at noon one would hark to the shriving bell to go to church. One batty lady heard the bell while tossing pancakes (to use up eggs) and ran to the church with pancake and pan. Hence the tradition. *Shrove Tuesday (date varies, day before Lent starts, related to variable Easter).*

PANCAKE GREAZE At 11am, a strange procession is seen crossing the medieval Westminster School tucked behind Westminster Abbey. The cook in his white hat and jacket is preceded by the verger, carrying a silver mace. The cook carries a frying pan containing a pancake. In the Great Schoolroom, there is a 16ft-high iron bar which used to mark the division of the Upper and Lower parts of the school. The cook has to toss the pancake over this bar and as it falls on the other side the boys scramble to get a piece in a massive scrum. In fact, the whole school used to take part, which ensured sore heads if not broken limbs. Now representatives of each form do the job. The boy who gets the biggest part receives a guinea from the Dean. The cook also receives a fee for getting the pancake over in one piece – presumably he can't get to practise much – although it is more than 60 years since the pancake infamously stuck to the bar, requiring a second toss. Not open to the public. *Shrove Tuesday.*

TRAIL OF THE PYX Held in the Goldsmiths' Hall, London. The exact and serious purpose of the ancient trial, despite its Peter Pannish name – it dates from at least 1280 – is to provide independent scrutiny of the quality and size of coins of the realm made by the Royal Mint in the previous year. Officers of the Mint are required to place samples in the Pyx (a box) and these are brought before a jury of goldsmiths sworn in by the Queen's

Remembrancer (a shadowy figure who appears in the Horseshoe and Faggot Cutting Ceremony, see *October*, page 17). Not open to the public. *February or March.*

MARCH

ORANGES AND LEMONS SERVICE At St Clement Danes in The Strand. Schoolchildren given one of each (see *Nursery rhymes*, page 99). *Early Sunday.*

DRUIDS' CELEBRATION OF THE SPRING EQUINOX Cloaked pagan types meet in Tower Hill, London, to celebrate spring equinox. *21 March.*

EASTER

Date fixed by Golden Numbers – dead complicated, ask the Pope for explanation. Always after 20 March. Covers period from Maundy Thursday until Easter Monday and, related to the feast, Ascension Day, which occurs 40 days after Easter Sunday.

ROYAL MAUNDY MONEY DISTRIBUTION At Westminster Abbey in even-numbered years, other great cathedrals in odd years. Monarch gives sets of specially minted coins in special purses to as many old people as years of the sovereign's age, travelling by royal train to further cities. The coins are legal tender but rarely spent, as they are much treasured by the families who receive them, which is just as well, as most people would be puzzled to be offered a fourpenny piece.

This is an ancient, complicated and fascinating ceremony for which tickets have to be sought well in advance. The name Maundy Thursday originates from a command, *mandatum* in Latin, from Jesus on the night of the Last Supper. He washed the feet of the apostles and said:

If I then, your Lord and Master, have washed your feet; ye also ought to wash one another's feet. For I have given you an example, that ye should do as I have done to you.'

(John 13: 14–15).

Throughout the Middle Ages, monarchs, princes and bishops across Europe treated the poor to feasts and literally washed their feet. English monarchs used also to give their gowns to the poor, but as these were of

5

little use, Elizabeth I substituted purses of coins at the 1572 ceremony at Greenwich Palace. There are records of sovereigns until James II and William III personally washing the feet of the elderly poor. At Somerset House, the records stated that on Maundy Thursday 1685 'our gracious King James the 2nd wash'd, wip'd and kiss'd the feet of 52 poor men with wonderful humility'. In the modern tradition, the washing is merely symbolised by the carrying of nosegays and towels in the procession. The Yeomen of the Guard, the Queen's bodyguard, are also present and two of them carry the great trays on which the purses are piled. Tickets to the ceremony may be obtained from the Abbey or those cathedrals concerned. *Maundy Thursday (three days before Easter).*

HOT CROSS BUN CEREMONY Widow's Son pub, Devons Road, Bow, London E3, noon. A sailor or Wren adds a bun to the somewhat stale collection going back at least 150 years to the time a widow, whose only son was at sea, put out a hot cross bun on Good Friday expecting his return for Easter. He never came back but each year she laid out another, refusing to take any away. *Good Friday.*

BEATING THE BOUNDS Boys of St Dunstan's beat on the City's boundary markers with willow sticks in an ancient ritual. Starts at 3pm at All Hallows' by the Tower. For more about bounds and the extraordinary St Clement's ceremonies, etc, see page 138. *Ascension Day (following Thursday).*

APRIL

THE BOAT RACE From Putney to Mortlake. It's a little odd that perhaps a quarter of a million people turn out to watch just two boats in a sport few people are interested in – rowing – from two universities most have no connection with over a course they can only see a small part of for a result they will probably miss and aren't particularly interested in. Plus Hammersmith Bridge, which (if the IRA haven't blown it up again) would be the ideal spot to watch from, is usually closed on Boat Race day for some daft reason. But as one Londoner said: 'It's the first day out beside the river in the year, and it's free, so why not if it's a nice day?'

The course goes upriver from the University Stone, just upstream of Putney Bridge, to Chiswick Bridge. The pubs such as the Dove, the Rutland and Blue Anchor on the north side, just west of Hammersmith Bridge, would be good vantage points, but crowded, ditto the White Hart on the

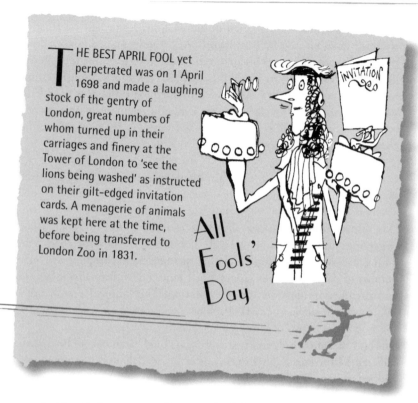

THE BEST APRIL FOOL yet perpetrated was on 1 April 1698 and made a laughing stock of the gentry of London, great numbers of whom turned up in their carriages and finery at the Tower of London to 'see the lions being washed' as instructed on their gilt-edged invitation cards. A menagerie of animals was kept here at the time, before being transferred to London Zoo in 1831.

All Fools' Day

south side a little upriver in Barnes, which has more room and a generous sweep of the river. So well ingrained that in cockney rhyming slang, 'nice girl, pity about the boat' means she's ugly but otherwise charming [race = face]. *First Saturday (or sometimes last one in March).*

CHANGING OF THE QUILL Learned address to statue of 16th-century historian John Stow, including changing the pen in his hand by either the Lord Mayor of London or the Master of the Merchant Taylors' Company, after a special service at the Church of St Andrew Undershaft, London EC3. Every three years (2014, 2017, etc). Noon. Open to the public. *5 April (approx).*

BEAT THE TUBE RACE The idea of chartered surveyor Richard Guthrie as a tribute to first four-minute-miler, Sir Roger Bannister. You may feel after another ordeal stuck in a crammed Central Line Tube that it would be a stroll to beat the Tube on foot, but in normal service it would not be that easy to outrun a Tube train. A group of determined young professionals, wearing braces and pinstripes, board a Victoria to Wimbledon train, get off at South Kensington and sprint like hell down the Fulham Road to try to get back on it at Fulham Broadway, 1.6 miles and four stops down the line. Few of them make it unless the Tube stops for some inexplicable delay at Earl's Court (now would they do that, I ask you?). An easier course would be to cut across the Circle Line from Farringdon down to Blackfriars where you can virtually see the other end. You could do it on crutches, or pogo sticks and still beat the train. Too easy for Mr Guthrie and his chums … *Second Monday (approx)*.

LONDON MARATHON The world's most popular; 29,000 people pound the pavement for 26 miles from Greenwich to the Mall, many dressed as circus clowns, gorillas, waiters with trays of drinks (glued on), a two-man rhinoceros, etc, but also many serious runners, and almost all raising staggering (and they do at the end) amounts of money for charity. In 2001's race, Angela Stratford ran in her wedding dress, complete with race number of course, and her groom Nigel Jones ran in formal suit (except both dress and trousers were on the short side). They stopped after 25 miles at Cleopatra's Needle on the Embankment and took their vows in front of a bishop and a crowd of friends. They had met at a running club and she told him that she'd only marry a man who could catch her, so he trained and trained and made the distance. After the service, they continued and finished wearing 'Just Married' placards.

In the following year, a deeply eccentric character called Lloyd Scott set out in a full old-fashioned diving suit including 22lb lead boots. He took six days to finish, gaining the world marathon record (slowest, that is). *Third Sunday.*

QUEEN'S BIRTHDAY 41-gun salute in Hyde Park to mark Queen's birthday. They make a hell of a noise and rarely hit anyone. (If Chaz has taken over by the time you read this, it'll be 14 November). *21 April, noon.*

ST GEORGE'S DAY On England's national day, the English – who gamely go along with the St Patrick's Day shenanigans about Ireland, or eat a wee haggis beastie on Burns Night for Scotland – eccentrically do precisely nothing. Shakespeare, who contrived not only to be born on St George's Day but patriotically to die on it too, wrote in *Henry V* about the Battle of Agincourt:

> *I see you stand like greyhounds in the slips,*
> *Straining upon the start. The game's afoot:*
> *Follow your spirit; and upon this charge*
> *Cry 'God for Harry! England and St George!'*

He needn't have bothered, frankly. A society dedicated to the saint holds a banquet; certain St George's pubs might offer a free pickled onion or something. The reason for this apathy is not so much the very eccentric choice of saint – an obscure Palestinian famed for not killing a non-existent beast somewhere far away – as a severe and prolonged lack of oppression of the English, and a healthy suspicion about nationalism unless there's a dire emergency. 23 *April.*

MAY

Moon Walk Thousands of London lasses brave a cold front, and walk a half or full marathon (13 or 26 miles) around Central London, starting from Battersea Park, in just their bras. Plus trousers or skirts, of course. These bras are decorated with feathers, tinsel, tassels or whatever, and whether the Moon Walk takes place after midnight to spare participants' blushes, to save passing drivers being distracted, or because it's cooler and less crowded, it is one of those strangely life-asserting and courageous events. It is in aid of Breakthrough Breast Cancer and some of the walkers are survivors of that all-too-common disease. The bra firm Playtex gives Wonderbras or Balconette bras to participants, which as *Evening Standard* writer Kate Rew wrote at the 2000 event, would be frankly the last thing you'd want if you'd had a mastectomy or prosthesis. She – the daughter of a survivor of the disease – raised the question of whether it's a stunt in bad taste, but as with all such in-your-face events which raise hundreds of thousands of pounds for research, if the victims and their families join in, one has simply to admire their guts (metaphorically, if not literally). And, as it is after midnight, no-one is forced to see it. There's a minute's silence for the victims of the disease that touches so many families today. *Second Saturday.*

For sponsorship and participation details, contact: Walk the Walk, Britannia Wharf, Monument Road, Woking, Surrey GH21 5LW.

Mr Punch Service It's almost beyond belief. Dozens of Mr Punches (as in Punch and Judy) sitting in pews in church, listening to a sermon which they subject to irreverent and cheeky interruptions. They hit each other, or their puppetmasters ('professors' is the strict term), for Mr Punch will not sit still. This is the crowded scene at St Paul's church (the actors' church) in Covent Garden where the annual Punch service takes place at 11.30am. The day includes a brass band procession of Mr Punches around the area beforehand at 10.30am and a May Fayre including non-stop Punch and Judy performances, and other forms of puppetry, all afternoon.

The procession to honour the deeply politically incorrect wife-beater and baby-batterer Mr Punch – Chelmsford and Chesterfield have tried to ban him in recent years – is accompanied, strangely, by his worst enemies, the uniformed bobbies, and includes a toast to the immortal puppet at a plaque to him at St Paul's. This is the very spot where Samuel Pepys made the first recorded sighting of Mr Punch in Britain in May 1662.

He wrote (in his own secret code, of course) that he saw '...an Italian puppet play, that is within the rails there, which is very pretty, the best that I ever saw, and great resort of gallants'. See also page 141. *Second Sunday.*

BEHEADED QUEEN'S ROSES Just north of the Tower Green in the Tower of London is the church of, appropriately, St Peter in Chains (or St Peter Ad Vincula). Here an intriguing and strange annual ritual takes place on 19 May, when a florist, acting for a strictly anonymous party, puts a dozen red roses on the grave of Anne Boleyn, Henry VIII's queen, whose head was struck from her body outside the church on the same day in 1536. She protested her love for, and loyalty to, the king with her last words on Tower Green. The blood-red roses have been arriving annually at this sad spot for at least 160 years and are thought to be sent by members of either her family, or possibly the Percys, ancient Dukes of Northumberland, one of whom the king ousted in Anne's affections. The secret admirer has never been identified, although several theories have been advanced. *19 May.*

OAK APPLE DAY Veteran soldiers at the Christopher Wren-designed Royal Hospital, Chelsea, parade with oak sprigs in their best uniforms and dress the statue of founder Charles II in oak to commemorate his escape in the Civil War by hiding in the Royal Oak. Setting up the hospital for old soldiers was reputedly rollicking royal mistress Nell Gwyn's idea. *29 May.*

JUNE

FORGOTTEN GEMS IN THE SHADOW OF ST PAUL'S The City Churches Trust takes guided walks round some of Europe's finest architecture, including some churches normally closed, plus Britain's oldest and lavishly decorated synagogue. A must for Wren and Hawksmoor fans. *Early June midweek.*

☎ 020 7626 1555

SECRET GARDENS UNLOCKED London Garden Squares Day offers a chance to enter hundreds of these intriguing hidden oases of peace and quiet. *Second Sunday.*

Tickets for all and details from LHPGT, Duck Island Cottage, St James's Park, London SW1A 2BJ, enclosing £5 and an SAE.

CHARLTON HORN FAIR There's a lusty origin to this fair in SE7. It dates from when King John had his wicked way with the local miller's wife, and in desperation at facing the cuckolded husband, said the miller could hold an annual fair, which locals naturally called the Horn Fair. It became so lewd that it was banned eventually, but not before Daniel Defoe complained in the 1720s:

> ...*the women are especially impudent for that day; as if it was a day that justify'd the giving themselves a loose to all manner of indecency and immodesty, without any reproach.*

It's been revived but, I'm told, includes some elements of the old event, with a procession involving King John, the Miller and some horn decorations. *Late June weekend.*

GARTER CEREMONY At St George's Chapel, Windsor Castle. It is peculiar that the oldest English order of chivalry, the highest such order in the world, revolves around a modest female under-garment, and odd that such Knights of the Round Table-style malarkey carries on in all seriousness in the 21st century. On this day the monarch and 24 Knights of the Order of the Garter process with spectacular robes and hats to mark this oldest order of chivalry and a useful, if humble, garment. A few tickets can be booked. Even odder is that the highest and best of the land should parade in what look like Gilbert and Sullivan comic opera outfits of peacock and heron feathers, badges, ribbons and glorified velvet pyjamas (plus of course a prominent garter worn below the left knee) 700 years after its origin, but that's eccentric Britain for you. It originated in 1348 when King Edward III, in picking up a lady's fallen garter at a dance, turned on sniggering noblemen and said in defence of the red-faced lady (possibly the Countess of Salisbury): '*Honi soit qui mal y pense*', now the official motto, meaning: 'Shame on him who thinks bad of it'. The court operated half in Old French at the time and he added in English that he would turn

11

the embarrassing garter into the most honoured garment ever worn, which he did.

The knights have banners which in Arthurian times would have been carried before them into battle but which hang in St George's Chapel, Windsor, where they have their own named stalls. Although generally dukedoms, baronetcies, earldoms or whatever are higher than mere knights, this order is regarded as superseding them all. For example, after Winston Churchill saved the entire world from slavery (not single-handedly, of course), it was suggested that the title Duke of London should be given to him but he asked merely for a 'park for children to play in, that kind of thing'. Later the young Queen Elizabeth offered him Knight of the Garter and he could not resist. Or as he said to a close friend: 'I only accepted because I think she is so splendid.' *19 June.*

KNOLLYS ROSE CEREMONY An odd quit-rent, Mansion House, City of London. Every 24 June a single red Knollys Rose is carried on a velvet cushion by churchwardens of All-Hallows-By-The-Tower in the City of London to the Lord Mayor at Mansion House. This quit-rent was a penalty imposed on Sir Robert Knollys in 1381 because he built a gallery bridge between two of his properties – now long gone – across narrow Seething Lane. Naughty man, he's still paying for it six centuries later. *24 June.*

LONDON MARDI GRAS Annual festival celebrating gay and lesbian life in London, usually at Finsbury Park. Preceded by a Pride March in Central London. The event is described as a carnival of kitsch with over-dressed drag queens and has major bands performing plus blessings for gay marriages. Tourist chiefs hope the Mardi Gras will become a success à la Sydney, claiming the pink pound is worth £750 million a year, a figure that sounds as if it's come from Keith Waterhouse's Department of Guesswork. *Last Saturday.*

www.londonmardigras.com

SMALL SHIPS RACE The great days of full-rigged sailing ships return to London's waters, in this case the Round Pond in Kensington Gardens, in front of Kensington Palace. Beautiful models with sensational curves – sailing boats, I mean – plus warships with working guns, tugs, fireboats and speedboats take to the waves, and to the deeps if two radio-controlled sets are on the same frequency, as happened recently. The little boats often appear on the Round Pond on other Sundays. The swans, and coots which nest on the lifebuoys, seem unperturbed. A word of advice if you chat to the amiable old coots who sail the things: not every tall-masted sailing vessel is a ship, that's a particular type. And a barque is not the same as a barquentine. If you don't want a salty sea-dog to fix you with a glittering eye, don't even think about commenting on the rigging. The Round Pond, by the way, isn't round, but then the Derby isn't at Derby but at Epsom, and Leeds Castle is not at Leeds but in Kent. Trinity Square is a crescent and Finsbury Park is, of course, nowhere near Finsbury. Ho hum, you get the idea. *Fourth weekend (approx)*.

WIMBLEDON TENNIS TOURNAMENT Like the Proms, a very English event with some fanatical queuers sleeping out all night in Wimbledon Park. Tens of thousands of tennis fans, young and old, arrive and leave without the least trouble. When it's crowded in the grounds, the gentle murmur is probably 100,000 middle-class people politely saying 'sorry' as they push past each other. In the Navy, anything that doesn't move gets painted grey (and if it does move, salute it); here everything's a dull matt green, which seems to have a calming effect. No advertising hoardings, everything very restrained and apparently uncommercial. The atmosphere is somehow like a suburban tennis club in Betjeman's *Metroland*, when in fact it's a megamillion pound international media fest.

Once in a blue moon there's a hunky young star such as Borg and a few adolescent tennis groupies will wait by the players' entrance, but it's not really a big deal. They don't push or shove or scream much. The red-top tabloid press whips itself into a frenzy about whoever the latest sexy young female is and endlessly discusses details of their underwear – Kournikova for example – but the true Wimbledon fans wouldn't dream of mentioning such things. Being England, quite often Wimbledon's totally screwed up by rain (notwithstanding the new Centre Court roof), in which case tens of thousands of people travel from Cornwall, Carlisle or wherever, politely shuffle around the even more packed grounds, watch ten minutes' play when the rain seems to have stopped, and perhaps participate in a sing-song or, really daring, a small Mexican wave if sitting in one of the big show courts. Then they have their sandwiches and eventually good-naturedly go home without a spot of trouble, saying what a good day out it was. They don't even get their money back if there's some play.

Tickets are expensive and for Centre Court vastly oversubscribed. If they were soccer fans they'd have burned Wimbledon down, filled the streets with broken bottles and litter and vandalised the Tube. They're a completely different race, tennis fans. Nice people like Sir Cliff Richard and Sue Barker. *Last week of June and first of July.*

☎ 020 8946 2244

JULY

Doggett's Coat and Badge Race Less well-known than the Oxford and Cambridge boat race, for some reason, but all the more fascinating for its early origins and strange survival. See Southwark walk, page 262. *Mid-July (date depends on tides).*

Black Cherry Fair In Windsor Street, Chertsey, Surrey, on the second Saturday in July. This is ancient, dating from a charter granted by King Henry VI to John de Harmondesworth, Abbot of Chertsey Abbey, and although it originally celebrated St Anne's Day in August, it now coincides with the supposed great Surrey cherry harvest, which of course doesn't exist and would anyway be at a different time of year if it did. *Second Saturday.*

The Proms Mostly, but not entirely, in the Royal Albert Hall, the world's biggest and best celebration of classical music, ancient and modern, eagerly followed by the young promenaders who make a gloriously anachronistic, jingoistic extravaganza of the Last Night of the Proms in September (making a rare exception to the comments above about St George's Day and nationalism). Tickets for that are as hard to come by as those for the Wimbledon tennis final – a lottery based on loyalty to the preceding concerts – but in recent years the thing has also been shown live to a huge crowd in adjacent Hyde Park. Also on TV. *July onwards (until September).*

Greenwich Mela All day, Greenwich, SE7. The largest Asian festival in southeast London, with a wide variety of Asian music, entertainment and stalls. Great food, great music, great clothes. *Late Sunday.*

Swan Upping This astonishing and complex ritual starts from the premise that all swans in Britain are royal birds and belong to the Queen. Except those belonging to the Dyers and Vintners' companies, of course. The ritual involves catching all the swans on the Thames, marking them as to whom they belong (as if it mattered). For the full but rather unbelievable story, see page 53. *20–24 July.*

AUGUST

Notting Hill Carnival Held in Portobello Road and Ladbroke Grove, this is always promoted as the biggest street festival in Europe, with up to two million revellers (who counts them?). It is supposed to be where efnic meets yoof, innit, and multi-cultural London's social mix is celebrated with a Caribbean theme. The reggae is loud, the dancing exuberant, the Jamaican food tasty, the floats and fancy dress spectacular, whatever the weather. The police try hard to get it right and are traditionally accused of being too light-handed or heavy-handed or both.

Many of the trendy trust-fund rich kids, film stars and right-on politicos who have colonised once-poor Notting Hill in the last decade find an excuse to go to their country homes that weekend. Then Tory leader William Hague and his then fiancée, Ffion, visited in 1999 and were ridiculed for the white patches on their wrists showing where their watches had been removed to foil the rampant Rolex robbers. Actually you'd be a total prat to wear a watch worth the price of somebody's house to such an event (or, arguably, at all). *Last weekend.*

SEPTEMBER

GREAT RIVER RACE About 200 traditional boats of many different kinds, carefully handicapped against each other, race a gruelling 22 miles right across London from the Isle of Dogs in Docklands to leafy Surrey's elegant Ham, west of Richmond. It grew out of a challenge in 1987 to beat the winners of Doggett's Coat and Badge (see July). In keeping with the Company of Watermen & Lightermen's traditional role of licensing boatmen who were, when the roads were primitive, the London taxis of the era, a passenger must be carried by each competitor, whatever their style of boat – and that certainly varies, although each must have at least four oars or paddles.

They have included in recent years: Viking longboat, Norwegian scow, Canadian C-8 canoe, Chinese dragonboat, numerous Cornish pilot and other gigs, skiffs, cutters, naval whalers, a magnificent 54ft replica Bronze Age Greek galley, traditional canvas and tar Irish boats, a new shallop and a Thames wherry (both built specially for the race) and the world's oldest racing rowing boat, the two-centuries-old *Royal Oak* built in County Down, Northern Ireland. They all take on the Watermen's cutter for the prize, which they keep for a year, of a trophy featuring a real Watermen's Badge (the equivalent of a present-day cabbie's badge) issued to William Savage of Gravesend in 1803. Crews have included policemen, cadets, teenage Sea Scouts, firemen, soldiers and sailors, pub teams of both sexes, along with international entries from America, Canada, Holland, Sweden, France, Germany, Ireland, and the Channel Islands. And me, in 2011, in a whaler. We rowed through two thunderstorms, saw a double rainbow, and caught no whales – what a blast! *First Sunday.*

www.greatriverrace.co.uk

BRICK LANE MUSIC FESTIVAL An annual free festival in Brick Lane, E1, with a world music stage, amazing street entertainment, delicious food, craft stalls and a special children's play area. If you've had too much balti, hail a rickshaw wallah. Celebrates the area's successive waves of immigrant communities: Huguenot, Jewish and, principally, Bangladeshi. Now this area is known as London's Bangla Town and well worth a visit anytime. *Usually the third weekend in September. Free.*

www.bricklanefestival.org

BROWNING REMEMBERED Browning fans from around the world – that is, admirers of the poet Robert Browning not the equally great, in his way, machine-gun manufacturer – gather at the Browning Chapel at St Marylebone church, on the corner of Marylebone High Street and Marylebone Road. It was here that he and Elizabeth Barrett wed in secret in one of the great love affairs of London literati. People still ask to see the marriage register and buy copies of their certificate. *12 September.*

HORSEMAN'S SUNDAY Service on horseback, with the minister on horseback too, in St John's, Hyde Park. An annual service where the packed congregation comprises dozens of horses sounds too bizarre to be true, but for a sight of a priest in his vestments on horseback intoning to the gathered dozens of horses – or, perhaps, their riders – make the trip to St John's, Hyde Park, in Hyde Park Crescent, W2, at noon. Horseman's Sunday is the occasion when the assembled posse can be seen bursting into a stirring blast of the hymn 'Jerusalem', after a veritable sermon on the mount, before the horses take a trot round the block and then are announced one by one and given a rosette. *Third Sunday (approx).*

LONDON OPEN HOUSE DAY Once-a-year access to intriguing buildings of architectural value that are closed to the public for the rest of the year – from futuristic offices to Art Deco masterpieces, from secret bunkers to private homes to the Bank of England. Fascinating and free. *Third weekend (approx).*

See public libraries or www.londonopenhouse.org.

CLOG AND APRON RACE At the Royal Botanic Gardens at Kew, where late each September dozens of horticultural students thus garbed have to clatter their way down the 373-yard-long Broad Walk. *Late September.*

OCTOBER

PEARLY HARVEST FESTIVAL At St Martin-in-the-Fields, off Trafalgar Square. Lots of folklore cockneys in their strange coats covered with pearly buttons playing ukuleles or just singing their hearts out. For more on pearly kings, see page 52. *First Sunday.*

HORSESHOE AND FAGGOT-CUTTING CEREMONY Deeply bizarre quit-rent, High Court, The Strand, London. This ceremony is unbelievably old and unbelievably meaningless. It must be held on a Wednesday afternoon late each October ('between the morrow of St Michael and the morrow of St Martin'). The City Solicitor cuts hazel rods with two knives, which he then presents to the Queen's Remembrancer, who pronounces 'Good service'. This is the rent for a piece of ground called The Moors at Eardington in Shropshire – or rather it was the rent once, but no one is sure precisely when or which bit of land. Then six very large horseshoes and 61 nails are counted out and the Remembrancer pronounces 'Good number'. This was the rent agreed after Walter le Brun was granted land in 1235 for a forge in St Clement Danes parish, probably where Australia House now stands. The horseshoes are given straight back and kept for next year, as far as I can gather. This little-known event, which you can witness if you apply to the courts, may be the oldest surviving English ceremony, apart from the Coronation. Actually it's deeply bizarre being the Remembrancer for something the purpose of which is totally forgotten. One other duty – he has to receive the Lord Chancellor's Great Seal – a wax one, not a flippered one – when he resigns or dies. *Variable Wednesday.*

LION SERMON At St Katharine Cree in Creechurch Lane, in the City. Everyone recalls the Roman slave Androcles who was spared by a lion in the arena because he had once extracted a thorn from its paw. Few recall a London Lord Mayor who, bizarrely, had a similar experience. On every 16 October at 1pm for more than 350 years, the Lion Sermon has been preached at the church of St Katharine Cree. Sir John Gayer, a trader and outspoken Lord Mayor who was once imprisoned for refusing City money for the Parliamentary army waging civil war, came face-to-face with an enormous lion in the Syrian Desert. Perhaps remembering Daniel rather than Androcles, he fell upon his knees and prayed for mercy. The lion came up to him, checked him over and walked off. Oddly, Sir John was Master of the Fishmongers Company, so what he was doing in the desert is anyone's guess. If he did have a box of kippers with him to monger, perhaps it put the lion off. Whatever the explanation, a grateful Sir John gave money to a number of charities, endowed the church to preach his annual sermon, and gave it a splendid font, inscribed with his coat of arms. Cree, incidentally, is not short for creed, as Archbishop William Laud wrongly records in his diaries, but for Christchurch, a medieval predecessor. *16 October.*

NOVEMBER

GUY FAWKES NIGHT Londoners blow tens of millions of pounds, worth of fireworks into the sky to celebrate defeat of the 1605 Gunpowder Plot to blow up Parliament and King James I. Organised displays in various parks, etc, are often on the nearest Saturday. Beefeaters still search the cellars of Parliament on this day, looking for barrels of gunpowder and Catholic conspirators with lanterns in black cloaks. Being multicultural, London also echoes to fireworks for **Diwali**, the Hindu festival of lights, at about this time. There's a big gathering in Trafalgar Square – the date for that floats a little according to the Moon. *5 November.*

LONDON TO BRIGHTON VETERAN CAR RUN Odd in that only cars built before 1 January 1905 are eligible, which means that there are not too many and that their chances of getting to Brighton are a bit ropey. The context of this run was to celebrate the 1896 abolition of the rule whereby a man had to walk in front of any motor car with a red flag, limiting them to about 3mph. Millions of hedgehogs have since flatly denied that this was a good idea. Starts from Hyde Park Corner and ends hours later in Madeira Drive, Brighton. Thousands line the route. *First Sunday.*

LORD MAYOR'S SHOW It involves 6,500 participants, both civilian and military, together with 67 floats from organisations across the country, 200 horses, 20 bands and 20 carriages, making a two-and-a-half-mile procession. Ever since 1215, the new Lord Mayor has made his or her way to the Queen's Bench to pledge their allegiance to the Crown. That's 786 years and counting, come plague, famine, civil war, Blitz – nothing stopped it.

Here you can see the gilded state coach, pikemen in armour and the strange giants Gog and Magog (see *London beasts*, page 206). Plus there are fabulous fireworks on the river in the evening: best viewpoint – in front of the Oxo Tower on the South Bank. *Early November, usually second Saturday.*

☎ 020 7606 3030

DECEMBER

PETER PAN SWIM In the Serpentine lake in Hyde Park on Christmas Day. Dozens of men and women vie for the Peter Pan Cup, first presented by author of the children's classic J M Barrie. Everyone has a chance of winning because less able swimmers have a start on the rest. The temperature is usually about 40 degrees Fahrenheit (just above freezing) and as they're a friendly lot there's no need to break the ice. An American visitor who took part in a recent dip quipped: 'I thought it would be really cool... Just how cool I didn't realise!' A large crowd watches at the usual start time of 9am and there are many very fit-looking elderly ladies in the event. In praise of colder women, as it were... *25 December.*

NEW YEAR'S EVE CELEBRATIONS Beneath the Christmas tree in Trafalgar Square. For people who have already had too much to drink, there's plenty more to drink in the fountains. Meanwhile various official bodies hurl tens of thousands of pounds' worth of fireworks into the sky, oblivious of the fact that it's midwinter and midnight on a rainswept Atlantic island where no sane person would celebrate outside. It's usually a damp squib, with the rockets exploding unseen in the rainclouds but sometimes wonderful. *31 December.*

DAILY EVENTS

CEREMONY OF THE KEYS This has taken place at the Tower of London every day for more than 700 years. At 9.53pm, the Chief Warder in Tudor uniform, carrying a lantern and the Keys, sets off from the Byward Tower to meet the Escort of the Key all bedecked in Beefeater garb. They tour the various gates, ceremonially locking them. On returning to the Bloody Tower archway, however, the party is challenged by a sentry with the words: 'Halt! Who comes there?' as if he wouldn't know after 700 years.
The reply is bellowed out:

19

'The Keys.'
'Whose Keys?'
'Queen Elizabeth's Keys.'
'Advance Queen Elizabeth's Keys.'
'All's well.'

The party passes through the arch and the Chief Warder raises his hat, saying: 'God preserve Queen Elizabeth.' All reply: 'Amen.' A bugler plays the Last Post and the Keys are carried to the Resident Governor of the Tower for the night.

The only time the Keys were late was in September 1941 when the Tower suffered several direct hits from Nazi bombs. It was delayed just half an hour.

Note: Admission to the Keys Ceremony is only by written application and invitation. The monarch may change.

Apply to Ceremony of the Keys, HM Tower of London, EC3N 4AB
☎ 020 7680 9004

INFREQUENT EVENTS

CEREMONY OF THE CONSTABLE'S DUES This 600-year-old ceremony reiterates the Tower of London's ancient right to tolls from ships wishing to moor close by. The crew of a visiting Royal Naval vessel, for example, are escorted by Yeoman Warders and a corps of drums to Tower Green, where the Constable of the Tower receives his dues, in this case a barrel of Navy rum.

Any major naval vessel must make this tribute – it happens four or five times a year – and it is far from the only perk of being Constable of the Tower. Never mind company cars, he is also entitled to any cattle, sheep, pigs or horses that fall off London Bridge; a penny for every foot of livestock that falls into the tower moat; and two old pence per pilgrim landing to visit the shrine of St James. Actually, as Freemen of the City of London have the legal right to drive sheep across London bridges, and at least one of them occasionally does, this may not be entirely pointless.

THE SWEARING ON THE HORNS A strange rite of passage – like that of ship passengers first crossing the Equator – was for people first passing through the inns of Highgate, where there have always been plenty of taverns (19 in 1826, fewer now), being both on the road to the north from London and also a pleasant day's horse ride out from the city to a village high up in clean air. The newcomer is paraded before the pair of cow or stag horns in a pub such as the Flask, Highgate West Hill, Highgate, and made to swear an oath vowing never to drink small beer (weak brews, that is) unless he liked it better than strong. Or eat brown bread when he could get white – unless he preferred it. Or make love to the maid when he could get the mistress – unless he preferred her. The sheer nonsense of such a conditional vow gave much opportunity for humour and ribaldry among the coach parties – horse drawn, then motor coaches – that it has never completely died out. After swearing on the horns you have to kiss them, and then can kiss any girl in the pub that you fancy (if she's willing). The Wrestlers in North Road has details of the oath displayed and undertook the ceremony twice a year when I was a student.

The horns here seem to be antlers of – appropriately – a stag, and their version of the Highgate oath seems to suggest kissing the maid *and* the mistress, if you could get away with it. Byron certainly referred to the ceremony in the 19th century and if you think it's the kind of thing Dickens would have put in *Pickwick Papers*, well Dickens and family stayed next door to The Red Lion and Sun, which also regularly ran the ceremony, in 1832. Another pub involved in living memory was the Gatehouse. People used to say of a fellow 'he's been sworn at Highgate', which meant he's been around a bit, he's a man of the world.

ECCENTRIC LONDONERS

ECCENTRIC CLUBS AND COLLECTORS

There is every kind of collector and specialist society in London. Just a few of the more esoteric ones run by Londoners include: the **United Kingdom Spoon Collectors Club**; the **United Kingdom Belleek Collectors Group** (an Irish pottery, it turns out); the **Guild of St Gabriel** (who collect only stamps with religious aspects); the **Spode Society** (the English pottery); the **Bookplate Society** (those printed labels inside books); the **Thimble Society**; the **Indian Military History Society** (based, not inappropriately, in Southall); the **Great Britain Postcard Club** (enquiries by letter presumably not so welcome); the **Crown Imperial Society** (military medals and badges, Allies only); the **Military Heraldry Society** (cloth insignia such as shoulder flashes); the **Trix Twin Railway Collectors Association** (only for the model railways of that brand manufactured 1935–37); the **International Map Collectors Society**; the **International Banknote Society** and the **Playing-Card Society**. Then there are Appreciation Societies – one each for **Moustaches**, **Bubble Wrap**, **Clouds** and **Corduroy**. The latter group became excited by the date not long ago of 11-11-11 because they thought it most resembled their favoured cloth. You wonder how they can wait another century…

THE STAMP OF THE TRUE COLLECTOR

There are clubs for types of people too: the **Left-Handers**, the **Tall Person Society**, the **Talbot Association**. And there's a lot you can learn from organisations such as the **Letter Box Study Group**, for example. Did you know that the first British pillar boxes were introduced in the Channel Islands in 1853, or that they were the idea of novelist Anthony Trollope, then a clerk for the General Post Office? Or that the standard Victorian colour for pillar boxes was green, the first red ones not appearing in London until 1874? That airmail used to have its own light-blue boxes – there's still one at Windsor.

TRAINER COLLECTORS: ECCENTRIC TO THE SOLE

Pillar box collecting, as Arthur Reeder used to do in Harrow, seems sane to me, in a crazy kind of way, but other equally obsessive collectors leave me cold because the thing collected seems deeply uninteresting. I don't mean things like sickbags – there's a family doctor who has thousands of them (unused) from all over the world – because that's funny, and you get them free on airlines.

But what about trainers? Those unlovely, largely plastic, shoes that the youth of the world would die for but the smell of which would soon make the rest of us die too?

There's a guy somewhere in London called Jeremy. He won't give his last name, he won't give his location, such is his fear of someone stealing his 1,587 different pairs of trainers.

Girlfriends have threatened to leave him over the trainers, but then relationship problems are not unknown for a certain kind of eccentric. 'Shoes don't answer back,' he told the TV crew, tellingly. And one more Jeremy-the-sneaker-freak-geek fact: he has a Nike emblem tattooed on his ankle. 'I'm branded for life.' Now that *is* weird.

SCOOTER TOOTER

One of the many eccentric collectors of unusual things in London who is a man after my own heart is Robin Spalding. Robin was a teenager in the late 50s/early 60s, when motor-scooters were the thing. Now if you asked the average Joe today for the name of a scooter manufacturer, he'd probably say Lambretta or Vespa. If he was particularly knowledgable, he might name a couple of British ones of that era: Triumph, for example. But Robin has done us all a great service by collecting an astonishing 45 different British-built scooters – that's at least one from all 25 firms that went into production. It was all the fault of someone who wouldn't sell him a secondhand Vespa back in '59, he says. 'I ended up with a British machine with a 250cc twin Villiers engine – it was a lot faster than the Italian one,' he says. Well he grew up and graduated to cars, as many of us did, but he never forgot that romantic sixties era of chrome-trimmed cars, juke boxes, transport caffs, beehive hair-dos, teddy boys, mods ... and of course scooters. The scooter went completely out of fashion for 20 years after that, but Robin, who lives on the Surrey edge of London, was slowly acquiring his collection. Every year he rides one or two to vintage shows, and hopes to leave his impressive collection to a national collection – if they can kick-start the fund-raising to build an exhibition hall large enough.

CRACKPOT CONTRAPTIONS

Londoner Maurice Collins has a deeply odd collection of weird gadgets, mostly from the Victorian era. They include a skirt-lifter, a hat-measurer and a pre-electric version of the later famous Teasmaid alarm clock, in which the clockwork sets off the alarm, pushes a lever, strikes a match on some sandpaper, lights a lamp, boils the water, pours it out and makes the tea. It's *Chitty Chitty Bang Bang* come to life, and the Muswell Hill-based enthusiast has not only mounted several exhibitions of his fascinating collection but also written books on the subject. Mind you, some are probably not that much use nowadays, such as an 1810 machine that tattoos deserters with the letter D on their foreheads, but they are all ingenious and intriguing.

NORTH LONDONERS: SERIOUSLY WEIRD AND WIRED

No offence intended, but most South Londoners believe true weirdos start at the river, going north. Of course, there are some normal people, but many north-of-the-river types have gone off the scale on the eccentricity meter. They're not on the same planet, Janet (Street-Porter, for example). Just a couple of eccentrics, marked by plaques of the unofficial sort, will suffice.

ISLINGTON'S FINEST: HOW JOE ORTON BECAME JOE OUGHTN'T

Most writers would like to make an impact on their local library; but none has ever done it quite like Joe Orton. The gay sixties author and playwright used to hang round Islington Central Library and deface other people's books in extraordinary ways.

He and his partner/flatmate Kenneth Halliwell swapped around illustrations, so a gardening book had an extremely ugly monkey where a beautiful rose should be, or they typed outrageously rude reviews carefully to fit in the dustjackets of popular novels. These contained obscenities, and Orton and Halliwell would watch with pleasure as people picked up the respectable volumes and recoiled in horror at the foul language in the reviews. Naturally the library became a little miffed with books being defaced by this rather fifth-form toilet humour and kept watch.

Having worked out it was probably Orton and Halliwell, they – rather clever this, so don't *ever* belittle librarians for lacking imagination – sent the two a fake letter from the town hall complaining about a dumped car near their flat in Noel Road. Halliwell sent back a rude riposte, composed on the same typewriter. It was easy to prove (from the worn-down F, presumably) that the same machine had been used to deface the books, and the pair got six months in jail for stealing 72 books, defacing 44 and removing 1,653 pictures. And 18 shillings and four pence in overdue book fines.

Orton, born John Kingsley Orton in 1933, went on to write some hit plays such as *Entertaining Mr Sloan* (1964) and *Loot* (1966). Then, on 9 August 1967, came an abrupt end to his CV. He was murdered by his partner, Halliwell, who then killed himself.

In his book about Orton's life, *Prick up your Ears,* John Lahr gives a rather gruesome description of exactly what Halliwell did. Suffice to say it involved a hammer, Orton's cranium, much exercise and a lot of re-decorating. There's a kind of grim comedy about it. The film of *Prick up* (written by Alan Bennett) has a scene where Orton's sister mixes the ashes of Orton and Halliwell together. As she does so she says: 'I think I'm putting in more of Joe than of Kenneth.' 'It's a gesture, dear, not a recipe,' replies Vanessa Redgrave, playing Orton's agent.

Orton would by now have been a grand old man of literature and, ironically, the same Islington library now carefully preserves those obscene gender-bender addenda as an archive of a local literary great. I know it's wrong of me, but I hope that somewhere, deep in the library's reserve collection, there's an outrageous alteration waiting one day to shock the stuffing out of a little old lady.

A similarly amusing wheeze with books came about in the 1990s when a London paper, fed up with all the pretentious twaddle that won literary prizes such as the Booker, set out to find if anyone actually read all this claptrap (not all the books, of course, were like this – just most of them). They snuck into bookshops and inserted between pages 100 and 101 a note saying a fat cheque would be given to any reader who sent the note back to the paper within a year. The note was jammed up by the spine so it wouldn't fall out unless you actually turned the pages. The journalists checked that the books were actually sold and then sat back for a year. Their money was safe.

THE SPOOKY LINKED DEATHS OF JOE MEEK AND BUDDY HOLLY

Another North Londoner who met a premature end was Joe Meek, the great record producer of the late 1950s and early 1960s. He inhabited a strange flat in Holloway Road, filled with wiring and half-assembled electronic devices – more like a mad inventor's retreat than a sound studio – but it's fair to say he was Britain's first independent producer with his own sound. He was seriously wired as well as seriously weird. The Chinese restaurant two doors away would rock with the sounds of his playbacks, and the little brown door that led up the stairs to his flat was for a while a place of pilgrimage for would-be rock stars.

Oddly, Meek wasn't very musical, but he was great with the technical side. People can remember amazing lash-ups with old valve amps, biscuit-tin lids held with Sellotape, dangerous uncovered wiring and weird electronic effects that only Meek could create. The arch example of this is the still amazing sound of the hit *Telstar* (which sold five million) and other hits such as *Have I the Right?* It's fair to say that the recording industry was changed by Meek's innovation and high standards, and better-known producers, such as Phil Spector in America, followed in his general direction. Even today, people use some of his revolutionary technical ideas.

But Meek's obsession with American rock star Buddy Holly and Holly's own tragic end was spooky and, ultimately, insane. Meek, a great spiritualist, met Holly in 1958 and told him an earlier Tarot-card reading had worked out that Holly would die on 3 February 1958. This was a little after that date, so a relieved Meek told Holly how pleased he was that the cards' figure was wrong. Holly was, of course, killed in a plane crash on *3 February* 1959, exactly a year later than Meek's prediction.

Meek was, as the 1960s went on, not a happy bunny. This Meek was not going to inherit the earth, what with drug addiction, paranoia, low self-esteem, problems in facing his own sexuality, and career failure all prompting him finally to flip and kill first his landlady, and then himself, on *3 February* 1967!

THE MOLE MAN OF HACKNEY

Hackney Council became somewhat perturbed when sections of its pavements started collapsing in recent years. It turned out that William Lyttle, 'the Mole Man of Hackney', had been burrowing tunnels all over the place from his home in Mortimer Road. After a court battle he was evicted from his home, which was condemned as unsafe because of the tunnels, and the council cleverly installed him in a top floor flat on the De Beauvoir estate, to curtail the tunnelling, while they trucked in concrete to shore up his former home. Or not so cleverly – he was soon found to have tunnelled through the walls of the flat, with holes everywhere and piles of rubble. He died aged 79 in 2010, leaving the council with a lot to look into.

TALES OF THE UNDERGROUND

We're used to Brits being sentimental about steam engines (with 100 steam lines run by volunteers at weekends it's no small phenomenon) and paddle steamers, but electric Tube trains are hardly up there with the *Flying Scotsman* and the *Orient Express*. In fact many people hate the hot, noisy and claustrophobic things. But not everyone...

THE MAN WHO TOOK THE LAST TUBE HOME

When London architect Mike Kelly left the City for rural Herefordshire he missed one thing: the Tube trains he had ridden to school, to college and to work. And not just any old Tube train. He was quoted as saying: 'I do have a sentimental attachment to the London Underground and to the 1959 Tube stock in particular.' So he was horrified when he heard all 1959 stock was heading for the scrapyard at the end of the 20th century.

He remembered his favourite type of train but also the number of one of the favourite cars he rode in as a child: car 1304. He tracked down this very car mouldering in a North London siding, bought it, and had it installed in his Herefordshire garden on a bit of track. It still says on the front that it's going to Finchley Central via Bank (aficionados will know we are on the Northern Line), but it'll never get there again. It makes a great garden ornament, he believes, and a good venue for a party ('Mind the gap, vicar!').

Not that he's alone in loving 1959 Tube stock, as I discovered while checking this wasn't all a leg-pull. There was a website dedicated to the 1959 trains, which included a picture of Mr Kelly's, and was all edged in black. I guessed that this was a symbol of mourning for their demise. But then I read: 'This page remains on a black background, in recognition of the Line on which these wonderful machines ended their days.'

POEM-POWERED TUBES AND A PINT OF BITTER, *BITTE*

Given that the London Tube passenger will famously avoid eye contact with every other person in a crowded carriage (unless he is a foreigner, a loony or a drunk, which increasing numbers are, in which case he may even start a *conversation*, for goodness sake), then the passenger has to look somewhere else. That leaves those curved card advertisements above passengers' heads, which consequently get read far more than they deserve.

One development of this was the series of **Poems on the Underground**, which some worthy person suggested – and why not, if it gets people to contemplate a bit of Andrew Marvell instead of 'Buy Biffo's Soap Powder'? In turn, that led to a rather good spoof in the book *Poems Not on the Underground* by someone called Straphanger, which included such gems as *Mind the Gap Rap*, or *To his Coy Train Operator*. You get the idea.

The **real ads** can be funny too, of course. At least, if you understand the Basil Fawlty don't-mention-the-war mentality of many Brits. (In other words, do mention it, but make people laugh.)

The great Kentish brewery Shepherd Neame (who have a beer, and a pub – the beer is elsewhere too; the pub isn't – in Smithfield, by the worrying name of Bishop's Finger) were promoting their jingoistically named Spitfire beer with the slogan: 'Downed all over Kent, just like the Luftwaffe.'

Better was a mock wartime aircraft recognition card with a British pint glass and a German stein in black silhouette, captioned 'Ours' and 'Theirs'. Yet another had a cryptic code message: 'The goat and the marmoset play all night by the river in the spring and later summer.' Certain letters had been ringed by a decoder to spell out 'German beer is pants.'

So the 'Bottle of Britain' went on, with 'Spitfire beer – No Fokker comes near' keeping the tone well lowered. It ended with the predictable mock German accent creeping in – 'Votz zo funny about zeez posters?' – and an eventual ban from London Underground chiefs who said they failed 'our taste test'. The taste test should perhaps have been applied to Spitfire beer, which is spiffing (as of course are many great German beers in their own way). Now the offending poster cards have become collectors' items. They've just been driven, well, underground ...

MURDEROUS LONDON

SITES OF THE CAPITAL'S MOST MACABRE KILLINGS

I wouldn't worry too much about being murdered in London: it very, very rarely happens to visitors. In fact you are 64 times less likely to be rubbed out here than in Washington, DC. But if you were, would it be any comfort to know that you might be knocked off rather eccentrically (to judge by the following examples)?

BLEEDING HEART YARD

At the **Bleeding Heart Restaurant** in Clerkenwell, you can savour your bloody steaks, bloody Marys or other food in the knowledge that on the very cobblestones you have just walked across, a most gruesome killing took place. As Charles Dickens recalls in *Little Dorrit*, the case involved the 17th-century society beauty Elizabeth Hatton, who, in 1626, had jilted the Spanish ambassador. The couple were seen at a ball just after this, whirling round most energetically, and then disappeared. The ball guests speculated that they had made it up, and were entwined limb-to-limb. Actually, Lady Hatton was being ripped apart. As Dickens relates, 'At dawn the body of Lady Hatton was found in the courtyard behind the stables torn limb from limb with her heart still pumping blood on to the cobblestones.' This offal history doesn't seem to put people off dining at this rather good, rather old-fashioned restaurant.

BLEEDING HEART YARD, Greville Street, EC1 ☎ 020 7242 2056

MOSSLEA ROAD, PENGE

Penge in South London has, to outsiders, a rather comic name. But what happened in Mosslea Road was so unfunny it shocked respectable Victorian London to the core and caused the name of the road to be changed out of shame. It is a macabre murder tale, but a crime whose solution came about because of two factors: that the centre of this road was then the boundary between the counties of Kent and Surrey, and a million-to-one chance encounter in a post office on, of all days, a Friday the 13th.

The victim was **Harriet Staunton**, born in 1841, who, when she was 33, being rather plain and weak-minded, had accepted the proposal of marriage from Louis Staunton, a lowly clerk. He was better-looking, and ten years younger, so why did he do this? She had an inheritance of £4,000 (ten years' pay for some people) and was expected to inherit more. Louis Staunton, under the laws of that time, took possession of this money.

He also had a mistress, and his aim seemed to be to get rid of his wife fairly quickly and enjoy her money. They married in 1875 and settled in Brixton. Louis Staunton quickly moved his mistress, Alice Rhodes, into the house under some pretence. Harriet had a son, born in 1876, and the household employed a servant – as middle-class families did at that time – who was Alice's cousin. Attempts by Harriet's worried family to see her were continually rebuffed.

By the end of 1876, Harriet was imprisoned and starved in a cottage in Cudham, Kent. The doors were locked and the windows nailed shut so she could not cry for help and her clothes taken away to discourage her from running away and to hasten her death in the freezing house. Louis Staunton, who steadfastly refused his miserable wife's pleas for a crust of bread, lived with his mistress in the same village. The baby boy was also being starved, but it is thought the servant fled with him to save him.

By April, the formerly healthy Harriet weighed just five stone (70lb or 33kg). Her ruthless husband realised that her death would attract attention in a small village, so, seeing the end was near, he hurriedly moved her by train to a house in Penge – in Forbes Road, as Mosslea Road was then called – where he had rented rooms. She died the day afterwards.

Louis Staunton was unsure about whether that house, an even number, was in Kent or Surrey, so he visited the corner post office to ask where to register a death. Standing in the queue behind Staunton was a certain Louis Victor de Casabianca who just happened to be in the area and needed a postage stamp. He was married to Harriet's sister and knew her family were frantically trying to contact her at Cudham.

The man in front of him in the queue gave the deceased woman's age and said she came from Cudham, Kent, which aroused Mr de Casabianca's suspicions. He found the name of the doctor who had just signed the death certificate and visited him, discovered it was his sister-in-law who was dead, and called the police. He identified the body which, according to the Press, was reduced to skin and bones, and crawling with lice.

Louis Staunton, Alice Rhodes, and Staunton's brother and his wife (who seemed to have gone along with the plot or done nothing about it) were all found guilty of murder and sentenced to be hanged.

Oddly, the death sentence was never carried out. An appeal was launched and Louis Staunton was sentenced instead to 20 years in prison. His brother had already died in jail, the brother's wife served just a few years and Alice Rhodes was released.

It was too late for poor Forbes Road. The lurid Press coverage had done its damage and house prices plunged in notorious Penge. The road name was changed to Mosslea Road in an attempt to shake off the gloom. But for the astonishing coincidence of Mr de Casabianca's need for a stamp that day – Friday 13 April 1877 – Louis Staunton could have enjoyed a comfortable early retirement instead of the grimy hell-hole of a Victorian jail.

HILLDROP CRESCENT, TUFNELL PARK

A quiet suburban road that fascinated and horrified the whole country in 1910. Here was the home of **Dr Hawley Crippen**, who was responsible for the particularly gruesome murder of his wife, Cora, a former music hall singer and dancer, and, after a dramatic transatlantic chase and some unlikely disguises adopted by the fugitive's mistress, the first man to be caught as a result of Mr Marconi's newfangled wireless telegraphy on ships.

It seems sexy Cora, who danced under the name Belle Ellmore, wasn't the woman Dr Crippen had thought when he married her. She was unfaithful with various entertainers and taunted Dr Crippen about this. So Crippen, an improbable Lothario or murderer, being a respectable, short, meek, balding 48-year-old dentist who had come from America to promote his medicines, began an affair with Ethel Le Neve, the typist at his Oxford Street offices.

In January 1910, Crippen ordered hydrobromide of hyoscine, a deadly poison, but a sedative if used in tiny quantities, from his chemist. Being a dentist, this was easily done.

On 31 January, Dr Crippen mixed his wife a hot toddy, including the poison, it was later surmised, because Dr Crippen never admitted to his actions. Cora, once sedated, would die peacefully and then he could call a colleague – whom he had primed with stories of Cora's supposed illness – with the shocking news of her death the next morning.

However, hydrobromide of hyoscine is a sedative only in small doses. Dr Crippen, had he been any good at his job, should have known that in larger doses it causes hallucinations, violent fits, vomiting, hysteria and screaming. It's not the behaviour you want from someone you are trying to murder discreetly.

He panicked, grabbed a pistol and shot his ranting wife through the head. This rather ruined the plan for calling a colleague to check the corpse. Unfortunately, although neighbours heard the sound, they did nothing. His next problem was how to dispose of the large corpse of a stout woman. Here, Dr Crippen's medical training came in handy and this is the macabre bit that absolutely fascinated Edwardian Britain.

He put her in the bath and filleted her, taking out the bones and burning them in the kitchen stove. He could then pulverise the ashes later. Left in the blood-filled bathtub was a floppy 'rubber woman', like a deflated balloon. He cut out the torso and buried it under the stone flags of the cellar. He put her limbs, organs and head in a box in the yard. Having fallen asleep, he woke early and burned his bloody clothes and cleaned up any other traces, then went to work as normal.

That evening, he dropped the box of internal organs in a nearby canal, weighted with bricks. His troublesome wife was gone. But how to explain her disappearance? The next day he told his mistress Ethel that his wife had left him, and surprised her even more by giving her Cora's jewellery. She chose some and he later pawned the rest in Holloway, near his home, for £3,195 – a heap of money then.

At this point Dr Crippen started making silly mistakes. He asked Ethel to deliver a letter to the local Ladies' Guild, of which Cora was the honorary treasurer. Purporting to be from Cora, it informed the society that she had been called urgently to America by the illness of a relative, and would therefore be resigning her post and returning their books. The Guild members suspected it was not her handwriting, nor her likely actions.

The next mistake was to use the spare ticket for the Guild's ball on 20 February to take Ethel. Dr Crippen said that as Cora was out of town, he might well bring his secretary. Clearly as they danced it was evident that this was more than a professional relationship, and suddenly the eagle-eyed Guild ladies noticed Cora's favourite brooch on Ethel's dress. The scandal grew.

In March, Dr Crippen told friends that his wife had been taken ill in California, and that he was expecting very sad news. On 24 March he further telegraphed them that Cora had died. He was, in fact, in Dieppe, having a weekend with Ethel.

Dr Crippen's next mistake was to tell the Ladies' Guild that there would be no funeral as Cora had asked to be cremated. They knew, as she was a Catholic, that this was quite impossible. The doughty matrons of the Ladies' Guild were less than convinced and swung into action like so many Miss Marples.

The Guild members tracked down the only shipping company that had a ship that should have sailed on the date Dr Crippen gave for Cora's departure to the States. The ship was out of action on that day, under repair in dock. They then contacted the Californian authorities about the date of death Dr Crippen had given. No such woman had died on that day either.

They sent for the police who called on Dr Crippen, and he told them it was indeed a fabricated story, to cover up his runaway wife's unfaithfulness. The detectives were, oddly, convinced.

The Ladies' Guild didn't give up that easily. They inquired after the doctor at his Oxford Street surgery and found that he and Ethel had both suddenly disappeared. They had taken a train to Harwich in Essex, intending to take a ferry to Rotterdam and meet a liner going to Canada. Ethel claimed in her later memoirs that she still did not know Cora was dead, and was told it was to escape the malicious gossip.

The police called again at Hilldrop Crescent and, at long last, made a search of the house, where they found that one of the cellar flag stones could be raised easily.

They dug a hole and soon came across what appeared to be revolting animal remains. But a pathologist pronounced them to be a woman's boneless torso. Traces of poison were also found. An operation scar matched one Cora was known to have had.

An **arrest warrant** was issued for Dr Crippen and Ethel le Neve. This is another extraordinary part of the story. They disguised themselves as father and son, Mr and Master Robinson, travelling on the SS *Montrose* to Canada.

But the ship's master, Captain Harry Kendall, was suspicious about the 'boy' in his ill-fitting clothes. The feminine sway of 'his' hips was not right.

By chance, the captain had a newspaper featuring pictures of the two suspects. When he was well past Land's End, going into the Atlantic, he sent the world's first radio message to result in the capture of a fugitive to his base in Liverpool. The Morse code message read:

Have strong suspicion that Crippen London Cellar Murderer and accomplice are among saloon passengers. Mustache taken off growing beard. Accomplice dressed as boy. Voice manner and build undoubtedly a girl. Both travelling as Mr and Master Robinson. Kendall.

Scotland Yard's Inspector Walter Dew, a sergeant and two female prison warders got on an overnight express for Liverpool and picked up a faster ship that was just leaving for Quebec and would probably arrive a day earlier – a real cliffhanger that the Press followed with verve. The 'Robinsons' sunned themselves on the deck unaware of the meaning of the buzzing of the Marconi aerial strung over their heads. (Wirelesses were a recent invention and you had to hire Marconi men to operate them. Not many months later one such machine would play a crucial role in the *Titanic* disaster.)

The story got even better. Ethel became a heroine when a little Belgian boy playing on the deck slipped through the rails and would have fallen to his death had not Ethel grabbed his ankle. The scream 'Master Robinson' gave, officers noted, was definitely that of a girl.

Dr Crippen seemed to suspect the game was up. As the ship approached Quebec, a launch met it, and Crippen was stopped by a tall man saying: 'Good morning, Dr Crippen.' He replied at once: 'Good morning, Inspector Dew.'

Crippen was brought back, tried, and condemned to 'be taken from this court to a place of execution and there hanged by the neck until dead'. He tried to make an appeal and sought a reprieve through the Home Secretary, Winston Churchill, but the execution was set for 23 November 1910.

Inspector Dew was so upset by the case that he resigned, aged only 47, before Dr Crippen was hanged. Ethel returned to Canada, and worked there until 1916, when she came back to England under a new name and married a Croydon accountant who looked like Dr Crippen. She had children and her husband eventually died, never having known her part in the most notorious killing of the era. She lived at Addiscombe, Surrey, as a quiet, respectable, needleworking grandmother until she died in 1967.

Top o' the Morning pub, Hackney Wick

The Top o' the Morning pub at 129 Cadogan Terrace (☎ *020 8985 9917*) hides a macabre secret. It was here that **Thomas Briggs, victim of the first railway murder in England**, was brought to die of his wounds in 1864. At the time, the story was an absolute sensation, not least because of the dramatic transatlantic chase that ensued. In this respect and others it was a strange precursor of the Crippen case (see above).

Given the pessimism the rapid spread of railways in the previous 40 years had brought – with doomsayers predicting murder, rape, suicide, theft of luggage, etc, plus the transport of the lower 'criminal classes' to areas where they had been hitherto rare – it is perhaps surprising that this was the first recorded murder on a train, particularly as they were, by the 1860s, conveying many millions of people per year. And particularly when you consider that passengers were conveyed in compartments without connecting doors or corridors – the terms coach, guard, etc, had after all been adapted from the horse-drawn variety whose design was simply copied – and there was no emergency communication cord with which panicking passengers could stop the train.

On the evening of 9 July 1864 there was still some light in the sky as the 9.50pm North London Railway service left Fenchurch Street terminus. By the time it arrived at Hackney at 10.11pm there were just the last glimmerings, and two bank clerks got into an empty first-class compartment. One of them put his hand on a seat and felt something damp. It was blood. They called the guard who checked the compartment, and found blood all over the cushions and the further door. He locked the compartment and telegraphed ahead to Chalk Farm Station, where the carriage was detached for police examination. There was also a black hat, a stick and a bag as clues.

Meanwhile, an alert driver travelling in the opposite direction from Hackney to Bow Station spotted what seemed to be a body between the tracks. He stopped the train and the severely injured man, whose head had been battered in – and who turned out to be a 70-year-old bank clerk, Thomas Briggs – was carried to a nearby pub, where he died. The murder – which had obviously involved robbery, as Briggs's gold watch and spectacles were missing – caused outrage at the lack of protection for railway passengers. An official reward was offered.

The first help resulting from this publicity came, oddly enough, from a **Mr Death** – a jeweller who had been offered some of the victim's belongings. This in turn led to a cabbie who knew a German tailor called Franz Muller who became the suspect. Muller had a jeweller's box marked – a macabre touch – 'Death' and had fled across the Atlantic on 15 July aboard the sailing ship *Victoria*, bound for New York, as the hue and cry over Briggs intensified.

Warrants were issued and the newspaper-reading public was agog as detectives boarded a faster steam ship on 20 July. This meant that they were able to overtake the fugitive and arrest him on arrival in America. Muller was brought back, tried – his alibi of being with a prostitute at the time led to the judge's observation that 'little reliance should be placed on a clock in a brothel', which leads one to wonder how the judge knew – and publicly hanged on 14 November of the same year. So many drunks crowded and fought to see the hanging, and there were so many robberies in this thick crowd in the Old Bailey outside Newgate jail, that this contributed towards the end of public executions in 1868. At least 50,000 people attended the hanging, and one of the beneficiaries of such macabre fascination was, ironically, the railway companies, which ran special excursion trains.

The case had another consequence. The public clamour for more protection aboard trains led to the communication cord, which was originally a cord or chain running inside the roof that any passenger could pull to apply the brakes.

CRANLEY GARDENS, MUSWELL HILL

One of the most macabre serial killers in London's history was uncovered by an unpleasant drain problem. Read no further if you are squeamish.

In February 1983, tenants at flats in Cranley Gardens, between Highgate and Muswell Hill, complained of their toilets not flushing and vile smells. A drainage clearance company discovered rotting meat and bits of flesh with hair on it in the drain, which they discussed with the tenants. When the police looked the next morning most of the evidence had been cleared away but sufficient traces confirmed their human origin.

When **Dennis Nilsen**, who was born in Scotland but had a Norwegian father, returned from work in a Soho employment office, detectives waiting to question him found their task unexpectedly easy. One of them said: 'Don't mess me about, where's the rest of the body?' The first great surprise was that Nilsen said straightaway: 'In the wardrobe. I'll show you.'

The second great surprise came in the car back to the police station. Nilsen was asked casually by a detective how many bodies were involved. 'One or two?' Nilsen calmly replied: 'About 15 or 16.'

It transpired that he was preying on young male vagrants or gays whom he picked up in public toilets and offered a warm meal and a bed for the night in exchange for sex. He then strangled them at his flat. The first was killed at his previous address in Melrose Avenue in 1978 and, quite some time later after being hidden under the floorboards, burned in the garden. There followed several similar victims – one a Canadian tourist.

After moving to a flat with no garden – here's a 'gruesome bit' warning! – Nilsen resorted to using the butchery skills he had learned in the Army, boiling the flesh in cooking pots so it would go down the drains. Evidently this plan did not entirely work. Nilsen was there when the drain clearance man arrived and knew he was likely to be exposed. On the day of his arrest, he told a colleague at work: 'If I'm not in tomorrow, I'll either be ill, dead, or in jail.' They laughed like drains.

Later that year, Nilsen, who pleaded not guilty to murder on grounds of insanity was found sane and convicted of six murders. He was sentenced to life imprisonment with a minimum of 25 years. He was not encouraged to do the cooking in prison, but his stove and favourite head-boiling pan are preserved as they were found in Scotland Yard's Black Museum, open only to the police.

THE GOAT PUB, KENSINGTON HIGH STREET

John George Haigh, who had a polite, impeccable English manner, committed a series of grisly murders in London that horrified and fascinated the public, when the facts came out, because he thought he had the perfect way of disposing of bodies. Like Dennis Nilsen, he was proved wrong. Haigh, born in 1909, had a very strict Christian upbringing (he later said he had nightmares about forests of crucifixes dripping blood). He moved to London in the 1930s and was involved in the car trade and petty scams, taking him in and out of prison.

He was a chauffeur for the McSwann family before one such term in jail and bumped into William McSwann again in 1944. The two went for a few drinks at **the Goat**, still a popular pub in Kensington High Street today. Haigh took McSwann under some pretext to one of his nearby workshops where he smashed his skull in. He put the body in a **barrel full of acid**. After trying to fool McSwann's parents for a while that their son was hiding from military call-up, he murdered them too, then impersonated William Donald McSwann in order to gain control of their property.

In 1947 he meted out the same treatment to a wealthy couple called Henderson whom he'd met during a property transaction. He gave them 'acid baths' at his new workshops at Crawley, Sussex. Haigh came undone with the case of widow Mrs Olive Durand-Deacon, 69, who in 1949 lived at the same boarding-house as Haigh, the **Onslow Court Hotel** in South Kensington. Haigh met her at mealtimes and had told her he was an inventor. When she wanted to demonstrate an idea of hers, Haigh took her to the Crawley workshops in his impressive grey Alvis sports car and shot her too. After taking her jewellery and fur coats, she was dumped into an acid barrel and Haigh returned to the Onslow Court Hotel for a relaxed three-course dinner.

Other guests were soon anxious about Mrs Durand-Deacon, and Haigh said he had failed to meet her and was worried too. He offered to accompany one of the others to Chelsea police, who were also unconvinced.

The next day Haigh drove to the Crawley workshop and dumped the acid sludge into the yard. He also made the mistake of taking Mrs Durand-Deacon's jewels to a Horsham valuer. When he returned to the hotel, the police – who had traced his full criminal record – were waiting to question him. He maintained his story but the police had also discovered the address of the Crawley workshops, where they found heavy rubber gloves, empty acid jars, a gas mask and a cleaning receipt for a fur coat like the victim's. Plus a recently fired army revolver.

Faced with this evidence, Haigh confessed, adding in the McSwanns and the Hendersons, and saying he used acid baths to dispose of the bodies. But he added chillingly: 'How can you prove a murder if there is no body?' He also claimed to have drunk some of his victims' blood, but this was never proved and was regarded by some as an attempt to escape the noose by pleading insanity.

He had not reckoned with the mute testimony of normally insignificant parts of the human body: gallstones. That and the painstaking, if gruesome, work of Home Office forensic pathologist, Dr Keith Simpson. Simpson found an acid-proof hatpin in one barrel. In the yard, he was looking around the messy sludge when he noticed what he thought might be a gallstone from a human or an animal. He had the pool of sludge collected and taken to police laboratories. Here analysts found a set of dentures and two more gallstones. The dentures were identified by Mrs Durand-Deacon's dentist. Justice was swift. Haigh's trial at Lewes, Sussex, lasted just two days in July 1949, the jury taking around ten minutes to find him guilty on all charges. The famous hangman, Albert Pierrepoint, was waiting for Haigh at the trapdoor in Wandsworth Prison, South London, on a fine morning in August.

GHASTLY CRIME AND CAPITAL PUNISHMENT

Before Tyburn became the place of common execution, **Smithfield** in the City was where most hangings took place, not far from where they eventually ended up at Newgate (the Old Bailey). In the 16th century Smithfield became known for religious persecution: Roman Catholic 'Bloody' Mary Tudor burned 49 Protestants there for refusing to acknowledge the Pope.

Mary's final tally, according to Foxe's *Book of Martyrs*, was 314, including widows, labourers and even two blind girls and two infants. How infants could be Protestants and how anyone burning them could be Christian is a question even the worst bigot would find hard to answer.

Perhaps they were among the 16 he records who died in prison or the 12 who were buried alive in dunghills.

Earlier in the 16th century a poisoner called Richard Rose was boiled to death in a cauldron here. Cruelly, like the best-boiled eggs, he was cooked from cold, so it took two hours to kill him. Smithfield was also the site of the execution of Scottish leader Sir William Wallace, lionised as Braveheart in the film of that name. He was hanged, drawn and quartered (castration thrown in free) here in 1305.

GOING WEST, BEING ON THE WAGON AND PERVERTED POSH LADIES

When **Newgate prison** stood where the Old Bailey now is, many a prisoner, be he highwayman, Catholic martyr or whatever, was forced to walk the three miles to **Tyburn**, now Marble Arch, to be hanged on the 'Tyburn tree', set up in 1571 (see also *Lost rivers*, page 129), or was taken there by cart. Thus they would pass **St Giles's High Street** (before St Giles Circus, the junction of Tottenham Court Road and Oxford Street).

Here a **strange ceremony** would ensue. Matilda, queen of Henry I, had founded St Giles as a leper colony (he is their patron saint) and left money

in her will for a cup of charity to be given to the condemned marching in chains to Tyburn (the origin of '**going west**'). By the end of the Middle Ages, it had become the custom for the **Bow Tavern** to give the condemned a pint of ale and they would sit there being cheered on by all the leering low life of London.

Another custom of this time was that if the executioner rode in the cart, he didn't get off to drink alcohol, hence the phrase being '**on the wagon**', a term for someone abstaining. Usually, the condemned would dress well and walk with a swagger, a practice recorded with complete astonishment by foreigners. The standing joke of the condemned was that they would pay for the drink on the way back.

Jonathan Swift pictures in his poem *Clever Tom Clinch Going To Be Hanged* (1726) another example of the criminal being executed as a kind of popular hero – with more than a frisson of excitement for the ladies:

> As clever Tom Clinch, while the rabble was bawling,
> Rode through stately Holbourn, to die in his calling;
> He stopt at the George for a bottle of sack,

And promis'd to pay for it when he'd come back.
His waistcoat and stocking, and breeches were white,
His cap had a new cherry ribbon ty't.
The Maids to the doors and the balconies ran,
And said, lack-a-day! He's a proper young man.
But as from the windows the ladies he spy'd
Like a beau in the box, he bow'd low on each side…
And when his last speech the loud hawkers did cry,
He swore from the cart, it was all a damned lye.

Instruments of torture and other gruesome devices

PROBABLY THE WORST HELL-HOLE in London's history of torture and brutality was the White Tower at the Tower of London, where every possible instrument of torture was collected, and used. There was the **rack** for stretching victims until the ball joints dislocated like a barbecued chicken leg being snapped off. Another demonic device was **'Skeffington's Daughter'**, named after a 16th-century governor of the Tower, which compressed the prisoner's body within boards until blood spurted from every orifice and, ultimately, the skull cracked. Nice. Or as an alternative, you might just possibly, conceivably, confess to something you hadn't done.

Then there was a particularly vile punishment, a cell called **'Little Ease'**, in which you could neither stand up nor lie down at full-length. If you've ever suffered a 14-hour flight in economy class, imagine that going on for 14 months without being able to get up and walk around the cabin. You'd end up looking like Danny de Vito.

The gates of London, including those at London Bridge and Temple Bar, were equipped with **spikes** to take the parboiled heads of traitors. One such was that of Catholic martyr **Bishop St John Fisher** (1485–1540), executed at the Tower, and whose head, a witness said:

The hangman for pardon fell down on one knee;
Tom gave him a kick in the guts for his fee…

I record elsewhere how society beauties would swoon after highwaymen (see page 132), but there was a more macabre, even perverted, scramble at Tyburn once the horses had been whipped to pull the carts clear and leave the prisoners dangling and twitching on the infamous Tyburn tree (they died slowly of strangulation, by the way, the trapdoor and slip noose which breaks your neck being more modern). When the bodies were cut down,

…being parboiled, was pricked upon a pole and set high on London Bridge. And here I cannot omit to declare unto you the miraculous sight of this head which stood up to the space of 14 days upon the bridge… daily it grew fresher and fresher, so that in his lifetime he never looked so well, for his cheeks being beautified by a comely red.

If they'd left it up any longer, he would have started preaching.

Occasionally, in a storm, the decayed head of a traitor would blow off and roll past the feet of shrieking ladies. By the 19th century, the spikes had been removed, which is just as well, as the Queen has to stop at Temple Bar (or where it stood) before she may enter the City. I don't suppose Her Majesty would ever shriek at a rolling head, but let's not put her to the test. The spot is marked by a particularly fearsome griffin statue (see Fleet Street walk, page 229).

Probably the last beheading was outside Newgate in 1820 when the five Cato Street conspirators had their heads removed with knives after being hanged. The Cato Street conspiracy was a rather amateur attempt at revolution in the early 19th century. A small group of conspirators believed that if they assassinated government ministers and paraded their heads on poles around the poorer districts of London, a popular uprising would put the conspirators into power.

Their bid to put their plan into action was known to the police, who surprised them as they were preparing their hopeless attempt in a **Cato Street apartment**. They killed a police officer while resisting arrest, so four of the conspirators were executed at Newgate on 1 May 1820.

ON THE WEST (left) side of New Bridge Street, which leads to Ludgate Circus from Blackfriars Bridge, can be seen the old gatehouse of **Bridewell Prison**. This House of Correction was opened in 1555 and eventually replaced in the 19th century by Holloway Prison in North London.

Public whippings

This was a House of Correction aimed at the chastisement of mischievous apprentices, unruly orphans and loose women who broke the law. A popular amusement for Londoners was to see the inmates being whipped in a black-draped cell, particularly the women, who were stripped to the waist before being thrashed. So many wanted to watch this that a gallery was built to accommodate them.

there was an unholy scramble to get at them. For one thing, the common people believed the touch of the newly dead would cure anything.

The *London Encyclopaedia* records how one young woman, a beauty 'all pale and trembling… submitted to have her bosom uncovered in the presence of thousands of spectators and the dead man's hands placed upon it'. The hand would have been still warm, if not twitching.

As well as those wanting to touch the corpse, there was a ready market for freshly hacked-off hands of the dead (for curative purposes) and, of course, good prices were paid for fresh corpses by medical schools.

FROM TYBURN TO THE OLD BAILEY

The abolition of executions at Tyburn in 1783 wasn't because of any great moral squeamishness about bunches of people dying before thousands of cheering, jeering, laughing onlookers, but – typically, in terms of priorities – because the rich people moving into Oxford Street and Mayfair in the late 18th century objected to the crowds of common people turning up in their droves to pack Mother Proctor's pews, a specially constructed

THE MOST UNWELCOME SOUND in London's history was the sound of a church bell. A very particular church bell. If you look in **St Sepulchre's church**, off Snow Hill and Holborn Viaduct in the City, there is an old bell mounted in front of the pulpit. This was used on the eve of an execution at the nearby Newgate Prison, where the Old Bailey now stands (see next page). The St Sepulchre bell-ringer would visit the condemned at midnight and rouse them with this bell and urge them to make their peace with their Maker while time allowed. So there you are, having bribed the guard to get you a bottle of cheap booze to send you to sleep after your last supper, despite all your nerves, and some nincompoop from St Sepulchre's comes in and makes an awful din.

To make matters worse, they often intoned a dirge-like verse:

> All ye that in the condemned hole do lie
> Prepare ye, for tomorrow ye shall die
> Watch out and pray: the hour is drawing near
> That ye before the Almighty must appear
> Examine well yourselves, in time repent
> That ye may not be to eternal flames sent
> And when St Sepulchre's Bell in the morning tolls
> The Lord above have mercy of your souls
> BONG BONG! PAST TWELVE O'CLOCK! BONG BONG!

Bloody racket. It might be enough to make you blaspheme, I should imagine, rather than beg the Almighty's mercy.

As recounted in the Fleet Street walk (see page 229), to add insult to injury, on the way to Tyburn the next morning the procession would stop outside St Sepulchre's so that the condemned could be presented with a nosegay (just when they were looking forward to a free pint). I imagine it was not unknown for a priest to get a good kick in the conkers from the condemned man for his troubles. After all, what could the authorities do? Hang him twice?

The knell of doom

grandstand next to the infamous Tyburn tree. After Tyburn's black role was ended, hangings took place right in the **Old Bailey outside Newgate Prison**, making the last journey of the condemned across London unnecessary.

In fact, moving from Tyburn did not decrease the crowd's appetite for macabre spectacle, only the space available to them, so that sometimes on a hanging Monday, more people died underfoot than on the gallows. Around 100 people died or were seriously hurt at a double-hanging in 1807, for example.

The aristocracy were not above such voyeurism – they rented rooms at the adjacent Magpie and Stump pub to watch the hangings.

The **last public hanging at Newgate** was of Michael Barrett in 1868, an Irish terrorist convicted of blowing up six people. After that, executions were carried out within the jail.

Dickens was instrumental in getting public executions stopped. He wrote a letter to *The Times* in 1849 complaining of the 'atrocious bearing' of the spectators at the double-hanging of a Mr and Mrs Manning at Horsemonger Lane Prison in Southwark.

The present 19-court Old Bailey on Newgate's site was opened in 1907 and hosted some of Britain's most notorious and spectacular trials.

THE LAST HANGINGS THAT MADE HIT FILMS: BENTLEY AND ELLIS

The last few hangings in London – by then taking place in various jails – were deeply controversial and included that of **Derek Bentley** in 1955. He was a simpleton hanged for being with a youth who, during a burglary, shot a policeman after Bentley allegedly said: 'Let him have it.' The only problems were that Bentley could have meant either 'shoot him' or 'give him the gun', that there was little evidence he ever said anything of the sort, and that his accomplice who fired the fatal shot, being too young for the rope, was merely imprisoned while the mental-defective Bentley was hanged for being party to the crime.

At long last, in 1998, Bentley's conviction for murder was quashed and he was given a posthumous pardon. The reaction of his accomplice Christopher Craig seemed genuinely heartfelt. He was quoted as saying: 'I am truly sorry that my actions on 2 November 1952 caused so much pain and misery for the family of PC Miles, who died that night doing his duty. Also, for the Bentley family, I regret that Iris, Derek's sister, who fought all those years for Derek's pardon, died recently before this appeal was concluded.' See the excellent film *Let Him Have It*.

Also in 1955, **Ruth Ellis**, a much abused victim who shot her cheating lover, David Blakely, outside the **Magdala pub in Hampstead**, swung for it at Holloway, despite huge public sympathy. The sorry story was also made into a rather good film, *Dance With A Stranger*, starring Miranda Richardson and Rupert Everett.

Ruth Ellis was the last woman in Britain to go to the rope, amid some protest, although one voice that dissented from the general sympathy expressed in the newspapers (see the *Daily Mirror* clipping inside the Magdala pub) was the woman passer-by who had bullets whizz past her. She thought it quite right that Ellis was hanged.

Hanging finally ended in 1964, to the regret of a sizeable proportion of the public – at times a majority. As in the next case…

WELCOME TO WORMWOOD SCRUBS

Wormwood Scrubs. Relish it, roll it round your tongue, spit it out, growl it with sinister intent. It's a name a Hammer Horror writer would make up for a grim, rain-swept prison, or a blasted heath on the edge of clanking railway yards and grimy industrial scrapyards. Tatty gangland streets where merciless shootings take place, a grim Cold War venue for treachery and escaping spies.

In which case the writer would be dead right. That is exactly what the Scrubs is, or at least has been.

If it feels a bit of a geographical no-man's-land, then history has certainly given that impression. It currently belongs to the Borough of Hammersmith and Fulham, the latter place being a million miles away socially and not a few literally. Immediately to the east of the open space of the Scrubs, there's North Kensington, which is a detached and wholly different experience from other parts of Kensington. It is somewhere many posh Kensington or South Kensington types wouldn't be seen dead in, or perhaps fear they *would* be seen dead in.

The A40 expressway flyover marks the rough boundary – the emphasis being on the rough – between shabby North Kensington and the deeply trendy Notting Hill where all kinds of stars, trust-fund trendies and politicos such as David Cameron have to be seen to hang out. The contrast between chavs and the chav-nots is so extreme that straying across the boundary has, from time to time, led to gruesome results.

To add to the confusion, this area was long ago a detached outstation of Chelsea, another area as different from here as chalk from cheese, and was known as the Chelsea Outlands. It was a forest for pigs to root for acorns.

Linking the Scrubs to North Kensington is the wonderfully named **North Pole Road**, and nearby there was an old-fashioned railway signal box called North Pole. I'd always wanted to get a picture of it in snow, or take a children's Santa Special train there for a treat.

The whole North Pole thing is because of a pub of that name, but is not inappropriate as the Bible refers to bitter wormwood at the end of the world.

Back to Wormwood Scrubs. What a great name. Can you imagine a developer coming up with a name like that now? Shepherd's Mead, Green Acres, Fair Lawns, Palace View… give me Wormwood Scrubs any day. One authority says the Wormwood name originates in a snake-infested forest.

The Scrubs was put on the map in a big way when the Army built **Wood Lane** up to here from the south and leased the land so the Life Guards could exercise in the open space, something they have done ever since. Some of that land, 20 acres, was sold in 1873 to the Director of Convict Prisons where the jail, built by convict labour, still stands. It was designed by Sir Edmund Du Cane, the penal reformer, so the prison stands in Du Cane Road.

Another major step in the story of the Scrubs came at the turn of the 20th century when local people were scandalised at the sight of poor men and women, often more than 100 of them, sleeping in the open on Shepherd's Bush Green because they had nowhere else to go.

The Guardians of the Poor were impelled by the outrage to open a new hospital near Wormwood Scrubs in 1905. It was so well appointed that it was nicknamed the 'Paupers' Palace'. Eventually that became the famous **Hammersmith Hospital** that stands there today.

Another landmark for the area came with the 1908 Olympic Games, which were based at **White City**, which still has its own Tube station on the Central Line (haven't they all gone home yet?). Later the **BBC Television Centre** was built on the site.

Other claims to fame, or infamy, of the Scrubs have included the Braybrook Street shootings in 1966, which took place on the west of the Scrubs, and the escape of spy George Blake a few months later.

THE BRAYBROOK STREET SHOOTINGS

The Braybrook Street shootings were particularly horrifying and this was one of those crimes that transfixed the whole country from the day it happened to the end of the villains' trial. Indeed, as I write 45 years later, public anger still seethes and letters to newspapers still pour in when the release of the gang from jail is discussed. The brutal killings came at a time when hanging had just been abolished and arming the police was being discussed, so the crime was politically explosive too.

A monument in Braybrook Street marks the place where, in August 1966, a car carrying a gang of three low-lives on their way to commit an armed robbery was stopped by three policemen doing routine checks for such minor things as expired road tax discs. The police were, of course, unarmed and it was, for them, appalling luck to have stopped this Standard Vanguard car. No mercy was shown to PC Geoffrey Fox, Sergeant Christopher Head and Detective Constable David Wombwell who were, one by one, shot dead.

People were appalled that our unarmed bobbies could be murdered like this. Scotland Yard received 50,000 letters and calls of sympathy from the public and the then huge sum of £70,000 was raised within days to help the grieving families.

The murder hunt obsessed the nation as, one by one, the villains were hunted down. The capital's cab and lorry drivers vowed collectively to find the Standard Vanguard car and it was soon located in a railway arch in South London.

The names of the suspects were published and one newspaper headlining the story '50,000,000 detectives' was not far off the mark. Fellow criminals, disgusted by the gang's callousness, handed the police information and within weeks two of the gang, John Duddy and Jack Witney, were arrested. The last of the villains, Harry Roberts, was tracked down in a forest near East London, living rough in a camouflaged makeshift shelter. Roberts was unearthed by armed police who combed the forest with dogs from end to blockaded end.

Many of those who had opposed the recent abolition of capital punishment doubted if the criminals would have shot the policemen if a noose had been waiting for them. We will never know that, but Duddy died behind bars while Witney was found in a pool of blood at his Bristol home just after being released on licence after serving 25 years. These three never showed any genuine remorse; in fact one of them had a tattoo boasting of the killing. Roberts was interviewed by a London *Evening Standard* reporter in 1995 and, according to its report, expressed no personal remorse for what he had done: 'I had to do what I chose to do.' He thought he should spend his 'retirement' fishing. What a pity a retired PC Geoffrey Fox, Sergeant Christopher Head and Detective Constable David Wombwell couldn't go fishing.

COLD WAR SPY ESCAPE: ECCENTRIC ESPIONAGE

Wormwood Scrubs was the scene of one of the most sensational spy stories of the Cold War, putting this grim bit of northwest London on the map with around-the-world front-page news. **Double agent George Blake**, who had worked for Britain's MI6 monitoring spying in eastern Europe while all the time passing top secret information to the Russians, was caught. He escaped dramatically from Wormwood Scrubs Prison in October 1966.

The seriousness of Blake's treachery has been debated by pundits ever since he was caught. Some said the 42-year jail sentence he received reflected just one year for each agent killed as a result of his revelations. Blake, speaking in Moscow later, denied he had killed any agents personally, but admitted he had passed their names to the Soviets. So what did he think the KGB would do? Give them tea and biscuits or torture or murder them? Any guesses, George?

The entire British spy network in the Middle East was also compromised and destroyed because of the work of this – in some ways – James Bond-like man: suave, dark-haired, athletic and charming to men and women alike.

On the day after his escape, the Shepherd's Bush area was swamped with police, and all airports and seaports were closely watched. Was it a top-level Russian-controlled escape?

Well, no. The escape itself was rather amateur. The authorities found the bars of his cell had been sawn through with a smuggled-in file or hacksaw and that a rope ladder made with nylon cord and knitting needles had been thrown over the prison wall from the outside. It later emerged that Blake had been smuggled to East Germany by two British sympathisers in a camper van, aided by an Irish adventurer.

The two men behind Blake's escape turned out to be 'peaceniks' – idealistic peace campaigners who met him in the Scrubs after being jailed for protesting inside an American airbase in Britain.

They 'sprang' Blake with no pressure from the Soviets and no financial inducements, because they believed in the communist system. They were among those whom the Soviets called 'useful idiots'; had Stalin taken over Britain they would doubtless have been among the first to go to the death camps.

After getting Blake out, they didn't know what to do with their hot potato. They took him round a series of the houses of friends who in horror said: 'Isn't that the man hundreds of armed police are searching for?' and moved him on. It was farcical. In the end, with Blake hidden in the floor of their campervan, they got as far as the East German border from where the double agent made his way to Moscow.

CAREER ECCENTRICS

LONDON'S ODDEST AND OLDEST JOBS

London has the daftest jobs in the world: The Queen's Swan Marker, Rouge Dragon, Blue Mantle. And who has to disobey a direct order from the monarch? How do you get to be a Pearly King and who are they? What's the vilest job in London? All will be revealed…

BEADLES The Burlington Arcade, an exclusive and elegant walk of shops – one daren't use such a common phrase as 'shopping mall' – off Piccadilly has uniformed Beadles who patrol the street much as they did 200 years ago. They are all tall, former army officers and their duties are to enforce the rules against singing, dancing, opening umbrellas, carrying large packages or running. But then no one of any standing would carry large packages, would they? What an outrageous suggestion!

THE EARL MARSHAL, HEREDITARY MARSHAL OF ENGLAND Thanks to William the Conqueror, who created this job, there is always someone to lead the monarch to Parliament at State openings, to the throne at coronations and to the grave at royal funerals. The Howards, Dukes of Norfolk, have just about got used to the task as they have been doing it since 1483, so they have rather more experience of kingship than most kings have. Come to think of it, when the cartoon character Andy Capp said he was a treacle-bender (so the employment authorities couldn't ever find him a job) he might have done better to say he wanted to be Marshal of England. No chance. The Howards have somehow managed to maintain their allegiance to the Roman Catholic Church through the periods when this faith was persecuted. One of their most magnificent seats has for centuries been Arundel Castle in Sussex, superbly sited to command a strategically important gap in the South Downs. By tradition, the Duke of Norfolk's eldest son is always the Earl of Arundel. One of the Earl Marshal's little-known jobs is to sit as judge in the Court of Chivalry. This court within the College of Arms has legal jurisdiction over heraldry, the titles and ranks of aristocrats, etc. It is dusted and maintained beautifully but has not been used since 1954, so it's only part time (being convened once every 50 years or so). The Earl Marshal also appoints the King of Arms.

GENTLEMAN USHER OF THE BLACK ROD, SECRETARY TO THE LORD GREAT CHAMBERLAIN AND SERGEANT-AT-ARMS OF THE HOUSE OF LORDS This is a rather long-winded way of saying 'doorman' or 'usher', as in cinema usherettes: someone who ushers people in and out of places, opening or closing doors.

This particular doorman (traditionally, these roles are combined) has a hell of a lot of history hanging from his short black staff, however. Edward III wanted someone to keep the Knights of the Garter in order, and mind the doors while their annual ceremonial took place at Windsor (as it does today), so an usher was appointed in 1348 and given a black rod made of blackthorn. Pay: twelve old pence a day for life (that's 5p, not allowing for inflation).

While he still performs this function, Black Rod is better known for his role at the State Opening of Parliament. Here the tradition is that the Queen (or King) arrives by coach and a magnificent procession takes her into the House of Lords, where her throne awaits her. She then sends Black Rod to command the House of Commons to attend and hear her speech as to what 'my Government' has in mind for legislation. Black Rod approaches the door of the Commons, only to have it slammed shut in his face. He then beats his rod on the door with crashes that echo through the building – and presumably dent the woodwork – when he is admitted to the Commons.

He conveys the Queen's command to 'attend upon Her Majesty immediately in the House of Peers'. If she wants them immediately, why do they slam the door in her usher's face? On the answer to this question hinges a lot of blood spilled and heads chopped off, including that of Charles I, in the Civil War between king and Parliament, and the key issue of how democracy can thrive in a monarchy.

On 4 January 1642, Charles I burst into the House of Commons to arrest five Members of Parliament who had disagreed with the king and were therefore, in his opinion, treacherous. He wanted to fling them in the Tower and probably execute them. There was a convention that parliamentary privilege prevented the arrest of any elected MP, but Charles told the Speaker that this did not include treason. The MPs were outraged, and the five wanted members were nowhere to be seen. Charles demanded to know their whereabouts and the Speaker famously, and courageously, replied: 'Your Majesty, I have ears to hear and eyes to see only as this honourable House shall command me.'

A furious Charles said: 'I see all my birds have flown,' left the chamber humiliated, with MPs yelling 'privilege' at him. It was the beginning of the Civil War and years of misery, brother fighting brother, whole towns, armies, churches and castles being destroyed before things got back on an even keel with the Restoration of 1660. One of the first things Charles II did, not being a total prat like his father, was to get himself a Black Rod to summon the Commons for him. It was a lot less troublesome.

THE KING OF ARMS People who wish to use heraldry, that is coats of arms, etc, to show their titles, lineage and status on their buildings, documents, knickers, carriages or servants' liveries – I know, it's *such* a chore fixing your servants' liveries – depend entirely on this figure to grant their rights. Otherwise you could have all kinds of bods inventing their own titles and coats of arms, couldn't you? You know how pretentious the *nouveau riche* are. There are also Heralds of Arms and Pursuivants of Arms in Ordinary and Extraordinary. It gets more complex, as you would expect. There are three kings of arms: the chief **Garter King of Arms**, named after an intimate item of ladies' underwear (see page 11); **Norroy**, who looks after England north of the Trent; and **Clarenceaux**, who looks after the south. The Heralds, whose original job was to cry out the names of knights at jousting tournaments are fairly boringly called Richmond, Chester, Lancaster, Windsor, York and Somerset. But the four Pursuivants are given wonderful names: **Blue Mantle**, **Rouge Croix**, **Rouge Dragon** and **Portcullis**. (What do you want to be when you grow up, Jimmy? An engine driver? No, dad, Rouge Dragon.) Their quite gorgeous uniform is a tabard of velvet, silk and damask on which the royal arms are lavishly embroidered.

THE LORD GREAT CHAMBERLAIN The Lord Great Chamberlain was the royal manager at the Palace of Westminster, which doesn't need him, as it's not really a palace any more, except when the monarch visits, in which case he makes the arrangements. For ceremonial occasions, he wears a golden key on his hip over his heavily embroidered red frock coat to symbolise his housekeeping role, and a sharp sword on his other side, lest the Yeomen of the Guard should miss an attempt on the monarch's life. Or possibly to kill himself if he breaks the great white stick he carries prematurely – a real possibility as he has to walk backwards with all this paraphernalia while leading the monarch to the House of Lords at the annual State Opening of Parliament. The correct time for him to break this thin 6ft-long wand is over the grave of the monarch after a royal funeral. The **Lord Chamberlain**, a totally different position, is by contrast the full-time manager of the royal household and hence a major employer in a multi-million pound concern. Bizarrely, the Lord Chamberlain was, until 1968, responsible for theatre censorship. If he didn't like a play, he could take it off.

PEARLY KINGS AND QUEENS, AND THE FLASHEST BOY OF ALL The Pearly Kings and Queens of London, a tradition much-beloved of cockneys, through which each district of cockney London has its own king and queen dressed in elaborate sequin-, pearl- and button-covered costumes, is an eccentric custom whose origins ought to be lost in the mists of time, started by we-know-not-whom for purposes only to be guessed at. It's that kind of tradition.

Surprisingly, its origin, originator and purpose can be precisely fixed. It's all down to orphan **Henry Croft** who grew up in the 19th century in Somers Town, a poor district near King's Cross. He was a small lad, born in 1862 without many prospects. He left his orphanage aged 13 to become a rat catcher in the Somers Town market. Yet he ended his life known and respected across London.

The young rat catcher soon became popular throughout the market with the market traders, or costermongers as they were then known (they knew the coster this, the coster that). Now this is the vital bit: some costermongers wore special outfits – the 'flash boys' – to make themselves stand out from the others. If you got a good cucumber and a smile from the one with the top hat, say, you'd go there next time. Some of the 'flash boys' would sew pearl buttons down their sleeves or whatever – it became a kind of uniform.

Henry Croft had a brainwave. He'd help all the boys left back in the orphanage by making them a lot of money and he'd do it by being the flashest flash boy ever – he'd completely cover a suit with pearly buttons. It took ages to make, but when he appeared at the local fair, people flocked round him to marvel at him, and the costermongers rallied round to his cause. He became so much in demand for charity fund-raising that soon every borough had its own Pearly King and Queen. By the time Henry died in 1930 he'd collected a fortune for charity. His funeral procession to Finchley, where he is buried, was enormous. The entire Pearly monarchy –

some 400 kings and queens – followed the hearse and the occasion made front-page news around the world, as well as going on cinema newsreels.

The tradition thrives with an annual pearly harvest festival on the first Sunday in October (see page 17). Most London parades, carnivals and fêtes that might not attract the regular Queen of England will feature a Pearly King or Queen, the titles being handed down within families. The Somers Town Pearly Queen at the time of writing, for example, is Henry Croft's great-granddaughter.

QUEEN'S REMEMBRANCER A shadowy figure involved in various duties such as collecting ancient and bizarre quit-rents for ancient properties which no one can, er, remember, any more. A quit-rent is a service or tribute payable when payments of a normal cash rent have been avoided, let off, or forgotten. It's totally and wonderfully absurd. See page 17.

QUEEN'S SWAN MARKER Almost all swans in Britain are royal birds in that they belong to the Queen. There are heavy penalties for harming them, in theory: a year and a day in jail for stealing a swan's egg, and if one is killed, the miscreant must pour sufficient grain on the dead swan, hung from a ceiling vertically, to cover it completely. This grain could then be used to feed live swans, presumably.

Personally, considering that when a yob kills a swan, its partner must live alone and palely loitering (because swans mate for life), I'd string the yobs up by their beaks too. Quite why the Queen owns swans is debatable: certainly people used to eat them. Perhaps it's because the lovely bird is simply the grandest in the kingdom and deserves some special protection. But being Britain, things don't stop there, not by a very long chalk.

The Queen's Swan Marker, with his splendid red uniform and a crook on the end of a long pole for catching them by the neck, supervises the astoundingly old and mind-bogglingly complex and pointless ceremony known as '**Swan Upping**'. This is all down to Edward IV being in money trouble in the 15th century. He had to borrow some money quickly from the wealthy Dyers and Vintners' companies in the City, and the price of the 1473 deal was that the Dyers and Vintners' could own some of the swans on the Thames.

The trouble was that big swans tend to have little swans, or cygnets rather, and the nit-picking ninnies in charge decided these, too, needed to be divided into those belonging to the monarch and those belonging to the Dyers and Vintners'. So it is that more than 500 years later, once a year an unbelievable procession of six rowing boats sets off from Sunbury up the Thames towards Abingdon.

Some of these boats are controlled by the Queen's Swan Marker and his swanherds (you just couldn't make it up), and others by the Swan Wardens of the Worshipful Company of Dyers (ditto Vintners). The Royal Swanherd's boat looks particularly fab with two grand flags, the one in the bows with the Queen's initials (her signet, one could say) and a crown upon it so that any oiks swanning about on the river know he is a big cheese, and one at the stern depicting a swan with raised wings. The other boats are allowed only one flag each.

Their task, undertaken with utmost seriousness and requiring great skill to avoid injuries to bird and swan wardens, is to capture these strong and sometimes angry birds, determine the ownership from previous marks in their beaks and mark the offspring accordingly. So it's not just a case of: 'This swan's for you, mate.'

Now the Dyers' birds get one nick in their beaks and the Vintners' get two nicks, punched out rather as railway tickets used to be punched by inspectors. If a mixed marriage, as it were, has taken place, then half are marked with one mark and half with the other. By the way, if you see the funny-sounding pub name The Swan With Two Necks, it comes from two *nicks*.

What about the Queen's swans? Well they need no marks as the law states they obviously belong to the monarch, and very majestic they look too. It is possible, by a 540-year-old law, for a person to own the swans on a closed lake or pond within his land (provided the land is worth at least five marks, whatever that is), but not on open water. These are all royal birds.

The whole process takes at least a week and involves not a few visits to the riverside pubs. The former cygnet pies and swan banquets are no longer eaten, as the whole thing is seen as some sort of conservation effort nowadays. But one tradition is upheld: As they pass Windsor Castle the Swan Markers propose a toast: 'To Her Majesty the Queen Seigneur of the Swans.'

In 1947 a member of the Labour government, dedicated to soaking the rich and helping the working classes, asked why on earth the state paid £600 a year – then a good salary – for someone to look after the king's swans, who could perfectly well look after themselves. Poor, naïve fool… as if ancient British traditions need any point to them.

ROYAL RAVENMASTER His job, at the Tower of London, is to make sure these creatures are content and not likely, by virtue of clipped wings, to leave the Tower. If they ever do, legend has it, catastrophe will strike England. It's raven mad…

SEARCHER OF THE SANCTUARY AND HIGH BAILIFF OF WESTMINSTER ABBEY
The medieval Abbey owned considerable lands nearby, much of it, such as Soho, wild countryside – London was still confined to the City, and Westminster was a completely separate place. Certain religious sites were able to offer inviolable sanctuary, for a limited time, for those accused of various crimes. Part of the Abbey's lands were deemed sanctuary, particularly the side towards what is now Horseferry Road and the river.

However, if the usual authorities had no jurisdiction here, the Abbey needed to act in their place; hence the job of the Searcher of the Sanctuary was to check through all the sanctuary-seeking miscreants, fugitives, wronged innocents and murderous types to make sure they didn't overstay their welcome. But the concept was abused and gradually the sanctuary, originating as an expression of holiness and mercy, became ironically an area of debauchery, prostitution, gambling and murder known as 'the Devil's acre'. This was an irony much repeated south of the river in Southwark (see page 262), but there is still a red-robed Searcher of the Sanctuary and High Bailiff, just in case you should loiter too long in the cloisters for the wrong reasons. More on Westminster Abbey, page 144.

SILVER STICK IN WAITING Another of those curious ceremonial posts for courtiers, often ex-army, such as Brigadier Andrew Parker Bowles, the man who famously laid down his wife for his country. He shared the anguish of Diana, Princess of Wales, that Prince Charles was more attached to Mrs Camilla Parker Bowles. In fact this kind of carry on was totally normal for British royals until around 100 years ago, historians will tell you.

AND THE VILEST JOB IN LONDON… Mortuary assistants and bomb disposal experts? No, it's having to clean the grids in the sewers of a kind of congealed waxy stuff consisting of fat poured down the drains from restaurants blended with human excrement.

DEAD ECCENTRIC LONDON

LONDON, MORE DEAD THAN ALIVE

London, more dead than alive, has been a macabre problem at certain points in the city's history. The **Black Death of 1348**, having marched steadily across Asia and Europe, landed at Dorset and, when it reached the capital, swept through the overcrowded, unsanitary medieval city and killed perhaps 30,000 here. There were not enough living to bury the dead properly, so plague pits were dug and corpses cast in them willy-nilly – then the plague mysteriously went away.

In **1665**, **bubonic plague** returned, with its grotesque symptoms of swelling under the arms, black patches on the skin and fairly rapid death for most of those infected. The churchyards were so 'stuft with corpses,' wrote clergyman Dr Thomas Vincent, 'that they are in many places swell'd two or three feet higher than they were before.'

This wasn't enough, as 68,576 died by official figures – the actual total was almost certainly far more than that. Again, plague pits were used. You may have walked over some while strolling round the City of London. There was no time for coffins. Cartloads of people, Defoe writes in his *Journal of the Plague Year*, were shot semi-naked into heaps, rich and poor, young and old alike.

So, when the **Great Fire of 1666** helped kill off the plague, London's graveyards were full to bursting. Things got worse for the next 150 years. That picturesque bulge of the churchyard above the level of the paths takes on a sinister appearance: Dickens notes this several times, at St Peter on Cornhill, for example. Some churchyard walls were being over-topped, some complained, as the freshly dead were being shoved in on to the hardly decayed.

It is said that the tiny churchyard of **St Martin-in-the-Fields** somehow absorbed more than 60,000 bodies. There is a notice at the top of the crypt stairs at this church that reads:

> *Ordered that in future no Graves be Dug in any of the Vaults under the Church as a Practice thereof will be Prejudicial to and in time endanger the Foundation of said Church and also ordered at a Vestry Held the 31 Day of March 1774 that in future no corps be buried in any of the Vaults under the church but what are in leaden Coffins.*

Inside the churches, where once only the rich and powerful were buried, the dead were increasingly jammed, with flagstones and pews going awry as the coffins and graves gradually collapsed. The middle classes were scandalised – Pepys wrote of going to see the gravedigger about his brother's funeral in 1664:

> *But to see how a man's tombs are at the mercy of such a fellow, that for sixpence he would (as his own words were): 'I will jostle them together but I will make room for him,' speaking of the fullness of the middle aisle, where he was to lie.*

By the 19th century, the living London poor were stealing coffin wood from recent burials for fuel. Human bones from paupers' graves were being shipped north and ground up for fertiliser. Fresh bodies could always find ready takers, if not undertakers, for use in anatomy classes, and for rich rewards; crooked clerics could sell the bodies of the dead at one gate and their broken-up coffins for firewood at another. The dead were crowding out the living in London.

By the 19th century, Parliament was told in medical evidence presented to it that piles of decomposing bodies were crammed into the vaults of churches just under the feet of living worshippers. At last, in the can-do Victorian era, something radical was done, just as freshwater pipes and sewerage systems were built in that era to improve the city's public health too. These latter measures sharply reduced the pressure on the graveyards by curbing outbreaks of cholera and similar diseases, so that the great graveyard crisis passed – for the time being.

Radical solutions

Parliament decided massive **new private cemeteries** on an unprecedented scale on the fringes of London would provide the answer, and these were built at places such as **Highgate** (see page 68), **West Brompton** (see page 221), **Kensal Green** (see page 61), **West Norwood** (see page 60), and further out of town still, linked to the capital by an extraordinary railway for the dead, the massive **Brookwood Cemetery** (see below).

One of the key figures in all this was **Sir Edwin Chadwick** (1800–90) who campaigned tirelessly to stop the stuffing of bodies into the bulging churchyards and under the floors of churches. His publication, *The Practice of Interment in Towns*, did much to promote the properly laid out cemetery as an alternative. Ironically, he is laid out in the Old Mortlake Cemetery in South Worple Way, not a particularly good example of what he was on about. But the commercially run cemeteries – shocking, said the clergy, who had been making money out of the death business for years – soon became extremely fashionable, with their sweeping drives, massive tombs, impressive monuments, neatly gravelled paths and leafy green spaces. They put life back into gravedigging.

Brookwood and a Death Railway

One of the Victorians' solutions to the 19th-century problem of London's literally bulging cemeteries was the macabrely fascinating **London Necropolis Railway**, which started running to Brookwood in Surrey in 1854.

It was exclusive, in that you only travelled once and then only in one direction. The service was run mainly for the dead, so the 'coffin tickets' issued right up until the 1950s were not available as returns.

Funeral trains to Brookwood ran from the discreet London Necropolis station adjoining Waterloo (in fact jammed right next to a turntable for locomotives), where steam power hoists would raise coffins to the level of the hearse vans. In the spirit of the age, these vans were segregated between Anglicans and the rest, as were the mourners' waiting rooms and carriages. In later years, the entrance to the London Necropolis station was marked by a discreet stone-built entrance. Everything was done to maintain dignity and avoid the view, expressed by the Bishop of London when the scheme was first floated, that it was improper to convey corpses by anything as fast as a steam train.

At Brookwood, a part of Woking, a vast city of the dead was laid out with every possible nationality and creed catered for; judging by the number of graves marked 'resting' or 'fell asleep', waking Woking might still be a possibility.

If today you take the pleasant and fascinating walk along the route of the long siding into which these mournful trains were directed, reversing back from Brookwood station, to two smaller but truly terminal stations (one Anglican, one for the rest), many interesting things will come to light.

Such as why the further station is now home to Orthodox monks, incongruously established with their chickens on a former platform for the dead in deepest Surrey. (They are venerating the relics of the English king Edward the Martyr, an important saint for them, in the nearby special chapel.) There is a fascinating collection of people to discover who finally met their Waterloo, as it were, at Brookwood, so a stroll round makes a happy day out, if you like that sort of thing. There are sections here for every kind of religion and every sort of dead.

Freddie Mercury (1946–91), rock star of Queen, was born in exotic Zanzibar but ended his days at Brookwood; the deeply eccentric explorer **Gottlieb Leitner** (1840–99) is responsible for there being a mosque the other side of Woking station; Turkish aviators killed in World War I; American sailors; the feminist author **Rebecca West** (1892–1983). Great people – but dead people. Brookwood also pioneered cremation.

🚂 Brookwood from Waterloo

THE PERILS OF PYRAMID SELLING

One really radical solution for getting rid of London's dead not pursued at the time of the 19th-century crisis was **Thomas Willson's pyramid**, proposed in 1829. Unlike the pharaoh's pyramid, or indeed the many fascinating smaller ones scattered around the English countryside, Willson's vast pyramid wasn't designed for just one person. It was to accommodate *five million*.

It would have dominated the view from almost every point in London, just as Canary Wharf does today. It was to have been taller than St Paul's and was to have a huge obelisk set on its summit. The vaults would have been brick arches arranged on 94 floors and the whole thing was to be faced with granite. Steam-powered lifts would have been included, but this was not a place in which the poor would have ended up: the cost of a family vault would have been prohibitive.

The profits, had the scheme gone ahead and received public support, would have been many millions of pounds. I can't quite see people visiting the dead up in the skies of north London, somehow, but it would have been a fabulous landmark. In the end Parliament went for the underground option with the massive new cemeteries listed here.

WHERE TO FIND SOME DEAD GREAT PEOPLE

The greatest cemeteries are known as London's Magnificent Seven: Abney Park, Brompton, Kensal Green, Highgate, Nunhead, Tower Hamlets and West Norwood. They are great for peaceful greenery, wildlife, wacky monuments and dead famous celebs. Here's a selection…

WEST NORWOOD

Norwood has many claims to fame, such as being the temporary home of Impressionist painter Camille Pissarro during the 1870 Franco-Prussian War. Or being where I got into an X-rated film at the Norwood Regal when aged about 13, by the odd trick of inserting penny chews in the heels of my shoes until I looked old enough. You can come unstuck like that, you know. But the dead of Norwood are far more interesting. Here lie people who really changed our lives – making them sweeter, tastier, shorter and noisier.

There's **Sir Henry Tate** (1819–99), whose sugar sweetened the Empire, and whose Golden Syrup still bears that macabre image of bees feeding on a dead lion ('out of sweetness came forth strength', as if golden syrup were made from honey). He collected a good few pictures and founded the **Tate Gallery**, which replaced the notorious Millbank Prison in Pimlico on the Thames. His marketing of cube sugar created the sugar-tong industry and it was soon popular all over the world. The eventual merger with someone called '& Lyle' made one of those enduring partnerships like Marks & Spencer or Burke & Hare – and gave a lifetime's work to thousands of dentists.

One who doubtless increased the demand for his products, **Mrs Beeton**, as in her *Book of Household Management*, is also here. One imagines her – well, I did – as a fussy old matron, but her grave shows that she died aged a mere 28 in 1865 and was a lively (until that point, obviously) young journalist who published her book as a serial in *The Englishwoman's Domestic Magazine*.

Sir Henry Bessemer (1813–98) changed our lives more than many people realise. Until he perfected his Bessemer process for **steel-making**, it was more than 100 times slower and far more expensive to make a decent bit of steel. Mass production of this useful metal made possible stronger bridges and railways, ships, cars, fridges and cookers, skyscrapers and all kinds of tools that we now take for granted. He has many a school and road named after him, but then he created much of the modern world.

Dedicated to shortening lives in the most efficient way possible was **Sir Hiram Steven Maxim** (1840–1916), Maine-born inventor of the Maxim gun, plus various military fuses and gunpowders. His primitive machine-gun was good enough to fill quite a few cemeteries in its time.

🚂 West Norwood, then up Norwood High Street to the north a little and on the right

KENSAL GREEN

This cemetery, close to Wormwood Scrubs (see page 45) in between the Great Western mainline, the West Coast mainline and the West London line, is a superb site for the graves of those great London engineers, **Isambard Kingdom Brunel** (creator of the Great Western Railway and much else) and his father **Marc Isambard Brunel** (who built the first tunnel under the Thames). But there's much more to discover in this cemetery, which, oddly, has a working canal running alongside it.

There's that chum of Charles Dickens, lawyer-turned-author **Wilkie Collins** (1824–89), who just about invented the detective story and is most remembered for *The Woman in White* and *The Moonstone*. Here, too, is **Anthony Trollope** (1815–82), writer of the *Barsetshire Chronicles* and inventor of the pillar box.

Also, although lost in undergrowth when I looked, is **William Makepeace Thackeray** (1811–63) – don't those Victorian names just roll off your tongue? – who wrote *Vanity Fair* (1847).

There's also **Charles Babbage** (1792–1871), the inventor of the world's first computer (he called them 'analytical engines' – for what happened to his brain, see page 64), and the last man you'd expect to find here dead of natural causes, **Charles Blondin** (1824–97), the world's greatest-ever tightrope walker. It was French-born Blondin who not only astonished the world by crossing Niagara Falls on a tightrope, but who did it again blindfold. Pushing a wheelbarrow, on stilts, in a sack, stopping midway to fry an omelette. He was a great hit in London, performing at the Crystal Palace. Perhaps his greatest feat was persuading a man to be carried on his back across that Niagara rope – would you have done it for him?

For **Brompton Cemetery** at Earl's Court and its fascinating inhabitants, see page 221.

🚇 Ladbroke Grove, Hammersmith & City Line, walk north up Ladbroke Grove for almost a mile; look for entrance on left by junction with Harrow Road. Or Kensal Green, Bakerloo Line.

Taking a grave exception

THERE'S NOTHING SO FUNNY as when a pompous inscription on a grave is wrong. One such is in Westminster Abbey where a slab proclaims gushingly, 'O rare Ben Johnson.' Rare indeed, as everyone else spells it Jonson (unless one is talking about the runner disgraced at the Seoul Olympics, Ben Johnson, not an obvious candidate for Poets' Corner).

Elizabethan dramatist Jonson, playwright of *The Alchemist*, is buried upright under here, just a stone's throw from where he was educated at Westminster School. And knowing that lot, the stone was probably thrown.

Jonson was always poor, and there is said to have been a conversation between the Dean of the Abbey in which the Dean asked if Jonson had ambitions to be buried in Poets' Corner. Jonson replied:

I am too poor for that and no-one will lay out funeral charges upon me. No, sir, six feet long by two feet wide is too much for me: two feet by two feet will do for all I want.

You shall have it, said the Dean.

There would have been no mark at all of the grave (in fact in the north aisle) had Jack Young not been walking past when the paving stone was being tapped back into place and asked whose grave it was. He gave the stonemason 18 pence to carve the name (wrongly, as it turned out). Later the stone was moved to a wall, where it may be seen, but the grave itself is marked by a small grey stone.

A macabre confirmation of the fact that Jonson was buried standing up came in 1849 when an adjoining burial was being made. Jonson's two legs, or rather the bones of them, were seen sticking into the sand, and a skull rolled down with some red hair visible. It was stuffed back. Alas, poor Jonson, Shakespeare knew him well.

Mind you, how many playwrights can have had Shakespeare in his opening night cast, as Jonson did with *Every Man In His Humour* in 1598? Rare indeed.

Putney Vale

This is not a very old cemetery/crem but it has seen off some remarkable people, including, briefly: **Jennifer Paterson** (1928–99), one of the eccentric 'Two Fat Ladies' who went round in a motorcycle sidecar doing TV cooking; **Hattie Jacques** (1922–80), the great *Carry-On* actress; film star **Kenneth More** (1914–82); Dr Who **Jon Pertwee** (1919–96); *Titanic* owner and controversial sinking survivor **Bruce Ismay** (1862–1937); radio presenter and *Desert Island Discs* inventor **Roy Plomley** (1914–85); World Cup-winning footballer **Bobby Moore** (1941–93); and Russian prime minister **Alexander Kerensky** (1881–1970), whose brief time at the top came between the Tsar and Lenin. What a bunch!

🚗 Beside the A3 in southwest London 🚌 85 and 265 from Putney centre

Golders Green Crem –
it's cool to be cremated

There's one seriously cool place to be cremated, if that's possible, and that's Golders Green Crematorium, pioneer in the once shocking art of taking that ashes to ashes stuff rather literally. Actually Brookwood (see page 58) pioneered the idea, but Golders Green with its proximity to Hampstead had a ready supply of dead free-thinking agnostic or atheistic radicals who didn't go along with grave burial, such as **Sigmund Freud** (1856–1939), father of psychoanalysis.

As the underground became unfashionable with the dead North London intelligentsia, so Golders Green became their favourite last stop. Around 300,000 cremations have been carried out here, and the advantage is that the place can never become full.

Among those who went up the chimney here at Britain's busiest crematorium are the following:

Writers Children's writer **Enid Blyton** (1897–1968), creator of Noddy and much loathed by some North London literati whom she outsold by millions; the creator of Dracula, **Bram Stoker** (1847–1912) – jolly good name for a crematorium, really; **Kingsley Amis** (1922–95), splendidly curmudgeonly creator of great novels such as *Lucky Jim*; sexologist **Havelock Ellis** (1859–1939), whose books were as likely to be burned as he was; **Rudyard Kipling** (1865–1936), writer of Britain's favourite poem for many years, 'If', creator of the *Jungle Book* and chronicler of the Empire.

A CONTROVERSIAL EXHIBITION AT LONDON'S Serpentine Gallery in 1995 included, beside a totally naked actress sleeping in a box, the pickled brain of mathematician **Charles Babbage** (1792–1871). Babbage's brilliant ideas on devising calculating machines in the early 19th century laid the groundwork for today's computers more than a century before such machines were actually made to work. But the bizarre preservation of his brain – it normally resides at the Royal College of Surgeons of England – isn't at all unique.

Not far away, the embalmed body of philosopher **Jeremy Bentham** (1748–1832) sits in state within a glass case in **University College, Gower Street**. In the 19th century his head was replaced with a replica, as disrespectful students had the macabre habit of playing football with the real thing, even if this followed his

Pickled Babbage and a kick-about brain

COMPOSERS **Sir Arthur Bliss** (1891–1975); **Eric Coates** (1886–1957), who wrote 'The Dam Busters' March'; **Ralph Vaughan Williams** (1872–1958), composer of the 'London Symphony'. Well at least they're not decomposing.

DANCERS Modern dance exponent **Dame Marie Rambert** (1888–1982), who has a blue plaque in Kensington's Campden Hill Gardens; ballerina **Anna Pavlova** (1885–1931), who, like Nellie Melba, was immortalised in a pudding, and was also good at dying swans.

famed principle of utiliarianism – matters should be arranged to be useful for 'the greatest happiness of the greatest number' (astonishingly, no one had thought of this before). Well at least he made a few football-crazy students happy.

People get very pompous when writing their wills and Bentham was no exception. He directed how his body was to be displayed in great detail:

> ...my executor will cause the skeleton to be clad in one of the suits of black occasionally worn by me. The body so clothed shall together with the chair and staff in my later years bourne by me he will take charge of and for containing the whole apparatus he will cause to be prepared an appropriate box or case and will cause to be engraved in conspicuous characters on a plate to be fixed thereon and also on labels on the glass cases in which the preparation of the soft parts of my body will be preserved... etc etc

Not only does this suggest the eccentric Bentham's lectures might in real life have been less than riveting, but that he had that delusion of the self-appointed great and the good that the world's fascination with them cannot possibly end with their death. Does that remind us of anyone today?

SCIENTISTS Sir Alexander Fleming (1881–1955), whose chance discovery of penicillin saved more lives than anyone else in the last century (and a great name for a man curing chest infections); **Sir James Dewar** (1842–1923), who proved life was a picnic, by inventing the Thermos flask; **Sir Bernard Spilsbury** (1877–1947), the brilliant pathologist who detected the undetectable by discovering the means by which Dr Crippen (see page 31) poisoned his wife. Ironically, in depression, he poisoned himself in his laboratory.

COMEDIANS Peter Sellers (1925–80), original Goon, Dr Strangelove and creator of Inspector 'Ees it a beumb?' Clouseau; **Tommy Handley** (1892–1949), the man behind the radio smash-hit *ITMA*.

And that's just a selection of the luminaries who have added to the atmosphere – literally – of this special corner of North London. There is no charge for admission; guided tours are sometimes available.

TOOTING'S ODD LINK WITH GANGLAND

There were at least two Charles Wilsons in London in the past 50 years, and it was a good idea not to get the two mixed up. One was a Glaswegian editor of *The Times* (formerly married to TV presenter Anne Robinson). The other was a member of the notorious **Great Train Robbery gang**, who brilliantly yet ruthlessly coshed their way to several million quid on a mail train in 1963. They faked a red signal for the Glasgow–Euston train, slugged the driver and moved the train to where they could unload the mailbags. This **Charlie Wilson** did his time in jail before coming to a sticky end in 1990 in his retirement in Spain. He was murdered by some low life. If you are fascinated by British gangster chic – and the film industry certainly is – you can pay your respects at **Streatham Cemetery**, Tooting.

Streatham Cemetery: ◉ about half a mile up Garratt Lane from Tooting Broadway

CITY: ST GHASTLY GRIM AND PEPYS AT THE PAST

The ghastliest gate in London is definitely that at **St Olave's** in **Hart Street**, **EC3**. It is grimly festooned with skulls, bones and spikes. The records show this slightly predates, oddly, the churchyard being used for mass burials of 326 people in the Great Plague of 1665.

The explanation is that intimations of mortality, death and decay were then acceptable ornaments and even regarded as a good thing for concentrating the minds of the living on the hereafter. Many a 17th- and 18th-century grave showed Death carrying his scythe, hourglasses running out, skulls, and warnings such as '*Tempus fugit, vita brevis*' – 'Time flies, but life is short'.

To quote Dickens, who used St Olave's for a fictional location in *The Uncommercial Traveller*:

> It is a small churchyard, with a ferocious strong spiked iron gate, like a jail. This gate is ornamented with skulls and crossbones, larger than life, wrought in stone; but it likewise came into the mind of Saint Ghastly Grim, that to stick iron spikes a-top of the stone skulls, as though they were impaled, would be a pleasant device. Therefore the skulls grin aloft horribly, thrust through and through with iron spears. Hence, there is attraction of repulsion for me in Saint Ghastly Grim.

PERHAPS THE ODDEST CASE of its kind concerns a woman who never reached her grave at all. When the first wife of the king of 18th-century eccentrics, **Martin van Butchell**, died in 1775, he had her embalmed with turpentine and camphor, fitted with glass eyes, coloured to appear lifelike and mounted in a display case in the front room of his Mayfair home. She was wearing full wedding dress and van Butchell charged the public to see her.

Van Butchell, who made a fortune supplying dentures and trusses to the gentry, although qualified in neither field, refused to visit his rich clients despite, in one case, being sent a horse and carriage and the small fortune of 500 guineas. On the other hand, he regularly visited Newgate jail to treat prisoners free of charge.

Eccentric's wife who was never buried

His bizarre preservation of his first wife's corpse may have been brought on by her will stating that her fortune was to go to a distant relative 'the moment I am dead and buried'. She had been offered, incidentally, the choice of wearing black or white for the rest of her life on her wedding day – she chose black – and when van Butchell married his second wife (his maid Elizabeth – perhaps so he had no longer to pay her a wage), she chose white.

Still the first wife was not buried. In 1815 van Butchell's son Edmund offered the body to the Royal College of Surgeons. There she remained unburied until blown to bits by a Nazi bomb in the Blitz of 1941. From dust to dust...

Among those buried here at St Ghastly Grim – I mean St Olave's – is the great diarist **Samuel Pepys** (1633–1703). He – a ghastly character himself when you get to know him – had his own pew erected so he didn't have to mix with hoi polloi. But consider that phrase 'the attraction of repulsion': Dickens foresaw the whole horror film industry.

◆ Tower Hill

Highgate: freeze, partner! Preserving the dead

Highgate Cemetery, in two sections either side of Swains Lane, is renowned for its rambling Victoriana, celebrity dead and for the kitsch of death – there's a piano tomb – and for the tomb of **Karl Marx** (1818–83). But Highgate's oddest death was surely that of Elizabethan philosopher, writer, politician and scientist and, some say, real author of Shakespeare's plays, **Francis Bacon** (1561–1626).

Bacon, a former lord chancellor in the government, was out in a coach with some friends one snowy morning in 1626 when, at the top of Highgate Hill, he made the coachman stop. He had had a brainwave and wanted to conduct an experiment and, typically, thought there and then the best time for it. He bought a hen from a woman in a nearby hovel, disembowelled it, then stuffed it with snow. He had a strange new idea, laughable to his friends, that freezing could preserve meat.

Unfortunately it was soon a case of frozen Bacon as much as chicken. He fell ill and was taken to the Earl of Arundel's house nearby. There they put him in a bed but it was a damp bed not used for a year or so, and Bacon caught pneumonia and soon died. Hence Bacon's Lane here next to the cemetery, and hence, eventually, a whole new industry for people like Mr Clarence Birdseye.

Meanwhile Highgate Cemetery has acquired a seriously spooky atmosphere, and has often been associated with **occultism**. Tombs have been broken into and bones removed for weird rituals and once, in the 1960s, a local resident opened his car door to find an exhumed corpse in the passenger seat. Not my idea of a joke. By day it has some fabulous monuments to examine and is well worth a visit.

The architecture in the well-laid out grounds is extraordinary. At the top of Egyptian Avenue there is a street of the dead called the Circle of Lebanon. Little family houses line this grassy road with half a dozen people in each. Dead ones, that is.

Famous residents also include **Douglas Adams** (d 2001), of *Hitchhiker's Guide*, novelist **George Eliot** (1819–80), scientist **Michael Faraday** (1791–1867) and Leftie writer and *Private Eye* stalwart **Paul Foot** (d 2004) who, appropriately enough for a die-hard socialist, is buried just yards from Marx's tomb.

⊖ Archway (Northern Line): walk up Highgate Hill (steep, or get bus 271) to green-domed church past hospital, enter Waterlow Park on left and go downhill across park (past duck ponds) to Swains Lane exit. The cemetery is either side of this lane in two halves. Note the West Cemetery is by booked tours only in weekdays, or tours you queue for at weekends ☎ 020 8340 1834; the East Cemetery is open at a small charge.

The bizarre Bolan family tree

LONDON'S ODDEST MEMORIAL is a tree in Barnes. It is the one pop star Marc Bolan, formerly of T-Rex, hit in his Mini in 1976, causing his untimely death. Unlike, say, Jimi Hendrix who died not far away, he didn't become a much bigger star after his death than before. But nevertheless the flowers, photos and loving messages tied to his tree loyally almost every single day since make this London's most enduring and extraordinary unofficial memorial. The effect is a little spoilt by the crash barrier in front of the tree, but given its history, I suppose that's understandable.

There is no footpath on that side of this fast and narrow road, so view the tree from the opposite side unless you wish to join Mr Bolan prematurely. Bolan's body was taken to Golders Green Crematorium in northwest London, last venue of many a British star of stage and screen (see page 63); he was joined by Keith Moon of The Who only two years later.

In fact the far side of what was for a long time a place of informal, spontaneous tribute, approached by a path from Gipsy Lane, now has a proper marble memorial and a better view than the main road side. When Marc Bolan's fans aren't putting flowers on this memorial they're sometimes listening to a tribute band featuring, bizarrely, his son Rolan Bolan.

For a while some local people resented the T-Rex pilgrims turning up and there was even a sacrilegious attempt to hack down the tree in question. The great headline writer Willy 'Three Puddings' Bloch punningly headed a paragraph about this 'Tree Wrecks'. Insensitive, some fans may feel, but brilliant in its way.

69

GONE FOR A BURTON IN DEEPEST MORTLAKE

The most eccentric tomb in London must be that of **Richard Burton** – not the one who kept marrying Elizabeth Taylor (eccentric in itself) but the great explorer (1821–90) who opened up the vast and unknown lands of Arabia to the eyes of an enchanted Western world. Thus, a full-scale Arab sheik's tent – complete with stone folds of cloth frozen in mid-flap of a desert breeze as if touched by a Narnian witch's wand – stands somewhat incongruously in a sleepy corner of suburban Mortlake.

Aptly, finding Burton's mausoleum is something of an exploration in itself. It is not in the vast municipal Mortlake Cemetery, nor in the graveyard of the confusingly named St Mary the Virgin church fronting Mortlake High Street near the Thames. But behind there, through a labyrinth of paths such as Tinderbox Alley lined by Victorian cottages, lies St Mary Magdalen, a Catholic church, where the extraordinary monument can be found by following a well-worn track through the undergrowth.

Close up, one can see an iron star romantically hidden in the foliage above the tent, a well-over-the-top valedictory poem typical of the era and, behind the tomb, its most fascinating aspect: a window in the tent's roof with a handy steel ladder enabling one to peer at the coffins of Burton and his wife surrounded by some of their favourite objects from his explorations, along with some well-withered wreaths, a century of dust and decrepitude having failed to spoil the oddly cosy, domestic scene.

🚂 Mortlake from Waterloo 🚌 209 from Hammersmith almost to the church gate and walk a bit further alongside the railway 🚗 North Worple Way from the level crossing in White Hart Lane, Mortlake

AND ONE LAST SPECIAL PLACE... ST PANCRAS

It was in the old St Pancras graveyard that **Mary Shelley** (1797–1851) plighted her troth to poet **Percy Bysshe Shelley** (1792–1822) over the grave of her mother, **Mary Wollstonecraft** (1759–1797). If that seems a little spooky, then remember the younger Mary wrote *Frankenstein* and the older one was an early feminist whose other daughter poisoned herself. Later, younger Mary dug up older Mary and moved her to Bournemouth, which she might have enjoyed more if she had been alive.

The other great grave here is that of eccentric architect-collector **Sir John Soane** (see page 80). The strange, domed roof of the tomb, cut off to make a square base, may remind you of the classic British phone box. In fact it's the other way round: the phone box designer got his idea from here.

THE LONDON RESURRECTION MEN AND GRAVE CRIMES

The grave-robbers who by the end of the 18th century were making a healthy £4 per fresh body (less for a 'short', that is a child's body, which would be paid pro rata per foot) were also known as the 'resurrection men'.

They had various ways of getting fresh corpses. One was to mingle with mourners at a funeral and note the grave. Relatives could, as a counter-measure, set markers in the soil to see if it had been disturbed or use watchmen, spring guns and primitive landmines as booby traps – at least one killed a resurrection man. A rare case of the dead killing the living.

The job of digging a corpse up from six feet under in the dead of night was arduous; the favoured method was to make a small hole using short wooden shovels (metal ones being too noisy) and then crack the coffin lid and pull the corpse up through this, leaving the rest of the coffin lid intact.

Given all this effort, it seemed inevitable that grave-robbers would sooner or later cut out the middle man – the funeral – and kill people to order. In 1831, two known London resurrection men, **John Bishop** and **James May**, tried to haggle for the price of a body at King's College Hospital, arguing it was exceptionally fresh. So it was, but as it also had suspicious marks on it, the surgeons pretended to dither while police were called. The body was of a well-known street urchin who had been seen with Bishop, May and another man, Williams, two days previously. Evidence of murder at the three's homes was quickly found, and it transpired that they had killed and offered for dissection at least three people by first drugging them.

Bishop and Williams were convicted of the killings and, by a neat bit of justice, were not only hanged but then dissected by surgeons.

This particular crime was instrumental in getting the **Warburton Bill** against the selling of bodies by grave robbers through Parliament. Any body not claimed within 48 hours could be lawfully given for dissection, if no objection had been stated by the deceased, but corpses could not be sold in the previous manner.

The bottom fell out of the corpse market (perhaps not the best choice of words). Thus workhouses, for example, saved themselves the expense of conducting even a pauper's funeral and the grave-robbing era, which had transfixed and terrified a nation, was over.

ECCENTRIC PASTIMES

LONDON'S ODDEST MUSEUMS

London is famed globally for its fabulous and unbeatable range of mainstream museums and galleries, from the huge **British Museum** in Bloomsbury (whose courtyard is now covered with what appear to be bulging fishnet tights) to the incomparable South Kensington Group of museums (the **Science**, **Natural History** and **Victoria & Albert museums** being the most famous), from the free **National Gallery** on Trafalgar Square to the pioneering and also free **Tate galleries**, both at Millbank and Bankside. All of these are well known.

But much of the capital's charm lies in around 250 myriad, odd and eccentric museums lurking on backstreets and in quiet suburbs, each with a fascinating story to tell. Here's a selection of just some of them, with travel information, phone numbers and 2011 adult entry charges. As usual, because museums can close for changes, etc, I recommend checking before setting out, if you have to travel any distance to get to them.

MUSEUM OF TRAMS AND TUBES

Many people have heard of the **London Transport Museum** at Covent Garden, and very good it is too, with its ancient Tube trains, buses and trams. But it is a small site and the linked **Acton Depot** in West London, more a collection of odd junk and memorabilia than a theme park, is equally fascinating. Where else in the world can you see the remains of a spiral escalator, for example? Nowhere, because there was only one. Did it work? How would the steps get back down again? These are vital questions I cannot live without the answers to.

Covent Garden, 39 Wellington Street, WC2 7BB ☎ 020 7379 6344
🖳 www.ltmuseum.com; admission £13.50 ● Covent Garden

MUSEUM OF BLOOD-SOAKED SURGERY

Return to a land of hope and gory, and to a time when still-conscious, screaming patients endured – or not – butchery that often killed them while sawdust soaked up the blood, all this in front of a theatre (as in operating theatre) audience. **The Old Operating Theatre and Herb Garret**, near London Bridge, dates from 1822 and offers a fascinating insight into surgery before the days of antiseptics and anaesthetics. If this makes you feel faint, there's always the fan museum (see page 76).

9A St Thomas's Street, near London Bridge, SE1 9RY ☎ 020 7188 2679
🖳 www.thegarret.org.uk; admission £5.90 ● London Bridge

MUSEUM OF THE BLOWN-OFF LEG

The **National Army Museum** traces the glorious, muddy, frightened, disciplined, heroic, horrific life of the British soldier from Agincourt to Afghanistan. Aimed at the general public, not just military types. One of the odder displays, indeed a somewhat grisly one, must be the scene where a blood-soaked surgeon removes the remains of the first Marquess of Anglesey's leg. During the Battle of Waterloo, as the cannon roared, the Marquess (then merely Lord Uxbridge, but later elevated for his heroism) cried out: 'My God, sir, I've lost a leg!' The Duke of Wellington, the British commander, remarked: 'Have you, by God!' and carried on observing the French lines through his telescope. It is not recorded whether the Iron Duke dismounted to lend a hand, as it were, but amputation was performed in the field and the aristocratic leg buried under a willow tree with full military honours. The actual blood-stained saw and a once-white glove are included in the museum's display. If you like blown-off legs, or this particular one, there's a museum to the Marquess's artificial leg (among other things) at Plas Newydd on the Menai Straits in Wales. There's also a monument where the real leg is buried at the real Waterloo in Belgium. Three monuments to one leg end, not bad.

Royal Hospital Road, SW3 4HT ☎ 020 7730 0717 🖳 www.nam.ac.uk; admission free ● Sloane Square, walk past Peter Jones down King's Road a little way then left on Smith Street to end (10 mins) 🚌 11,19, or 22 to Smith Street on King's Road

MUSEUM OF TRIUMPHS AND FAILURES

The **London Motorcycle Museum** is for fans of Triumph motorcycles mainly: an astonishingly detailed collection of all the great British bikes and the odd prototypes and one-off engines that you might have heard of but never actually seen. Plus lots of other ancient British bikes and motor scooters – many of them useless failures, but some heroic race-winners. There's a notice: 'Parking for Triumphs only. All other makes will be crushed.'

If you come on your Yamhonkawaduki 1500, be a good boy or girl and park it round the corner…

Ravenor Farm, Oldfield Lane South, Greenford, Middlesex UB6 9LD
☎ 020 8575 6644 ✉ thelmm@hotmail.com 🚌 South Greenford, from Paddington 🚗 Off the A40 west of the North Circular. You need to pretend to take the A4127 southwards but instead rejoin the A40 going west, then the turning is on your left. You can't turn in from the A40, just the sliproad.

MUSEUM OF TALLY-HO GINGER!

If you like military history, there's also the **Royal Air Force Museum**. Real planes from the Battle of Britain and more modern times. Tally ho, Ginger!

Grahame Park Way, Hendon, NW9 5LL
☎ 020 8205 2266 ✉ www.rafmuseum.org.uk ◉ Colindale

MUSEUM OF THE NARROW-MINDED

The colourful history of canals, the tunnels, the navvies, the horses, canal art, and the canal characters, they're all here. Get narrow-minded at the **London Canal Museum**. Or you can tie up here if going by boat. The museum's also part of the history of ice cream, because this was the ice warehouse of Carlo Gatti, the great ice-cream pioneer. Before refrigeration, ice was brought from Norway and stored here for use in hot weather.

12/13 New Wharf Road, N1 9RT ☎ 020 7713 0836

🖾 www.canalmuseum.org.uk; admission £3 ✪ King's Cross, walk (5 mins) north up York Way on the east side of the main station and then right into Wharfedale Road, then left into New Wharf Road

MUSEUM OF SKETCHY IDEAS

Should be a good draw (groan) and I'm glad someone is taking laughter seriously. **The Cartoon Museum** boasts hundreds of cartoons and caricatures including the earliest and the burst-out-laughing variety, plus biting political satire some people would rather forget.

35 Little Russell Street, WC1A 2HH ☎ 020 7580 8155
🖾 www.cartoonmuseum.org; closed Monday; admission £5.50 adult
✪ Holborn, cross Kingsway and go west down High Holborn. Turn right into Museum Street and Little Russell Street is on your left after crossing another main road. It's close to the British Museum and next to a rather good Pizza Express (well, they're all the same but the building's rather good).

MUSEUM OF SOMETHING MISSING

It ain't crystal, it ain't a palace and it ain't here anyway. **Crystal Palace Museum** is a local museum with an interesting story to tell – how gardener Joseph Paxton's dream of a giant glasshouse to house all the best things in the world came to fruition in 1851, how it was moved to Upper Sydenham and how it met its dramatic end in 1936. Plus TV was invented right here.

Anerley Hill, SE19 2BA ☎ 020 8676 0700 🖾 www.crystalpalacemuseum. org.uk; open Saturday, Sunday and bank holiday Monday only 🚌 3 from Oxford Circus and Central London 🚂 Crystal Palace overground

MUSEUM OF THE ECLECTIC AND PECULIAR

A very unusual museum. At the **Cuming Museum, the Museum of Southwark's History** you'll find a Red Indian scalp from North America, a bit chipped off the ceiling of the room where Napoleon died in St Helena and part of the waistcoat Charles I wore to his execution. It's all down to two eccentrics, **Richard Cuming** (1777–1870) and his son **Henry Syer Cuming** (1817–1902), who collected this remarkable lot of bric-a-brac. Henry left 100,000 objects and the money to display them, and the new museum opened in 1906, covering every field of knowledge in a scatter-gun kind of way. It was billed as the 'British Museum in miniature' at the time. It really is eccentric. I mean, the Cumings not only collected fakes, knowing they were fakes, but also the sawn-off leg of an Egyptian mummy.

75

It was all the fault of Richard Cuming's aunt who gave him three fossils when he was five years old. That was it. The enthusiasm of these people and their boundless curiosity shines through.

First floor, 151 Walworth Road, SE17 1RS ☎ 020 7525 2332; closed Monday, Sunday and bank holidays; admission free ⊖ Elephant and Castle

MUSEUM OF THE STUFFED WALRUS

Another absolutely fantastic collection is at the **Horniman Museum** in South London. Tea magnate and MP for Falmouth, Frederick Horniman, who died in 1906, started this collection, which now offers 6,500 musical instruments (the world's best collection, and kept right up to date), 60,000 items from remote peoples, and 250,000 specimens from nature. Five years before his death, he handed over this amazing collection, and a purpose-built museum, to the people of London. Unlike Pitt Rivers (who created a similar museum in Oxford), Horniman travelled the world to collect much of the material himself. Big on Africa and on recreated environments such as riverbeds and beehives. The stuffed walrus (and the aquarium) are a particular hit with children.

London Road, Forest Hill, SE23 3PQ ☎ 020 8699 1872
🖳 www.horniman.ac.uk; admission free 🚌 185, 122
🚃 Forest Hill overground

MUSEUM OF GREATEST FANS

Folding, not footie ones, thankfully, and the **London Fan Museum** contains the world's biggest collection of more than 3,000 of them. A special exhibition of rather pretty Art Nouveau jobs opened in 1999, perhaps permitting the pun 'Fan de siècle'. Plus advertising fans. Teashop with napkins folded in guess what shape. It's just an eccentric thing to do, frankly.

12 Crooms Hill, Greenwich, SE10 8ER ☎ 020 8305 1441
🖳 www.fan-museum.org; closed Monday; admission £4 🚃 Greenwich overground, from Charing Cross. Included in Greenwich walk, page 306.

MUSEUM OF FROCKS AND FURBELOWS

Yes, *dahling*, Zandra Rhodes's cherished dream to celebrate London's role in fashion over the last half century and also to showcase the newest and best from all over the world has come true at the **Zandra Rhodes's Fashion and Textile Museum**.

83 Bermondsey Street, SE1 3XF ☎ 020 7407 8664
🖥 www.ftmlondon.org (lots of pink on this one when I looked)
⊖ London Bridge

MUSEUMS OF GREAT WRITERS

If you're a great fan of Dr Johnson or Charles Dickens and don't know their London houses have been preserved as museums, check them out.

DICKENS HOUSE MUSEUM 48 Doughty Street, WC1N 2LX ☎ 020 7405 2127
🖥 www.dickensmuseum.com; admission £7 ⊖ Russell Square

DR JOHNSON'S HOUSE 17 Gough Square, EC4A 3DE, off Fleet Street ☎ 020
7353 3745 🖥 www.drjohnsonshouse.org; admission £4.50 ⊖ Blackfriars (more in Fleet Street walk, page 229)

MUSEUM OF MASSIVE GUNS

Guns that could sink a navy threateningly dominate the forecourt of the absolutely fascinating **Imperial War Museum** in Kennington, near Waterloo (aptly). But it's not just the sexy guns, planes, bombs and torpedoes you'll find here; you'll also find that the experiences of the British Tommy in the trenches, of the jolly Jack Tar in the Royal Navy and of the 'Few', the Battle of Britain air aces, are brought back to life by the memorabilia displayed here. Great for scholars – I wanted to find out about the disastrous siege of Kut in Mesopotamia (Iraq) in World War I, because my grandfather was involved; a typical bit of British humour (or bureaucratic bloody-mindedness) emerged. A letter home said: 'We are camped amidst the [hole cut in paper] palms. We enjoy eating the [another hole].' It transpired that the military censors had been told to cut out all *dates*. Later, British and American bombers in the Gulf War of the 1990s took out the same bridges my grandfather had built.

Lambeth Road, SE1 6HZ ☎ 020 7416 5321 🖥 www.iwm.org.uk;
admission free ⊖ Lambeth North

MUSEUM OF LOADS OF MONEY

The amazing confidence trick whereby instead of giving us a pound's worth of gold we were given a note with a promise to pay that amount and then that promise is abandoned so only the worthless bit of paper has a value is a staggering thing when you stop to think about it. At the **Bank of**

ECCENTRIC PASTIMES

England Museum you can see the early bank notes, written out by clerks in longhand and individually signed by the cashiers, in this, the Museum of the 'Old Lady of Threadneedle Street'. Originally every country bank around Britain would issue its own bank notes but these were only as good as the bank they were drawn on. Whereas the Bank of England's notes were as safe as, well, the Bank of England. Now only a few Scottish banks provide their own notes. Here you can learn about the evolution of devices to prevent forgeries and the success or otherwise of the counterfeiters – the most severe penalty for counterfeiting being, of course, the gallows. They probably won't tell you about the sexy female financial journalist and the high official who had to resign a couple of years ago after headlines such as 'Bonk of England' appeared about their love-making on the Bank's carpets and the leather-topped desks. Ouch – watch out for staplers. But forget mere sex – who isn't fascinated, just a bit, by piles of gold and money?

Bartholomew Lane, EC2R 8AH ☎ 020 7601 5545; closed weekends; admission free ⬤ Bank, unsurprisingly

Museum of Moorish paradise

At the **Leighton House Museum** you will find an Arab fountain tinkling with water, beautiful original Moorish tiles and a shuttered window balcony overlooking it, furnished with plump cushions, fit for a harem. Plus the sensual paintings by Lord Leighton, the Victorian painter, and the only one honoured with that rank. Not near Holland Park Tube but off Melbury Road which goes north off Kensington High Street between High Street Kensington Tube and the nearer Olympia. More rave comments in Kensington walk, page 341.

12 Holland Park Road, W14 8LZ ☎ 020 7602 3316 🖳 www.rbkc.gov. uk/leightonhousemuseum; closed Tuesday; admission £5 🚌 8, 9 ask for Melbury Road or Commonwealth Institute ⬤ Olympia (District Line or overground from Clapham and Willesden Junctions)

Museums of shoving, hitting and throwing

Places of reverential pilgrimage for serious rugby, tennis and cricket fans must be the museums at **Twickenham**, **Wimbledon** and **Lord's** respectively. If you want to see how Victorian ladies played tennis in long dresses so they wouldn't show an ankle, and the strange things balls and racquets were once made of, plus Pat Cash's sweaty headband, plus videos of the greatest moments of the world-famous championships, Wimbledon's the place. If you'd like to have a go with a rugby scrum machine, tour the

78

stands, and recall how that boy picked up the ball and ran with it at Rugby School, then it's Twickenham for you. And if you'd like to see a painting of how a well-struck six, soaring from the bat in 1936, killed a passing sparrow, plus the actual ball and the stuffed bird, and of course the real Ashes (a burned bail of 1882), then it's got to be Lord's.

WORLD RUGBY MUSEUM, Twickenham stadium (Gate L), off the A316 main road leading from Central London to the M3; Rugby Road, Twickenham, TW1 1DZ ☎ 020 8892 8877 🖳 www.rfu.com; closed Monday, and Sunday after match days; admission £6, £14 including stadium tour 🚃 Twickenham, overground from Waterloo

WIMBLEDON LAWN TENNIS MUSEUM, Church Road, SW19 5AE ☎ 020 8946 6131 🖳 www.wimbledon.org; admission £11 ● Southfields (cross over and walk down Wimbledon Park Road for a half-mile)

MCC MUSEUM, Lord's, NW8 8QN ☎ 020 7616 8595 🖳 www.lords.org; admission for the Lord's tour including museum £7.50 ● St John's Wood

Museum of torture and imprisonment

When you go down the steps into this prison that gave its name as a nickname for all others – into the Clink – you have an uneasy feeling that getting out again might not have been so easy for some of those who preceded you. Punishment was one of Southwark's biggest industries, and there were major prisons round here which lasted for centuries, but the **Clink Prison Museum** features the chains and manacles, and the harrowing stories, recreated, of inmates. You will learn that whereas men could be hanged, drawn and quartered, women were more gently treated: they were just drowned or burned at the stake. One of the most fascinating devices here is the 'scold's bridle', a device that allowed a flat metal plate to be fitted over the tongue of a woman who talked too much, to keep her quiet (watch out Ruby Wax), plus puritan branding irons for prostitutes (a B on the forehead meant Bawd, not a second-rate one).

1 Clink Street, SE1 9DG ☎ 020 7403 0900; admission £5.50 ● London Bridge, then go past Southwark Cathedral or through Borough Market

Museums of terrific toys

Pollock's Toy Museum is full of bizarre 19th-century gadgets for children, great puppets and dolls' houses and the real story of Teddy bears. Plus an Egyptian clay mouse which could be the world's oldest toy. The **Bethnal Green Museum** is a branch of the Victoria & Albert Museum. Zillions more toys, pedal-cars, puppets, mechanical toys, spinning tops, lead soldiers, model trains, children's clothes, and toys you can actually play with. Baby and nursery equipment. Nostalgia for any generation.

> **POLLOCK'S TOY MUSEUM**, 1 Scala Street, W1T 2HL, near Tottenham Court Road ☎ 020 7636 3452 ▦ www.pollockstoymuseum.com; admission £5 (imaginary friends go free) ◉ Goodge Street

> **BETHNAL GREEN MUSEUM OF CHILDHOOD**, Cambridge Heath Road, E2 9PA ☎ 020 8983 5200 ▦ www.vam.ac.uk/moc; admission free ◉ Bethnal Green

MUSEUM OF A TRUE ECCENTRIC

Sir John Soane's House is a quite extraordinary testament to the passions and private life of Georgian England's great architect (1753–1837) whose simple, unadorned style can still be seen in his buildings, which include the Dulwich Picture Gallery and the Bank of England. But what interests us here is why this house holds a human skeleton and Roman cremation urns, a three-yard-long Egyptian sarcophagus, an eccentric collection of architectural bits and bobs from around the world and the marble tomb of Fanny, his favourite dog. The front of the building, designed by Soane, of course, includes two stone statues made to the indestructible Coade formula for making artificial stone (as in the Coade lion, page 210). The reason for this house being frozen in time is that Soane fell out with his two sons who didn't want to follow him into architecture. When one of his sons wrote an anonymous attack on Soane's architectural style, and Soane found out who'd written it, that was it. He virtually disinherited them, put his money into a trust for preserving this house and even obtained a private Act of Parliament to set the thing up in perpetuity. This decrees that nothing must be changed, so it isn't. Here you can see the models Soane made of great buildings and ancient monuments, and his entertaining rooms, decorated in the original style. Note the experimental use of domed skylights to shed light as required and compare this to his brilliant achievement at the Dulwich Picture Gallery.

> 13 Lincoln's Inn Fields, WC2A 3BP ☎ 020 7405 2107 ▦ www.soane.org; closed Sunday and Monday; admission free ◉ Holborn

MUSEUM OF SWASHBUCKLER'S TREASURES

The amazing **Wernher Collection**, surely one of the greatest private collections of art ever assembled by an individual, was saved for Britain in

2001 and found a home in the lovely Ranger's House in Greenwich Park. The man who collected the 650 works, now on 125-year loan to English Heritage, was Julius Wernher, a swashbuckling empire builder from the days of Cecil Rhodes. In 1871 the poor young German sailed for South Africa to make his fortune, arriving amidst scenes of violence and filth. He set up business in the rough and tough diamond town of Kimberley and worked hard for a London firm. He married a society beauty and heiress and bought the massive stately home of Luton Hoo in Bedfordshire, meanwhile starting his art collection which, like everything else he did, was done with shrewd success. He ended a remarkable rags-to-riches story with a baronetcy and a remarkable and eccentric collection of gems, fakes, and heavily restored pieces. English Heritage, for once, have vowed to keep the collection in its original flavour, with the odd eccentricities intact telling of a man who seems to have stepped from the pages of a Kipling or Rider Haggard adventure. The 1723 house, once home to a princess, is itself worthy of a visit.

Ranger's House, Greenwich Park, SE10 8QX ☎ 020 8853 0035
⌨ www.english-heritage.org.uk; admission £8.30
➲ Blackheath (mainline or DLR, walk 3/4 mile up through park)

Museum of Victorian interiors

Linley Sambourne's House has an almost completely unchanged late Victorian interior. Headquarters of the Victorian Society and once home to the famed *Punch* cartoonist Linley Sambourne, an ancestor of another famous Kensington resident, the Earl of Snowdon, who married Princess Margaret (and their son, twelfth in line to the throne, is furniture-maker Viscount Linley). He – the ancestor – drew his cartoons by getting various comely young ladies to pose in position, undressed for reasons we can only surmise. Note this house is open for a guided tour by appointment only, and it's an intimate experience: you feel you really get to know the family. The guide is sometimes a costumed actor speaking in role. They can also arrange joint tours with nearby Leighton House (see *Museum of Moorish paradise*, page 78).

18 Stafford Terrace, Kensington (a couple of streets north of the middle of the High Street) ☎ 020 7602 3316 ext 300 (11.00–17.30 Monday–Friday), 020 7938 1295 (weekends) ⌨ www.rbkc.gov.uk; admission £6 by appointment only ➲ High Street Kensington 🚌 9 from Strand, 10 from Oxford Street and King's Cross

THE LONDON LIDOS – ART DECO OASES?

Just occasionally, this windswept island of grey skies and umbrellas and southwesterly gales experiences a heat-wave, when, for a few days, it's too hot to be comfortable and the newspapers run headlines such as 'Phew wotta Scorcha!'.

Better than that is when the hot weather gets stuck in a groove of endless summer days, blue skies, people walking around in shorts and T-shirts, children with no shoes, sunglasses and car windows wide open. It only happens about once every five years, but this is the only time we Poms can risk planning a barbecue more than a few days ahead, as our more fortunate cousins Down Under are able to do.

At these times, an extraordinary London institution comes into its own: the lido. These enormous open-air pools were mostly laid out in the 1930s when 'fresh air for health' was promoted across Europe (even for the Hitler Youth), when some Art Deco houses were built with outside sleeping areas, even in this country (there's one at Amersham).

Many foolish seaside communities have filled in their **1930s' lidos**, but strangely a large number have survived in London. The hard core of serious, up-and-down, 50-length swimmers get an adrenalin rush from the cold. They are mostly far too big to heat (the pools, not the swimmers) – but they only really get busy in a heat-wave or a really good summer.

Then the regulars, with their serious Speedo swimwear and rubber hats, look askance at the families pouring in, at the naked toddlers weeing on the pavements and dropping half-eaten ice creams, screaming while their mums, and teenage boys, with acne-ridden faces, hopelessly eye the hourglass figures of girls posing as *Baywatch* extras, where lido meets libido.

When there is blue sky overhead it's never as unpleasant as a noisy, crammed indoor pool on a hot day.

You'll usually find some eccentric pensioners whose floppy bodies, painfully awkward and slow on land, move gracefully through the water with ease that comes from years of practice and who put the rest of us to shame with their effortless 40 lengths.

Going to the lido was, for many working-class Londoners in the days before package tours, the closest thing to a holiday and an escape from the discomfort of a city heat-wave they were likely to get. Exposing their bodies to sunshine gave them much-needed Vitamin D. This could prevent rickets, a disfiguring bone disease common in the slums just a few years before.

When I was a child at **Brockwell Park Lido**, between Dulwich and Brixton, I recall the surface of the water stretching endlessly to the horizon, punctuated by floating dead flies and lolly sticks. I couldn't really see the other end – it seemed like an ocean to me. Probably there were some serious swimmers in the deep bit, but I didn't see them. I just saw the small bunch of children who had claimed a small patch of the shallow end as their own, because there was so much of it to go round.

Now I've gone back on a scorching day as an adult and, yes, the pool's only half the size it seemed to be then. There are still brazen teenagers in skimpy bikinis and spotty youths who haven't quite switched from Toblerone to testosterone. It's still bloody freezing when you get in, but on a scorching day that's exhilarating and all the more reason to get out and bask in the sun once more. It's an instant beach holiday.

London's main surviving lidos

Tooting Bec Lido London's oldest, built 1906. Nice woodland setting, good for picnics. Not heated. Food: Café, picnics possible.

Tooting Bec Common, Streatham, SW16 1RU (off Tooting Bec) ☎ 020 8871 7198; open 26 May–end of September 🚊 Streatham

Richmond Pools on the Park Open air and enclosed pools; both heated. Food: Café, picnics possible.

Old Deer Park, Twickenham Road, Richmond, TW9 2SF ☎ 020 8940 0561; open all year 🚗/🚊 Richmond (overground from Waterloo and North London line, District Line Tube)

Park Road Pools Heated. Food: Café, picnics possible.

Hornsey, N8 8JN ☎ 020 8341 3567; open May–September 🚗/🚌 Finsbury Park, then a W7 bus drops off at the door

Serpentine Lido Food: Café next door; canteen on site. Mind the ducks … it's a lake. You can – if you're mad – even go on Christmas Day.

Hyde Park, W2 2UH ☎ 020 7706 3422; open 27 June–9 September 🚗 Knightsbridge or South Kensington

Parliament Hill Lido On the south edge of Hampstead Heath, beneath that hill with unmissable views over London. An enormous 58m by 27m.

83

Not heated. You occasionally spot local celeb politicians and nubile actresses. If you spot them together, even better. Food: Café on site, picnics possible.

> Gordon House Road, NW5 1LP ☎ 020 7485 3873 for a recorded message, or 020 7485 4491; open May–September usually; admission free between 07.00 and 09.00 🚋 Gospel Oak (overground, North London Line) ⊖ Tufnell Park (Northern Line), then three-quarters of a mile walk

HAMPSTEAD HEATH PONDS Not really a lido, but a very special place. None of the Art Deco concrete but instead a near-natural atmosphere. Men's, ladies' and mixed bathing ponds. A small charge was introduced recently but locals have resisted this. They even swim in the snow.

HAMPTON HEATED OPEN-AIR POOL Food: Café, picnics possible on lawns. Heated, with Christmas Day swimming. This is just lovely at any time of the year, so I'm reluctantly telling you about 'London's best-kept secret'.

> High Street, Hampton, TW12 2ST ☎ 020 8255 1116; open all year 🚋 Hampton, Hampton Court (overground from Waterloo) both about a mile distant 🚗 From Kingston past Hampton Court towards Sunbury, it's a turn on the right. (From the M3 north end of Sunbury go towards Hampton Court and it's on the left.) Go through village and pool's on the right.

FINCHLEY LIDO Both pools heated. Food: Café, picnics outside possible.

> North Finchley, N12 0GL ☎ 020 8343 9830; open May–September (open air); all year (indoor pool) ⊖ West Finchley, then three-quarters of a mile walk

BROCKWELL PARK LIDO This is a particularly enterprising lido, with classes for t'ai chi, on-site massage, scuba diving (obviously not very far, but hey, it's a start), a children's club, floodlit night swimming and barbecues most Friday nights. The pool has been used as a location for filming episodes of *The Bill*, fashion shoots, advertisements, pop music videos and documentaries; many a Brixton-based celeb can be spotted here. Icy cold. If you don't die in the first length, you will be so numb it doesn't matter, so keep going. Food: Café with comprehensive menu and picnics possible.

> Brockwell Park, Dulwich Road, SE24 0PA ☎ 020 7274 3088; open end of May–2nd weekend in September (weather depending) 🚋 Herne Hill (overground from Victoria or Blackfriars)

LONDON FIELDS LIDO I am delighted to announce that the tide has turned at last for lidos and this one, closed like so many others, was triumphantly reopened in late 2006 after a spirited local campaign supported by local

MP Diane Abbott. Where there was for 20 years a vandalised, derelict eyesore there is now a splendid heated pool. Well done Hackney, and other boroughs, dive in – there are about 30 other lost lidos that need restoring or recreating. I well remember a freezing plunge at Whipps Cross, and Purley Way, both long gone, as is the famed and huge Surbiton Lagoon. Bring them back!

London Fields, Westside, E8 3EU ☎ 020 7254 9038

THEATRE: A BETTER MOUSETRAP AND OTHER QUIRKS

The Mousetrap is the world's longest-running play, but it wasn't supposed to go on stage at all. The play, which opened at the Ambassadors theatre in 1952 and is now at **St Martin's Theatre** (☎ *08444 99 1515*) and which has thus lasted an incredible 60 years, staged at several theatres, was originally written by Agatha Christie as a radio play to mark Queen Mary's 80th birthday. But it was received with such acclaim by whodunnit fans that she decided to rewrite it for the stage.

She gave the royalties to her only grandchild, Mathew Prichard, as a birthday present. Some birthday present! When Mathew became captain of the cricket team at Eton, he took the entire side to see the play. It was a gift whose longevity and reward could only be matched by two I can recall – Handel's gift of the *Messiah* to the Foundling Hospital and J M Barrie's wonderfully apt gift of *Peter Pan* to the Great Ormond Street Hospital for sick children, which still receives income from Disney for its various versions.

The **Theatre Royal**, London's oldest, dates back to the time of Charles II and his mistress, actress Nell Gwyn (see page 145), and comes complete with a resident ghost. The man in grey appears to have been a gentleman horse-rider, for he wears a white wig, a tricorn hat and boots and carries a sword.

The story goes that such a man in the theatre's early days pestered an actress and was asked to leave the premises. A fight ensued, and the man was killed. His body was hastily walled up. In Victorian days, when rebuilding was taking place, a skeleton was found. It had a 17th-century dagger through its ribs…

The diarist Pepys, himself much taken with Nell Gwyn, attended the very first performance at the Theatre Royal when it opened in 1663, after the boring Puritans who had banned theatre were themselves banned and theatres returned to the capital. Though the theatre has been burned down more than once, it has always risen like a phoenix, so the show could go on.

85

The Irish playwright Sheridan owned it at the time of the third fire in 1809, and refused to hurry over, despite hearing the news; when he finally got there he calmly took a glass of port at Covent Garden. When onlookers protested at his composure in the face of the great disaster, he replied: 'Surely a man may take a glass of port at his own fireside.'

Actors are, as is well known, horribly superstitious, and will always refer to Shakespeare's … Scottish play … as 'the Scottish play' and never as … well, it would be bad luck, wouldn't it? They like to talk about 'thespians' and 'treading the boards' instead of actors and acting.

One of the less well-known thespian traditions takes place at the Theatre Royal, where on 6 January, a Baddeley Cake is consumed by the cast in memory of actor Richard Baddeley, who was a successful actor here. When he died in 1794, he left money to provide for a **Twelfth Night Cake** and wine to be shared amongst the company (but not the audience). So every 6 January, Twelfth Night, just for luck a cake is carried into the Green Room by bewigged attendants dressed in their 18th-century livery for the company, who drink Baddeley's health. After all, one doesn't want to break a leg. Especially not Baddeley.

If you're having a drink in the bar, you can contemplate the fact that Britain's most successful theatre producer of modern times, Sir Cameron Mackintosh, once scrubbed the floors and polished the brass here as a mere cleaner. It was just a stepping stone for the man behind such mega hits as *Les Misérables* which dominated the West End and Broadway for decades. He had wanted to be a theatre producer from the age of eight. (Personally, I thought for many years that 'Les Miserable' was French for Les Dawson.)

Perhaps the oddest thing that's ever existed off-stage in a London theatre was a royal railway that went from the foyer to the Royal Box in the **London Coliseum**, so the pampered princes didn't have to walk that small distance.

It was hard to know whether or not to believe this story, kindly pointed out by reader Jim Garrod, but on prompting he produced two sources of evidence. One was an old Coliseum programme that said:

> *Through the Grand Salon is the Royal Entry. Immediately on entering the theatre, a Royal party will step into a richly furnished lounge which, at a signal, will move softly along on a track formed in the floor, through the salon and into a large foyer which contains the entrance to the Royal Box. The lounge car remains in position at the entrance to the Royal Box and serves as an ante-room during the performance.*

A photograph accompanying this piece, which may not have come from the same source, shows a square box about ten feet long with no apparent wheels. The caption, crucially, says: 'The King's Car: on Edward VII's first visit it broke down ignominiously and was consigned to use as a box office in the Stoll Theatre.'

Mr Garrod goes on to point out that in *London's Secret History* by Peter Bushell (Constable, 1983) is the following:

> *Dominating the southern end of St Martin's Lane is the Renaissance-style Coliseum, opened in 1904 with a roof garden, the world's first revolving stage and a glass train which carried royalty to their box.*

Given Edward VII's predilection for mistresses (one famously being an ancestor of Camilla, Duchess of Cornwall), I am more likely to agree with Mr Garrod who comments:

> *In fact it is more likely that it was to hide the identity of the King's companion, since Bushell's description of a glass box is wrong. The photograph shows it to be of wood with small, curtained windows.*

Mr Garrod adds:

> *My wife was originally told about it some years ago by a long-serving member of the ENO staff who said the rails were still there under the carpet, at that time.*

Which turns out to be just as unbelievably believable as the London opera house powered by a German submarine. When the **Royal Opera** at Covent Garden was being done up in the 1990s it was decided to chuck out the old diesel engine that provided emergency power. Someone looked into where it had come from – a member of the orchestra told me it was from a German sub in World War I.

A further disaster befell the Coliseum a week after its royal humiliation when it was decided ambitiously to stage a play about the Derby horse race on its new triple-revolve stage. The plan was to use the revolving stage and real horses. One of the horses fell into the orchestra pit, killing the jockey and injuring musicians. The horse had to be put down. That's why orchestra pits in the West End today have safety nets over the heads of the band in case anything else falls off stage, pantomime or real horses included.

ECCENTRIC SHOPPING

THE SHOPS THAT TIME FORGOT

Guns

Since 1835 **Holland & Holland** has been supplying gentlemen with the best guns. Naturally, at this end of the market they are bespoke, tailored to your shoulder and eye. You can specify the engraving and the walnut for the stock, although, at £40,000 a pair, that's understandable.

> 34 Bruton Street, W1J 6HH ☎ 020 7499 4411
> 🖼 www.hollandandholland.com ◆ Green Park

Hats

James Lock & Co has been hatters since 1676 and invented the British bowler hat. 'A chap called Coke came in one day in 1850 and said he wanted a more practical, curved hat for his gamekeepers, so it wouldn't get snagged by branches,' says a spokesman for this family-owned firm. 'He wanted it strong so a blow from a poacher wouldn't do any harm, too. He had a rough design and we made him one. When he collected it, he jumped on it to test it. It was satisfactory.' Later, a firm called Bowler Bros started producing large numbers, hence the name. But don't call it a bowler at Lock's. For them it's still a Coke (pronounced Cook). 'Mad as a hatter' comes from the former use of mercury in the felting process, which made hat-makers a little odd. The days in the 1930s when a man would not dream of going out bare-headed have gone – then it was a flat cloth cap for a workman, a bowler for a tradesman and a topper for a gent.

Today, it's mainly top hats for Royal Ascot, panamas for Henley Regatta, and hats for society weddings. And the Coke family still send their gamekeepers here.

6 St James's Street, SW1A 1EF ☎ 020 7930 8874 🖥 www.lockhatters.co.uk 🟢 Green Park

SHIRTS

If you want an old-fashioned shirt, with a neck band that takes a separate, stiff, starched collar attached with brass studs (a public school torture you may not wish to revisit), **Harvie & Hudson** is the place for you. And starched front shirts for stuffed-shirt gentlemen. Plus more modern, bespoke shirts and ready-to-wear, of course. A splendid mid-Victorian shop-front at 97, by the way.

77, 96–97 Jermyn Street, SW1 6NP ☎ 020 7930 3949 🖥 www.harvieandhudson.com 🟢 Green Park

SHOES

George Cleverley & Co is where shoes are made by traditional methods using wooden lasts for each customer (stored upstairs like so many feet). You can be shod by the people who made shoes for Rudolph Valentino, Winston Churchill, Laurence Olivier, Humphrey Bogart, Sir John Gielgud, Gary Cooper, Clark Gable. The last word in shoes.

13 The Royal Arcade, Old Bond Street W1S 4SL ☎ 020 7493 0443 🖥 www.gjcleverley.co.uk 🟢 Green Park

TEA

Infused with history, **Twinings** has been on The Strand since 1717. How this gem of a shop survived the Blitz, etc, one wonders – with a good cuppa to steady the nerves, I expect. Note the extraordinary figures above the door and the ancient fittings inside. Definitely my cup of tea.

216 The Strand, WC2R 1AP (not near Trafalgar Square but up the other end, opposite the Royal Courts of Justice and therefore nearly in Fleet Street) ☎ 020 7353 3511 🖥 www.twinings.com 🟢 Temple

STICKS AND BROLLIES

The fantastically preserved, gloriously Victorian **James Smith & Sons** is absolutely worth a visit even if closed for the sheer look of the place. On first glance at one gorgeous window I thought they just made sticks and canes. Fine in the dandy days of between the wars, but hard to see how they'd make a living doing that nowadays. But then I discovered the umbrella-making aspect – bit more of a market in London, you may think – and found that prime ministers such as Gladstone bought their brollies here. Go east from the Tube and you'll have a treat.

53 New Oxford Street, WC1A 1BL ☎ 020 7836 4731
🖳 www.james-smith.co.uk ✪ Tottenham Court Road

WIGS

Ede & Ravenscroft produce not fashion wigs, or wigs for those who have lost their hair, but full 17th-century-style horsehair wigs for lawyers. It is stark staring bonkers that barristers and judges still need to wear 17th-century wigs, and therefore a good thing. They are curled with old-fashioned curling tongs and last for decades longer than most lawyers.

93 Chancery Lane, WC2A 1DU ☎ 020 7405 3906
🖳 www.edeandravenscroft.co.uk ✪ Chancery Lane

WINES

The rather unprepossessing, battered exterior – understated, one might say – of **Berry Bros & Rudd**, an apparently small shop, hides wine vaults with the best vintages in the world, extending for hundreds of feet. I'd like to recommend the 1928 Petrus at £9,000 a magnum, but I haven't tasted it. There are even late 19th-century vintages which may, of course, be undrinkable. But a tip: if you manage to get hold of one of them and it's as wonderful as it should be, drink it all straight away. It will go off rapidly.

3 St James's Street, SW1A 1EG ☎ 020 7396 9600 🖳 www.bbr.com
✪ Green Park

YACHT BITS

You might expect a shop like **Arthur Beale** in a port, but not in the heart of theatreland. I love these ship-shops – the smell of rope and tar, the bronze deck fittings, coils of rope, stainless-steel bits of rigging, galvanised anchors – a promise of more messing about in boats. But it should be about as useful here in West End's theatreland as a surfboard in the Sahara. Maybe actors pop out after the matinee and pick up a mizzen monkey's fist and a Cunningham cringle – don't ask – for the weekend. Less surprising, but still a wonderful Aladdin's cave, is the one at Putney on the river front, **Chas Newens Marine** (just across the river from Putney Bridge Tube, turn right (west, on the south bank, what a wonderful stroll up to Hammersmith Bridge!).

194 Shaftesbury Avenue, WC2H 8JP ● Covent Garden

BUTTONS

If you thought buttons were just a case of sewing one on occasionally, you couldn't be more wrong. People collect them and cherish them, and **The Button Queen** pushes all the right buttons for aficionados, with horn, shell, brass, leather, Bakelite, celluloid, wood and plastic jobs of all sizes and colours. A rare one could be worth £130, but more humble buttons are available.

19 Marylebone Lane, W1U 2PR ☎ 020 7935 1505 ● Oxford Circus

CAKES

Konditor & Cook offer cake creativity at its most fun. No staid royal icing swags, Corinthian columns or sugar rosebuds, but vibrant colours, zany designs, bright and delicious. Hand made, to the order of people such as Madonna and Jerry Hall. Irresistible. The cakes, that is. There's also a branch in Borough Market.

Cornwall Road, Waterloo, SE1 8TW ☎ 020 7407 5100
▦ www.konditorandcook.com ● Waterloo

FABRIC

Have you noticed how crazy economics have turned the concept of the homemade on its head? Even as recently as 30 years ago, those needing to save money made their own jumpers, jam, dresses and furniture. Now it's far cheaper to have it made by someone else on the other side of the planet. Only the well-to-do would consider making dresses, etc, now you can buy a ready-made one for the price of a couple of packets of fags, and the extraordinary **Joel & Son** is where they go to get the world's most gorgeous fabrics, anything from £40 to £2,000 a metre. Yes, £2,000 a metre, encrusted with crystals.

75 Church Street, NW8 8EU ☎ 020 7724 6895
🖳 www.joelandsonfabrics.com ⬥ Edgware Road

MUSIC

Chappell probably has the most comprehensive stock of music in the world. Sheet music, that is. You can settle old scores here all right! Full orchestral range of instruments from triangles to bassoons, and from cor anglais to French horns.

152 Wardour Street, W1F 8YA ☎ 020 7432 4400
🖳 www.chappellofbondstreet.co.uk ⬥ Oxford Circus

SPICES

It must have required enormous self-control to name this shop **The Spice Shop**. Not something corny like Basil & Rosemary's, Hot Stuff, Spice Odyssey 2001 or whatever. Well done! It's hard to imagine a spice or herb that isn't here. Dozens of chillis and paprikas. Also a market stall in the North End Road, which runs from Fulham to West Kensington, if you're cumin on a Friday and Saturday. As Obama nearly said: 'Yes, you cayenne.' Just don't get any on your cloves. Dang, I've given in to the ghastly spice puns! So sorrel...

1 Blenheim Crescent, W11 2EE ☎ 020 7221 4448
🖳 www.thespiceshop.co.uk ⬥ Ladbroke Grove

JAMES BOND STUFF

Spymaster is a kind of surveillance supermarket. Covert cameras, phone bugging stuff, listening equipment, shredders, body armour, etc. Great fun and none of it illegal. They'll get you an armoured car if you want one. Pop into the nearby bar afterwards for a Martini and say in a Sean Connery accent: 'Shaken, not shtirred...'.

3 Portman Square, W1H 6LB ☎ 020 7486 3885 🖳 www.spymaster.co.uk
⬥ The name's Bond. Bond Street, actually.

ALL THE TRIMMINGS

V V Rouleaux, founded by Annabel Lewis, specialises in passementerie, which the dictionary defines as: 'a decorative trimming of gimp, cord, beads, braid, etc.' It's an Aladdin's cave of ribbon, braids, feathers, buckles, brocade, tassels, cords and fringes: a mad dressing-up box for grown-ups.

'Sex on a spool,' as one customer put it. Rather good that.

102 Marylebone Lane, W1U 2QD (and 261 Pavilion Road, SW1X 0BP, next to Peter Jones IN Sloane Square) ☎ 020 7224 5179 📠 www.vvrouleaux.com
⊖ Green Park

A SHOCK IN STORE AT WHITELEY'S

An eccentrically brilliant London shopkeeper who has left his name writ large on the capital was **William Whiteley**. As you approach Central London up the A4 from the Heathrow direction, and rise over a humped bridge near Earl's Court, you notice his name on the old furniture depository on the left. And in Queensway, Bayswater, his name is still used for the flashy shopping centre on the site of his pioneering department store.

Whiteley (1831–1907), invented the modern department store. He boasted that he could get anything for his customers, and when he was tested by being asked for a pint of fleas and an elephant, he produced them in 24 hours.

His radical approach was to provide what the public wanted, not what the store wanted to sell. He had come to London from Yorkshire with less than £10 in his pocket, but having learned the trade in another shop, soon bought his own, and by buying adjoining houses gradually built up his shop with more and more departments until it covered everything from building work to wedding dresses – a concept he called 'the universal provider', but which we now call the department store.

Not that this made him popular with other traders. Local butchers who were undercut by his service burned him in effigy on 5 November. Several fires started in his stores during these years and no doubt some of these were arson. The other traders no doubt wished he would drop dead – a wish that would come true sooner than they imagined.

On 24 January 1907, the great William Whiteley, merchant prince of London as he was known, was shockingly shot dead in the very store that had made him famous. He was not popular as an employer – apprentices weren't paid at all in their first year. He made his 6,000 staff live in dormitories and enforced 176 draconian rules, expecting them to work from 7am to 11pm six days a week. Whiteley also had a habit of taking attractive females to Paris, promising them the earth, but delivering perhaps more direct signs of his desires.

On that January day, a young man, Horace Raynor, had turned up at

93

the store claiming to be Whiteley's illegitimate son. He asked to see the store owner and demanded money for his studies in America. Whiteley refused, and called the police. Raynor drew a gun and shot him dead, but was easily detained. The 29-year-old tried to kill himself shortly afterwards but recovered in hospital and was then charged with the murder in court.

The criminal was sentenced to be hanged, but was reprieved and served just 12 years, a sign, perhaps, that the authorities believed his yarn about his parentage.

Meanwhile, Whiteley had bought himself immortality. Not in the names on the side of the department store and the furniture depository, but in an idyllic woodland retirement village of Surrey almshouses he provided through his will with uncharacteristic generosity in Surrey, and furnished with a statue of himself, all at the then huge cost of £1,000,000. And the name of that village? Whiteley, near Walton-on-Thames.

One of Whiteley's employees, **John Barker**, left to start a small shop in Kensington High Street which became the great Barker's store whose magnificent Art Deco pile is still at the bottom of Church Street, although not used as a department store any more.

Another famous, not to say deeply posh, London store, **Fortnum & Mason** (at 181 Piccadilly for the past 300 years) has survived, thankfully, and has a curious history. A Palace footman, William Fortnum, was entitled to remove the candle ends from chandeliers and candelabra, and sold them on. This was at a time when poor people couldn't sew or read at night because they couldn't afford whole candles, so even a stub end would be welcome. He eventually became rich enough to start up in business.

The store was famous for delivering post anywhere before the penny post stamp was invented, and for feeding the homesick British around the Empire with familiar fare while bringing those countries' spicy, exotic recipes home to tingle the Londoners' palates. A certain young Mr Heinz lugged several cases to this shop all the way from the United States and introduced the British to perhaps their greatest love: the tinned baked bean. Which might be – who knows? – why the store has more royal warrants than just about anywhere on earth. 'More beans, Your Majesty?'

Part Two

THE ECCENTRIC CITY

IMMORTALISED LONDON

LONDON ADDRESSES IMMORTALISED

84 CHARING CROSS ROAD is the location of the bookstore made famous by Helene Hanff in her romantic book about her real-life correspondence with its manager Frank Dole, and by the feel-good film made of it. This area is still riddled with bookshops. Helene Hanff had a witty, acerbic and affectionate 20-year correspondence with the London bookseller whom she never met. Ironically, she was a poor struggling New York writer with barely enough to live on, yet her correspondence – her being brash and demanding, yet deeply sympathetic to the literature she discussed with Dole, at first British and reserved and then increasingly affectionate towards her – was a world-wide hit. He died before she was able to visit London; she died in 1997 aged 80. It's quite a story.

221B BAKER STREET is the address of the home of the greatest of all detectives, Sherlock Holmes. It was later parodied by Dorothy L Sayers in the address of her own hero, Lord Peter Wimsey, 110A Piccadilly. Today there's a museum at a fake 221B (actually at 239), which is a reconstruction of a film set of Sherlock Holmes's apartment, complete with the fire, the violin, the pipe and deerstalker hat. The actual 221B is the headquarters of the Abbey National bank, which receives some 90 letters a week from Holmes fans around the world, including an occasional one genuinely seeking help from the world's most famous detective as if he were real.

10 DOWNING STREET, an outwardly tiny terrace house, is home to the prime minister, who has a lot more power than the almost powerless monarch who lives in palaces and castles – so much for the British constitution (if there were one). George Downing created the street; he must have been a great political survivor, because he worked for Cromwell as a leading republican in the 1640s and 1650s, yet did equally well as a strident royalist after the 1660 Restoration of the Monarchy. Not the last unprincipled two-faced turncoat to live in this street, some may feel. I couldn't possibly comment. For the bizarre story of how his bequest led to Downing College, see my book *Eccentric Cambridge*.

23 RAILWAY CUTTINGS, East Cheam, is a fictional address immortalised for Brits of a certain age by Tony Hancock (1924–68) in the radio then TV comedy show in which he was paired with South African Sid James. The scripts have been published, but real fans don't need them and can recall Hancock's outraged tone as if it were yesterday – eg: in *The Blood Donor:* 'A pint? But that's nearly an armful!'

10 RILLINGTON PLACE is a book and a film. This address was where real-life simpleton Timothy Evans supposedly murdered his own baby girl in 1949, leading to his execution by hanging. The discovery that another occupant of the house, John Reginald Halliday Christie, was a serial murderer led to Evans being pardoned, posthumously, in 1966. Classic miscarriage of justice stuff.

79 CADOGAN PLACE was made notorious nationwide in 1886. The steamy divorce case that centred on this fashionable address caused outrage in the Press (so outraged that they gleefully printed every word of the evidence, day after day) and concerned 'What the butler saw'. It involved Lady Colin Campbell, née Gertrude Blood, a dark and gorgeous Irishwoman. Married in 1881, she soon caught syphilis from her husband and sued him for divorce on the grounds of adultery with a maid. He fought the case on the grounds of her promiscuity and the evidence that fascinated Britain was what went on in the drawing room at 79 Cadogan Place, involving the highborn sons of two dukes.

Among her ladyship's male visitors were the Marquess of Blandford (who had already been cited in divorce cases), a chief fire officer, Captain

Shaw, and a surgeon, Tom Bird. The butler told the court that he was told not to announce these men in the hearing of Lady Campbell's husband, Lord Colin (son of the Duke of Argyll). On one occasion, the butler found Lady Colin with Blandford (heir to the Duke of Marlborough), her dress 'disordered' and her face flushed. Yet again, by spying through the keyhole, he saw her lighting the fire, so to speak, of Captain Shaw.

> Butler: *'I saw Lady Colin lying down with Captain Shaw on the carpet.'*
> Counsel: *'Did you see her bust?*
> Butler: *'I certainly saw more than that.'*

There were arguments as to whether the heavy metal escutcheons (covers on the keyhole) would prevent this kind of spying, so the jury insisted on seeing for themselves. The court was solemnly taken to peer through London's most famous keyhole. The jury found that not only would the stiff escutcheons stay in any position but that they would not even cover the keyholes. Even more peculiar, the jury found none of the claims of adultery proven, so the Campbells remained married but separated until, unsurprisingly, they both died prematurely of syphilis.

A LONDON FLAT WAS SOLD to a Ukrainian chap in 2011 for £136 million. Yes, one hundred and thirty-six million smackeroonies. For a flat! Admittedly it wasn't any flat – it was two apartments in One Hyde Park that would be knocked together to make a penthouse suiting a billionaire. Still, for that price you'd get some pretty good fixtures and fittings, wouldn't you? Well, er, no. It was a bare shell and an estimated £60 million more was needed to do the place up (no popping down B&Q for some brilliant white, then?). The whole block had gone for a total of £1 billion. What recession, darlink?

London's most eccentric property deal

RHYME AND REASON

Are children's nursery rhymes harmless? Not a bit of it! There's a lot of horrid history of London – execution, plague, death, warfare and prostitution – in these ditties.

St Clement's, oranges and lemons, and a right old ding-dong

A New Zealand friend told me about the day when, first arrived, she walked down Fleet Street to where The Strand splits from the Aldwych. There she heard the bells of St Clement's ringing 'Oranges and Lemons', a song sung in school playgrounds around the world. 'It was a nursery rhyme come alive,' she says, 'a magic moment.' And indeed, every March, schoolchildren are given oranges and lemons there.

The shorter version of the rhyme, which has more variations than J S Bach could have dreamed up, goes:

Oranges and lemons,
Say the bells of St Clement's;
You owe me five farthings,
Say the bells of St Martin's;
When will you pay me?
Say the bells of Old Bailey;
When I grow rich,
Say the Bells of Shoreditch;
When will that be?
Say the bells of Stepney;
I do not know,
Says the big bell of Bow.
Here comes candle to light you to bed,
Here comes a chopper to chop off your head;
The last, last, last, last man's head.

It's a rhyme beloved of children in playgrounds many miles from London's bells for many generations because of the simple metre and catchy tune, plus the game where two of the children form arches with their arms and the rest run through in a line with linked hands.

There's a suitable amount of menace – which children love – in not knowing who will be caught by the chopper of the arms coming down and capturing a child. In the oldest versions of the game the trapped child is asked, out of earshot of the rest, which he prefers, oranges or lemons, and then he must stand behind one of the chopping pair who secretly agreed to be lemons or oranges. The process repeats until the children are divided into two teams, who then compete in some other way – such as a tug-of-war.

Why should such a game have evolved at all? It's certainly very old. It was probably long established when printed in a 1744 book with hardly a word different except one line reading: *Ring Ye bells at Fleetditch*. It is known that the various London parishes met for sporting challenges in the Middle Ages, including just such tug-of-wars, and a rhyme about the parishes involved may have followed this long-forgotten custom.

On the other hand it is undoubtedly macabre with its reference to execution – the candle to light you to bed being a funeral torch, public executions being a popular event for children as well as adults for many centuries. All such topical events were made into rhyme, just as London's football fans today chant insulting doggerel about their opponents.

Which St Clement's is the one in the song is in serious doubt – today it is assumed by most visitors that St Clement Danes in The Strand is the church involved, but **St Clement's Eastcheap** near the north end of London Bridge in the City could have a better claim. It was here that oranges and lemons unloaded from ships would be carried from the river to the market by porters who, on New Year's Day, gave each tenant a fruit and some more to the church.

St Clement Danes, a wedding-cakey Christopher Wren church, was after all then outside the City, although both churches claim to be the one in the rhyme. Adding weight to St Clement Danes's claim is the idea that fruit porters rested their loads there on their way from the wharves of London to Clare Market nearby.

A clue to the confusion lies in a colourful character called William Pennington-Bickford, minister of St Clement Danes in the 1920s, who installed a new carillon of bells to ring out the famous nursery rhyme. He started the annual presentations of oranges and lemons to schoolchildren and had the carillon's tune broadcast on radio. Did he then appropriate another church's history and tune for his precious bells? No one can say for sure, given how old the rhyme is, and the fact the Reverend Pennington-Bickford is long dead. Either way, it's a right old ding-dong. For more on St Clement's, see page 138.

RING-A-RING OF ROSES AND A HORRIBLE DEATH

Another apparently harmless childhood rhyme is 'Ring-a-ring of roses', and again it is full of the blackest, most macabre London history.

Ring-a-ring of roses,
Pocketful of posies,
Atishoo atishoo,
We all fall down.

At the first line the children circle round with joined hands in a ring, at the third they stop and do exaggerated sneezes and at the fourth they fall on the floor. Children of about three or four love it.

There's no need to tell them, until they're well grown, that 'ring-a-ring of roses' refers to the skin discoloration that the Black Death brings, that 'pocketful of posies' refers to the herbs people carried to try to ward off the dreaded plague, that 'atishoo, atishoo' describes its remarkably rapid onset and 'all fall down' the inevitable end, death, then being tipped from carts into pits of quicklime. The poem probably started with the 1665 Great Plague. For more about plague, see page 56.

THE GRAND OLD DUKE OF YORK AND KITTY FISHER

Everyone knows the magnificent curve of Regent Street as it approaches Piccadilly Circus. Beyond the brash and vibrant Circus the road continues a little into the rarified air of St James's (yet another example of how the atmosphere of London can change totally in 100 yards or so) and then peters out as it crosses Pall Mall, changing into Waterloo Place. The massive column looking like something out of imperial Rome is a monument to someone not terribly important, **Frederick, Duke of York**, forgettable second son of mad George III, and commander-in-chief of the army.

It was this duke who, in the words of the nursery rhyme, insanely marched his men up and down hills. As well as being fed up with all this marching, the army had to suffer every man having a day's wages stopped to pay for this ludicrously tall monument.

The Grand Old Duke of York,
He had ten thousand men,
He marched them up to the top of the hill,
And marched them down again.
And when they were up, they were up,
And when they were down, they were down,
And when they were only half-way up,
They were neither up nor down.

At the time it was said to be built so high to keep the Duke of York away from his creditors, as he owed the enormous sum of £1.9 million at his death.

There is another amusing link between money, this part of London and a previous Duke of York, that is, the younger brother of George III. He liked to visit the upmarket courtesan **Kitty Fisher** at her home in nearby Carrington Street, off Shepherd Street north of Piccadilly, in the early 1760s. She notoriously charged 100 guineas a go – £105, an enormous amount of money then – to her gentlemen, mostly married figures of high social standing. When the duke gave her a mere £50, her contemptuous reaction was to stick it between two slices of bread and eat it. (Oddly, it was just about this time that the fourth Earl of Sandwich, gambling near here, ordered thin pieces of meat to be placed between slices of bread so he could continue his game uninterrupted for 24 hours. Just because he was a nob, the thing became known as a sandwich. We could just as reasonably ask for a cheese and tomato Kitty.)

There is also a rhyme about Kitty Fisher, contrasting her wealth as a successful courtesan with the poverty of a lower order of the same profession (Lucy Locket), which goes as follows:

> *Lucy Locket lost her pocket*
> *Kitty Fisher found it*
> *Not a penny was there in it*
> *But a ribbon round it.*

LONDON BRIDGE, PILLAGING RAIDERS AND A VIRGIN'S BONES

This very well-known verse is clearly about London's history, but it's astonishing how many centuries of it. It sounds innocuous enough; it starts:

> *London Bridge is broken down,*
> *Broken down, broken, down,*
> *London Bridge is broken down,*
> *My fair lady.*

Various solutions are tried:

> *Build it up with mud and clay,*
> *Mud and clay, mud and clay etc*

and problems encountered:

> *Mud and clay will wash away etc*
> *Iron and steel will bend and bow, Silver and gold will be stolen away, but*
> *stone so strong will last ages long*

the song eventually concludes.

The last part was true if we consider the extraordinary history of this bridge, the one key factor in the whole 2,000-year history of London. The **Romans** saw how the hills where the City now stands caused the wide marshy river to narrow and built the first bridge right here. The Romans believed in river gods and would often throw into a river inscriptions aimed at appeasing them, or make sacrifices to them. In fact in pre-Christian Europe a child sacrifice was thought particularly effective, so sometimes infants were walled up alive in the bridge stones. It is said by various chroniclers that the **timber London Bridge** had a virgin's bones in its foundations in line with this legend.

The **Vikings**, under Olaf the Norseman, managed to pull down the timber London Bridge in 1014 as part of their rape and pillage campaign against the Saxons and it is probably this event that is remembered by the rhyme. Fascinatingly, there are Norse rhymes told to children on the other side of the North Sea celebrating exactly this event a millennium ago.

The **stone London Bridge**, begun in 1176 by a monk, Peter of Colechurch, took until 1209 to finish and lasted, amazingly, until the 19th century. For nearly all this time it was London's only river crossing and thus its survival was critical to the City.

The London Bridge we generally picture was the 1176 stone one, built with stone arches on a series of boat-shaped artificial islands called starlings. These arches had to be repeatedly strengthened, making the channels between them narrower, so when the tide was at full flood, or ebb, it roared through with white water. For boatmen, shooting the bridge was a risky business. It could also slow the water upstream enough, in the right conditions, for the river to freeze deeply enough to hold a Frost Fair on it (see page 270). This bridge lasted, with many repairs and embellishment, until 1830.

Taking it down had two unlikely results. Firstly a cutler on The Strand bought all the steel straps strengthening the stonework and made the best cutlery of the day out of them, and the elm timbers were made into thousands of souvenir knick-knacks such as snuff boxes. Secondly, two stone shelters on the bridge somehow survived and can be seen even today in Victoria Park, Hackney, by St Augustine's Gate.

The **four-pier stone bridge** which replaced it was completed by 1831, and it survived heavier and heavier traffic, German bombs and the ebb and flow of the river until 1967, when an American squillionaire bought it to put over a specially created river in Arizona. Famously, and probably apocryphally, he was said to have thought he was buying the medieval bridge with houses on rather than the somewhat boring 19th-century job. This has been denied, but today we have a steel-arched thing that is functional and even graceful but not curious, giving a 330-foot clear span. Same place, fewer piers and wider spans sums up the 2,000 years so far.

Now the great and the good are thinking of another bridge nearby with – guess what – lots of shops and houses on it.

HALF A POUND OF TUPENNY RICE

This strangely pleasing rhyme is probably not so very old and has puzzled generations of children who wonder why weasels should go pop. However, as is fairly widely known, it is a tale of hand-to-mouth working class life in Islington, north of the City, where there's indeed a pub called the Eagle and a City Road.

Round and round the cobbler's bench
The monkey chased the weasel,
The monkey thought 'twas all in fun
Pop! Goes the weasel.

A penny for a spool of thread
A penny for a needle,
That's the way the money goes,
Pop! Goes the weasel.

A half a pound of tupenny rice,
A half a pound of treacle.
Mix it up and make it nice,
Pop! Goes the weasel.

Up and down the City Road,
In and out of the Eagle,
That's the way the money goes,
Pop! Goes the weasel.

I've no time to plead and pine,
I've no time to wheedle,
Kiss me quick and then I'm gone
Pop! Goes the weasel.

To 'pop' something is to pawn it, to take it to the shop with three golden balls outside (there are still some around London and one indeed opposite the Angel pub, Islington) where money would be handed over for valuables which could be redeemed later, if the person produced the money, plus a little more no doubt, and the ticket. If not, the valuables could be sold. It's much the same the world over.

A weasel was a kind of ironing and clothes-making machine that would have provided an income for a family in the rag trade, as London's famously badly paid clothing industry was, and is, known. The irony captured by the rhyme was that once the weasel had gone, so had much of the family's income. Hard times.

UNKNOWN TO MANY, London contains a Nazi Government memorial – or rather one put up by its ambassador. It commemorates Giro, the faithful hound of the German ambassador Leopold von Hoesch (not, I'm told, a Nazi himself), who was buried in February 1934, complete with tombstone near the then German embassy at 7 Carlton House Terrace.

The memorial, with touching epithet *Ein treuer Begleiter* (a true companion), is tucked under a tree at the top of the steps from the Institute of Contemporary Art on the Mall up to Waterloo Place, perhaps somewhat cheekily given that the area is laden with such vast monuments to heroes of the British Empire.

Indeed, the statues show serious bomb damage inflicted by Giro's master's master, Hitler, fewer than ten years later. Giro's tombstone, however, was undamaged – as was the splendid Nazi interior nearby designed by Hitler's architect Albert Speer – and has been encased in glass to preserve it further. Every February someone puts flowers on the little mutt's grave. That the simple love of a faithful dog has survived all this terrible history is, in its way, reassuring.

London's Nazi-era monument

LONDON'S ROAD TO ECCENTRICITY

LONDON'S ECCENTRIC ROAD AND PLACE NAMES

ABBEY ROAD Everyone's heard of the eponymous Beatles album, but why is Abbey Road in St John's Wood linked to Kilburn High Road by the oddly named Quex Road, with the equally unlikely Mazenod Avenue running off it? Urban myth has it that these road names, made with black-and-white tiles as on the Beatles cover, were the last throw of a desperate council department with a few odd street-name letters left over, like a losing Scrabble player. In fact Mazenod is a Catholic saint and Quex is connected to a stately home in Kent (don't ask me how).

BATTERSEA The English name ending -ey, or -ea, meant island. Battersea was St Peter's ey, an island in the marshes where monks from Westminster Abbey of St Peter would retreat. No doubt Chelsea, Marshalsea and Bermondsey are named for similar reasons – long before the Thames was finally confined within Victorian embankments it was a wide marshy estuary (the north shore being where Buckingham Palace now stands).

BELGRAVIA Though the origin of Belgravia is well known – the Grosvenor family who own so much land here had an estate at Belgrave, Leicester – the derivation of neighbouring Pimlico is, bizarrely, a total mystery.

BLOOMSBURY Named after a Norman noble to whom William the Conqueror gave land here. The Dukes of Bedford still own large chunks of Bloomsbury and the street names recall them and other aristocrats who developed the squares and terraces: Russell Square, Bedford Square, Tavistock Square and Woburn Place. More recently, Bloomsbury has become associated with intellectuals, the British Museum, London University, student residences, bookshops and publishers, and the early 20th-century bunch of writers called the Bloomsbury Group.

BROMPTON Incredible though it seems standing in today's Brompton Road (you wouldn't live long if you did) with its Kensington-style house prices, this was once a country lane which crossed common land covered in the yellow-flowering broom. Hence the hamlet along it came to be known as Broom-ton.

BUNHILL FIELDS Bunhill Fields, off City Road, EC1, is actually a corruption of Bone Hill. Not surprising when you consider that 120,000 Londoners are crammed into the cemetery here.

CANNON STREET Cannon Street was originally Candle Street, until the candle makers who boiled their animal fats there were expelled to the countryside because of the vile smell their trade created.

CARTING LANE Talking of pongs, Carting Lane, off The Strand, WC2, was once listed as the less than fragrant Farting Lane. However, this simple typographical error had a whiff of truth about it, for the gas lamps there were once lit by the gases rising from the sewers of the Savoy Hotel.

CLARIDGE'S The London residence of many a king and president (and often spelt without that apostrophe), Claridge's is also the most frequently used and thinly disguised location in crime fiction. According to an excellent book for whodunnit fans, *London: Mystery Reader's Walking Guide* (Passport Books, Illinois) by Barbara Sloan Hendershott and Alzina Stone Dale, it has appeared as Alridge's in Anthony Berkeley's *The Piccadilly Murder* as somewhere 'where the air cost several pounds an hour to breathe' and as Harridge's in Agatha Christie's *The Golden Ball*: 'Who in England did not know Harridge's where notables and royalty arrived and departed as a matter of course.' Complete with apostrophes, of course.

CLOAK LANE Cloak Lane, EC4, sounds pleasant enough but it means 'open sewer street', as in Rome's Cloaca Maxima.

FITZROY SQUARE Fitzroy Square could have been Royal Bastard Square, although that's not quite so elegant as an address. The prefix Fitz often meant 'illegitimate son of' (not in current holders of the name, *of course*), so Fitzroy meant the king's bastard. In fact this whole area, known as Fitzrovia, is linked to yet another of randy Charles II's mistresses, the voluptuous and sexually insatiable **Barbara Villiers** (1640–1709), much fancied by diarist Samuel Pepys, among others. She had many other lovers at court, which Charles didn't seem to mind, and many street names in this area, such as Euston, Warren, Southampton, Grafton, and of course Fitzroy are taken from titles created for the offspring of this most fruitful woman's loins.

FRYING PAN ALLEY, E1 A City name that probably has more to do with its shape than its function. Or was an ironmonger's shop here?

GLOUCESTER ROAD Gloucester Road in South Kensington was originally the rural, winding Hogmore Lane or even Hogmire (pig pooh) Lane. But it was felt this was too lowly a title when the Duchess of Gloucester moved there in around 1800, so it was changed to something posher. Oddly, during the boom in recreational gardens of around 40 years before – with Vauxhall Gardens being the most famous of them – there was one here in what were semi-rural surroundings. Florida Gardens, situated where Stanhope Gardens is now, was a popular pleasure ground for ladies and gentlemen who weren't always quite the ladies and gentlemen they should have been. The Legoverland of its day.

HA HA ROAD, SE18 A ha-ha is a boundary for country estates. It's a dry, grassy ditch in which the side of the ditch nearest the house is built up with brick or stone. The idea is you get a fenceless boundary that makes the view from the house more pleasant: you can't see the join between the lawns which surround the house and the fields beyond where deer or cattle graze, and it stops them from straying on to your lawn. And if anyone comes across the ditch unexpectedly, they would say: 'Ha ha!' Well, they might have in the 18th century.

HAYMARKET Yes, once the place to get hay for the capital's thousands of horses, but later a highly disreputable part of town. Even Dostoevsky was appalled by how the Haymarket prostitutes put their young daughters to work: 'Little girls, aged about 12, seize you by the arm and beg you to accompany them.' Haymarket was notorious for its louche drinking salons until the late 19th century.

HOUNDSDITCH Just what it says: a stinking ditch, notable for dead dogs floating in it.

Kensington Gore This slightly vile-sounding name for a rather posh road turns out to be completely innocent. There was a triangle of land, whose apex was near the Knights Bridge (see page 110) and covering where the Albert Hall now stands, which was seized by King Henry III, when it was said to be worth 12 pence per acre per annum (now, of course, it's some of the most valuable real estate on the planet). A 'gore' is a triangular piece of cloth, so this triangular piece of land became known as the 'Kinggesgor'. So a gore is a sewn-on patch of cloth. They're lucky it isn't called Kensington Gusset.

Kew The earliest reference to Kew is in a 1440 court case involving 'Richard Hunte of Shene and his wife Alice in Kayowe'. It has also been called Kayhough, Kayhowe, Kaio, Kaw, Keyhowe, Keyo, Kayo, Cayo, Kaw, Cewe and Kewe. They probably all derive from 'quay' or 'key', a landing place. It's the home of the fabulous **botanic gardens**, once a royal park popular with the unpopular Georgian kings and princes beginning with Frederick, Prince of Wales in the 1730s, who had popular composer Handel pop over to play for him. Once, writer Alexander Pope brought him a gift of a dog. On the dog's collar Pope had engraved:

> *I am his Highness's dog at Kew,*
> *Pray tell me, Sir, whose dog are you?*

This Frederick, part of a bitterly divided family of squabbling Hanoverians, was to die young in 1751 after catching a chill walking at Kew and from an abscess that developed after he was hit by a tennis ball. But his wife's closest companion played an interesting role: Lord Bute. He was always hanging around the princess, and the prince, who took a mistress himself, once said: 'Bute, you are the very man to be employed at some small proud German Court where there is nothing to do.' But Bute didn't take the hint, and after the Prince's death, Horace Walpole recorded bitchily of Bute and his scandalously indiscreet relations with the princess:

> *The favoured personage, naturally ostentatious of his person, seemed by no means desirous of concealing his conquest... the beauty of his legs was constantly displayed before the poor captivated Princess. The Prince [so he could have a quick one with his mistress] used to bid the Princess walk with Lord Bute. As soon as the prince was dead, they walked more and more, in honour of his memory.*

The widow devoted herself to her son George, future mad King George III, and to Bute who lived at King's Cottage near the church and who was appointed to the ancient office of Groom of the Stool. This, literally, means 'cleaner of the king's excrement' but someone more lowly usually actually carried out the royal potty. Still, some thought it an apt job for Bute. And whatever you think of that Prince of Wales and his wife, they left some amazing gardens at Kew; it was stuffed with far more pagodas, temples and follies than survive today. But there's still one superb pagoda left – a birthday present for a spoilt princess.

KING EDWARD STREET, EC1 This sounds better than its two previous names: Blowbladder Street after the unsavoury practice among crooked butchers of inserting bladders into the orifices of dead animals and inflating them to make them look bigger. You got your turkey big enough for six home, it passed wind like the cowboys in *Blazing Saddles* and suddenly you had only a chicken big enough for two. Charming. Then it became Stinking Lane because of the awful offal the butchers left around. No wonder they changed it to something more fragrant in time for King Edward VII to open the General Post Office here.

THE KING'S ROAD Fashionable, sixties, egalitarian hang-out of hippies and nobs alike, this road was until 1830 an entirely private road for the king to reach the countryside without having to share his road with hoi polloi.

KNIGHTSBRIDGE Knights heading off for the Crusades or whatever had to ride to the Bishop of London's Palace at Fulham (hence today's Fulham Palace Road) and cross the Westbourne stream at this point, hence Knights' Bridge. Actually, given its extreme Harrods-and-Harvey-Nicks poshness nowadays, it is odd to recall what a scummy low-life dump Knightsbridge used to be. For one thing, it was all mud and it was difficult for people to wade through to the village of Kensington. There were rich pickings for highwaymen this close to London, so every night in the late 18th century a convoy system would operate, with pedestrians waiting at Hyde Park Corner to run the gauntlet to Kensington in large enough numbers to put the blackguards and cut-throats off.

LITTLE BRITAIN, EC1 Nothing to do with the TV series. Little Britain actually refers to the Bretons who lived here.

MAIDEN LANE, WC2 Again, this sounds nicer than it was. It's named after middens: rubbish and dung heaps.

MAGGIE BLAKE'S CAUSE By the 1980s and 1990s the great Victorian wharves and warehouses on the South Bank of the Thames just east of Tower Bridge had received their last cargoes and fallen into disuse. Smart property developers grabbed their chance and they are now trendy riverside apartments. Part of this process was the insertion of trendy restaurants – some of which have gained international reputations and have had Tony Blair and François Mitterrand as diners – and these meant walkways or promenades in front of the old wharves. Not surprisingly, some of the developers wanted these walkways to be for the rich and powerful using the cool restaurants and the fashionable flats; equally predictably, local people – led by Maggie Blake – wanted to share the access to the wonderful river views being created. In the end they won and without going all socialist on you, this is what town planning should do. Let the rich and powerful make money, but on terms that suit the people, not exclude them. Anyway enjoy the walk east from the south end of Tower Bridge and when you are in **Shad Thames** – itself a fascinatingly Dickensian path between former warehouses and crossed by frequent bridges above you – look out for the passage to the left marked **Maggie Blake's Cause**. Tip your hat to the lady as you go through to share some of the best riverside views in the world.

THE MALL AND PALL MALL Does any tourist think these parallel roads are shopping centres? Pall Mall is named after a French game once played there, *paille maille*. The Mall is the grand royal processional route from Admiralty Arch to Buckingham Palace, an area laid out in a brief period of imperial pomposity that thankfully didn't spread throughout the whole of London. Lesser countries with less well-run, smaller, less useful and more corrupt empires, flattened entire cities to lay out imperial boulevards giving views of self-important temples to national grandeur and commemorate battles of little consequence, and sometimes to create useful fields of fire to mow down potentially hostile populations. All very well with new cities, such as Washington and New Delhi, but here, not very British, in my view, and not very eccentric.

MAYFAIR The poshest corner of the Monopoly board. Odd to recall that the original May Fair, on open ground east of Park Lane (now Curzon Street), was so raucous and raffish that it was banned in the late 18th century. Maybe it was just the snobbery of the rich and powerful, for it was about this time that London's aristocratic centre of gravity shifted westwards.

NEWGATE STREET Well, it was new once, in the 2nd century. Compared to Aldgate (old gate), that is.

PARK ROAD You'd think someone would have tried to avoid repetition of London road names. This one takes the biscuit for confusion, there being 62 of them.

PETTY FRANCE, SW1 'Petit' being the French for 'little', this area was a hang-out for Huguenots driven from France by Louis XIV.

PICCADILLY A piccadil was a collar or ruff, and a tailor called Robert Baker, having made his fortune with them, bought this patch of then countryside as a site for his mansion, named Piccadilly Hall, in 1612.

PORTOBELLO ROAD, W10 A farm here was renamed Porto Bello in 1739 to celebrate the British capturing a town of this name in the Gulf of Mexico.

PUDDING LANE, EC3 Famously where the fire of London started; the spot is marked by a monument. Again, 'Pudding Lane' sounds a lot nicer than it was. 'Pudding' was the slang name for the butchers' offal that slopped down here.

SCOTLAND YARD Great Scotland Yard was where kings of Scotland would stay while visiting kings of England. When James VI of Scotland became James I of England in 1603, this became unnecessary, but its name lives on, spreading to New Scotland Yard when the police moved there from Great Scotland Yard.

SEETHING LANE, EC3 A more interesting name than its origin, this time. Seething comes from an Anglo-Saxon word for the chaff blown across here from a nearby cornmarket.

SEVEN SISTERS ROAD, TOTTENHAM Robert the Bruce, King of Scotland, had seven daughters and asked them to plant seven elm trees here. The trees, and then the road, and then the Victoria Line station, became known as Seven Sisters.

SHERBORNE LANE This street in the City is nothing to do with the fragrant West Country town, but is a cleaning up of its medieval name, Shitteborwe, ie: the public bog, khazi, longdrop, loo, outhouse, or whatever.

SHRAPNEL CLOSE Not the most friendly address, but then this road in Charlton is close to Woolwich's historic Arsenal and nearby roads are called Gun Park, Master Gunners Place, Ordnance Road and Artillery Place, so it fits in. British soldier Henry Shrapnel was the inventor of the artillery shell which blew up on impact into many lethal fragments, shredding anyone nearby.

SOHO Sohoposedly named after a hunting call, for these were hunting grounds before London spread west. But the only hunting round here for the past century or two has been for two-legged quarry. For more on Soho, see page 251.

SPITALFIELDS Unusually, less horrid than it sounds. The 'spital was a hospital for mental patients set up in 1197.

TURNAGAIN LANE, EC4 Nothing to do with Dick Whittington, but an alley which turns back on itself and crosses the Fleet River.

TURNHAM Despite featuring in a rude schoolboy's ditty about London which ends with the place names 'Turnham Green and Peckham', Turnham Green probably originates as the rather boring 'Turnum' or medieval court of the hundred, a unit of local government.

XX COURT Supposed to be in the City of London somewhere, but I've never seen it. Let me know if you spot it.

ZETLAND STREET, E14 Zetland is a variant spelling of Shetland, the Scottish and once Norwegian island. Or is that Zcottish? Hence the Marquess of Zetland.

CHIMPS AND BABIES ON BUSES

A chimp once escaped from the chimpanzees' tea party at London Zoo and clambered onto a red double-decker bus that had stopped nearby. Urban myth? No, I heard it from the driver's daughter and it was a No 53 in 1951. Sadly her father died in 2010, but he'd told her he ended up on someone's balcony, beating his chest like King Kong (the chimp, not the driver). Of course if it had been urban myth – or a PG Tips tea ad – he would have put on the conductor's hat and ticket machine and taken the fares for the rest of the journey to Hampstead.

And at least two babies have been born on London double-deckers. In October 2009 Emiloju Fatimah Lawal had a son on a No 394 in Hackney, and then in July 2011 Joanne Terry gave birth on a No 145 in Dagenham. The driver evacuated the bus while a female fellow passenger helped safely deliver little Joaquin. Just don't try it on the No 3 route. Having grown up there, I recall the buses always seem to be twins or triplets – and well overdue.

LONDON'S EARLIEST ACCIDENTS

HARROW ON THE HILL It didn't take long for the motor car to produce its first fatal road crash in 1899, and Harrow on the Hill, with its steep roads, was the place. The army's top brass had hired the eight-seater Daimler wagonette and thought a test run from Whitehall to Harrow for a spot of lunch would make an excellent trial for the horseless carriage, as it did, because it showed the car's weakness. Refreshments at the King's Head went well enough – too well, possibly – and they set off down Grove Hill so they could test the brakes. Reaching the dizzy speed of perhaps 20mph, the driver, Edward Sewell, braked at the corner. The wheels collapsed and the car turned upside down. Sewell and a brass hat were killed.

CRYSTAL PALACE Not that this was Britain's first horseless carriage fatality. Three years earlier a Mrs Bridget Driscoll was knocked down and killed in the grounds of Crystal Palace where the Anglo-French Motorcar Corporation had been invited to demonstrate its machine in August 1896. Crowds of curious sightseers flocked to see the machine. The driver insisted he had been keeping to the regulation 4mph and had rung his bell furiously but Mrs Driscoll had seemed bewildered and froze to the spot in his path. Some backed the driver, Arthur Edsel, and others said he'd been driving recklessly. There were notices all around to warn the public of the new hazard, but no one had yet decided whether motorcars should drive on the right or left, so he kept to the middle. The driver was cleared of any blame and Mrs Driscoll became the first of hundreds of thousands of road victims, human hedgehogs flattened by human road-hogs.

ALTERNATIVE TRANSPORTATION

Decades after the hippie counter-culture, Carnaby Street, oriental gurus and all that befuddled London with its joss-sticks and dresses for men, something of that era is returning to the capital's transport system.

London's freakiest accidents

Woolwich In 1929 an electricity generating station in Woolwich suffered a freak accident. The load on a Bellis & Morcom high-speed steam engine was disconnected so the thing oversped. The heavy flywheel flew apart due to enormous centrifugal forces and a large lump of it smashed through the roof and soared across the Thames in a graceful parabola, landing with a crash in North Woolwich Gardens. No one was hurt.

Silvertown A few years before, there was a massive explosion at a Silvertown chemical factory nearby which was processing TNT for use in World War I. It flattened the factory, killing workers and destroying nearby homes. Careful detective work proved it was not the explosives that had gone up, however, as their handling had been carefully controlled, but a little-understood by-product of the manufacturing process that was given off as vapour, then crystallised in the roof space as a highly explosive and unstable danger which the slightest knock could set off.

Macclesfield Bridge Macclesfield Bridge on the Regent's Canal near London Zoo is supported by massive cast-iron pillars higher and broader than a man. These have grooves in them, like all canal bridge pillars, where thousands of tow-ropes pulled by horses have rubbed against them. But why do the pillars have grooves on the landward side? An amazing gunpowder barge accident blew the place to pieces in 1874, and threw the pillars weighing many tons aside. To even up the wear, they put the massive pillars back the wrong way round. Hence its nickname, Blow-Up Bridge.

I don't mean the official London Transport system, although frankly you might at times imagine dope-heads run the Tube. 'Wow man, signals problem at Baker Street. Heavy stuff – better close the Circle, Metropolitan and Jubilee lines. I can't handle this. Freaky!'

1 The **first London bus service**, from Paddington Green to the Bank, was by horse-drawn coach and cost one shilling. Newspapers were included, for the journey could take three hours.

2 Savoy Court, the road that joins the Savoy Hotel to The Strand, is the only road in Britain where, because of its angle to The Strand, you are required to **drive on the right**.

3 Under many London **crossroads** lie the corpses of those who committed suicide. Suicide was a mortal sin, which meant that victims could not be buried in consecrated ground, and custom had it that they be buried in a pit under a crossroads, covered with quicklime to eat away their flesh, and even, sometimes, with a stake driven through their hearts à la Count Dracula. De Quincey wrote about one such burial, at the junction in Wapping of Cable Street and Cannon Street, in his gruesome essay *On Murder Considered as One of the Fine Arts*.

4 London's **first toll gate** was in Highgate; the last is in Dulwich (see page 294).

Did you know?

5 Juxon Street in Lambeth was the home of the **first motorised taxi**, which was registered in 1897. So that was the destination of two Japanese taxi drivers who made a 12-week, 30,000-mile pilgrimage to mark the centenary which made the *Guinness Book of Records*. Hope the meter wasn't running. They were greeted by 32 London black cabs sounding their horns. These taxi drivers saw London as the birthplace of the cab.

6 You can catch a bus from **World's End to World's End** in London. It is No 328 and passes the Camden pub of that name and ends at the Chelsea one, intriguingly shown as the destination on the front of the bus. I don't know if people going to the 'world's end' or 'the four corners of the world'; have ever noticed, but it doesn't really have any – it's round. But it does, eccentrically, on London buses.

Be that as it may, those who miss – or completely missed – the hippie culture can travel around London in laid-back style with **Karma Kars**, a strangely alternative cab company. Never mind the old joke about 'my dogma has been run over by my karma', it seems inconceivable that you could come to harm in the inner peace of a Karma Kab.

For one thing, the interior is opulent, covered in embroidered silks, etc, with satin cushions, joss-stick incense and twanging sitar music to lull you into deep relaxation.

For another, an effigy of the Hindu god Ganesh sits on the dashboard. He – the remover of all obstacles – is the same god painted on the front of thousands of lorries in India which hurtle down the pot-holed, buffalo-strewn roads with apparent impunity (even though many of their drivers, one study has shown, could be registered as blind in Western countries).

And third, you can't imagine the main driver and man behind the idea, Tobias Moss, ever reaching a speed that would create a crash. 'Motorways are too fast. I won't go to Gatwick or anywhere like that,' he says. Creating an impact with the populace, however, is what his old Ambassador cars – an Indian reincarnation of the 1950s British Morris Oxford – certainly do as you pass it serenely by. Not drug-induced serenely, of course. 'I've been there and wasted enough time on that,' says Tobias. So, I ask, the slogan on the Karma Kars calendar, 'All Trips Considered', doesn't mean what it would in the hippie heyday? He laughs.

Where did the idea come from? 'I was sitting in a bar in South India with Robin Brown, author of a book about travelling around India on an Enfield Bullet motorbike [another great British design still made in India]. He said: "As you love India so much, Tobias, you shouldn't be driving Mercs around London, you should use these Indian cars." It was one of those moments where everything clicked.'

What about karma in a religious sense? 'We are on this earth to redeem ourselves for a past life,' begins Tobias. Hang on, isn't that a bit weird, for a 56-year-old North London Jew? 'Well, I was raised as a Jew, but I first went to India when I was 24 and have lived in both Buddhist and Hindu temples. You could say I'm confused, but I'm not into dogma and rituals.'

Well, that's cleared up that then. But how laid back and hippie *is* Karma Kars, and what is it for? 'I don't like going fast, motorways and so on. I'm not interested in airports apart from Heathrow. We're not really a cab company, we're a form of entertainment, and experience. If someone rings up wanting to get somewhere in a hurry, I tell them to get a taxi.' So, at £40 an hour, and if he likes you – 'I refuse a lot of people, you don't have people you don't like in your home, do you, and this is my home, not just a job' – Karma Kars will take you in style to wherever you like, within the

M25. The Orient, for example – Leyton Orient, that is. Nirvana, if it's within the M25. But the destination is not the thing, says Tobias. 'The journey is more important than arriving,' says Tobias. 'Life's a journey.'

☎ 020 8964 0700

HAIL A RICKSHAW WALLAH

Another Indian method of transport doing well in London is rickshaws. Not the running-man sort that poor, sweating, short-lived rickshaw wallahs pull in steamy Calcutta, but modern pedal-powered ones, or pedicabs. Or – if you can bring yourself to say it – **Bugbugs**, the rather cutesy brand name under which they have been brought to London.

They are a fun way to get to a restaurant, show or just have a ride around the West End, and the place to pick one up is Old Compton Street in Soho. Being 21st-century pedicabs, Bugbugs are equipped with mobile phones, and are made in the US, or Manchester in the case of the four-wheeled model, which is truly bug-like.

'We get lots of bookings for hen nights and stag nights, but some people just want to cruise around without causing pollution,' says manager Liz Harrison. 'Everyone loves them and it adds a bit of fun to a night out.' But are they safe in modern traffic? 'We think so because in the 18 months since the first one went out we haven't had an accident, and the drivers are trained and insured. Maybe because they're bright yellow, motorists give them a wide berth.' That and disbelief that anyone would ride one of these things up Park Lane.

☎ 020 7353 4028

Sailing Private Ryan

Fancy a tour round London where the driver has to obey not only the rules of the road but the rules of navigation too? Where the bus has lifebelts? Amphibious trips using London streets and the River Thames are run by **London Duck Tours** using a World War II-style amphibious military vehicle, adapted for carrying passengers.

The organisers say the yellow-painted 'frogs' (old military types call them Ducks, or DUKWs) are tested and certificated by both the rules for buses and for the river, which must be a headache. The 80-minute tour leaves from behind County Hall and goes round the streets before driving, lemming-like, down a ramp into the river. The tour company had about a dozen of the vehicles last time I checked, but was intending building a more modern version. Perhaps they should go the other way, and go for authenticity. Give customers tin helmets to wear and dummy rifles to hold while coming ashore through fake explosions...

☎ 020 7928 3132 📠 www.londonducktours.co.uk

London's forgotten transport system

Amazingly, it is possible to get round London even slower than on the Circle Line: you do the **London Ring canal trip**, which takes at least two-and-a-half days. I've done it and it's very odd, because you cross over or under all the teeming arteries leaving central London – all the rail routes and roads – but you hardly meet a soul. It's a deserted system – we didn't meet one boat between Camden, North London, and Limehouse, where the Regent's Canal reaches the Thames in East London. You also see the great Thames bridges from the undersides and buildings such as Somerset House and the Houses of Parliament from the angle they were designed to be seen from. It's also pretty spooky going through long tunnels such as that under Islington, as there is no tow path.

As it's pretty difficult to arrange without your own boat nowadays, thanks to boatyard closures, I'll restrict myself to mentioning that the Hanwell flight of locks in West London is picturesque and well worth a visit on foot.

BENEATH THE ECCENTRIC CITY

DIFFICULT-TO-BELIEVE TUBE EXPERIENCES

It may be inconceivable, looking at today's Tube, to imagine on that system a dining car rolling past with waiters serving gents in tail coats sitting at tables covered in white damask, the glint of heavy silverware reflecting the glow from gilt table lamps. But this Pullman level of luxury could be regularly seen passing Baker Street in the early days of the Metropolitan Line as wealthy commuters from leafy outer suburbs such as Northwood and Rickmansworth – the gin and Jag belt today, or Metroland, as it became known in the 1930s – tucked into full English breakfasts on their way to the City. The staff knew their regular gents so well they'd have the table laid for certain customers and serve their eggs or kippers just after they sat down to peruse *The Times*. The cars were given names such as *Galatea* and were just as luxurious as those on the British version of the Orient Express.

The **Metropolitan Line** was unlike any other. Its cranky creator, **Sir Edward Watkin** (1819–1901), dreamed of great things – he started building a Channel Tunnel to take it to Paris, and his line reached out to remote Verney Junction near Buckingham in its attempts to reach the Midlands. He even became a director of railways in northern France in his bid to achieve what was eventually done in the 1990s.

Another Metropolitan branch snaked across country to end at Brill, a sleepy hamlet which became a sleepy terminus for the rambling country tramway – people would load pigs for market here, while Londoners would bring their horses for hunting by the train – perhaps the Met dreamed of reaching Oxford but never quite got there.

Of course the Met lines run mostly on the surface or just below it, so its carriages are as big as normal railway trains. How much more difficult would be catering on the tiny trains of the deep-level Tubes?

Yet this happened – and was done well – in the extreme circumstances of the World War II Blitz, when people sheltering from the massive German bombing campaign forced the authorities to open more and more of the Tube as shelters. Previously only disused bits of the system were being used as shelters. Here, people could sleep relatively safely; I say relatively, because if a bomb did penetrate the crowded tunnels, the results could be horrifying. One bomb that fell on Bank Tube in January 1941 killed 111 people.

An excellent book on this period called *The Shelter of the Tubes* by John Gregg (Capital Transport, 2001) quotes a Hungarian doctor who was called to the horrific scene at Bank station:

> *You English people cannot appreciate the discipline of your own people. I want to tell you I have not found one hysterical shouting patient. I think this very important, that you should not take such things as given – because it does not happen in other countries. If Hitler could have been there for five minutes with me he would have finished the war. He would have realised he has got to take every Englishman and twist him by the neck – otherwise he cannot win this war.*

In October of the previous year a bomb caused a tunnel collapse at Balham – you may have seen the almost comical picture of a London double-decker which drove into the crater, but you may not have realised that 68 people died down below.

But for the hundreds of thousands sleeping in the deep-level Tubes during the raids, the London Underground had suddenly to provide lighting, fresh air, water, toilets, and food. Six catering trains were hastily organised and ran all night, bringing hot drinks and food to all stations, with the American aid committees stepping in at Christmas and loading trains with a toy for every child huddled in the tunnels.

Something of the spirit of those days is conveyed by a contemporary poster headed: 'Tube Refreshments'. It read:

> *This Depot supplies Service Points, Stations and Feeds People. They rely on us for food and drink night and morning. We must not let them down.*

And they didn't, even when damaged tracks meant they had to carry the food through the blazing streets. It's all food for thought as we ride the same tracks today.

F YOU ARE AN alpha male between 18 and 38, have you ever wondered why that woman on the Tube is holding her phone at an odd angle? The answer could be that she is photographing you for TubeCrush.net, a website where the capital's lovelorn females put pictures of men they find cute or hunky with often comic commentaries – made-up lives of the 'victims'. Only men who are 'six-of-ten hot or above' make the grade, they tell me. It's highly sexist and ageist of course: thank God there isn't one of women on the Tube! And it can go wrong.

Journalist Ailsa Leslie, then 23, found that out on the Victoria Line. She recounted: 'I saw a very beautiful man on the platform at Brixton. So my friend and I did some tactical boarding, to be in the same carriage as him. But training your camera on someone at an angle, sort of mid-air, while they sit opposite, isn't very subtle. As I hit the capture button mid-tunnel, my flash went off in his face. We had to get off at the next station – the shame!' So disable the flash function next time, chappesses. And you thought Tube travel was boring!

Getting in a crush on the Tube

TEN FASCINATING BITS OF UNDERGROUND LONDON

1 MINISTRY OF THE INTERIORS

The wine cellar to Cardinal Wolsey's London palace, York Place, renamed **Whitehall Palace** after Henry VIII dumped Wolsey and seized the building for himself in 1530, survived the great fire of 1666 that destroyed the palace above it.

In the 1940s this area had to be cleared for the building of the new Ministry of Defence and road widening, but the royal wine cellars were saved by ingenious engineering. The entire structure was exposed to foundation level, a concrete collar inserted, the resulting 1,000-ton block being rolled sideways on rails and lowered into a pit. Now the 60 foot by 30 foot structure is in the middle of the much bigger basement of the new ministry, and not a stone was dislodged.

Unfortunately, security means we civilians can't pop in for a look at any old time. But the **London Open House weekend** (see page 16) sometimes offers a tour.

2 TARDIS WINE VAULTS

The Tardis, you will need to know if you are not a fan of TV's *Dr Who*, is a time machine that is as small as a phone box on the outside but as big as a house on the inside.

Berry Bros & Rudd, the long-established wine merchant in St James's that has supplied the crusty old gentlemen's clubs in that area for decade after decade, manages the same trick. On the outside, it is a small, worn-looking shop but inside, hundreds of feet of cellars stock perhaps a quarter of a million bottles of wine, including the rarest 19th-century ports and Cognacs.

The explanation is the network of cellars under adjoining properties that the burrowing Berry Bros borrowed over three centuries, accessed through a trapdoor in the shop. You can walk at street level around the corner into Pickering Place, or as far as Pall Mall, and still be above rows of dusty bottles – maturing nicely.

DISTRICT LINE TRAINS go faster between East Putney and Southfields because this stretch used to be owned by British Rail. So the electric supply is 100 volts too much – 750 volts DC, suitable for mainline trains. The proof: mainline trains are sent round this way every morning from Clapham Junction to get them back to the sheds at Wimbledon without cluttering up the main line, to the surprise of people waiting for Tube trains. And, rather charmingly, the frontage of Southfields and Wimbledon Park stations incorporates in the brickwork, if you look carefully, the monogram of the mainline company that built them, L&SWR.

Odd Tube fact 1

3 KING WILLIAM STREET TUBE

There are more disused Tube stations in London than many a city has on its entire network – an amazing 48 in all where only **ghost trains** call. Some of these were little more than above-ground halts that were later closed or moved, or stations on the annoyingly cluttered Piccadilly Line, which has, thankfully for passengers heading for Heathrow, lost Brompton Road and Down Street in Central London, plus six other suburban stations. Not all trains stopped there, but 'Passing Brompton Road' became such a familiar cry for passengers (like today's 'Mind the gap') that a play called *Passing Brompton Road!* became a surprise hit at the Criterion Theatre in 1928. Older people may remember British Museum station on the Central Line.

Other ghost stations are on sections of line completely abandoned, the first and oldest being at King William Street in the City. The **City and South London Railway**, the world's first electrically operated Tube, opened from Stockwell in South London in 1890. Because of Parliament's insistence that the newfangled Tube should not burrow beneath buildings, even in the tightly packed City, the King William Street terminus was badly laid out and its approach was so steep and twisting that trains sometimes had to have several runs at it; access for passengers was poor too.

Nevertheless, such was the success of this railway that an extension from Borough to Moorgate (now the City branch of the Northern Line) was opened in 1900, making 1,267 yards of former track to King William Street redundant.

In World War II, as Nazi bombs rained down on London, it was obvious that it would make an excellent **air-raid shelter** and large new entrances were provided for workers from adjoining office blocks to pour in. Bunks were erected in the tunnel, but signals and a signal box remained from the station's short life 40 years before. After the war, these were sealed up again. Twice in the more than a century since the station closed, the building above, Regis House, has been replaced, but the station slumbers on with wartime posters warning 'Careless talk costs lives' recalling its short revival as a bomb shelter.

4 ALDWYCH TUBE'S THEATRICAL HISTORY

That such abandonments of whole sections of expensively built Tube railway in good working order can still take place was shown in 1999 when the relatively new part of the Jubilee Line from Green Park to Charing Cross was closed, to enable the south and east extension of the line through Westminster to Greenwich and Stratford to open.

A little-used branch line, which nevertheless ended right in theatreland and which closed in 1994, had a very peculiar history. It was the **Aldwych branch**. If you get a chance for a station tour – arranged occasionally through the **London Transport Museum** (see page 72) – it's well worth it. Because the station was on a sleepy, one-station branch of the Piccadilly line at Holborn, it was relatively unaltered by station interior revamping diktats and retains much of its original **Art Nouveau-style tilework**.

It opened as The **Strand station** in 1907, and was to have been the terminus for the Great Northern and Strand Railway, linking the river to King's Cross and Finsbury Park. That line's merger with the Brompton and Piccadilly Circus Railway made a through route, giving rise to the even more cumbersomely named Great Northern, Piccadilly and Brompton Railway (now thankfully the Piccadilly Line), leaving this station on a dead-end branch. It was for a while intended to make a river crossing to Waterloo from here, but it never happened.

The station served a few hundred people each day, and was closed for seven years during World War II, becoming a **bomb shelter for Egyptian mummies**, etc, from the nearby British Museum. Early on, from 1917, one of the sets of tracks was ripped up, so the through theatre trains from the suburbs could come in, but not leave again (not rejoin the 'mainline' in one movement, that is) which was daft. So the service was reduced to a shuttle from Holborn, usually just two coaches, which was plenty.

The kind of **architectural detail** Tube history buffs love is typified by the lifts here, original wood-panelled Otis jobs with Art Nouveau ventilation screens designed by Leslie Green. (Ironically it was the need to spend £3 million replacing these lifts that led to the station's closure in 1994.)

5 LONDON'S EIFFEL TOWER WENT LOCO

Wembley's famous soccer stadium, old and new, has had a steam railway locomotive buried under its pitch for 80 years. It's to do with an all-but-forgotten scheme dreamt up by eccentric visionary railwayman **Sir Edward Watkin** (see start of this chapter) to transform London, and Wembley in particular.

In 1893 he started building a Wembley rival to the Eiffel Tower (known of course as the **Watkin Tower**), which was designed to be 170 feet taller. It reached the first stage by 1895 but because of financial problems the tower never went any higher, although thousands of people ascended the bit that was there.

> MARC GAWLEY IN 2011 gained the world record – there is one, honestly – for visiting every single London Underground station in the shortest time. He made it to all 270 in 16 hours, 29 minutes and 57 seconds. Cost, if he'd bought station-to-station single tickets, £1,076, or with a Travelcard or Oyster Card, £15. You have to get a train that stops at each station, so rattling through won't do. To prove this, he made video clips of the entire thing. That'll be a fascinating day and evening's TV! www.thetubechallenge.com/

Odd Tube fact 2

It was demolished for scrap in 1907, and the land levelled for redevelopment. During this process the locomotive used in the rebuilding works either fell off the tracks into a muddy morass, or being beyond repair was tipped in as part of the landfill, depending on whom you believe. But it's definitely been there all these years, through dozens of FA Cup Finals, buried deep under the hallowed turf.

6 THE UNDERGROUND LINE FOR GHOSTS

London has the world's most complex underground railway, but there's a whole mothballed separate system down there on which no one ever rides, or, in fact, ever rode. Until 2003, 50 trains ran 19 hours a day along 23 complicated miles of track, yet no member of the public ever travelled on them, heard them or saw them.

This was **Mail Rail**, the Post Office's own 2-foot gauge system of driverless trains, opened in 1927, which for more than 70 years carried four million letters a day that would otherwise have been in little red vans snarled up by London's traffic. One end is at Paddington, and the other at Whitechapel, and it is still there. It mostly runs 70 feet (21 metres) underground, although it ducks and soars from time to time to pass normal Tube lines and other underground features.

There are a couple of battery locomotives in siding tunnels for emergency and repair staff to use, so in truth a very few people *have* actually travelled through this unique system, and one lady who braved the darkness from one end to the other said how very bumpy it was. But it was very reliable. Yet in 2003 the system was closed down and consequently the little red van population of London was redoubled.

7 BOADICEA'S GRAVE AND HARRY POTTER

The grave of Boadicea (or Boudicca), the great warrior queen, is located under platform 9, or perhaps 10, at **King's Cross station**. There is a fab sculpture of her in full charge on her chariot at the north end of Westminster Bridge. Oddly, that queen of children's fiction, J K Rowling, used a **platform 9¾** for the departure point of the *Hogwarts Express* from the station here in her globally successful *Harry Potter* series. And so it was that platform 9 was temporarily redesignated 9¾ so that a steam engine representing the *Hogwarts Express* could draw in a promotional train carrying Ms Rowling, rattling old Boadicea's bones. Ah, these indomitable British women… Meanwhile, some wag has put up a platform 9¾ sign with a trolley half-way through the wall.

8 SECRET SPARE TUNNELS

One of the most apparently ludicrous of the myths and legends of secret bunkers and tunnels under London – and of course there are plenty of both – seemed to be the one about various Northern Line station tunnels having **duplicate tunnels** underneath them. I mentioned this once to an LT press officer when I was preparing a newspaper article and received a nervous laugh, as if they had been asked about UFOs at Uxbridge or trolls at Turnham Green.

A couple of days later, I received the oddest call back from the press officer. 'You know those duplicate tunnels under Northern Line stations such as Belsize Park? Well they *do* exist, it's just that I didn't know and didn't believe it either. Something to do with air-raid shelters.'

I'd like to find out more, so if you recall sheltering in one of them in World War II, for example, drop me a line. The idea might have been that the trains could continue to use the existing tunnels, while people sheltered beneath in spare tunnels. If these tunnels are indeed there, why not join them up with each other, creating a non-stop express route in from Golders Green to Camden Town to speed rush-hour commuters from the outer suburbs past slower stopping trains?

9 THE TUBE STATION THAT NEVER WAS

Insanely, there is one station on the Tube that never made it to the surface, although it *was* constructed underground. Still known unofficially to

Underground staff as the Bull & Bush after the pub (which inspired the song), **North End station** would have been near that pub, between Golders Green and Hampstead on the Northern Line. You can still see a widening of the tracks where the platforms should be.

This bizarre state of affairs is usually blamed on doughty philanthropist, Mrs Henrietta Barnett, an eccentric battleaxe who realised that the new Tube would logically mean housing sprawl extending over Hampstead Heath, one of London's premier open spaces. She was in the process in 1903 of securing 80 acres north of the station as an extension of the heath and wasn't going to let the Charing Cross, Euston and Hampstead Railway spoil things. Politicians at the London County Council were unimpressed by her munificence, thinking no doubt that well-to-do types at Hampstead already had enough green space and that ordinary people needed houses.

The doughty Mrs Barnett – who wasn't opposed to the Tube as much as to urban housing sprawl – then changed tack and proposed the construction of Hampstead Garden Suburb, an estate laid out on land nearer the Finchley Road and on the revolutionary 'garden city' principles then being tried out in Letchworth, Hertfordshire. This would be an improving and healthy environment for the 'industrial classes', she argued.

This did the trick and the Garden Suburb was laid out, although the chances today of any industrial type getting a home there among the millionaire celebs without winning the Lottery first are as remote as their chances of finding a way out of the Tube station that never was. The Tube bosses, having dug out the station tunnels and cross passages, gave up on the station because there wouldn't have been enough custom to pay for the expensive lifts. Its above-ground site became a house, No 1 Hampstead Way. Perversely, in recent years a small lift *has* been installed, for maintenance access.

10 GREATHEAD AND HIS SHIELD

Just near the Bank of England, in Cornhill, is a statue of the Victorian, **James Greathead** (1844–96), the man who made tunnelling under London's rivers and gravel beds possible. It's appropriate that he's standing on what seems to be a vent for an Underground line. His invention was a framework with a top shield that was pushed forwards from the tunnel sections behind with rams as the digging progressed, when new sections were bolted in.

You can see near here a 19th-century Greathead shield used in the digging of the Waterloo and City Line. Take the Waterloo and City

THE UNDERGROUND FEATURES IN many films: from *An American Werewolf In London*, to *28 Days Later*, to *Sliding Doors* (which like most of them make mistakes with the type of train or possible destination). For period pieces, the closed but preserved Aldwych station makes a useful background with its lovely Art Nouveau tiling. On TV, Dr Who and the Daleks have used the Tube, and a whole fake Underground station called Walford is maintained in up-to-date style for the TV soap *EastEnders*. Although it is on the District Line (on maps in the programme it is where Bromley-by-Bow should be) it is in fact at Elstree studios in Hertfordshire. Long tunnels, clearly!

Odd Tube fact 3

to Bank, then follow the signs to the Docklands Light Railway, and you'll see it in the former Waterloo and City overrun tunnel. There's the shield, painted red.

THE LOST RIVERS OF LONDON AND THEIR LEGENDS

There's something truly fascinating about London's **14 lost rivers**. Most of the seven to the north, and the seven less notable ones to the south, are entirely forgotten even by Londoners, until one floods, collapses or blows up (as the Fleet did once, because of sewer gas, demolishing a few houses).

Yet even today you can plot their sources, their routes and their outfalls by a number of methods. Controversially, a London hospital doctor once showed you could trace their courses by the incidence of disease on the ground above, particularly respiratory problems brought on by dampness and sewers. It is also claimed that you can plot them by the incidence of ghosts – there are supposedly more murders and suicides by water than in dry places.

More concretely, their old courses are given away by the road names above – **Brook Street**, **Bridge Road**, **Bourne Street** ('bourne' meaning stream, and revealing the former presence of the Celts here), etc – or by the river names being directly incorporated into the street map, as in: **Effra Road** in Brixton; **Fleet Street** in the City; and **Westbourne Grove** in Notting Hill.

Also, if you can get a vantage point high enough, you can see how the hills and valleys of London's landscape, difficult though they are to see today, still reflect the hidden watercourses below – Farringdon Road on the course of the Fleet being a clear example. And yet there are places where the authorities don't know where the lost rivers go, except that they reappear further along. Another, eighth, North London river seems to have formed itself under Soho after the area was built up, although experts debate whether the so-called Cranbourn exists or is just an abandoned sewer which has made a new route for itself. All of these rivers carry a lot of strange history with them, swirling in the darkness, much forgotten, much not.

THE LOST RIVERS OF NORTH LONDON

1 THE FLEET – FROZEN CORPSES AND EXPLODING FILTH

One of London's lost rivers that still influences today's landscape is the Fleet. It rises near the Jack Straw's Castle pub in **Hampstead**, goes into the Vale of Health and into the ponds, disappearing underground at **South End Green**. It is soon joined by a tributary from **Highgate ponds**, which starts at Kenwood House. In fact, if you climb Parliament Hill on Hampstead Heath for the excellent view, you will be standing between the two branches of the Fleet.

The Fleet flows under the **Regent's Canal** at Camden Town, past **King's Cross** and along the obvious river valley that is **Farringdon Road**, discharging into the Thames beneath Blackfriars Bridge. The Saxon *fleete* is said to mean 'float', a navigable river, so pedantically the upper reaches of the Fleet should take the river's other name, the Cent or Cant.

Holborn viaduct, which bridges this Fleet valley (over Farringdon Road), shows how steep it really is; the name 'Holborn' itself means 'stream in a hollow'. Eventually, the river, or the Fleet Ditch, as it became known, became so choked with sewage sludge that people who fell in would suffocate, not drown, as frozen corpses with their legs up in the air sometimes revealed the next day. In 1862 so much foul gas had collected in the covered-over river that it blew up, throwing brickwork all over the place and causing traffic havoc.

The Fleet was once a wide river, 60-foot wide at one point in Camden Town, discharging into a massive basin 500-foot wide below the bridge, which stood where **Ludgate Circus** now is. Ludgate was once at the western edge of the City, so as it was necessary for the shunned professions of journalism and law to be outside but near the City, their position across the Fleet was ideal. Some cynics will believe a sewer full of rats, vermin and parasites fed by fetid gutters of filth was the ideal spot for journalists and lawyers! As a Fleet Street journalist myself, I couldn't possibly comment.

2 THE TYBURN – WALKING TO DOOM

Tyburn is a fascinating area, forever associated with death, crime, retribution and martyrdom thanks to the Tyburn tree (see page 39), a **three-sided gallows** that stood at the junction of Tyburn Road (now Oxford Street) with Edgware Road, near where the Marble Arch now stands.

Before the gallows were taken down in 1783, an estimated 40,000 people met their ends here. Tens of thousands of people would turn out to see a murderer strung up. Tickets would be sold for stands – the nobility would book the best spots in overlooking houses. The deaths would have been slow because the modern noose and trapdoor were not used. Instead people waited for 'the turning off' where the prisoners would be turned off their ladders or carts if they refused to jump and then choke to death agonisingly slowly.

But after the 16th-century Protestant Reformation, and the associated paranoia about Popish plots, the Tyburn tree saw more than 100 Catholics go to their deaths here, sometimes on the flimsiest of pretexts.

The **Tyburn convent** was established early in the 20th century off Bayswater Road and although the main chapel is public, there is also a shrine to the Tyburn martyrs, who met their deaths here as a result of Protestant persecution, complete with a replica of the triangular gibbet.

Each year, on the last Sunday afternoon in April, the **Tyburn walk** led by a Catholic bishop retraces the three-mile last walk of the martyrs from Newgate Prison in the City to the Tyburn shrine for a special service.

Maps of early 18th-century London show **Tyburn Road** as being on the north edge of London, with open fields towards Marylebone to the north, and **Tyburn Lane** (now Park Lane) facing open country (then, as now, Hyde Park), so what is now Marble Arch was the very northwest corner of London.

The Tyburn rises on **Haverstock Hill**, which leads up to Hampstead from Chalk Farm. It flows down through **Swiss Cottage**, over the

Would you mind awfully? Your money or your wife!

THE TYBURN CARRIES with it the history of the dashing French highwayman, **Claude Duval**, the very handsome, young, courteous and honourable (apart from being a thief) terror of the rich in the 1660s. He stalked the lonely hills near Hampstead village, often right at the Tyburn's source and, having held up a coach at gunpoint and with many apologies relieved the gentry inside of their baubles, he would then sometimes ask the ladies to dance in the moonlight, with much bowing and courtesy. He was arrested while blind drunk in the **Marquess of Granby pub** in Chandos Street, Covent Garden (or rather in its predecessor, the Hole in the Wall).

He was hanged at Tyburn in 1670, and his lying in state, as it were, at a pub in St Giles drew huge crowds, many of them fascinated females. His subsequent funeral at St Paul's, Covent Garden (see page 141) was attended by several society beauties. What his connection with these ladies was is something we have to guess at, but a stone once said to be at St Paul's perhaps points us in the right direction:

Here lies DuVall:
Reader if male thou art
Look to thy purse;
If female to thy heart.

Regent's Canal in a large conduit pipe near the northwest corner of the Park. Authorities disagree whether it feeds the Regent's Park lake or not, but the Tyburn certainly continues under **Marylebone High Street** and beside the consequentially winding **Marylebone Lane** (the village of St Mary's by the Bourne), across **Oxford Street** (further east than the Tyburn tree), **Mayfair**, **Berkeley Square**, under **Buckingham Palace** and eventually falls into the Thames off Grosvenor Road, west of Vauxhall Bridge. So much of it leaks into the Tube near Victoria that a pumping station sucks out a million gallons of water a day.

On the other side of Vauxhall Bridge, on the south side, is the outfall of the **Effra**, one of the lost rivers of South London (see page 135).

Once, long before manmade embankments narrowed the Thames, a wide marsh surrounded the river and the Tyburn entered this marsh at the edge of the firm ground where Buckingham Palace now stands. There's an amusing record of a much later Victorian boating trip up the Tyburn: when the boatman said that they were now under Buckingham Palace, the passengers stood up and sang the national anthem. Lucky they didn't fall in the pooh.

3 WALBROOK – SKATING ON BONES

The Walbrook, the stream of the walls of London, was sacred to the Romans, which is why in 1954 a Temple of Mithras was discovered in Queen Victoria Street, which in Roman times was on the banks of the Walbrook. The nearby **Museum of London** (150 London Wall, EC2, ◉ Barbican) has Roman relics on show.

Because it goes through the oldest part of London, the City, the Walbrook was the first to be lost. It runs from **Old Street** south and a look at the ground levels around the Bank of England shows that it runs under the skirts of this, the 'Old Lady of Threadneedle Street'.

A similar dip in **Cannon Street** reveals its course, now much diminished, although in the 16th century still strong enough to carry away a youth who was trying to ford it and drown him when he hit a cartwheel at Dowgate, where the river then poured into the Thames.

In the 12th century the river was recorded as flooding **Moorfields**, then freezing, when City apprentices tied animal bones to their shoes and skated on it. Moorfields was so marshy that the road name Finsbury Pavement records a causeway that was the only firm footing here.

The river itself is remembered in a City street name, **Walbrook**, which still leads into Dowgate, and a lovely, light and airy Wren church, **St Stephen's, Walbrook**. It runs unseen a few feet beneath Cannon Street Tube. This church, by the way, contains the grave of the 18th-century playwright and architect **Sir John Vanbrugh** (1664–1726) who was good but not brilliant at either career. His tombstone, now gone, was inscribed by rival (and better) architect Nicholas Hawksmoor (1661–1736), who said pithily:

Lie heavy on him Earth! For he Laid many heavy loads on thee

4 Counter's Creek – up the creek in a forgotten canal

A once-clear stream edged with healthy watercress, and rising near **Kensal Green**, Counter's Creek flowed down the west edge of **Kensington**, forming its boundary, as it still does, unseen. The stream was once crossed (by what is now **Fulham Road**) by a sand ford, later bridged, hence Sandford Bridge, now **Stamford Bridge**. It became known as Chelsea Creek by the time it hit the Thames.

After hundreds of years of trickling along in rural peace, during the 19th century Counter's Creek underwent several huge revolutions. First, Lord Kensington, impressed by the **canal boom** of the preceding 30 years, canalised the creek from the Thames to the Grand Union Canal at Paddington not with a mere narrowboat canal but with one capable of taking 100-ton freighters.

There were locks to allow for the change in height, one being at **Cromwell Road** (where the hump-back bridge on the A4 is). It was opened with a stately barge procession, brass bands, a banquet and much pomp in 1828, just in time for the railway boom to make it completely redundant. Later, with the development of the huge **Brompton Cemetery** (see page 221) alongside the canal, there was a suggestion that funeral parties could arrive by boat, but with the speeding up of roads and railways, this notion was soon, er, dead in the water.

By 1839 it had switched to being a carrier of sewage, which it did for around 20 years until, condemned because of an outbreak of cholera in Fulham which might have been caused by the creek, it was ordered to be filled in. Soon afterwards, in 1863, railway tracks were laid over it. Now known as the **West London Line**, the route still forms the boundary between Kensington and Hammersmith.

5 The Westbourne

The Westbourne is another of London's lost rivers that rises on **Hampstead Heath**, in a small detached part of it near **Whitestone Pond**, flowing under **Branch Hill** as an infant rivulet.

Curvy **West End Lane** towards Kilburn was once a rural route beside this wandering stream that was also known as the Kilburn. Eventually it goes into the **Serpentine** and then underground again.

This pleasant lake, named because of its snake-like shape, was once a scene of Victorian horror when dozens of people skating on it were drowned when the ice gave way. After that it was supposedly filled in so you can stand up all the way across – but don't take my word for it.

Oddly, thousands of commuters unknowingly pass daily under the Westbourne at **Sloane Square** station, where it passes over the tracks and platforms in a massive pipe that thrums with a gentle vibration when the river is in full flood. Eventually it reaches the Thames by Chelsea Hospital.

6 **STAMFORD BROOK – RUNNING WITH BLOOD**
Probably the least substantial of North London's seven lost rivers, Stamford Brook not only has a road in Hammersmith named after it but a whole Tube station of its own on the District Line. It was also the site of a bloody battle in the Civil War.

7 **TYBURN BROOK – DIFFERENT FROM THE TYBURN**
This is the last lost river of North London, but is in fact a small tributary of the Westbourne. Further out you get proper above-ground rivers: the Lee (north and east) and the Brent (west).

THE SEVEN LOST RIVERS OF SOUTH LONDON

Briefly, from the east, they are the **Peck** (as in Peckham), the **Neckinger**, the **Effra**, the **Falconbrook**, the **Wandle** (OK, this one wasn't lost as in being buried, but was lost in pollution terms until recent years, and is home to an eccentric lady who paddles a coracle up and down it), the **Graveney River** and the **Beverley Brook**. That last one sounds like it was named last year after a reality TV star. In fact it was more than 1,000 years ago when beavers were around in Barnes and 'leigh' meant place, hence the name.

ECCENTRIC
CHURCHES

SECRET CHURCHES
AND HIDDEN PUNS

Many London churches are so hemmed in by later development that they are accessible only by narrow passages, and located in secret churchyards, or tiny courtyards, and are easily missed.

One such is **St Mary-at-Hill** off **Eastcheap** in the City, although the church is not as old as its churchyard, being a modern rebuild after a fire. Another, not visible from the road, **St Bartholomew the Great** (see page 237), is accessed through a curious medieval gate, surmounted by a Tudor beamed building, from **West Smithfield** (⊖ Farringdon), also in the City. St Bartholomew's was a priory before Henry VIII destroyed the monasteries in 1536, but its name lives on in the famous Bart's hospital nearby.

The interior of St Bartholomew's is pure Norman, with massive pillars, curved Romanesque arches and chevron (zig-zag) moulding. But one fascinating feature is the **rebus** (visual pun) on the oriel window projecting over the choir. It has carved on it a barrel (a tun in old usage, as in Three Tuns pubs' names) with a crossbow bolt shot through it – Bolt-tun; the name of the prior in charge at the time was Roger Bolton.

More of these jokes can be seen around London if you know where to look. Why is the famous **statue of Eros** at Piccadilly shooting his arrow downwards, as if to *bury* the *shaft* of his arrow in the roadway? Because it was a monument to the Earl of Shaftesbury. Not convinced? There is a tomb in Westminster Abbey, of the last Abbot of Westminster, showing a man slipping from a tree. Did he die like this? No – but his name was I slip – John Islip in fact.

Still not convinced? Try the puzzling **rebus milestones** between London and Eastbourne on the A22. These give mileages but no written destination at all except a bow and some bells. Bow bells... the bells of the church of St Mary-le-Bow, which was the traditional measuring centre of London. Freaky or what?

COCKNEYS WITH BELLS ON

It would be no exaggeration to say that **St Mary-le-Bow** (◉ Bank, walk down Poultry to Cheapside) has an impact on the aural, and oral, heritage of London, the nation and even Europe.

For one thing the Bow Bells define who is and who is not a cockney. Those born within hearing of the bells – the biggest being a two-ton job called the 'Great Bell of Bow' – are by definition cockneys. This means that a lot of luvvable cockneys born in the outer suburbs, or dare I say it, beyond the M25, either have superb long-range hearing or are fakes. (The posh ones, by the way, who pretend to be prolier than thou, are speaking 'Mockney'.)

It was these same Bow Bells that famously called back **Dick Whittington**, the real medieval lad who came to London to make his fortune, failed and set off home dejectedly. He reached Highgate Hill – the spot is today marked with a stone – when he heard the Bow Bells saying:

Dick Whittington, Dick Whittington, Thrice Lord Mayor of London.

Well, he did become Lord Mayor of London, three times, but I'll have a pint of whatever he was drinking because the rhythm of the bells could have just as well have been saying:

Dick Whittington, Dick Whittington, You useless dozy half-wit.

More seriously, recently, accurately and poignantly, the sound of Bow Bells was broadcast in World War II to the peoples of Europe enslaved by Hitler. How much this meant to them can be seen from the Norwegian chapel in the church, a beautiful place that recalls how the sound of far-off bells could keep alive the hope of liberation.

And, lastly, that name. Is it anything to do with the district of Bow in East London? No. It is an ancient church, destroyed at least twice, once by the Great Fire of 1666 and once by the Blitz of the 1940s. Yet part of the original medieval church remains undamaged – look in the crypt for the arches, or bows, that gave the church the nickname that has stuck for 1,000 years. Just as in Bow Street, a bow means simply a curve.

THRASHED CHOIRBOYS
AND PILLAGING DANES

Another church whose bells have gone into legend is **St Clement Danes**. St Clement Danes (➍ Temple, walk up Arundel Street) is a most unusual church for many reasons, not just its role in the ancient rhyme *Oranges and Lemons* (see page 99). Not only does it stand isolated, hemmed in by rushing traffic like a rock in a torrent, but it looks to the sky – it's the church of the Royal Air Force. The men and women of the RAF, and the thousands of them who perished during World War II, are remembered here.

St Clement Danes was gutted in that war and left a blackened shell. Of Sir Christopher Wren's fabulous legacy of 51 churches, built to replace 98 destroyed in that earlier disaster, the Great Fire of 1666, just 27 remain more or less intact. Much of the City of London was reduced to rubble, thanks to the 417 high-explosive bombs, thousands of incendiaries, 13 parachute mines and 2,498 oil bombs that were dropped on it.

A sea of yellow ragwort grew in the roofless interior of the bombed-out church, although Wren's lovely steeple survived. The bells, rehung after World War I and used in the carillon beloved of the rector in the 1920s, the Reverend William Pennington-Bickford, had been taken down and stored in a pile of sand at the bottom of the tower for safety during the Blitz as so many churches were being hit. Sadly, when the firemen fighting the fire that destroyed the roof of the nave played their hoses on the tower to save it, the cold water cracked the hot bells. Having been destroyed by aerial bombardment, it was apt that the church was restored as the RAF's church, when this parish was merged with that of the almost adjacent church of St Mary-le-Strand, now also stuck on a traffic island.

Yes, that's **Strand** as in shoreline – St Clement Danes was indeed once at the waterline. Its squat tower had cannon on it for firing at sea raiders or unruly mobs. It is claimed that, even further back, when the Danes were finally driven out of England by the Anglo-Saxons, those who had married Englishwomen were compelled to live between the isle of thorns (now Westminster) and Ludgate – in other words, here. It could be the origin of the word 'Danes' in its name.

St Clement Danes was a few hundred yards west of the line where the Great Fire stopped, so Wren helped rebuild it – for which he charged no fee – because it was decrepit, not because it was burned down.

One great loss from all these changes was the ending of St Clement Danes's version of the ceremony of beating the bounds, surely one of the very best versions of this ancient custom. **Beating the bounds**, which still goes on in many a British parish, involves the clergymen on Ascension Day taking young people such as choirboys to the boundary stones of the parish and beating them – usually the stones – to drum into the next generation exactly where the parish boundary lay. (No wonder children today are said to lack boundaries.)

St Clement Danes had one of the most colourful versions of these ceremonies. Its parish line on one side went right down the middle of the Thames, so the boys were bizarrely taken out to thrash the water with willow wands. On land the boys thrashed various markers on the ground – you can still see an ancient iron anchor mark with 'SCD' on it in Strand Lane, and there are more in nearby Devereux Court. I'm told one of the marks was in a building that had been raised higher than the old street level so a choirboy had to be lowered headfirst into a dark hole and bumped on the relevant stone. It's the sort of eccentric tradition that the British usually cherish, and it's a shame that small matters such as the Danes raping and pillaging, the Black Death, Great Fire, Plague and the church being destroyed by Nazi bombs and the parish disappearing, should have allowed a good pointless tradition to lapse here.

And why *do* the remaining parish marks have an anchor on them, including the one you can see on the side of the tower? Because it was a shoreline parish? Not a bit of it. It's because St Clement, the patron saint of blacksmiths, was martyred in AD100 by being thrown into the sea with an anchor tied to him.

FASCINATING FEATURES AND MARVELLOUS MARBLES

The most over-the-top Victorian church, festooned with layers and layers of decoration for its own sake, can be found at **All Saints** in Margaret Street, W1 (✷ Oxford Circus) where the walls positively drip with colour. The multi-coloured stone pulpit is just insane. It is as if you'd tried to paper your house using pages torn from hundreds of wallpaper sample books – there's every kind of marble imaginable here in architect William Butterfield's psychedelic 1850 creation.

This is High Church Anglo-Catholicism at its most decorative and about as far as you could possibly get from the plain, whitewashed simplicity of the Puritans' churches 200 years before.

Staggering out into the sunshine I had a sensation similar to that of coming out of richly decorated Chinese temples in Hong Kong or

ECCENTRIC CHURCHES

Singapore and straight into a modern city. But then I walked across the road and by chance into the Fo Guang Temple (see page 149).

WEIRD NAMES THAT TELL GREAT STORIES

You couldn't make up names like those of some London churches: St Vedast; St Mary le Stocks; St Peter Ad Vincula (St Peter in Chains, appropriately in the Tower of London); St Cyprian (Clarence Gate, Marylebone); and St Lawrence Jewry-next-Guildhall.

Near Blackfriars, a few paces up Victoria Street, is the quaintly named, Narnia-esque **St Andrew-by-the-Wardrobe**. There's been a church here since at least the 13th century but it's been through a few upheavals, to put it mildly. Formerly known, only slightly less eccentrically, as St Andrew juxta Barnard Castle after the old fortifications nearby, its name changed when the royal apparel stores were moved nearby. It was destroyed by the Great Fire of London in 1666 and rebuilt by Sir Christopher Wren. It was then gutted by bombs in 1941 and its interior rebuilt in the 1960s.

Other churches in the City with unusual names include **St James Garlickhythe**, **St Margaret Pattens** and **St Ethelreda's Chapel** (Roman Catholic). Going without is perhaps saintly, but we have a **St Botolph Without Aldersgate**, **St Botolph Without Aldgate**, and a **St Botolph Without Bishopsgate**. Their names simply refer, of course, to their position outside the old City gates. Ditto St Giles Cripplegate. Equally, the distinction between **St Bartholomew the Great** and **St Bartholomew the Less** refers, of course, not to two saints, but to the relative status of these two churches, both in the Smithfields area.

Oddly, few of the City churches are open on Sunday. The population has shifted and City workers, since the advent of the train, tram and bus, now live further afield and go to their own local Sunday churches, while the few working-class inhabitants of the City have moved to estates in the surrounding boroughs. The City is largely a ghost town at weekends.

So what do all these 47 churches (about half the 109 crammed in here in 1665) actually *do*? They are, in fact, at their busiest during the week when the City population is huge. Services, prayer meetings and concerts thrive. On a Sunday only around eight churches – including St Paul's Cathedral, of course – need to open.

The reason why there were originally so many churches in the City is not entirely clear, as they must have always exceeded in capacity the number

140

of worshippers. Perhaps rival monastic orders pushed their own churches, like competing half-empty supermarkets do today. And then there was the medieval Catholic cult of the saints. People believed – some still do – that contact with, worshipping and touching relics of saints would bring protection and admission to heaven in the afterlife. A great city's insurance policy, as it were, would include churches dedicated to all the powerful saints in the Christian calendar.

But why did having 109 churches fail to protect the City from the Great Plague of 1665 and the Great Fire of 1666? Well, it may not work like that, but remember that the Puritans and republicans who took control of the City in the Civil War about 20 years before, banned the cult of the worshipping of the remains of saints, chopping off the heads of their statues and obliterating their paintings and names from churches. Asking for trouble, you may think.

Among the City's lost churches, but remembered today as a street name, was **St Mary Axe**, which displayed the axe with which St Ursula and a bunch of virgins were said to have been martyred. (Another opportunity for Sir Richard Branson's Virgin brand? If Virgin cola and Virgin trains, why not Virgin virgins?) The road, where the Gherkin stands, is pronounced Simmery Axe.

ACTORS, A HIGHWAYMAN AND THE HANDSOMEST BARN

It was at **St Paul's, Covent Garden** (● Covent Garden), the actors' church, not the other grander one, that **Samuel Pepys** (1633–1703) made the first recorded mention of the great Mr Punch puppet in Britain, and thus it is here that the annual Mr Punch service takes place, which sees the extraordinary spectacle of numerous Mr Punches and their professors sitting in rows while another Mr Punch interrupts the sermon (see page 9).

Talking of professors, it is here that Shaw's Eliza Doolittle meets Professor Higgins in *Pygmalion*, the play which became the hit musical *My Fair Lady*.

The area in front of the church also figures in Hitchcock's horror film *Frenzy*, notable for the way its killer says '*lovvly*' as he strangles women, just as cockney flower and veg sellers used to say 'lovely caulis', or whatever, until the Covent Garden flower, fruit and vegetable market was moved to a different part of London.

Many a famous 'luvvie' is buried or commemorated here, including **Vivien Leigh** (1913–1967), **Noel Coward** (1899–1973), **Charlie Chaplin**

(1889–1977), **Terence Rattigan** (1911–1977) and, strangely, **Claude Duval**, the handsome highwayman (see page 132). Plus a certain William Henry Pratt, better known as **Boris Karloff** (1887–1967) of horror film fame.

Samuel Butler (1612–80), satirist, left instructions that he should be buried here in the churchyard with his feet touching one of the outside walls. We can be sure of this because his friend, John Aubrey, recorded it:

> *His feet touch the wall. His grave, 2 yards distant from the pillaster of the dore (by his desire) is 6 foot deep. About 25 of his old acquaintance at his Funerall. I myself being one of the eldest, helped carry the Pall.*

He should perhaps have been buried at Westminster Abbey with the other literati, but died in poverty so had to be buried locally. He eventually got a rather heartless monument in the Abbey:

> *The poets fate is here in emblem shown:*
> *He asked for bread and he received a stone.*

The history of this rectangular, spireless building that is St Paul's, Covent Garden, is that when Francis Russell, Earl of Bedford was developing land at Covent Garden (formerly the garden of a convent that the Reformation had put into the Russell family's hands) into an Italian-style square in the early 17th century, he asked the superb architect of the day, Inigo Jones, to build him a church. He warned that it had better be a barn-like structure to keep the costs down. Jones responded:

You shall have the handsomest barn in England.

The great Tuscan portico facing the piazza shows how the whole building is the wrong way round. Jones wanted this to be the entrance and the altar to be at the far, western, end. But the church authorities insisted that the altar should be, as usual, at the eastern end, that is nearest to Jerusalem, so the entrance is round the back. There is something Italian about the massive eaves, but when all's said and done, Russell was right. If you prefer your churches Gothic, with a steeple, you might well think this is just a blooming big box.

Perhaps the most unlikely memorial round here is at the **Jubilee Market Hall** and it is to donkeys. About 100,000 of these humble beasts toiled here for three centuries until about 1970, pulling carts laden with produce about and adding to the malodorous niff of the neighbourhood. Oddly, they sometimes appeared on stage in nearby theatres. Their carts were often gaily coloured and the beasts themselves festooned with their headpieces and horse-brasses gleaming brightly. On the other hand, a good many of them were tatty, drab and miserable, which donkeys do rather well.

CLASSIC DING-DONGS AND A GOTHIC HORROR SHOW

But, at least St Paul's, Covent Garden, is honestly classical (ie: not Gothic) and, therefore, doesn't have a spire, which is from the Gothic tradition. Greek and Roman buildings didn't have spires, did they? Did Sir Christopher Wren take the medieval spire of old St Paul's Cathedral and stick it on his new classical replacement after the Great Fire? No, he gave it a dome, a properly classical topping.

The severest possible contrast between these two styles can be seen in the difference between **Westminster Abbey's** supremely Gothic soaring heights and the **Methodists' Central Hall** opposite, which is in the classical style. To many eyes, it doesn't look like a church and could have been a railway station or a bank. In fact one end of it *was* my bank. I suppose there's Methodism in their madness.

But it was felt that many of the rest of London's hundreds of classical churches (such as **St George the Martyr**, Southwark, see page 262) should have spires despite their not fitting in with classical-style porticos and so on, and some very odd hybrids resulted, but then at least it was somewhere to stick the bells.

The oddest spire in London could be the stepped pyramid at **St George's, Bloomsbury** (⊖ Holborn), which is said to be based on a classical mausoleum described by Pliny, the Roman writer. It's almost as if architect **Nicholas Hawksmoor** (1661–1736) is desperately saying, 'It IS classical, honest!' while breathing a sigh of relief at having found something resembling the steeple most English people demand of a church.

Hawksmoor's efforts at **Christ Church**, Spitalfields, is a much more honest and successful attempt to stick a Gothic spire on a classical building. Actually, Wren wasn't immune from this problem. Those in his fabulous set of City churches that don't have square towers often feature spirish things that are a fancy attempt to marry the two, frankly almost incompatible, traditions. Talking of marriage, it is not surprising that Wren's tower of **St Bride's, Fleet Street** (⊖ Blackfriars, walk away from the river, up New Bridge Street, left on Fleet Street), looks to us today the very image of a wedding cake. All the tiered wedding cakes in the world were modelled on this inspired creation of Wren's, perhaps because of the aptness of the name of the saint to whom the church is dedicated.

The elaborate 230-foot spire of Wren's **St Mary-le-Bow** is beset with pillared drums as if to apologise for its existence. They almost hide the spire within, rather like those prim Victorians who allegedly put trousers on table legs because they thought bare legs rather rude.

Absolutely fabulous, though, is the much more honest effort at **All Souls, Langham Place** (⊖ Oxford Circus), in front of Broadcasting House, at the top of Regent Street. A clean cylinder of columns that could have come straight from ancient Greece is given a needle-sharp spire right through the middle, wallop. Architect **John Nash** (1752–1835) makes no apologies for putting the two together. Brilliant. The contrast with the plain rectangular body of the church behind is to my mind deliberate and geometric. But one website church fan imagined Nash saying after building the superb foyer: 'I've had enough of this now. Stick a big box on the back for the rest of the church. I'm off down the pub.' It makes you like Nash all the more.

THE PECULIAR ABBEY HABIT

Just building **Westminster Abbey** on the Isle of Thorns in the empty, soggy marshes alongside the Thames, west of London, was a deeply eccentric decision, but one which decided the shape of London for all time.

Edward the Confessor was, on 3 April 1043, the last king to be crowned at Winchester, capital of England under the Saxon kings. He had a vision in which St Peter told him to build the Abbey on this boggy island, and a palace as well.

The building of the Abbey took up the rest of Edward's life, and he was buried there in 1066, his death sparking off the Norman Conquest by William the Bastard (later the Conqueror). After this, all monarchs have been crowned in this massive Abbey, which is a 'Royal Peculiar', a church decreed by the royals to be neither a church nor a cathedral.

You can visit part of Edward the Confessor's church, although the main structure is of an obviously later date. In fact, the brand-new Abbey had two coronations in its first year – Harold's being followed by that of William the Conqueror on Christmas Day 1066. The Norman guards asked the surrounding population to acclaim him as king, whereupon some reluctant Saxons half-heartedly cheered. Other Norman troops took this strange noise to be rebellious resistance to the Coronation and promptly burned down the Saxons' homes all around. It was an ominous start to Norman rule. So much for Norman wisdom. For the story of Westminster Hall, see page 166.

ST MARTIN-IN-THE-FIELDS, A HIGHWAYMAN AND ROYAL WHORES

St Martin-in-the-Fields (⊖ Charing Cross) is a church known around the world by the broadcasts and recordings of great classical music made by the famous orchestra, the Academy of St Martin-in-the-Fields. More down-to-earth, literally, are the characters buried here, who include the highwayman **Jack Sheppard** (1702–24), King Charles II's mistress the actress **Nell Gwyn** (1650–87), and **William Hogarth** (1697–1764), who chronicled London's whores, drunks and pickpockets with such humour in his 18th-century cartoons.

Jack Sheppard was so bad that he was rather good. Born in 1702, and brought up in a City workhouse, he took to crime to satisfy the demands of his loose-living wench, Edgeworth Bess. He was soon robbing people almost daily around London and, in the extraordinary year of 1724, he was captured twice and escaped twice, captured a third time and tried at the Old Bailey but escaped again with Bess's help, caught again and chained to the floor in Newgate jail, escaped up the chimney, was caught again when blind drunk and quickly hanged at Tyburn before he could sober up enough to escape again. He was still only 22 when he died. He has stayed put since he came to St Martin-in-the-Fields.

Salisbury Hall between Hatfield and St Albans in Hertfordshire, was where 'buy my lovely oranges' **Nell Gwyn** and the king would spend naughty weekends together. She gave birth to their bastard son in this house, and as the baby took its first breath and yelled, Nell asked the king to give him a title. He refused, so Nell hung the mewling infant outside the bedroom window, threatening to dash his brains out in the courtyard below if he wasn't worthy of a title.

The panic-stricken king looked past her at the mighty St Albans Abbey on the sky-line, and blurted out 'Someone catch the Duke of St Albans!' Feisty girl… but a risky way to start a dukedom. Nell, who is buried here at St Martin-in-the-Fields, not far from where she was born in an alley off Drury Lane, is remembered by the Nell of Old Drury pub near the great Drury Lane theatre with which she and the king were associated.

She had started as an orange-seller but soon became a great hit on the stage, as Pepys records several times. 'Pretty, witty Nell,' he enthused in his diary. She was also popular with Londoners, partly because she was 'one of us' and partly because she was not French and not Catholic, unlike Charles's other main mistress, Louise de Keroualle, a voluptuous woman who was placed in Charles's gaze by the French government.

This led to an amusing Nellism at Oxford in 1681 when, during the anti-Catholic unrest known as the Popish Terror, she sought to reassure the mob who stopped her coach of her good character: 'Pray, good people, be civil. I am the *Protestant* whore.' A huge cheer went up.

On his deathbed in 1685 Charles begged his brother, about to succeed him as James II, 'Let not poor Nell starve'; she was given enough of an estate to keep her in style, with plenty of oranges, for life, which was not long. She died in 1687 aged just 37, so Nell never had the chance to grow old disgracefully, as she surely would have. One legacy of hers was that the only house on the south side of Pall Mall that was not a Crown Estate freehold was hers, because she cannily levered the title to the land out of the besotted Charles.

LOST AND WANDERING TOWERS, A CRYPT ASCENDING TO HEAVEN

Not a few London church towers are lost like orphans or even wander around by themselves, it seems. Besides the isolated towers like that at **St Anne's**, Soho (see page 260), and towers that have become homes (at Wood Street, City of London and Gipsy Hill), some of them have actually moved.

The tower of **All Hallows** in Chertsey Road, Richmond (Richmond from Waterloo: right out of station, follow Whitton Road to the end, turn right 🚗 the A316, the main road linking the M3 to London), must strike many motorists heading for the M3 as looking surprisingly like a classic Wren City of London job. It is. It was moved from All Hallows, Lombard Street, in 1938, when that church was demolished. Although the main body of the later church is not even slightly Wrenish, it contains many of the original fittings (panelling, ceilings, that kind of stuff) from its predecessor.

Another church tower that has moved, unbelievably, from its original location, is the 14th-century tower and 12th-century crypt of **St James-in-the-wall**, now in Mark Lane, EC3 (● Tower Hill), moved in 1873 because they were in the way. Even the brash Victorians sometimes had a conscience about knocking down such treasures.

But how do you move a medieval church? Get lots of bubble wrap and string? I once had a slightly surreal demonstration. I was in the men's lavatories high up in the old *Daily Mail* building off Fleet Street, looking out of the window over the ground where the *Sun* building had just been knocked down, and discussing the world with the chap at the next urinal, ace headline writer, Willy 'Three Puddings' Bloch. It had been a beery lunch – such things were possible before computers – but even so we were aghast to see a medieval crypt, complete with arches and pillars, rising past our window. An angel or two would have helped us cope with the concept.

It was the old 13th-century crypt of the **Whitefriars Monastery**, which famously was located in the bowels of the *Sun* and *News of the World* building's printing works. It had always been a trick up the sleeve of a desperate rival news editor that he could covertly send a religious-looking reporter to demand to see the crypt (and, hopefully, the rival paper's next day's front page) at any time. Even more bizarrely, real Carmelite monks would occasionally turn up to look at the crypt, maybe inadvertently catching sight of pictures of naked *Sun* page three girls in the process.

The crypt had been forgotten about for a few hundred years after the destruction of the monasteries that covered the area before Henry VIII's time. Then in 1867 someone rediscovered the lost crypt, a damp, decaying haunt of rats and skulls. It was used as a coal cellar for 30 years but in the 20th century was conserved, though the presses thundering overhead probably didn't do it much good. Eventually, as the Murdoch newspapers fled to Fort Wapping, redevelopment of the site loomed. The crypt was protected, yet the foundations needed to be rebuilt. How to solve the two problems – lift it out and rebuild, then put it back again.

So the 13th-century crypt was lifted out in a steel cradle high into the heavens above the office blocks and later returned to its original position. But the heart and soul of old Fleet Street, sadly, has never been craned back into position since the great papers left.

LONDON'S MOST EXOTIC PLACES OF WORSHIP

Amid London's truly wondrous heritage of mainstream Christian churches, there are here and there some astounding, beautiful, surprising or just curious edifices constructed by other religions. Here's just a selection:

1 **THE SWAMINARAYAN HINDU TEMPLE, NEASDEN**
Built on a cathedral scale, this stone and marble edifice stands out like an exotic oriental gem in this, the dreariest of North London suburbs, with its vast, shining pinnacles rising incongruously near the North Circular road. Built by Indians using traditional methods (and traditional rates of pay, one of them pointed out), this is a rather special place. The most unlikely way to construct a building like this would be to quarry a load of Bulgarian marble, ship it to India where it would be carved, then ship it back across the world to Britain where it would be painstakingly reassembled like a monstrously complicated Ikea kit temple (we are yards from the Ikea furniture store here, after all). So that was exactly how they made it. Has to be seen to be believed. Believers in the Swaminarayan sect, a division of Hinduism, say the building will last more than 1,000 years because it is all stone, with no steel or wood.

> Between North Circular A406 and Brentfield Road. Car parking available. Neasden (Jubilee Line) Stonebridge Park (from Euston).

2 **THE BUDDHAPADIPA TEMPLE, CALONNE ROAD, WIMBLEDON**
Only a good lob away from the tennis courts, this beautiful, glittering building sits serenely in a bubble of unlikely oriental tranquillity. The exquisite murals inside are fascinating in their blend of Buddhist teaching and the Western environment.

> Signed off Wimbledon Parkside, which is south off A3 at Tibbetts Corner, Putney Heath. /Wimbledon station (District Line or mainline from Waterloo) then bus 93 through Wimbledon village.

3 **RUSSIAN ORTHODOX CATHEDRAL, CHISWICK**
An incongruous and definitely unorthodox sight for visitors to London arriving up the M4, this onion-domed cathedral is tucked in beside the M4 flyover at Chiswick, after the part with flashy buildings (coming in to London). Finished only in 2000, with its gold and blue decoration, it adds a completely new dimension to this patch of West London.

 Gunnersbury Park (District Line)

4 PEACE PAGODA, BATTERSEA PARK

This startling riverside apparition makes the point that those on the receiving end of the ultimate warfare weapon, at Hiroshima, wish to promote global peace. Elegant and peaceful.

 Between Chelsea and Albert bridges on south bank of Thames.
 Battersea Park station (from London Victoria one stop) then cross park to river.

5 REGENT'S PARK MOSQUE

The glittering gold dome of this cathedral of Islam, or the London Central Mosque, to give it its proper name, with its 140-foot minaret, is one of London's most stunning landmarks. People are often willing to show you around this 1969 building, which arose from a suggestion that Islamic troops who were in London during World War II should have somewhere to worship. It is austere but beautiful.

 Baker Street (Circle, District, Metropolitan, Hammersmith and City, Bakerloo lines)

6 ST ARKIS ARMENIAN CHURCH, KENSINGTON

This is a little gem of a building, so prettily perfect it is almost like a divine jewellery box. Built in 1922, with Armenian script above one entrance, and English above another, it is tucked away just off Kensington High Street, down Wright's Lane, and right into Iverna Court.

 High Street Kensington (Circle and District lines). Also featured in Kensington walk, page 341.

7 FO GUANG TEMPLE, SOHO

Situated on Margaret Street near All Saints church (see page 139), this is a most surprising and rather wonderful Chinese Buddhist centre. It is an extraordinary experience, having removed your shoes and sought permission, to enter the Main Shrine, dedicated to the Sakyamuni Buddha, with its three large statues, in total tranquillity – yet we are only 100 yards from Oxford Street's incessant commercial bustle.

The walls and ceilings are covered with the Buddhas of Five Directions and Eight Tathagatas respectively, with the lighting designed to highlight this. You can see from name plaques attached to these hundreds of Buddhas that individuals have sponsored them. It is a friendly yet intense atmosphere.

🚇 Oxford Street (Central, Bakerloo, Victoria lines). Also in Soho walk, page 251.

8 BEVIS MARKS SYNAGOGUE, CITY OF LONDON

Britain's oldest synagogue, for although Jews and this country go back to Roman times, their expulsion in the late Middle Ages meant that their history began again only when they were allowed back during Cromwell's 17th-century interregnum. These were Jews mainly from the Spanish and Portuguese traditions. This building was put up in 1701. The Quaker architect waived his fee rather than profit from the building of God's house, and Queen Anne gave a massive oak beam from one of her warships. It is not, today, the busiest synagogue in London but it is the most interesting. The 12 columns of the gallery are said to represent the 12 tribes of Israel. Bevis Marks is also the name of the road.

🚇 Liverpool Street or Aldgate (Circle, Metropolitan lines)

9 SOUTHALL, WEST LONDON

Not so much one place of worship but a **collection of temples** where one can be the only chap not wearing a turban in a busy street (if one is a chap and one doesn't wear turbans, that is). If you visit the area, the authentic Indian food at authentic Indian prices, the shops glittering with gaudy Indian brassware, spices, carvings, over-the-top Ali Baba shoes and endless Indian clothes, will make this a cultural experience.

🚗 Just south of A4020 (from Shepherd's Bush to Uxbridge). From M4 J3 take A312 north, then A4020 east (right) 🚂 Southall from Paddington

Note: If you are reading this book you have clearly got considerably more than the usual two brain cells to rub together (flattery gets you everywhere), but even so I feel compelled to remind you that these sites are not tourist destinations, or theme park ornaments, but places of worship. Make sure you have permission to enter any grounds or buildings; observe rules about removing shoes, taking photographs, etc. I've seen enough Westerners – and other tourists in our own churches too – wandering in chewing gum, smoking, showing off bare flesh or with screaming brats who fiddle with sacred ornaments, or photographing people praying, to be thoroughly ashamed of them. Don't be like them…

LONDON: HOME OF ECCENTRICS

PLAQUE TO THE FUTURE

Immortality here on Earth is available to Londoners through the medium of official oval blue plaques, those 'Joe Bloggs lived here' things that are stuck on the exteriors of many a house. Candidates are selected by a special committee and English Heritage. They must have been dead for at least 20 years, which at least frees us from the tyranny of the self-appointed great and good of the moment.

The official plaques are made by, and at, Armitage in Staffordshire (spiritual home of the modern lavatory) and unveiled in a small ceremony at the rate of about 12 a year. So in about 300,000 years, every house in London will have one (if some don't have two or three, which they already do).

In fact they're not all 'official oval'. Older ones are rectangular, even brown (as in Dr Johnson's at 17 Gough Square off Fleet Street and Thackeray's in Young Street, Kensington; Thackeray raises the question of the need for more than one plaque for the same person; having another one on a house in Palace Green just across Kensington High Street).

Unofficial ones are in Perspex, round, or whatever. There's a strange one to **George Orwell** in Pond Street, Hampstead, which has the writer of *Animal Farm*'s face coming out of the wall. The Dead Comics Society had one up for **Frankie Howerd** in Edwardes Square, Kensington, almost before the old chap ('titter ye not') was cold; they put another one up not far away in Eardley Crescent, Earl's Court, to commemorate *Carry On* star **Hattie Jacques** who lived there.

The interesting thing about plaques is: how much will the people they recall matter to future generations? I mean, and I parade my ignorance here, who was **Ugo Foscolo**, commemorated on the other side of the above-mentioned Edwardes Square? An Italian nationalist, apparently. Yes, perhaps it's good to remind us of people who really mattered once to Londoners. But if these nationalists need to be remembered, why don't they leave us a decent biscuit, like Garibaldi did? (Aptly, he fought against the Bourbons.)

In fact, Foscolo, who turns out to be a once-famous Italian patriot and poet, was buried at Chiswick churchyard where there is a rather flash cenotaph with a pompous inscription about how his remains were transported later to Florence: 'From the sacred guardianship of Chiswick … honoured custody for ever held in grateful remembrance by the Italian nation.' Flowery tosh. Actually he was an ineffective bore when in Kensington and the nobs at Holland House soon grew tired of extending him endless hospitality, so irritable and irresponsible did he become.

Does it increase the value of a property to have a blue plaque on it? This may not have been the motive, but a property developer stuck a blue plaque looking remarkably like the real thing on 64/65 Glebe Place, Chelsea, recently. Only by looking closely do you see the usual endorsement 'English Heritage' is missing – as well as, sadly, the final 'S' of the name **Sir Alfred Munnings**, an artist already commemorated by another unofficial plaque at Beldon House, Chelsea, as English Heritage rather sniffily pointed out.

There's the very peculiar story of a house on Bankside, just south of the river, which makes two impressive claims on a plaque that are both total fantasy, yet should have two real ones, which are missing, on page 272.

Nevertheless, genuine plaques are thicker on the ground north of the Thames than south. This is doubtless because most of South London has a history of only a century or two. But a Radio 4 wag, Arthur Smith, has another theory, less flattering to South Londoners:

Up in North London we have blue plaques to mark where famous people lived. Down in South London they instead have those yellow boards – you know, murder, stabbing, rape, appeal for witnesses, that kind of thing.

Charming.

Stamps of heroism collected in Postman's Park

Other people have suggested different ways of commemorating heroes. For example, at the **Postman's Park** off St Martin's le Grand (🔵 St Paul's, Central Line), in the City, there is a rather moving and extraordinary wall of plaques to 53 people who gave their lives trying to save others. The idea of a Victorian artist G F Watts and opened in the 1880s, it caught on only for a decade or so.

Daniel Pemberton, aged 61, foreman LSWR, surprised by a train while gauging the line, hurled his mate out of the track, saving his life at the cost of his own, 17 January 1903.

Thomas Simpson died of exhaustion after saving many lives from breaking ice on Highgate Ponds, 25 January 1885.

Frederick Alfred Croft, Inspector aged 31, saved a lunatic woman from suicide at Woolwich Arsenal Station but was himself run over by the train, 11 January 1878.

The memorial, which features some rather splendid tilework, is a typically British Victorian concept: the mawkish, melodramatic celebration of dead heroes – people who jump into lakes, save loads of people and then die themselves, trying to save just one more. The only sure way to British hearts was to die heroically failing to do something, such as Scott of the Antarctic. Shackleton, who achieved far more without losing one of his men, was clearly not dead enough to achieve immortality when he returned and was almost ignored by the population when he returned from his own Antarctic expeditions.

We Brits love our failures. (At the peril of sounding smug, when we were marking the 60th anniversary of the defeat of the British Army at Dunkirk during World War II, another heroic failure, I wagered we were making far more fuss about that than we would for the 60th anniversary of its victory at El Alamein the following year, where the British and Empire troops turned the whole course of the war, without the Americans having arrived yet. It was the end of the defeats and the beginning of the victories. And come that anniversary, I was right. Hardly a word was said about it.)

CHEYNE WALK – LONDON'S MOST BRILLIANT ROAD

Some locations in London positively thrum with genius past and present. **Cheyne Walk** (pronounced 'chainey'), in Chelsea, for example, is stuffed with an astonishing heritage of great people. What a creative pantheon, what a cornucopia of talent is revealed by a blue plaque attack of measles-like proportions! What stories they tell, of brilliant engineers, wonderful artists, mad Irish barbers, eccentric millionaires, recluses, pop stars, saints, sinners, and a possible living link to Jesus Christ.

It is said to be the street with the most blue plaques in Britain, and achieves that on only one side too – the other side suffers from a slight damp problem, as estate agents might say. That side is, of course, the River Thames, either side of Battersea Bridge's north end.

In numerical order of their addresses, the blue plaques are:

4 George Eliot (1819–80), novelist, wrote *Middlemarch*, *Mill on the Floss*, etc; the pen name George, although odd for a woman, was helpful at a time when some considered no lady should write novels. Jane Austen, for example, at the beginning of the same century, published her books initially without her name. Painter Daniel Maclise had this house before her.

16 Dante Gabriel Rossetti (1828–82), poet and painter. This house is also known as the Queen's House and is judged the finest in the row by some. Rossetti kept an odd menagerie of animals in the garden – strange ones for Chelsea – such as armadillos, a racoon and a kangaroo; a fountain nearby is dedicated to him.

16 Algernon Charles Swinburne (1837–1909), poet. Swinburne is greatly underrated, an Oxford poet tells me, but the latter poet's ex-wife's family included one who stood next to Swinburne in the urinals at the Athenaeum club and found he had virtually no penis. Hmmm, curious… ,

93 Mrs Elizabeth Cleghorn Gaskell (1810–65), a novelist who proved it was all right for women to write novels under their own names after all, as long as they had silly names like Cleghorn. Her first book, *Mary Barton*, drew the admiration of a certain Charles Dickens, who then employed her to write for his magazines.

96 James Abbott McNeill Whistler (1834–1903), painter and etcher, was buried at Chiswick church. American-born Whistler painted Battersea Bridge (well, pictures of it; workmen painted the actual bridge), which is within sight – not the present rather ugly 1887 structure but the previous wooden bridge of 1772.

There was a very funny court case in 1878 in which Whistler claimed he had been libelled by writer **John Ruskin** over a picture of Battersea Bridge at night. Ruskin had said it wasn't a correct representation at all. The case, which included long evidence about a waterman who rowed Whistler about in the moonlight, featured some classic exchanges between the artist and the judge, Baron Huddleston:

Judge (shown the picture): *'Which part of the picture is the bridge?'*
(Much laughter in court.)
His Lordship earnestly rebuked those who laughed…
Judge: *'The prevailing colour is blue?'*
Whistler: *'Perhaps.'*
Judge: *'And those figures on top of the bridge are intended for people?'*
Whistler: *'They are just what you like.'*
Judge: *'Is that a barge beneath?'*
Whistler: *'Yes, I am much encouraged at your perceiving that.'*

Whistler was always good for a pithy quotation. Hearing a witty remark, Oscar Wilde sighed: 'How I wish I had said that.' Whistler retorted: 'You will, Oscar, you will.' Another time, when Ruskin was appalled at Whistler asking a huge price for a work, Ruskin said: 'For two days' labour, you ask two hundred guineas?' Whistler replied: 'No, I ask it for the knowledge of a lifetime.' One more Whistler quote, about painting: 'Nature is usually wrong.'

98 SIR MARC ISAMBARD BRUNEL AND ISAMBARD KINGDOM BRUNEL (1769–1849 and 1806–59 respectively), engineers. This brilliant engineer father-and-son duo that contributed much to London, including its first under-river tunnel at Rotherhithe (the first underwater tunnel through soft soil in the world) and the Great Western Railway and Paddington station (son).

Although the Brunels were of French Huguenot extraction, the name 'Isambard' comes from Germany and appropriately means 'man of iron'. Isambard Kingdom Brunel was both brilliant, taking, for example, the chains from the Old Hungerford Bridge across the Thames near Charing Cross and creating the spectacular Clifton Suspension Bridge in Bristol out of them, but also a little crackpot.

His atmospheric railway in Devon (where trains were sucked along by a vacuum) didn't work too well, and his method of laying railway track (with longways sleepers attached to piles) was disastrous and had to be abandoned, as – eventually – was the broad-gauge rail track he insisted on.

On the other hand, his billiard-table-flat GWR is still the best laid out railway in Britain. There was a certain haughtiness about the GWR. For example, their horse drinking troughs were marked with the warning that only

155

GWR horses might drink there. Another favourite episode concerns a GWR train waiting at Reading for a branch train from Newbury to pull in at a nearby platform. A GWR director leans out of the carriage in his top hat and suggests to the guard that he blows his whistle to hurry up the passengers crossing to the London train. The guard replies: 'Sir, one does

ODDLY ENOUGH, THAT TRULY great painter of the Thames, J M W Turner (1775–1851), has no official plaque (though his influence is such that the the river hereabouts is called **Turner's Reach**). He lived here anonymously at No 119 Cheyne Walk, on and off from 1846 to his death in 1851 (he has an unofficial plaque).

Joseph Mallord William Turner (who, like Shakespeare, cleverly contrived to be born on 23 April, St George's Day, England's national saint's day) was indeed a little eccentric.

He was a great Impressionist about 50 years before the French think they invented it, and was very reluctant to sell his paintings, which he regarded as his children. Indeed, he would go into a sulk if one did sell.

His subjects include the Great Western Railway – the creation of another Cheyne Walk resident, Isambard Kingdom Brunel (see above) – in his superb painting *Rain, Steam and Speed*. Like Brunel, he sometimes got things wrong and in that painting, to be seen at the National Gallery at Trafalgar Square, Turner seems to have thought the loco's firebox was open at the front. Even Brunel would never have allowed that. Perhaps it was a flag or a coat-of-arms, but I'm sure it was supposed to be the fire. Have a look. Only a pedant would feel this negates the atmosphere of the picture. By the way, this bridge at Maidenhead, built by Brunel, has daringly wide and low brick arches, and the authorities were so worried that they insisted wooden arches be put beneath them for safety. This Brunel did, but he made sure the wooden supports didn't actually touch his arches by leaving an unseen gap, so eventually they rotted and fell down, unlike his daring

Oil, iron and brick: JMW and IKB

not blow whistles at people from Newbury.'

Isambard Kingdom Brunel was picked in 2000 as **Man of the Millennium** (admittedly by readers of *Railway Magazine*) and I borrowed his name for my son (not all of it, just the first bit). See also box, below, and for the Brunels' apt gravesite, see page 61.

arches, which are in their second century still holding up thundering express trains heading for Bristol and South Wales.

In fact, Turner often really studied his subjects with devotion. He once paid a fisherman a great deal of money to take him to sea in a storm, with him, the artist, lashed to the mast. It nearly cost him his life, but his raging seascapes are magnificent. At other times Turner was known to inhabit a room in St Mary's church, Battersea, and spend hours gazing at the Thames. Perhaps his most famous work is set on the surface of the Thames, *The Fighting Temeraire*, the sad, stately hulk of a sailing era man-of-war (once captured from the French, hence her name, or maybe one named after such a prize) being towed to the breaker's yard by a symbol of the exciting, brash new era, a smoke belching steam tug.

Late in his life the reclusive Turner – who had a very secretive private life, and no real friends except his father and who never married – fell ill and disappeared from his London home. After several months of searching, his housekeeper found him here in Chelsea, where he died the next day in December 1851.

Thanks to his possessive feelings towards his works, he was able to leave the nation 300 paintings, plus thousands of watercolours and drawings, many both brilliant and popular. Those two adjectives would seem to be a disqualification for the winners of today's **Turner Prize**, an annual prize worth £20,000 for the assiduously avant-garde who relentlessly try to shock a jaded public with such creations as the tediously risquée Tracey Emin's unmade bed (including, apparently, her soiled underwear – how flipping fascinating). The media, always short of a story at that time of year (therefore known as the silly season), always go along with the hype and pretend to be shocked, thus creating another instant celeb out of this year's *enfant terrible*. Not one of them will be remembered long enough to get a blue plaque, of course.

104 HILAIRE BELLOC (1870–1953), poet, essayist and historian. He wrote *Cautionary Tales* and a lot about Sussex, which he loved sincerely despite being half-French. He once featured in a radio show about someone who pronounced 'E's as 'O's as Hilairo Bolloc. He wrote about himself: 'When I am dead, May it be said, His sins were scarlet, But his books were read.' He is, it isn't, they weren't, but they are.

104 WALTER GREAVES (1846–1930), artist. A great follower of Whistler (see page 154) and a painter of Thames scenes. He once said: 'I never seemed to have any ideas about painting – the river just made me do it.' Honest, Guv.

108 JOHN TWEED (1863–1933), sculptor. Forgettable.

109 PHILIP WILSON STEER (1860–1942), painter. Forgotten.

120 SYLVIA PANKHURST (1882–1960), women's rights campaigner. For more on the Pankhursts' graves, see page 222.

FLOATING VOTERS AND THE CELEBS TOO NEW FOR PLAQUES

The other, river, side of the road does in fact have a few residents, at the west end, but these are the truly floating voters of Chelsea, with nothing more to affix blue plaques to than houseboats, which may not even last as long as the inhabitants (although I like the idea of beplaqued boats; one of them could be for politician Dr David Owen, now Lord Owen, who lived there for a while, and tried to make a home for the whole country's floating voters in his short-lived Social Democratic Party – which has since sunk with all hands. Boats such as these which took part in the miraculous evacuation of Dunkirk in 1940 *did* actually acquire plaques to say so).

Given that blue plaques usually don't go up until 20 years after the death of the great person, the present status of more recent inhabitants of Cheyne Walk may well lead to yet more plaques. It's still an intriguing mix, although being well-heeled is of course now more of a qualification than being a genius. Not that this makes all recent inhabitants of Cheyne Walk, all too fresh to have blue plaques, boring. Far from it.

Residents over the last few decades have included the following:

MICK JAGGER (in his **Bianca** years). Rock superstar. No need to explain him to anyone except perhaps a High Court judge.

J PAUL GETTY II (d 2003), son of the famous American billionaire, was a neighbour of Mick Jagger's. He was here in the early 1970s after taking the sixties permissive thing rather to excess. He was in quite a bad way – let's not go into details – and rarely went out. He recalled later how his salvation was neighbour Mick, who survived the sixties with less damage. Mick kept popping in for cups of tea – how English – and would chat to Getty, but put the cricket on the TV while he was there in case he missed anything in the Test matches. Getty recalled: 'I'd have to watch too.'

Eventually, while Mick patiently explained the finer points (such as when you're out, you come in, and someone else goes out to be in, and when they're all out, you're in, that kind of stuff), Getty became hooked:

I started watching even when Mick wasn't there. That was the turning point, the day I found myself watching cricket when no-one else was there.

It's so unlikely that it *has* to be true. Getty, deeply troubled, was reborn as an eccentric English gentleman with the help of Mick Jagger, cups of tea and cricket.

He turned out to be a great philanthropist and built a wonderful cricket ground at his later home, **Wormsley Park** in the Chilterns, where he bred red kite birds of prey, and famously became so British that he was knighted to become Sir J Paul Getty in later life. Amazing.

'SIR' BOB GELDOF (b 1951), saintly rock person and Live Aid inventor and all-round good egg. The 'Sir' is in quotes because he, unlike Getty, retained his nationality, in this case Irish, and so cannot be awarded an honour.

MICHAEL HUTCHENCE (d 1997), the late Aussie rockstar of INXS.

KYLIE MINOGUE (b 1967), Aussie pop kitten formerly of *Neighbours* soap opera.

PALOMA PICASSO (b 1949), the model-perfume person and daughter of the great painter.

KEN FOLLET (b 1949), Labour luvvie and novelist.

SIR JOCELYN STEPHENS (b 1932), English Heritage new broom and newspaper supremo.

NIGEL WEST (b 1951), the spy writer who doesn't exist and is really a former MP called Rupert Allason.

JANE ASHER (b 1946), actress for whom a new career in baking was the icing on the cake.

GERALD SCARFE (b 1936), the great cartoonist, who drew Asher down the aisle.

SIMON LE BON (b 1958), former Duran Duran pop star, and his model wife **Yasmin** (b 1964), if you include the adjoining Apollo Place. The le Bons are not the only ones on this list to be connected.

Unsung genius: Don Saltero

JAMES SALTER IS ONE of the unsung eccentrics of the Walk who have no plaque but perhaps should have. He ran a coffee shop here, at No 18, in the 1720s and called himself 'Don Saltero'. A bit rum for a skinny, small Irishman, but why not? He was known as a great wit and a philosopher, and as well as providing excellent coffee for his customers, would extract their teeth, play the fiddle to them, shave them and generally entertain them with the extraordinary collection of curios and oddities he called his museum. The exhibits included, he claimed, a petrified crab from China, a pair of nun's stockings, several pieces of the True Cross, a starved cat found in the walls of Westminster Abbey when they were being repaired, and one of Elizabeth I's chambermaids' hats. Among his customers were Jonathan Swift and Benjamin Franklin.

A MILLIONAIRE AND AN EXTRAORDINARY MOVING HOUSE

In modern Cheyne Walk, one of the most massive eccentrics, in terms of what he will leave to future generations, must be multi-millionaire **Christopher Moran** (b 1948). Supposedly very rich at an early age, he was a brilliant but highly controversial performer at Lloyd's insurance market, and a complex, intelligent and equally controversial character.

Moran has, with the rebuilding of **Crosby Hall**, achieved in a home – surely the most remarkable private residence in London – something on the scale of the recreation of the Globe Theatre or perhaps the restoration of Somerset House, at an outlay of tens of millions of pounds (one estimate was £25 million). It has window arches around 70 feet high, 30-foot oak portals, a fireplace big enough to live in, and a glorious Tudor painted and scissor-beamed ceiling.

Moran, whose business acumen from an early age was such that he sold cigarettes and the *Financial Times* at school and had a Rolls-Royce by the time he was 20, acquired the freehold to the 15th-century hall, once home of 16th-century Lord Chancellor and later saint, **Thomas More** (see the play and film *A Man For All Seasons*), in 1989 for a reported £100,000.

The incumbent Association of University Women, who had the leasehold, soon moved out. The Hall then underwent a massive restoration by the finest craftsmen, who releaded its oriel windows and cupolas, and gilded the weather vanes on the Tudor cupolas, taking down the 15th-century brickwork and replacing it with authentic materials, and building further matching wings. It took years.

Now, as you can see even from the exterior, it is a thing of real beauty, and it seems impossible that such a structure could have survived the ravages of London's fires, plagues, wars, and the pressures of development and whatever intact right here.

Well it didn't. In the 15th century, Chelsea was miles outside London and this house, built by a wealthy wool merchant and lord mayor, Sir John Crosby, in fact stood at **Bishopsgate** in the City of London. Crosby died in 1475 and is buried at St Helen's, Bishopsgate.

Threatened with demolition, Crosby Hall and its beautiful Tudor timber roof was taken apart beam by numbered beam and stone by numbered stone by London County Council in 1908, and re-erected on the embankment here, the clear intention being to save it for the public good. The stone hall itself, now on the right, was the only medieval part that survived 17th-century fires in its previous site, according to one source. I have seen it suggested that most of the convincingly Tudor-looking stuff at the front dates from 1927, built by a certain Walter H Godfrey. And of course substantial parts are brand new, so detailed has been the restoration.

In the complex history of the next 90 years of its development, the public access part of the original plan for the relocated building has somehow gone by the board, although it is undeniable that the building has been saved in a remarkable operation. A curt notice on the side door of Crosby Hall when I revisited it warned away those who think they may have a right to have a look.

Is the reclusive Mr Moran indirectly building a monument to himself? He can be sure this remarkable building will be here in Cheyne Walk many more centuries. It is quite a staggering thing to be undertaken by, and apparently for, one man and most surprising to find in Chelsea a massive medieval building the size of an Oxford college, looking virtually brand new.

MORE MORE AND A STRANGE HOLY RELIC

There is a lot more **Thomas More** (1478–1535) to the right of Cheyne Walk as you look at Crosby Hall (that is downriver). What was once Thomas More's orchard next door is now a sunken garden and if you are a Londoner of a certain age and see a garden obviously laid out in the late 20th century in a gap in a row of houses, you say to yourself 'bomb site'. Either you saw the smoking ruins or, if a bit younger like myself, you played in the marvellous weed-filled lands of adventure that such ruins offered. Mostly they've now gone, giving way to some ghastly 50s' or 60s' block stuck incongruously in a row of older houses, but occasionally the gap was retained for public use as in **Roper Gardens** here, offering peace and tranquillity – odd when you think of the violence that created them.

In the middle of this one is a fine statue of a girl – *Awakening* by Gilbert Ledward (1888–1960). She is looking up, perhaps watching for another parachute-mine like the one that flattened this place in 1941. At the other end of the garden is a much more cryptic sculpture by **Jacob Epstein** (1880–1959) whose former studio here was redistributed by the *Luftwaffe*. His brilliance, along with that of so many other great Jewish artists and musicians, we ought to remember, would have been extinguished for ever had the Nazi campaign succeeded, when all their works would no doubt have been destroyed.

Just a bit further on is a fine statue of **Sir Thomas More** in front of the Chelsea Old Church, looking not unlike the fine picture of him in the National Portrait Gallery, apart, of course, from the skin tone. The statue bills him simply as 'statesman', 'saint' and 'scholar'.

More's saintliness was, as I have mentioned, not only brilliantly portrayed by Paul Scofield in Robert Bolt's 1966 film, *A Man For All Seasons*, but was also confirmed by the Pope who canonised him in 1936. However, others think the above monument should have added to it: 'scheming politician, arrogant extremist and enthusiastic torturer.' At least, that's what a not-very-convincing BBC documentary tried to argue in 2001.

More wrote a good epitaph for himself shortly before his head was chopped off for refusing to agree that Henry VIII was now head of the Church. On the scaffold, Sir Thomas, by the way, pushed his beard to one side with the words: 'Well, at least my beard has not committed treason.'

His head, as was usual for those judged traitors, was stuck on a pole on London Bridge for a few weeks and then it was taken down and pickled in spices by his daughter. He had expected to be buried in the church here with his first and second wives, but was buried (minus his head, of course) at the church within the Tower of London, where he was executed in 1535, St Peter Ad Vincula (appropriately, St Peter in Chains). And More's own epitaph?

The King's good servant, but God's first

Not a bad CV and commendably concise too – unlike the gushing monument to **Sir Hans Sloane** at the right-hand side of the churchyard behind him.

Sloane (as in Square and by extension Ranger) may not have been a saint but was President both of the Royal Society and of the College of Physicians 'who [the monument tells us] in the year of our Lord 1753 the 92nd of his age without the least pain of body and with conscious serenity of mind ended a virtuous and beneficent life'.

Sloane's house nearby was flattened by the construction of Beaufort Street, running north from Battersea Bridge, but his collection of antiquities became the nucleus of the **British Museum**, a finer monument still. Sloane is crucial to the Cheyne Walk story because he bought the land from a Lord Cheyne and hastened the development of the area.

Don't miss, at the other corner of the churchyard (that is left as you look at Thomas More), an apparently insignificant-looking sapling. This just could be the most significant thing in Cheyne Walk, or in London, or indeed in your whole life. It could just be a living link to when Jesus Christ was on earth. Not convinced? Well, hear this. It's quite a story.

It was planted in 2000 to commemorate the second millennium of Christ's birth. It is a piece, I am told, of the **Glastonbury Thorn**, a legendary tree of that epicentre on Glastonbury, Somerset, of British ... British what? Spirituality? Sacred myth? Folklore? Hippiedom? Rock festivals? (Tick the box that says 'All of the above'.) This undoubtedly extraordinary place is linked to King Arthur, the past and future king who will return, it is said, and which is the focus of ley lines. (Ley lines? I haven't time to go into all that, but if you believe in astrology, corn circles, UFOs, pyramid power and Atlantis, you'll love them. If not, you won't.)

The important bit of the story they tell you in Somerset is this. When

Joseph of Arimathea, having arrived in Britain carrying the Holy Grail, first saw the Isle of Avalon (now Glastonbury Tor), he directed his boat there and thrust his hawthorn staff into the ground, where it took root and flowered.

It *is* possible for a piece of wood to root like this, but then miracles, if it was one, don't need to be possible. (I hate all that stuff newspapers blather on about; for example, 'Well, the Red Sea could have parted if there was a very strong tide and the wind was from the east, etc, etc.' If it's a miracle, it's a flaming miracle, for God's sake.)

A church was built there, **St John's, Glastonbury**, and when the monumentally po-faced Puritans came along in their inane, humourless republican way, smashing stained-glass windows and decapitating statues of saints (they went on to create whole cities across the Atlantic which some less fair people than myself still label 'irony-free zones'), they of course chopped the tree down as idolatrous.

They hadn't reckoned with a faithful priest who kept a cutting and replanted it. One thing that lends credence to this whole story – and I am merely telling you what is said – is that each reigning monarch takes care to have a sprig from this tree on his or her table each Christmas time. This very tree in Chelsea is one such sprig.

Chelsea Old Church itself was badly damaged by that parachute-mine in 1941, but parts, such as the south chancel rebuilt by More in 1528, were undamaged. There are more More monuments, plus a rather good one with effigies of Dacre of the South (d 1595) with his wife, and an unusual monument to Sara Colville (d 1631).

THE MISERABLE COUPLES AND A WRITERS' BLOCK

Back to the plaques. Between Cheyne Walk and King's Road, there are some fascinating streets and footpaths, mostly on an agreeably small scale and dotted with welcoming, if not cheap, pubs.

The main road north from the ludicrously pretty Albert Bridge is **Oakley Street**, home of heroic failure **Captain Robert Falcon Scott** (of Antarctic fame, 1868–1912) at **No 56**.

In Cheyne Row, a small street running north from the river just east of here, is the home of the 'sage of Chelsea', author and philosopher **Thomas Carlyle** (1795–1881), who wrote histories of recent great events such as the French Revolution. Others thought him not quite as fascinating as he did. Samuel Butler wrote:

> *It was very good of God to let Carlyle and Mrs Carlyle marry one another and so make only two people miserable instead of four.*

The house is now owned by the National Trust, having been bought by Carlyle's admirers in 1895, so you can inspect his study, the kitchen where he would smoke with Tennyson, and the grave of Nero, Mrs Carlyle's dog, in the garden.

At **21 Carlyle Mansions**, a block at the river end of this street, American novelist **Henry James** breathed his last in 1916. He wrote about London in his *Notebooks*:

> *It is difficult to speak adequately or justly of London. It is not a pleasant place; it is not agreeable, or cheerful, or easy, or exempt from reproach. It is only magnificent.*

His funeral was held in nearby Chelsea Old Church where he was a regular; **Rudyard Kipling** (1865–1936) was one of his mourners. Other literary greats who lived in this block included another American, poet **T S Eliot** (1888–1965)**,** and author **Ian Fleming** (1908–64), creator of James Bond. Can you conceive of two more different writers? Fleming lived like a would-be playboy while Eliot lived like a monk, sleeping in a bare cell of a room lit by one unshaded bulb. But then his poems aren't a bundle of fun, either.

I know it's frightful of me, but there's a great deal of pleasure to be had in contemplating the publication of Eliot's at times impenetrable *The Waste Land* by the equally over-serious Leonard and Virginia Woolf at their Richmond home press in 1923. This is because it was full of printing errors, but nobody noticed, least of all the entirely eccentric Eliot who was supposed to check it. Now wouldn't it be obvious if any normal poem were full of errors? Someone has written in my copy of *The Waste Land* a quotation from Byron: 'I wish he would explain his explanation.'

ECCENTRIC BUILDINGS

WESTMINSTER PALACE AND THE PERILS OF KEEPING TALLY

The story of Westminster Abbey, the inspiration of **Edward the Confessor**, is told elsewhere (see page 144), but what of his plans to build a palace at Westminster? It was indeed built and became home to England's conquerors, the Norman kings. It was extended by the unpopular **William II** (1056–1100, known as Rufus because of his ruddy complexion). He added **Westminster Hall** – the great medieval barn of a place still survives – before fate, in the form of an arrow ricocheting while he was out hunting in August 1100, intervened. That this great hall of history has survived fires, the Blitz, modernisers, etc, to be the scene of tragedy and treachery – with the trials of Guy Fawkes and Charles I, as well as the lying-in-state of Winston Churchill and the Queen Mother – is partly luck, and partly down to repairs.

Regarding the latter, I caught a fascinating radio broadcast in which an official recalled how the great hammer-beamed roof needed some new oak in the early 20th century. The only problem was that the exact size and shape of tree was hard to find. Experts scoured the southern counties, but it seemed all the suitable great oaks had been felled for the Royal Navy's great wooden ships in the six centuries since Westminster Hall was built.

They came to an estate near Wadhurst in East Sussex, where a stand of great oaks of exactly the right dimensions marched up a hill to a great house. They hastened up to the home and knocked on the door. The owner himself answered and the conversation – if I remember rightly – went something like this:

Official: *'We're very sorry to bother you, but it's about your oak trees. They are rather special, aren't they?'*
Owner: *'Oh, you'll be from Westminster Hall, then.'*
Official: *'What?'*
Owner: *'Westminster Hall, am I right?'*
Official: *'How on* earth *did you know that?'*
Owner: *'Well my ancestor supplied the original oaks, so he planted some more. He said they would need some more in about 600 years, when they would be ready, and here you are.'*
Official (staggered): *'Yes, here we are.'*

I have since heard another version of that extraordinary story, which confirmed that the trees came from the **Courthorpe family estate**. In that version, however, a despairing official looked up the original records to see where the original timber had come from all those centuries before and was thus led to Wadhurst, where a similar conversation took place. Either way, the centuries and centuries of foresight must be almost unprecedented anywhere on earth.

The rest of the **Palace of Westminster** became a government building, and the seat of Parliament, after Henry VIII moved his court to nearby Whitehall Palace. Westminster Palace was to fall victim to taxation, but not in the usual way. In the Middle Ages, taxes collected were recorded on a 'tally stick', a stick with notches cut out to show how much tax had been paid. The idea was that you could split the stick lengthways so that both the government and the taxpayer would have a record or receipt. Any argument, and the two halves could be joined again. It's a bit like indentures, where an apprentice's contract was cut with jagged, indented edges so both parties get a half that matches only the right document.

All very well, but what to do with the tens of thousands of tally sticks? Being civil servants, they filed them away in bundles under the Palace of Westminster for nigh on 1,000 years. Eventually, in 1834, someone decided the tally sticks would probably not be needed to settle 800-year-old tax disputes.

Charles Dickens retold what happened with one of his usual caustic observations:

It would naturally occur to any intelligent person that nothing could be easier than to allow them to be carried away for firewood by the miserable people who live in that neighbourhood. However, they never had been useful, and official routine required it that they never should be, and so the order went forth that they should be privately and confidentially burned.

That part rings true by modern civil service standards. The sticks were confidential documents so people couldn't be allowed to see one even 800 years later and let's get rid of them quietly without fuss.

This last objective wasn't achieved, however. The sticks were burned in a furnace under the House of Lords but the fire soon spread to the mountains of crisp, centuries-old sticks all around. The Palace burned down that night, 16 October 1834. The glow was visible all around London, and one man who spotted it from the North Downs was **Charles Barry** (1795 –1860), travelling towards London in a coach from Sussex. He wondered what it was. In fact, it turned out to be the greatest architectural job of that architect's life: he was awarded the contract for designing the new Palace of Westminster, the sublime Gothic masterpiece that is today's Houses of Parliament. That fire gave Barry a knighthood, and immortality.

11 ECCENTRIC LONDON BUILDINGS

1 THE ARK

This superb apparition next to the thundering A4 flyover in **Hammersmith** offers changing and different vistas from any direction. It is brilliant, elegant and avoids that cigarette-pack-shape cliché of most modern offices. Oddly, when a newspaper where I worked asked readers to nominate the ugliest building in Britain, this one made it into the top few. It's a matter of taste, I suppose, but there's no denying it is eccentric. I think it's a brilliant breath of fresh air in a jaded era. For full details, see Hammersmith walk, page 325.

⊖ Hammersmith

2 THE LLOYD'S BUILDING

Centre of London's insurance market, the building was designed by **Richard Rogers** (b 1933), later Sir Richard and Lord Rogers, but is much better and more durable than his Pompidou Centre in Paris, which, by comparison, looks like some tatty relic from a 1970s' Habitat store, the chief fault of the Centre being, in my view, its trashy colours.

The basic Rogers idea was that you don't have to hide all the ducts, lifts, escalators, etc, inside the building, but could instead put them on the outside, freeing up the interior and offering an exterior that is sculptural yet functional. Everything but the kitchen sink is visible on the outside (actually it would make about two million kitchen sinks if they demolished it).

The steel boxes on the outside are mostly lavatories, a humorous touch when you think how Victorian and 20th-century architects mostly hid these unmentionable things away in the bowels of a building. Actually it's more of a return to the medieval approach to the lavatory – *garderobes* were tiny chambers projecting from the outside walls of castles and great houses. But, standing beneath Lloyd's one hopes that the effluent of the affluent doesn't just drop out of holes in the floor and streak the walls as in those malodorous days.

Leadenhall Street, the City ⬤ Tower Hill

3 THE ALBERT MEMORIAL AND THE ROYAL ALBERT HALL

Kensington. Londoners may think they don't need to read this, so well-known are these landmarks. But how many have considered this pair in their extraordinary detail?

First, the overall scheme of things. I suppose you would expect the memorial to Albert, the much-loved consort of Queen Victoria, the Empress of the greatest empire the world has ever seen (well, she was about to become empress when he died) to be noteworthy. After all, wasn't the lovely Taj Mahal in India built by Shah Jahan in mourning for his wife? But here in Kensington these two structures of astounding contrast bedazzle the eye – the Memorial, a soaring arch-Gothic Victorian fantasy with every fantastic embellishment; and the Hall – across the road, epitome of restrained, unadorned and even severe classicism, neatly summarising the two incompatible roots of British architecture, Gothic and Roman, which are usually kept well apart, or horribly watered down to make them live together.

The **Albert Memorial**, recently restored at huge expense, was designed by Sir George Gilbert Scott (1811–78), great architect of the fantastic Midland Grand Hotel at St Pancras – and grandfather of Sir Giles Gilbert Scott (1880–1960), creator of the classic red phone box, Battersea Power Station and Waterloo Bridge.

Sir George, when he designed this structure, evidently had in mind the Eleanor crosses, soaring Gothic spires put up by the grieving King Edward I (1239–1307) at every spot where his beloved Queen Eleanor's coffin rested overnight on its 12-day journey back to London in 1290. The Albert Memorial, a soaring pile of expensive stonework, with hundreds of sculptures on it, is the same idea taken to ridiculous extremes.

Revealingly, two other ideas for the Albert Memorial were rejected. One was an obelisk, similar to Cleopatra's Needle, another was a great monolith, a massive slab that, *The Times* complained, would cost as much money as half an ironclad frigate. Both ideas were sarcastically attacked as: 'England may show she can do in the 19th century what the ancient Egyptians, and even the painted Britons, were able to accomplish in the Sphinx and Stonehenge'.

This is the nub of it. What the Albert Memorial reflects above all was the sheer confidence of the British at the time: confidence in their industry, their navy, their empire, their history, confidence that they were better than other ages or countries. That's also why socialist, post-imperial late 20th-century Britain found the Albert Memorial in such bad taste. Demolition was considered seriously in the 1960s, while restoration had to wait for the very end of the century.

The **Royal Albert Hall**, opened in 1871 and designed to hold 8,000 people, would not have looked out of place in ancient Rome as a place for gladiators to hack each other to bits, or, in its almost industrial severity, as a Victorian roundhouse for servicing giant steam locomotives. Victorian virtues are listed around the top of the outside walls of the building.

> ⊖ High Street Kensington, turn right out of station, walking east along Kensington High Street for just over half a mile

4 VICTORIAN TURKISH BATHS

When Ali Baba rubbed his lamp, a genie appeared and said:

Master, what is your will, for I can perform any task you desire?

Ali thought for a moment and said:

Take the money-changer's harem from the great bazaar at Baghdad and transport it to the infidel city beyond the sea called London.

Genie: *It shall be done, master.*

Well that's a plausible explanation of how this eccentrically oriental building came to be sandwiched between modern glass buildings on New Broad Street. What else could it be? Has Brighton Pavilion slipped up to London and pupped? Is it a lost sultan's bog? Actually, it has recently been a restaurant, but its origin in 1894 was as a Turkish bath, so builder Harold Elphick made it utterly Ottoman. It's still charmingly here, blending into the background as well as a bowler-hatted City gent at the Taj Mahal would. Wonderful.

New Broad Street/8 Bishopsgate Churchyard ⊖ Liverpool Street

5 TRELLICK TOWER

If you're going to have tower blocks, the Trellick Tower is the *tour de force*. No quarter is given to convention here, no pussyfooting around with apologising for being a concrete tower. God knows how it was ever permitted to be built. Wallop! It punches into the air near Paddington to remind us of the new brutalism of the sixties.

Generally, we came to hate the people who ripped the heart out of towns and terrace streets to make these brutal blocks. Being an old-age pensioner on the 17th floor wasn't fun when the urinated-in lifts broke down while elsewhere unseen thieves and vandals rampaged. We thought the architects monstrous hypocrites and blew up a lot of the towers (memorably, one in East London, Ronan Point, blew itself up).

This one was different. Far more radical than the boring boxy blocks elsewhere, it is so tall it would bridge the Paddington mainline or the Grand Union Canal (Paddington Arm) were it ever felled. Architect **Erno Goldfinger** (1902–97), unlike the usual bunch of architect-hypocrites, actually lived in one of his towers for a bit, although he preferred his low-rise Modernist house in Hampstead, now a museum. He scorned the whitewashed stucco Art Deco style of some houses: 'I want to be remembered as a classical architect, not a kasbah architect,' he said. (In fact, after Ian Fleming pinched his name for a James Bond villain, his name unfairly brings to mind an evil megalomaniac.)

Now that trendy Notting Hill is colonising the former combat zone that is North Kensington, flats in the Trellick Tower are becoming sought-after by those who fit the uncompromisingly trendy radical profile. Most of Goldfinger's urban renewal stuff has – in my view rightly – been blown up or refurbished. Trellick House is different. It is, on a somewhat Soviet or fascist monumental scale, an unashamed, powerful piece of sculpture. Long may it remain.

⊖ Westbourne Park

6 THE NATWEST MEDIA CENTRE

Have the Martians landed? Is the War of the Worlds about to start in exclusive St John's Wood? I don't know of any other building in the world that looks like this spaceshippy thing – but then its monocoque aluminium shell was built in a shipyard. It has suitably large sloping windows on the cricket side (ball proof?) but to the outside world it is exciting, alien, about to take off – and they say Lord's and the MCC are stuffy. For a picture of it, see colour section.

Lord's Cricket Ground, St John's Wood ⏺ St John's Wood

7 PECKHAM LIBRARY

Unlikely in that it is in Peckham and done on the cheap, this library, designed by Alsop and Stormer, avoids both the stamp of council mediocrity and the clichéd emblems of post-Modernism. It's different and it works. In 2001 Peckham and design were in the news again when *Angel of the North* sculptor, the otherwise brilliant Antony Gormley, created some immensely phallic bollards for the streets. What was that rude schoolboy rhyme ending 'Turnham Green and Peckham'? Answers in a plain brown envelope please.

🚂 Peckham Rye (from London Bridge)

8 THE GHERKIN

An icon for modern London, the Gherkin is instantly recognisable from its fat cigar – well, all right, gherkin – shape. The Gherkin is an ugly pickled cucumbery thing sold in British fish 'n' chip shops, and not to everybody's taste (although if you haven't tried pickled eggs, you haven't *lived*). Gherkins are like the French *cornichons*, only bigger, and if you cut the curved end off one and set it with the other end upright, you have the perfect Gherkin building shape. It might seem an eccentric name for a building, but it's an unofficial one, the official building name at the time of first writing 'the Swiss Re' – equally daft. It is, nevertheless, a fantastic building, designed by **Norman Foster** (b 1935), and uses far less energy than a normal office building. Not the tallest tower, at 180m it is slightly outranked by the nearby Tower 42 (which used to be the NatWest Tower) and the 237m Canary Wharf in the Docklands. And, across the river, its rival for startlingness, the **Shard of Glass**, the 303m London Bridge Tower.

30 St Mary Axe ⏺ Aldgate or Bank

9 THE GLASS HELMET – CITY HALL

Recognisably another part of the Norman Conquest of London (architect Norman Foster, that is), City Hall near Tower Bridge looks like a vast alien has put down his helmet, or is perhaps buried whole deep in the riverside. Despite the curved glass on a fishnet signature of Foster's work – which might become a horribly dated cliché one day but must have bought a few glaziers a nice holiday home – this tilted building is eccentric because of its spiral interior ramp that goes up around perhaps ten storeys like a demonic apple peeling. This design is said by the usual know-alls to 'symbolise openness, accessibility, democracy and transparency'. It could equally well be said to symbolise a huge waste of space, uneccessary and profligate duplication (we had a perfectly good County Hall, and needed another layer of government like a fish needs a new bike), elitist disdain for our culture and gesture politics. Anyone in a wheelchair who really takes that right-on ramp to the top deserves a medal. Be good for skateboarding, however.

Well I really like it, although cynical Londoners who came up with the Gherkin nickname have also called this the Glass Testicle. It's on the South Bank in Southwark, close to Tower Bridge. Another Foster triumph you must see is the indeed great **Great Court at the British Museum**, where the gap between the circular reading room and the surrounding building has been covered by another set of bulging fishnets. And as you look up, consider again the work for glaziers – are any two of those glass panes the same shape? Brilliant.

At the time of writing Lord Foster was vying to replace all London's airports with a megaport on an island east of the city, connected by new high-speed trains and motorways. Far-fetched? Well, it's what he did in Hong Kong.

London Bridge for City Hall ● Holborn for British Museum.

10 **University of East London Halls of Residence**

Great examples of clean, functional attractive modern architecture. They are also an antidote to those increasingly common riverside developments on the Thames that look as if rich people and Lego kits collided without an architect. These halls, situated in **Docklands**, are dramatic truncated cylinders, whose roofs are shorn off at an angle to shed London's rain (whatever fool thought flat roofs would work in this climate?). They are bold and clear about what they are doing, and don't pretend to be anything else or from any other period. The student rooms inside them are arranged, like pizza slices, in a long triangle, 12 to a floor. Economy is achieved by linking two such blocks so the stairs, etc, can be shared. They are brightly painted; like most organic and efficient things (and unlike most buildings), they are curved, presumably representing a well-rounded education. Great for spotty plane-spotters, too, as it is located opposite London City Airport on Royal Albert Dock.

Royal Albert Dock ● Royal Albert (DLR). Not open to the public.

11   LAUNCHING RAMPS

Well, they might be a bus station canopy, but this building (or sculpture) is deeply eccentric, with its undulating roof ending up in a pair of ramps which look suspiciously like those used for launching the V1 doodlebug rockets at London during World War II. When you bear in mind they could swivel round to aim directly at the MI6 Secret Service headquarters across the road, should we be worried about elderly teutonic types who want revenge?

Vauxhall Cross was known as the world's most unpleasant road junction before it was tarted up with this insane structure, and it has improved the area a little. Oddly, all Russian railway stations are called Vauxhall because the mainline from the southwest ended here before Waterloo was built and the Tsar, being shown round, said the Russians should get a Vauxhall for themselves. That may be apocryphal, but if so, the Russians probably named stations after the Vauxhall pleasure gardens nearby, because a pleasure park was called a Vauxhall in Russia at the time, and the first railway there went to one too.

⊖/🚂 Vauxhall

Are you 20th-century foxed?

I F YOU'RE A FAN of modern architecture, then the 20th Century Society (*www.c20society.org.uk*) might be for you. Originally called the Thirties Society, it saved a few art deco masterpieces, and failed to save a few more, such as the Firestone factory on the Great West Road, which was scandalously demolished just before it could be listed for preservation, and on a bank holiday Monday too.

The Thirties Society then found itself fighting to preserve fifties, and even sixties, architecture, which was confusing, so it changed its name to the 20th Century Society. Of course, as the 21st century continues, the same problem will arise but, like 20th Century Fox in films, they haven't got round to dealing with that one yet. Perhaps they should be the Not Before World War I But Anything Modern After That Which Is Really Nice Is Pretty Well OK By Us Society.

ART DECO, DREAM PALACES AND RECOGNISING A SUCKER

For the greatest quality Art Deco architecture, people go to Miami, perhaps to Napier, New Zealand… and to **Perivale, West London**.

Here, on Western Avenue, the extraordinary **Hoover building** stands testament to that confident era when pseudo-Tudor suburbs sprawled unrestrained, when grand arterial roads for the newly popular motorcar were being laid out, along which sprang up buildings in this astonishing architectural style, which looked forward to the supposedly bright future of the rest of the 20th century, and not at all backwards. It's a matter of taste, of course, but I think the Hoover building, with its odd glass angles and the tilework over the door is superb.

This example of Art Deco, on Western Avenue, is surely one of the best. Hoover products are no longer made here, but the building is part supermarket, part offices.

At a similar distance out of London on other roads can be found other examples of Art Deco buildings – the architecture that threw every previous notion out of its curved windows. They can be private homes, still with those strange bits of curved glass, often in ribbon development, which would now never be allowed, or cinemas, such as the **Regal** in nearby Uxbridge, or factories and offices, also situated along or near the A40 on the road to Oxford (and don't miss the old **Arsenal Football Club** building in Highbury, North London).

If the Regal stands out now, how must it have seemed to 1930s Britain with its predominantly Edwardian and Victorian stock of buildings? A bombshell.

Art Deco fans may have spotted its frontage, cast as a cinema supposedly in Doncaster in the TV film of Agatha Christie's Poirot story, *The ABC Murders*. The interiors of such splendid cinemas often survive too.

While we're on **cinemas**, the twenties and thirties saw the great dream palaces of this, the golden age of cinema, being finished with some very eccentric interiors. There was the elaborate Venetian palace interior of the **Granada Tooting** (1931); while the **New Victoria** (1928–29) had, and has, not only a striking Modernist exterior but also a fabulous underwater-palace-style interior complete with scalloped everything and fantastic lighting.

Then there were the **Astorias**, of which two have survived, at **Brixton** and **Finsbury Park**. The latter, which enjoyed a resurgence as a top rock venue in the later 20th century as The Rainbow, has a fountain court foyer and an elaborate Moorish interior, with lions on pillars either side of the stage, and a silhouetted-oasis roof-line of palm trees, minarets and houses set against a sky cleverly lit from below so that it faded through various blues and pinks to black, revealing twinkling stars set in it. Superb.

Other exotic themes used in these dream palaces included an ancient Egyptian temple at the **Carlton, Islington** (1930), and the wacky, Chinese-pagoda-style **Southall Gaumont** (1928) and the completely over-the-top Tsarist Palace interior of the **Kilburn State** (1937) – its exterior was art deco with tower. The cinema changed the face of architecture in London as surely as the great railway stations had 50 years before.

With their electrically driven trains, **Tube stations** were particularly suited to reflect the Art Deco vision of clean, suburban living – from the radical Modernist boxes that are the Tube stations at **Sudbury Town**, **Sudbury Hill**, **Acton Town**, **Turnpike Lane**, or the marvellous drums that are the stations of **Chiswick Park**, **Arnos Grove**, **Hanger Lane** (just before Perivale on the A40 heading out from London), or, one of the best in terms of detail, **Southgate**.

These still look modern today – in the 1930s they must have resembled science-fiction spaceports. To put it another way, the ultra-modern Jubilee Line extension, opened in 2000 – that is, the bits that run from Westminster eastwards – features some superb modernistic stations which, on first glance, look not unlike the Art Deco or Modernist counterparts of 70 years before.

So back to Perivale and the Hoover Art Deco palace, a landmark in London's architecture. Actually it should be called the Spangler Building. The inventor of the vacuum cleaner was an American boffin, Murray Spangler; William H Hoover was merely the canny businessman who recognised a great sucker – literally – when he saw one, and really cleaned up. So after a party, one should really say: 'I'm just going to Spangler the carpet.'

TOWERING ECCENTRICITIES AROUND LONDON

Eccentric towers – follies, indeed – are usually associated with the remote country estates of barmy barons, delinquent dukes and mad marquesses. But if you know where to poke around, there are some darned odd buildings around London too.

One rather strange triangular tower not only gives a superb view over much of southeast London, but also tells of a swashbuckling fight against pirates in the exotic east. **Severndroog Castle** in Castlewood Park off Shooters Hill, near Blackheath in southeast London, was built in 1784 for the widow of Sir William James as a tribute to the heroic attack led by Sir William, with four ships and thousands of men, on the original Severndroog Castle, a nest of pirates on the Malabar coast of India. That castle was taken in 1755. This one's still here.

A whole set of strange towers puzzles travellers going southwest from London along the line of the A3. They look as if Rapunzel might let her hair down from them. They are in fact **semaphore towers** for sending messages quickly back and forth from the fleet at Portsmouth to the Admiralty in London, in the days before the electric telegraph was invented. There's one you can visit at **Wisley** (see below), where the road crosses the M25, and, I was delighted to discover, one rebuilt into the **Telegraph pub** between Wimbledon Common and Putney, on the edge of Roehampton. Again it's on a hill, so it's a logical location – in fact in Telegraph Road, Putney Heath – and again it's next to the modern A3, which takes a similar line because it's also making for Portsmouth.

Go on down this road far enough and you will find **Tower Road** in **Hindhead**, Surrey, and a little further another **Tower Road** in **Liphook**, Hampshire. Coincidence? I think not. There was a chain of these things. That the Telegraph pub at Roehampton wasn't named after the electric telegraph is clear from the pub sign, showing semaphore signals. But this building has been hopelessly altered (although it's a good pub, and bears an astonishing plaque about how a bunch of Canadian firemen were killed by a doodlebug there, and is near the extraordinary fireplates obelisk – for details and direction, see page 183). You need to go to Wisley to see the real thing.

The **Wisley** tower, on Ockham Common, off Junction 10 of the M25, is, in fact called **Chatley Heath Semaphore Tower**. It is 60 foot high, was built in 1822, and could do six words per minute, the 15 stations taking about 20 minutes to reach Portsmouth.

But this system wasn't unique. In fact the French had 155 of these towers in Napoleonic times, and they thought Morse's electric telegraph unnecessary when it arrived. But the semaphore towers were expensive and slow compared with Morse's system. They were also easily spied upon, and didn't work well at night with lamps. And one further thought – the first railway signals of the waving-arms type appeared on the Brighton line in the 1840s and sprouted from the roofs of signalboxes just like the semaphore towers. I had a moment of clarity while gazing at the Telegraph pub sign (beer does that sometimes). They *must* have been influenced by the semaphore chains of only a few years before.

THE MYSTERY LOCATIONS

The fascinating thing about another little-known piece of architectural London eccentricity is that no one has a clue why it's there. Near King's Cross, where Gray's Inn Road and Pentonville Road converge (we're on the blue corner of the Monopoly board), there's what's known as the **King's Cross lighthouse**, which sits on top of a plain four-storey building. Some claim it was once a fairground helter-skelter tower but it would have to have been, impossibly and improbably, moved up there. How? Why? Inspections of the interior, say Camden Council, show that it can't have been a clock tower or a camera obscura. A thoughtful reader recently suggested it was to control the tram junctions below. Yes, you needed someone to do that and switch the points and the things guiding the electric pick-ups on the overhead wires onto the right route, but having examined one in Hong Kong, I'd point out it would be mechanically linked to the tracks with rods and therefore as close as possible, not on top of a building.

A sham, on the other hand, is a building that pretends to be what it isn't. One sham in Central London you could pass every day without noticing. If you deal with anyone who gives a London address at 23 or 24 **Leinster Gardens** – such a respectable street – you may be dealing with a con artist. The two houses appear there in the right sequence, but they are a thin sham without foundations or substance, even the windows being painted on.

When the wedding-cake-style five-storey terrace was broken in 1865 to make way for the South Kensington extension of the Tube railway, property owners demanded that instead of a yawning gap over the railway track, a phoney frontage be erected. At first glance, you hardly notice the join, though from the back – it is between Bayswater and Paddington stations – the thing looks like a film set. An utter sham, in fact.

FROM PHEW TO VIEW

One more bit of towering bonkersness is in **Arthur Road, Wimbledon**, where there's a domed thing that turns out to be an **Artesian well** (see plaque on the side, it is private property within). 'Blooming Artesians, comes over here, dig our wells,' a local no doubt grumbled at the time.

An Artesian well is where you have a basin-shaped landscape with a non-porous soil (London clay in this case) overlying porous rock (chalk). The rain falls on the hills round the edge and to get clean water spurting up you simply drill through the clay and, *bingo*! – no more hauling up buckets. If that's not easy to envisage, imagine making a small hole in the bottom of a washing-up bowl, then pushing it down into a bath of water until the brim is almost submerged. But, as 'any fule kno' (to quote the great British schoolboy Molesworth), the well has to be at the *bottom* of the basin to work. This one is on top of a hill, so it didn't.

Mind you, it was built at the command of the eccentric Earl Spencer family (the lot that gave us the late, lovely Diana) who had a rambling estate here before all these houses popped up – which is why almost any approach to here will have taken you past a **Spencer Arms** or **Earl Spencer** pub.

If you want more evidence of their endearing if not enduring barminess, walk a few hundred yards southwest to the mini roundabout and look at **Stag Lodge** with its ridiculous antlered ornament. It was lead, originally, and must have weighed tons. Scrap-metal thieves, please note: It's now a glass-fibre replica.

And while you are in the vicinity, go into **St Mary's churchyard** next door to lay a fragrant flower at the grave of **Joseph Bazalgette**, the man who saved more lives than any doctor (see page 335) and ended the Great Stink of London. His grave is at the far side of the charming graveyard and the views aren't bad either.

IF YOU WANTED a great eccentric day out, combine the Artesian well, Stag Lodge and St Mary's churchyard (see opposite and above) with the fireplates/pub/Buddhist temple (see page 183 and 177). Bus 493 links Wimbledon station and Southfield tubes to both these sites. If you just want to see the first three, there's a pleasant walk uphill from Wimbledon Park Tube, particularly if you take Inner Park Road and rejoin Arthur Road at the top.

An eccentric day out in Wimbledon

MONUMENTALLY ECCENTRIC

THE HISTORIC STONES OF OLD LONDON

STONE OF SCONE

You might think the veteran Rolling Stones, bless 'em, are the most ancient stones in London, but there are some even more ancient ones – real rock stars with legendary, mystic, king-making properties.

One of these you will no longer see in London, except at a coronation. The ancient and much-travelled Stone of Scone was the coronation stone of Scottish kings and has had quite a history.

Legend has it that this very stone was where Jacob rested his head in the Bible story. St Columba used it to crown Aidan in 574.

Eventually, this 'Stone of Destiny' ended up at Scone Palace in the Scottish lowlands – where Malcolm goes to get crowned at the end of Shakespeare's *Macbeth* – from where it was seized in 1296 by England's Edward I, the 'Hammer of the Scots'. It was then incorporated into the base of the nation's **Coronation Chair** in **Westminster Abbey** (see page 144).

All English (and, after 1603, British) monarchs since have been crowned at Westminster Abbey over this Stone of Scone. Even the republican, and hence anti-royalist, Oliver Cromwell sat on it in **Westminster Hall** (see page 166) when he was installed as 'Lord Protector', as if the stone had magic powers to legitimise him. Interestingly, when Charles II had himself crowned in 1651 at Scone during the Civil War but without the Stone, it didn't count.

Then on Christmas Eve 1950 a bunch of Scottish Nationalist students removed the Stone from Westminster Abbey and took it secretly back to Scotland – gaining much publicity for their cause. But it was back in Westminster in time for the coronation of Queen Elizabeth II in 1953.

In 1996, the Stone of Scone was taken back to Edinburgh, where it was installed with much pomp in the castle, with three of those 1950s students present to see their aim fulfilled. It may be brought back to Westminster for the next coronation, so it has not finished travelling yet. The Scone of Stone, on the other hand, was the name of a cake on offer in Dundee University Student Union from 1973 to 1975.

ENGLAND'S FORGOTTEN CORONATION STONE

Outside Kingston-upon-Thames Town Hall, completely forgotten except by local people, stands a massive stone that was the coronation stone of the Saxon kings of England. Kingston means 'king's stone', after all. The old kings of Wessex who were crowned on it, or perhaps next to it, included Edward the Elder, Edward the Martyr, Ethelred the Unready, Hagar the Flatulent, Ethelstan the Unreasonable and Geoffrey the Hysterical. I made up the last three of course, but the others were real; what is remarkable about these coronations that took place between 900 and 978 is how very little is known about them.

A MAD MILESTONE IN LONDON'S HISTORY

The **Brass Crosby Milestone** that is neither brass nor tells accurate mileages from where it is, despite distances shown on it being detailed down to the very last foot, can be found in **St George's Road, London**, **SE1**, right outside the Imperial War Museum. It tells a rather fascinating story.

It is named after the Lord Mayor of London, Brass Crosby, who became a national hero in 1771 when he refused Parliament's order to jail a printer who dared to report Parliament's proceedings in the press. Brass Crosby was thrown in the Tower but public outcry assured his release, and he eventually won his campaign for the free reporting of Parliament.

The milestone – more of an obelisk in size – was set up in St George's Circus, south of the Thames, where the roads from Blackfriars, Waterloo and Westminster bridges converge, as a memorial to him but was removed during rebuilding in 1905 to its present site. This may be only a few hundred yards southwest, but it does make the rather precise measurements it displays singularly and totally useless. The present spot may have been chosen because during Crosby's life, the War Museum was the original **Bedlam** (a corruption of 'Bethlehem') lunatic asylum. Crosby was appointed president of the asylum in 1772, helping the process of its reform.

So when people say parliamentary debates sound 'like Bedlam' on the radio, they are paying tribute to two different major steps forward in British life where Brass Crosby went the extra mile. Milestones, in fact.

An un-royal relic

Another obscure, obsolete obelisk is **Cleopatra's Needle**, located on the Thames embankment near to Embankment Tube. It's a strangely moving pillar but it had nothing to do with Queen Cleopatra. It is a fascinating 1400bc Egyptian relic, which survived being moved by the Romans in 14bc then being taken to England in 1878 in a sort of submarine and being nearly sunk in a storm in the Bay of Biscay, only to be covered in pollution and then damaged by German bombs after it arrived. You can see the shrapnel marks on it today. Its twin was erected in Central Park, New York, in 1881.

How to make beauty out of coal

In 1851, London was ringed by hundreds of **Coal Dues obelisks** and markers in four different designs to mark the point – you can't avoid the word – on every road, railway or canal at a distance of 20 miles from the General Post Office in St Martin's-le-Grand in Central London. It's all the fault of the Great Fire of London in 1666, which led to the City of London Corporation being empowered to levy tax on coal or wine brought within a certain distance of London to pay for rebuilding.

In 1851, because of the sprawl of London, an Act laid down that the distance should be that 20-mile radius, still marked with four types of iron pillar, post or obelisk, all bearing the City's coat of arms or at least their main elements: the crusader shield, red cross on white with a dagger.

To complicate matters, some of these markers were moved slightly in 1861 to coincide with the boundary of the new Metropolitan Police area, so posts such as that on Watling Street, Radlett, still have a function today... it marks where the Mr Plods of the shires take over from the Old Bill of the Met.

More impressive are the 14-foot stone Coal Dues obelisks such as the one alongside the London–Norwich mainline at **Chadwell Heath** on the boundary of Barking and Havering boroughs, or that beside the mainline at **Watford**, which refers on its inscription to the Coal and Wine Duties Act of 1861 (which must have updated the earlier Act) and which demanded a duty of 11d (4½p in today's coin, but then a week's pay for some) for every ton of coal which rolled past southwards.

Like most taxes dreamed up for a specific purpose, the Coal Dues carried on long after the original point of the obelisks was forgotten, and were finally abolished in 1889, although we have the splendid heritage of Wren churches such as St Paul's to thank them for.

MORE BLOODY OBELISKS

Even the dullest London suburbs are riddled with obelisks, if you know where to look, to testify to blood-soaked history and other excitements that once happened there. A foggy Sunday morning in **Barnet** doesn't sound too dramatic, but an obelisk at nearby Monken Hadley tells of the desperate struggle of 14 April 1471, when the Earl of Warwick's waiting army in the Wars of the Roses between the houses of York and Lancaster attacked under the cover of mist and drove Edward IV's men right back into Barnet town centre.

A swift cavalry counter-attack had the Lancastrians retreating; Warwick was caught on foot and slain close to where the obelisk stands. Some 1,500 men died.

The next Tube station to High Barnet on the Northern Line, by the way, is **Totteridge and Whetstone**. The latter takes its name from the high number of whetstones found there, discarded by soldiers after sharpening their swords and daggers before the Battle of Barnet.

More than 200 years later a very different rebellion, the **Jacobite rebellion**, was crushed in 1715 and the Earl of Derwentwater executed for taking part. An obelisk to his memory stands incongruously in the suburbia of Churchfield Road East, **Acton**, in a small park.

THE MAN WHO TRIED TO BURN DOWN A MAD KING AT BREAKFAST

In 1774, David Hartley invited the king and queen to breakfast at a spot now beside the thundering A3 at Tibbet's Corner, Putney Heath and while they were eating upstairs, tried to burn the house down. Was he torn to pieces by torturers in the Tower of London? Surprisingly, the **Fireplates Obelisk** here records that he was rewarded with £2,500 from a grateful Parliament and the Freedom of the City of London from the Corporation.

George III and Queen Charlotte had agreed to Hartley's daring experiment because he wanted to demonstrate his fireplates, which, he claimed, made a fireproof floor. To the great relief of courtiers, he was right.

George III was yet to become completely mad, but if the fireplates had failed Britain might have been even more grateful. The American colonies might not have been lost in the following nine years if a saner monarch had been on the throne. Come to think of it, maybe the Americans should build Mr Hartley an obelisk too.

Curiously there's a lodge from that era now in a housing estate about half a mile south of here on Princes Way – not particularly worth a visit in itself – and it bears metal plaques boasting of its 'fireproof' construction, proving Hartley was on the right track. The Fireplates Obelisk is part of a set of curiosities (see page 179) worth a visit in the area.

And if you're gasping for a drink there's a rather good pub beyond the obelisk, called the **Telegraph** with great stories to tell (see page 177).

 In woodland beside northbound slip road off A3 signed Putney, but you can't stop there. Instead, from Tibbet's Corner roundabout, at the A219/A3 Junction south-west of Wandsworth, SW19 6AN, take the exit signed Wimbledon, then turn immediately left into Withycombe Road. Park and walk back on the paths under the roundabout, to the far side, leaving by the exit marked Putney. Turn sharp left tight back on yourself along the northbound A3 sliproad, leaving the concrete path at the bend to go straight on a few yards. For the Telegraph pub, retrace your steps to path and turn left along fence (away from the A3) / Putney Bridge (District Line), then bus 39 to Tibbet's Corner, then follow directions above. You can afterwards walk to Buddhist Temple (Calonne Road, see page 148) or bus 93 from Tibbet's Corner. You can continue with that bus to Wimbledon village for additional curiosities (see page 179).

12 RATHER STRANGE LONDON SCULPTURES

London's got the strangest things tucked away here and there, and many have an intriguing story to tell. Here's a selection of the hundreds of such treats that await the urban explorer.

1 WATER TOWER SCULPTURE
There's a beguiling water tower sculpture in the middle of the diamond-shaped roundabout at the east end of **Shepherd's Bush**. When it's

working properly at night, the water flowing within it is a strange fluorescent blue; it must have puzzled and intrigued thousands of drivers coming down the motorway spur from Westway.

2 TRAFFIC LIGHT TREE

Pierre Vivant's strange and unexpected work, a **traffic light tree**, is at **Heron's Quay** in East London just south of Westferry Circus gateway to the Isle of Dogs. It features more than 75 sets of traffic lights and seems designed to give oncoming drivers apoplexy. Unveiled in February 1999, the strange sculpture seems at its best at Christmas time when its red and green lamps going on and off look rather festive. The world's first traffic lights, for horse-drawn traffic, were at the corner of Parliament Square and were gas-powered. Sadly, they eventually blew up and killed the policeman operating them.

3 EAST FINCHLEY TUBE ARCHER

This clean-looking lead-covered archer, located at one end of the station, combined with the elegant lines of East Finchley's Modernist station, evokes the best of 1930s style. The station, with its ship-like curved glass walls, was designed by Charles Holden and opened just before the outbreak of World War II. The Archer was by Eric Aumonier and has since become the district's emblem – the community newspaper is called *The Archer*. The ten-foot-high sculpture aims its massive bow at the mouth of the Northern Line tunnel, which goes all the way to Morden right across town in South London and was, until the building of the Channel Tunnel, Europe's longest. There should be a matching sculpture at the other end – a warrior holding up a shield with an arrow stuck in it, perhaps.

4 BRONZE COMMUTERS

At **Brixton station**, which stands at rooftop level in this vibrant Caribbean-cockney community, stands a surprising pair of passengers on opposite platforms, endlessly waiting for trains (you know the feeling). One looks a relaxed dude, the other a young housewife with her shopping bags. They know no colour bar – they're both bronze, after all – but they endlessly eye each other up, waiting for their trains that never come. Like many excellent sculptures, it seems a real moment frozen for ever.

5 THE WINDOW CLEANER

Allan Sly's sculpture (1990) at **Capital House, Edgware Road**, besides having a comic, almost Laurel-and-Hardy jauntiness, has the guy looking quizzically up at the vast expanse of glass above, a daunting prospect. Or maybe it's pride at having finished them. We'll never know.

6 GOLDSMITHS COLLEGE OF ART ROOF SCULPTURE

This is called **Scribble**, an honest name. On first sight it looks like a scrap metal merchant has dumped a load in a chopped-off two-storey-deep top corner of the rather boring, office block-style building that is Goldsmith's College roof on the **New Cross Road**, SE14 (that is if someone didn't just blow up that corner, leaving a twisted wreck, which may be an explanation).

A student there tells me that the college wasn't allowed to block someone's view otherwise the building would have been a complete box. The sort of thing students say, but why would anyone prefer a view of *this* to an office building? Anyway, for a college that produced *enfant* yawningly *terrible* **Damien Hirst** (b 1965) – the pickled shark guy, about whom the less said the better – then perhaps it is a fitting attempt to shock and produce a kind of high-level advertising hoarding saying: 'We're arty but not artistic, we're really rebellious but not so rebellious you stop giving us all that money.' Make up your own mind. Perhaps I just don't get it, like I don't get why a dead sheep or an unmade bed is considered art at all and is 'worth' many thousands of pounds, and don't get why we no longer transport such annoying people to Australia in chains. However, I do get that Goldsmiths has produced some brilliant artists over recent years, including **Antony Gormley** (b 1950), who made the *Angel of the North* and many other wonderful things. The architects of this sorry structure, Alsop and Stormer also produced the jolly creative nearby Peckham Library (see page 172). We all have off days.

7 FORTNUM AND MASON CLOCK

Is a clock a sculpture? The most delightful clock at Fortnum and Mason's, the royal family's grocery shop in **Piccadilly**, has, on the hour, little figures of Mr Fortnum and Mr Mason, which come out to the tune of the 'Eton Boating Song'. If the clock were new, it would be pronounced totally naff, kitsch or whatever, but as it isn't, it isn't. Afternoon tea here is one of those very English things, but be careful to whom you chat. For Sir Thomas Beecham's very odd encounter here, see page 260.

8 LITTLE BEN

Definitely a clock rather than a sculpture, but worth mentioning because it's little known, being stuck on a traffic island in front of **Victoria Station**, is Big Ben's counterpart, Little Ben. Big Ben, pedants will tell you, is correctly the name not of the tower at the Houses of Parliament, but of the deep-toned bell whose sound starts the news on millions of radio sets around the world. And if you thought you saw an identical Little Ben in the Seychelles, you were right.

9   SENTIMENTAL STATUES OF CHILDREN

There's an odd statue of a boy behind the London Planetarium, and another of a child on the Victoria Embankment. Several old schools are decorated with children in archaic uniforms, such as the Blewcoat School, Caxton Street, Westminster and high up on the wall beside Kensington church, on the intriguing footpaths north of the High Street Kensington Tube, and at St Andrew's, Holborn.

The Blewcoat School, a lovely building, is now a National Trust gift shop. Another charming pair of statues of children at St Botolph's church hall, Bishopsgate, are made of that indestructible Coade stone that the Coade lion is made of (see *London beasts*, page 206).

10   WELLINGTON ARCH

This massive monument at Hyde Park Corner commemorates the Iron Duke who made Europe safe by defeating Napoleon at Waterloo in 1815. It is a huge arch surmounted by the biggest bronze sculpture in the country, and is ignored by millions of people every year rounding this busiest of road junctions.

But it is neither what was intended or what was constructed, nor is it even where it was first put, and its story is one of bitterness and bickering. It was once topped with one of the world's ugliest sculptures, so hideous that the embittered architect of the triumphal arch left a huge amount of money in his will to get the blasted thing taken down.

Let's start in 1825 when the great architect **Decimus Burton** (1800–81) designed the arch, which was finished in 1828. It was aligned with the Hyde Park screen, making a processional route into Buckingham Palace, then being tarted up for George IV.

Burton had envisaged the arch being adorned with complicated sculptures and a *quadriga* (a four-horse job, as at St Mark's Cathedral in Venice), but to his complete consternation an immense statue of a mounted Wellington was instead erected with great difficulty there in 1846. This stiff, lifeless, clumsily colossal equestrian effort reduced the arch to a mere plinth or pedestal – the combination was ugly indeed.

When Burton died in 1881 he left £2,000 – a huge amount then – to have the statue removed. Queen Victoria, however, was careful of the elderly Duke of Wellington's feelings (after all, he lived at Apsley

House nearby) so nothing was done until he died. Even then, the real impetus was the opening of Victoria (the railway station not the Queen) in 1874 when the thing just had to be moved out of the way of the traffic to its present alignment. The opportunity was taken to whip the horrid horse off to Aldershot, where it remains in a more military setting. In 1891 another Prince of Wales, later King Edward VII, revived the four-horse idea having seen an excellent smaller work on these lines by sculptor **Adrian Jones** (1845–1938). Jones was set to work but his magnificent creation, *Peace Descending on a Chariot of War*, wasn't placed on the arch until 1912, two years after King Edward had died.

Perhaps Edward was lucky to miss the irony of the spectacle of this sculpture featuring Peace ringing to the sounds of the bloodiest conflict in our history just two years later. As a result, Peace is now an odd bedfellow to other sculptures at Hyde Park Corner, such as the massively military **Machine Gun Corps Monument**, the **Australian and New Zealand memorials** and the **Royal Artillery Monument**.

Poor Jones the sculptor lived on unrewarded and forgotten. The monument, his greatest work, was never even given an official unveiling, and he died embittered in 1938, not having even been fully paid for it.

Neither do many people know that during this era the arch housed London's smallest police station, complete with 18 officers and a cat called Snooks. This station was closed in the 1960s with the building of the road underpass leading from Piccadilly to Knightsbridge. From this point to the end of the century, the arch and sculptures suffered an ignominious period, both decaying slowly and in danger of collapse. It was only the massive intervention of English Heritage, when they'd finished the nightmare job of restoring the Albert Memorial (see page 169), that saved it; by November 2000 the Wellington Arch was restored to its full glory, with creative floodlighting dramatising the sculpture at night. Now the arch's interior is open to the public, which gives people a chance to enjoy the fabulous views over London once enjoyed only by PC Snooks.

11 **HEAD OF NEWTON**

This sculpture, located at **Butler's Wharf** in East London, is by **Eduardo Paolozzi** (1990). Does it suggest there's something mechanical about Newton, the man who reduced the orbits of the heavens, until then inexplicable, to mere natural laws of motion? Or perhaps it is a joke that, if he famously 'discovered' the laws of gravity by an apple falling on his head, this is what would result: a cracked nut. Either way, Newton's fame lives on in other ways too: if you have a £2 coin in your pocket (and aren't they satisfying things?) you'll see some of the great man's words around its rim. Heaped with praise, he said he achieved what he did because he was 'standing on the shoulders of giants'. There's another good Paolozzi bust of Newton at the **British Library** at **St Pancras**.

12 THE NAIL

At **One New Change**, a shopping mall next to St Paul's Cathedral in the City, a 40-foot-high rusty nail stick is at a five-degree tilt out of the pavement, the creation of **Gavin Turk** (b 1967). In fact it's made from bronze to look rusty. He said it was a tribute to the tiny object in a shopping development 'which probably contains no nails at all'. It could be a reference to the Cross, some say. Others are just waiting for the hammer of God that goes with it…

LONDON'S LOST AMERICAN CONNECTIONS

What could be more American than Pocahontas, Mark Twain, Harvard and Texas, for example? Here, you'll find the oddest connections with all of them, and more, and some strange stories to go with them.

POCAHONTAS

Pocahontas was that American Indian princess who famously saved the life of Englishman, Captain John Smith, who had been captured by the Indians and was about to have his brains bashed out; many people assume they fell in love with each other. She also conveniently came to stand for the empowerment of women and the proudness of Native American culture. Thus the much-misunderstood Indians themselves ensured the survival of America's first settlement by Europeans. Or so the popular misunderstanding of the legend goes, at least on this side of the Atlantic, encouraged by that rather catchy song and at least six monuments in London.

The truth was as extraordinary as, and more interesting than, the smoothed-out, politically correct version. What most people forget is that she actually became Mrs John Rolfe, not Smith, became a Christian, called herself Rebecca, and came to Britain. She's still here, having met her grave end in Gravesend from some ghastly English disease she was ill-equipped to resist. And that John Smith was more Danny de Vito than Keanu Reeves to look at.

There's very little evidence that the thing with Smith actually happened in Virginia in 1607, but then there wouldn't be. The scepticism arises only because he wrote one account not mentioning at all her role in saving him from the wrath of her father Powhattan, and then much later in 1622 wrote another that included it. Perhaps there was a good reason for this. Maybe he was embarrassed. Or maybe he had thought of a good yarn to immortalise himself. He was a known fantasist when it came to his adventures, although he was certainly a ruthless, wideboy adventurer who didn't balk at chopping off the heads of three Turks he captured on an earlier voyage.

Neither is there any evidence the legendary event did *not* take place. It was certainly the kind of hostage-taking and tit-for-tat stuff that went on, and still does in some countries. What we do know is that in the years following 1607 Pocahontas was often seen in Jamestown, Virginia, and did a great deal to reduce friction between settlers and Indians. By 1614 she had indeed become a Christian, called herself Rebecca and married John Rolfe with whom she had a son. The family arrived in London in 1616, where she was a great favourite at Court. Legend had it that she bumped into John Smith again while staying at the Belle Sauvage ('beautiful woman savage') pub in Ludgate Hill. Ironically, she died suddenly at Gravesend in 1617, just as she was about to return to her homeland; she is buried at St George's church in that town on the Kent side of the Thames Estuary. There is a statue of her there, erected by the people of Virginia. There is another, rather sexy, statue of her in offices in Vincent Square, SW1.

Not that **Captain John Smith** is forgotten. There is a statue of him in the City of London, in a garden once the churchyard of St Mary-le-Bow. He is also remembered in the **Church of the Holy Sepulchre Without Newgate** on Snow Hill, Holborn, where there is a memorial plate to him (he died in 1631) and a stained-glass window to him and Pocahontas.

This window makes Smith look like William Shakespeare, but in 2001 an extraordinary sequel emerged when crime novelist Patricia Cornwell declared she would erect new windows in the church to tell the full story. Cornwell lives in Virginia and had been in London to research her novel based here (in the Isle of Dogs).

John Rolfe, who had returned to Virginia, was killed in a surprise attack by the same tribe of Indians in 1620. They had pretended to be friends with the settlers, sharing their tables and playing with their infants, yet massacred hundreds of them that day, infants, women, children and all. So the story of the Indians ensuring the colonists' survival are a little off the mark. Their son, Thomas Rolfe, survived only because when his mother died, he had been put ashore at Plymouth to be brought up by his uncle in England.

There is also a riverside monument in **Blackwall** to the first settlers who departed from here to America on 20 December 1606.

TEXAS

Second, there's a little bit of London that is, or rather was, **Texas**. In the somewhat exclusive gentlemen's ghetto that is St James's, there was some real Lone Star Texas territory. If you go through the narrow timbered entrance on St James's Street, next to Berry Bros, you can enter **Pickering Place**, a hidden tiny 18th-century square that not many Londoners have ever seen. **No 3** was the embassy of the short-lived independent Republic of Texas for three years in the 1840s. There's a plaque on the north side. The nearby restaurant called the Texas Embassy, in Cockspur Street, complete with Lone Star flags, etc, never was the actual building. It could reasonably fly a one-star flag, however, having been the headquarters of the White Star shipping line. Yes, you should be able to eat Titanic burgers here (and you could say: 'I know I ordered ice with my drink, but this is ridiculous!').

THE FOUNDER OF PENNSYLVANIA

One of the baptisms at **All Hallows by the Tower** in 1644, in the Civil War era, was of a **William Penn** who, when he grew up, went on to found Pennsylvania. His father, Admiral Sir William Penn, was instrumental in saving this church in the 1666 Great Fire of London by blowing up houses around it to create a firebreak; he had also lent the cash-strapped King Charles II a great deal of money.

In return, in 1681 the King gave Penn's son, William, a licence to set up Pennsylvania, which he did, along Quaker lines. He also founded Philadelphia (without which we Brits wouldn't know what to call cream cheese), now one of Pennsylvania's principal cities, but he was regularly in trouble with the government in London over his radical religious non-conformity. He was as relentlessly serious as Quakers, bless 'em, sometimes are. 'No pain, no palm; no thorns, no throne; no gall, no glory; no cross, no crown,' he wrote in a 1699 pamphlet. Well, he may have been right, but would it have helped lighten things up from time to time to pop a whoopee cushion on his chair, one wonders.

He died in 1718 when Pennsylvania was well on its way and is buried just west of London at Jordans, the Quaker Meeting House near Chalfont St

Giles, Buckinghamshire. His tombstone is plain and assiduously self-effacing, as you'd expect from a broad-brimmed hat Quaker (apart from naming an entire state after yourself, of course). I've always respected Quakers whom I've met (as if my opinion mattered a jot) but I can't resist one more friendly poke at their seriousness. Victorian cleric Sydney Smith, told of a Quaker infant, retorted: 'Quaker baby? Impossible! There is no such thing, there never was. They are always born broad-brimmed and in full quake.'

THE FOUNDER OF HARVARD

Harvard's origins were humble. What could an inn-keeper's son do apart from enjoy a life of wassailing and brawling? Well, quite a lot judging by publican Robert Harvard's son, **John Harvard**, baptised in 1607 at Southwark Cathedral, then a mere parish church in the notorious South Bank district (for more about Southwark, see page 262). The infant Harvard's achievement was to found the first and most famous university in the New World. Or rather, to bequeath half his estate and his entire library of 320 books for the foundation of such a college, for he died of consumption in 1638, only a year or so after arriving in Boston. Most of his family had died from the plague in 1625, but he is remembered by a **chapel** and a **library** in **Southwark**.

AMERICAN PHILANTHROPISTS

Around London there are many homes for working people proudly labelled **Peabody Buildings**. These are a memorial to a truly great man, American banker and philanthropist **George Peabody**, saviour of the state of Maryland, the man who put the United States on the international financial map, improver of the lives and education of thousands.

George Peabody, born in 1775 in what was then South Danvers, Massachusetts, a very rich and prosperous merchant and banker, was a philanthropist.

Eventually, he moved to London and set up a soon-thriving merchant bank, helping the young United States enter the world's financial stage and rapidly making a vast fortune of $20 million which he quickly spent on others. He built libraries, museums and art galleries at Baltimore, Yale and South Danvers. In 1862, appalled at the slums and poverty in London, he gave $2,500,000 for the building of tenement blocks for working people. Many of these survive today.

He was the first American to be given the Feedom of the City of London and at his funeral in 1869, the carriages of Queen Victoria and the Prince

Everyone could use a hand parking in the city, but this giant aluminium helper may be more than you bargained for. Artist Lorenzo Quinn's vintage Fiat 500 gets a lift from his sculpture in a temporary art installation in Park Lane (d/5)

Attraction of repulsion: 'St Ghastly Grim' in the City is in fact St Olave's near Tower Hill (BL)

Christus vivere
Mors mihi lucrum
April 1658

I CAN'T BELIEVE ... IT'S NOT BUDDHA?

There are more varied, beautiful and surprising religious buildings in London than anywhere else. You just need to know where to look...

An unexpected slice of Japanese tranquillity on the South Bank – the Peace Pagoda with its gold Buddha. It was the first such pagoda to be built in any Western capital (both JR)

Just yards from Oxford Street is the surprisingly tranquil Fo Guang Temple. Please ask permission and remove shoes to view the splendid interior (BL)

This Russian Orthodox onion-domed cathedral provides a startling sight from the A4 at Chiswick. All we need now is a lot more snow, decent vodka and a sledge to Heathrow being chased by wolves (BL)

On a cathedral scale, the astounding Swaminarayan Temple, with its shining white pinnacles, has put the suburb of Neasden on the map – somewhere east of Mumbai, by the look of it (BL)

The most over-the-top Victorian church in London – All Saint's on Margaret Street – explodes with psychedelic patterns. You might need to blink a couple of times when you walk back onto the street to adjust to the grey... (RB)

Cosmic, man: Karma Kars, using Indian-built Ambassador cars imported by Tobias Moss, brings the exotic Orient to London streets (BL)

A Fortnum & Mason delivery trots through London; a refreshing change from Tesco vans hurtling along the streets (SS)

If you're a Harry Potter fan platform 9¾ at King's Cros means a lot to you, as it's there you have to rush at t brick wall with your trolley reach the *Hogwart's Expres* Looks like someone got stu half-way (BL)

ECCENTRIC TRANSPORT

Londoners sometimes feel public transport is insane. But even they would agree these examples are a bit bonkers.

Don't worry if you get confused by the flashing lights of Pierre Vivant's delightfully quirky *The Traffic Light Tree*, on the Isle of Dogs: it's designed reflect the restlessness of the nearby financial distri in Canary Wharf (JR)

hat would really cheer up
ey commuters trudging to
e station in rainy London?
now, how about a
ulpture of grey commuters
dging to the station in
ny London? *Rush Hour*, by
orge Segal (1987), near
erpool Street Station (BL)

Chiho Aoshima's painting of
anthropomorphic skyscrapers entitled
City Glow, Mountain Whisper has given
commuters at Gloucester Road something
to look at other than their papers (JR)

Oh, Christmas!
Stranger things
have happened
on the London
Tube, but don't
be surprised if
a tree comes
along for the
ride. Probably
a Metropolitan
branch (SS)

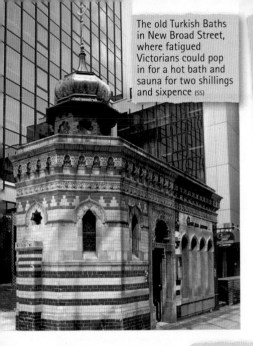

The old Turkish Baths in New Broad Street, where fatigued Victorians could pop in for a hot bath and sauna for two shillings and sixpence (SS)

A vivid splash of sunshine on the South Bank, this spiral yellow staircase takes you up to Queen Elizabeth Hall (NL/S)

PECULIAR BUILDINGS

The only thing that's predictable about London's buildings is that you will come across the totally unpredictable.

Gleaming galactic silver, the NatWest Media Centre looks like Martians have landed in leafy St John's Wood. Lord's Cricket Ground is ready for take-off... (SS)

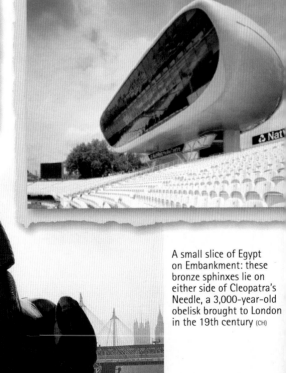

A small slice of Egypt on Embankment: these bronze sphinxes lie on either side of Cleopatra's Needle, a 3,000-year-old obelisk brought to London in the 19th century (CH)

One of the most recognisable buildings in the London skyline, the affectionately nicknamed Gherkin towers above the city's older buildings in a spiral of modernity (NR)

An iconic entrance to one of the world's finest museums, the Great Court at the British Museum is the largest covered square in Europe (AD/WC)

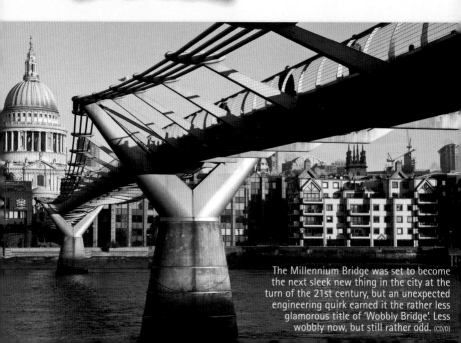

The Millennium Bridge was set to become the next sleek new thing in the city at the turn of the 21st century, but an unexpected engineering quirk earned it the rather less glamorous title of 'Wobbly Bridge'. Less wobbly now, but still rather odd. (CD/D)

FUNNY BUSINESS

Does London's global finance role make it boring? You shouldn't bank on it!

London businessmen are always trying to get a step above the competition, sometimes performing with a bit more panache in Covent Garden (ER/D)

The swirling interior of the new City Hall on t[he] South Bank near Tower Bridge is brilliant in a building without any real point, literally if no[t] figuratively (BL)

Deadline long gone at an Art Deco clock on a former newspaper building in Fleet Street (BL)

I N FASHION COURT, SPITALFIELDS, lived the young **Abe Saperstein**, founder of **The Harlem Globetrotters**. He was born in 1902 to a couple of the 100,000 Jewish refugees who had fled the pogroms of Poland, central Europe and Russia. His family, with ten children, struggled in poverty and so they migrated to America in 1905. You might not associate a five-foot-three-inch Jewish lad with basketball – a natural home for lanky often black guys – but he was excellent at it. In 1927 he took over the management of a struggling team called the Savoy Big Five and gradually the team – they were not allowed to play everywhere because of race segregation – fought its way up, winning the world title in 1940 and, arguably, making a major step forward in the battle for black people to be treated with equal respect around the world. It wouldn't have happened without, as he put it, 'the poor little Yiddish boy from the East End who made good.' Abe died on 15 March 1966 and is buried in Chicago.

How the poor little Yiddish boy from the East End made good

of Wales followed the hearse containing his coffin to Westminster Abbey. Vast crowds lined the streets, showing the respect Londoners held for Peabody. The Prime Minister was among the mourners.

After the funeral service his coffin was taken to his burial in the US at Danvers (by then renamed Peabody) by the Royal Navy's latest ship, such was the esteem in which this man was held. As he envisaged, his good works have survived into the 21st century, with 24 organisations on both sides of the Atlantic, including those housing 26,000 Londoners. A **statue** of him stands near the Bank of England in the City of London.

JACK LONDON SHOWS UP LONDON

He may not have had Peabody's money but the fearless, San Francisco-born explorer-journalist-novelist **Jack London** (1876–1916), showed the same concern for London's poor. Renowned for books such as *Call of the*

193

Wild, his courage in penetrating the most inhospitable and perilous wastes of the world came in handy when in 1902 he took a trip into the worst of **London's East End**. His resulting book, *People of the Abyss*, revealed to a wider world the desperate poverty, the over-crowding, the slums and the starvation of this area. Children starved (the word means 'to death') on the street just as they do in Third World disasters today, and with just as little need for it to be allowed to happen. His words rightly shocked the complacency and pride of Edwardian Britain. Just read this, describing a walk he took with a couple of London workmen up the Mile End Road, still, 100 years later, London's most deprived area:

> *Both kept their eyes upon the pavement as they walked and talked, and every now and then one or the other would stoop and pick something up, never missing the stride all the while. I thought it was cigar and cigarette stumps they were collecting, and for some time took no notice. Then I did notice.*

> *From the slimy, spittle-drenched sidewalk, they were picking up bits of orange peel, apple skin, and grape stems and were eating them. The bits of greengage plums they cracked between their teeth for the kernels inside. They picked up stray crumbs of bread the size of peas, apple cores so black and dirty one would not take them to be apple cores, and these things these two men took into their mouths, and chewed them, and swallowed them; and this, between six and seven o'clock in the evening of August 20, year of our Lord 1902, in the heart of the greatest, wealthiest and most powerful empire the world has ever seen.*

That was great writing and it was anger such as this, anger that the success of Britain's economy meant great wealth for a few and grinding poverty for many, that fuelled the country's great 20th-century social advances, such as the introduction of the 'cradle to the grave' Welfare State, the National Health Service, better schools, pensions, sickness benefits, etc.

BENJAMIN FRANKLIN IN LONDON

Benjamin Franklin, that splendid fellow who wrote the opening part of the American Declaration of Independence, wouldn't be a chap you'd expect to have skeletons in his closets. Certainly not ten of them. Yet the remains of four adults and six children were found at his London home in 1998 and they date from around the times he lived there: from 1757 to 1762 and again from 1764 to 1775.

The skeletons were found at **36 Craven Street**, next to Charing Cross station, when it was being refurbished and restored. So what is the answer to the mystery? This building, after all, was, *de facto*, the first American embassy in Britain, so it has a place in both countries' history. Could the founding father of American independence have been involved in some gruesome crime?

The answer, strangely, involves the eccentric bull-wrestler, buffalo collector and surgeon, **John Hunter** (see page 216). A clue lay in the skeletons themselves – most bones had been sawn, drilled or chiselled. This suggests anatomy classes for would-be surgeons, not to mention grave-robbing (see page 71), whose purpose was to supply bodies for those classes, that was rife at the time.

Franklin's landlady – the full details of their relationship are a little cloudy – had a daughter, Polly, who married a promising young surgeon, William Hewson. He was a close colleague of the anatomist, John Hunter. It seems that Hunter and Hewson may have run an anatomy school in part of the house while Franklin was in America or living further up the street.

The fact that the remains of the bodies, presumably dissected for students, were disposed of so surreptitiously suggests that those corpses were supplied, illegally, by 'resurrection men' – grave-robbers. The punishment for the crime of grave-robbing was hanging and in some cases, bizarrely, drawing and quartering – a form of dissection – as well. At the very least, those convicted of supplying or receiving stolen bodies could expect to be transported to some tropical hell-hole where life was short, hot and brutish. So under-floor burial must have seemed a sensible option. Whether the great philosopher and humanitarian Franklin knew of or condoned such

More American connections

- An astonishing story of a Red Indian chief – a Native American, that is – buried in Earl's Court, see page 224.
- For Americans, authors Henry James and T S Eliot, painter Whistler, and amazing billionaire J Paul Getty II who was saved by cups of tea, the rules of cricket and Mick Jagger, see *Cheyne Walk*, page 154.
- For Canadian links, see *Wolfe in Greenwich*, pages 306 and 177.

activities is not known, but it seems unlikely. Hewson was a pioneer in several fields of anatomy and must have learned his trade somewhere. In the end the dead got their revenge – he cut himself while dissecting a rotting corpse and contracted septicaemia, dying in 1774 aged 34.

Oddly, one of Franklin's visitors at this address included libertarian author **Thomas Paine** (1737–1809), whose bones also came to a peculiar end, this time in a pub (see page 348). **Franklin's house** is now fully restored and can be visited for studies by arrangement or as part of a 'historical experience', a re-enactment, at a cost of £8 per adult.

BENJAMIN FRANKLIN HOUSE, 36 Craven Street, WC2N 5NF
☎ 020 7930 6601 💾 www.benjaminfranklinhouse.org; or from the New Players Theatre round the corner, which acts as box office
☎ 020 7839 2006

THE ORIGINS OF DOWN UNDER

Australia, of course, has its historic links in London too. On the formal side, the church of St Mary-le-Bow in the City's Cheapside has a bust of **Admiral Arthur Phillip** (1738–1814), founder of Sydney in 1788. There is also a banner of the Order of Australia here. That's the official stuff, but the arrival of many in what was to be their home country, Australia, was a lot less comfortable than his, and undertaken rather more reluctantly: they were transported for life for, sometimes, quite trivial offences.

Millbank, on the Thames where the Tate Gallery now stands, was once the site of an area of brothels and drinking dens known as the 'Devil's Acre' plus a grim jail, Millbank Prison. Near the Tate Gallery, on the waterfront, Australians might ponder a squat **bollard** that marks the spot where thousands of prisoners in clanking chains passed 'Down Under' in a special tunnel under the road from Millbank Prison to barges which carried them downriver to ships waiting to take them to the other side of the world. This sad traffic ended in 1867.

So if it's that simple to find the origins of the expression 'Down Under', how come nobody seems to know why Aussies call the Brits 'Pommies' (or just 'bloody Poms')? The least convincing argument is that new arrivals would be Prisoners of Mother England, hence POMEs. Anyway, that would make Aussies the real Pommies, not those who stayed in Britain. I tried explaining that once in a rough drinking den in Kalgoorlie in Western Australia. The hospital food there is excellent.

ECCENTRIC BOOZERS, BEASTS AND BOGS

PECULIAR PUBS AND THEIR STRANGE STORIES

London was alcohol-soaked in the 18th century. For one thing, the water was unsafe to drink so even infants were given small beer, even for breakfast. The gin was cheap and strong, so much so that Hogarth's famed cartoon *Gin Lane*, with its drunken mother dropping her baby, was very close to the truth.

A survey of 1746 said there was one tavern to every five dwellings, and that at least one of the remaining four was a gin shop. Some 36 gallons of beer was brewed for every man, woman and child that year, while a barely comprehensible seven million gallons of gin were consumed. This was before laws limiting the strength of booze, the hours it could be served and the age of the customers allowed into pubs and gin shops. Pub landlords boasted that you could get drunk for tuppence. Free straw was provided for the unconscious in the back rooms.

So when people complain about drunken yobbery and debauchery nowadays, they haven't seen the half of it. Our ancestors would be astonished, and probably appalled, at our sobriety. It was not until World War I that the necessity to maintain munitions productions meant that pub hours and the strength of drink were strictly controlled.

Of course you don't have to get three sheets to the wind to appreciate London's wonderful collection of pubs, many of them deeply strange in their ways. Here are just a few of them:

I Am The Only Running Footman, Mayfair

This is unusual on three counts. First, it is Britain's second-longest pub name – the longest being the Green Man And Black's Head Royal Hotel in Ashbourne, Derbyshire – and London's longest. Second, its name is initially totally incomprehensible (actually, that isn't that unusual for pub names). Third, it has been taken wholesale for the title of a book by Martha Grimes, a murder mystery no less, which starts with a dead hitch-hiker in a Devon wood. In the book, another victim is found outside this pub in Charles Street near Berkeley Square, and the rest … well, you'll have to read it.

The pub itself eluded my attempts to track it down for some years until one day in desperation I said to a cabbie:

> Me: *'Take me to the I Am The Only Running Footman in Mayfair.'*
> Cabbie: *'Yer wot, Guv?'*
> Me: *'A pub in Charles Street.'*
> Cabbie: *'There ain't no pub there, Guv.'*
> Me: *'Well let's go anyway because I need to prove it doesn't exist.'*

The cabbie gave me a sideways look and probably thought about diverting to the nearest funny farm at this point but gamely went along with my delusions.

> Cabbie: *''Ere we are, no bleedin' pub, Guv.'*
> Me: *'What's that down the end?'*
> Cabbie: *'Er… looks like a pub, dunnit?'*

To my chagrin, the door merely had 'Running Footman' over it, losing the longest name in London title, so I went inside for a consolatory few pints and to read about its history.

Difficult though it is to imagine today, the nobs of Mayfair in early days required that a footman, dressed in full livery, should run before their coach or sedan chair, opening gates, paying tolls or whatever. Of course, the real reason for the presence of these 'running footmen' was to increase the pompous self-importance of their employer: 'Make way, here comes the Duke of Bombast! Make way!' That kind of thing.

There was also a group of liveried footmen whose job it was to walk behind the bigwigs to emphasise their importance even more. These equally pointless characters were known by down-to-earth Londoners as 'fart-catchers'. You get exactly the same kind of thing in big business nowadays – toadying executives hovering behind the big cheese, laughing noisily at his every joke – but not his inferior's jokes.

Anyway, the fashion for running footmen declined until there was only one poor sweating booby left, whose Mayfair master would not change with the times. Hence the pub name.

Fortified by the knowledge and its ale, I burst out into the adjoining street and was delighted to see the swinging sign still proclaiming in its full glory: 'I Am The Only Running Footman.' Saved!

Talking of sedan chairs, those rather ridiculous boxes on poles in which rich people somehow incapable of walking were carried about by poor people (quite fast too, by all accounts), there are several pubs named the **Chairmen** or **Two Chairmen** – I can think of one off Dean Street in Soho and another at the end of Queen Anne's Gate in Westminster. Naturally, you think of the wrong sort of chairman until you see the signs. There are also several pubs around Soho called the **Blue Posts**. This is to do with the blue posts located outside pubs, etc, where one waited for a chair in those days. (Why walk to a blue post when you could walk to wherever you were going?)

THE LAMB, LAMBS CONDUIT STREET

This was Charles Dickens's favourite pub when he lived at 48 Doughty Street, WC1, which can still be visited. It is a perfect example of a Victorian pub, has a bar equipped with small pivoting glass shutters designed to enhance drinkers' privacy, and, the last time I visited, truly excellent ale.

THE JOHN SNOW, BROADWICK STREET

This is famous for being the place where, yes, you've got it, John Snow solved the mystery of cholera by taking off the handle of the water pump outside. Now the beer pump handle inside is more interesting. Pictures and explanation upstairs. This is said to be Soho's oldest pub, but not vastly ancient by London standards. See Soho walk, page 251.

THE PACKHORSE AND TALBOT, TURNHAM GREEN

Goods coming into London, in this case along the old Great West Road, before the revenues raised by turnpikes allowed the roads to be improved, would often be carried on packhorses. The talbot was a hunting dog used to protect packhorsemen from the highwaymen that plagued this route. So when a traveller stopped to drink and eat at this inn, he would have left his packhorse and talbot outside, guarding the goods.

THE OLD MITRE, ELY PLACE, EC1

It may be impossible to find, but it's a gem worth seeking out. Let me

ECCENTRIC BOOZERS, etc

explain. In Holborn Circus are gates leading to Ely Place. This is so-named because it was the London residence of the Bishop of Ely so that, once past these gates, one was technically in Ely, so pickpockets and others escaping justice would head this way and nip inside during a hue and cry; the officers pursuing had to catch them before they entered or wait outside. More on this pub in the Fleet Street walk, page 239.

THE PROSPECT OF WHITBY, WAPPING WALL, WAPPING

This is a pleasant-sounding pub (named after a collier – a coal-carrying ship that brought coals from Newcastle past Whitby) that most Londoners will have heard of. But the pub's old name, the Devil's Tavern, gave a more accurate idea of its original clientele. Pirates, cut-throats, spies, loose women, coachloads of tourists, you name it. Nearby is Execution Dock where some of the pub's customers would end up being hanged; their bodies were then left in chains, tied to piles at low tide, for the tide to wash over them three times before they were buried. One such pirate, caught in the Americas, who was thus executed here has a new pub round the corner named after him in Wapping High Street – **The Captain Kidd**. The Prospect was visited by Dickens and the painter J M W Turner, both – in their own way – fascinated by the murky shadows of the river hereabouts and both of whom brilliantly captured something about the murky depths of Old Father Thames.

THE MAYFLOWER, ROTHERHITHE

The name recalls the founding fathers' ship that set sail from here in 1620 to found the New World (calling at Plymouth in Devon on the way, of course). The fact that John Smith had got to Pocahontas a few years before (see page 189) wasn't the point. This was the big one. The pub's wharf was the starting place and this building that dates from 1560 was then called The Shippe. The commander of the *Mayflower*, Captain Christopher Jones, brought his ship safely back in 1621 and its timbers were later used in rebuilding the pub, so it's not so much that the pub's part of history, but more that history is part of it. Captain Jones himself was permanently berthed in St Mary's churchyard in 1622.

THE WORLD'S END, CAMDEN

Called the **Mother Red Cap** for some 250 years; the histories tell the very strange stories of the first of the two Mother Red Caps who ran this house. The first Mother Red Cap had a child at 15 by a man called Gipsy George, who was hanged not long afterwards at Tyburn for stealing sheep. She then took up with a man called Darby, who disappeared after a few months of drunken quarrelling and was never seen again. Then her parents were convicted of killing a girl by black magic and were hanged. She took up with a third lover call Picher, who before long was found in her oven, burned to a cinder.

She was tried for his murder but acquitted after a witness declared that he often took refuge in the oven to escape her cruel tongue, and could well have been burned by accident. She then became something of a recluse, but was occasionally seen in the lanes and hedgerows, collecting herbs and berries.

During the Civil War (1642–49), she gave shelter to a fugitive, who knocked at her door one night begging for shelter. He had money and stopped with her for a few years, even though, from time to time, they were heard quarrelling. When he died there were whispers that she had poisoned him, but nothing was ever proved.

When she went out, she always wore an ugly grey cap and a grey shawl, and her huge black cat was never far behind. By this time people were convinced she was a witch, and most were too frightened to go near her, her only visitors being Moll Cut-purse the highwaywoman, and a few brave souls wanting their fortunes told or to be cured of some ill by one of her strange brews.

The night she died, people declared that they saw the Devil walk into her cottage, but no one saw him come out. She was found the next morning, sitting by a pot on the fire, her cat beside her. When the cat was given some of the contents to drink, its hair fell off in two hours, and it died soon afterwards.

The second Mother Red Cap was far more cheerful. She turned the place into an inn and brewed a rather potent ale there.

DIRTY DICK'S, BISHOPSGATE, EC2, CITY OF LONDON

This pub has a sad history of disappointment. One Nathaniel Bentley, an early 19th-century ironmonger who lived near here, was all set to marry a veritable beauty. He turned up at the church only to discover that his intended had dropped dead the night before. Desolate, he preserved the wedding feast that had been intended for the guests on the tables, spending his life in broken-hearted squalor, the cobwebs and dust gathering on the dining table as his wedding clothes turned to rags. Locally, he became known as Dirty Dick and was something of a legend. His dead cats were allowed to dry and become mummified, unburied, and eventually Dirty Dick died too.

That was the opportunity for the landlord of this pub, who bought the decaying contents of this strangely fascinating, nightmarish house and put

LONDON'S MOST EXPENSIVE BAR BILL yet was clocked up by an American gambler called Don Johnson at the One for One club in Park Lane in 2011. It included a midas of champagne (equal to 40 normal bottles) which at £120,000 might be the most expensive bottle of bubbly ever bought. That's after buying a methusalah (equals eight normal bottles) of the same at a mere £25,000, and a couple of mere magnums (two bottles). He sprayed some of the eye-wateringly expensive stuff all over the crowd, perhaps the most costly carpet shampoo in history. In contemplating the full awfulness of the bill, you might think how kind it was of them to give him the free soda water. Particularly as the service charge was more than £21,000!

Dom Perignon Luminous Magnum 2002	1 @ £750.00
Grey Goose Magnum Bt 1	1 @ £420.00
Red Bull	4 @ £5.00
Soda Water Complimentary	4 @ £0.00
Armand de Brignac Methusalah Bt1	1 @ £25,000.00
Armand de Brignac Midas	1 @ £120,000.00
SubTotal:	£146,190.00
Service (@ 15.00%)	£21,928.50
VAT:	£24,364.99
TOTAL:	**£168,118.50**

London's most expensive bar bill

them around the pub – even the dried cats. Sadly, they eventually fell to dust and were cleaned away.

However, one Charles Dickens thought the macabre story worth re-using in *Great Expectations* (probably his best book – I can't decide), where Miss Havisham is the one who never gets to eat her wedding breakfast.

THE OLD RED LION, HIGH HOLBORN, BLOOMSBURY

Another pub connected to gruesome dead stuff. When the English realised that, like royalty, republicanism sometimes stinks (and was even worse) and invited King Charles II back in 1660 for the Restoration of the Monarchy, this pub decided to do its loyal best. It exhibited the freshly dug-up corpses of some of the chief characters in the interregnum: **Oliver Cromwell**, or Lord Protector as he was styled; **Henry Ireton**, a relative of his; and **John Bradshaw**, the man who had issued the order to behead the new king's father, Charles I, just 11 years before. The bodies, which certainly pulled in the curious punters for a pint or three, stank not a little, and were the next day dragged off to Tyburn to be hanged and decapitated (the sort of penalty they have in mind nowadays for parking on those new red lines, I expect).

THE ANGLESEA ARMS, SELWOOD TERRACE, SOUTH KENSINGTON

This is where the plot was laid for Britain's most infamous – but not biggest – heist of the 20th century, the **Great Train Robbery**. Bruce Reynolds and an associate met here to decide how to rob a train. It appears they didn't intend to rob a mail train at all, originally, and not on the line from Euston where they eventually succeeded so famously. Their preferred target was a train taking a ton of gold shipped from South Africa to Southampton to the Bank of England. Exactly how they would have stopped it was not exactly clear, but when they arrived at the mainline near Weybridge in the early hours, when the train was due to arrive there they found the area swarming with police, also intent on keeping an eye on the train. But when the gang did stop a train, their plan was efficient and ruthless. They covered up a green signal on the main Glasgow–London line near Leighton Buzzard, wired up a battery to the red signal and brought the train carrying valuable mail to a halt. When the driver climbed down from his cab to phone the signalmen, he was coshed over the head and nearly killed. The gang then drove the train to a bridge over a lonely track where they threw out all the mailbags to waiting accomplices.

THE BUCKET OF BLOOD, COVENT GARDEN

This is the nickname for the **Lamb and Flag** (its modern name) where bare-knuckle fights used to see gore-a-plenty in times gone by. Today it can still be a bit of a bare-elbowed fight to get to the bar on a Friday night. The timber-fronted pub, where Floral Street meets Garrick Street and Rose Street, is said to be Covent Garden's oldest. Low beams, wood floor. Talking about fights, in 1679, the poet John Dryden was given a good thrashing just outside the Bucket of Blood for writing scurrilous stuff about the Duchess of Portsmouth.

Coach and Horses, Greek Street, Soho

London's rudest landlord, you may be relieved to know, retired in 2006. **Norman Balon** was the legendary and not-so-genial *minehost* (more of *mein führer*, frankly) at the Coach and Horses. His intellectual, writer, artist and actor regulars absolutely loved it. Here are some sayings from the great man:

> *You're barred, you're too boring to be in my pub.*
> *I don't care if you are a man or a woman, you can go now.*

To American tourists seeking sandwiches:

> *Leave now and don't come back.*
> *You're so ugly you're upsetting my customers.*

The attraction of the pub for a certain kind of grumpy English intellectual was huge in the second half of the 20th century. It was an extension of the nearby office of *Private Eye*, the satirical magazine, which held weekly lunches upstairs. It was the basis for the magazine's cartoon strip *The Regulars*. The pub interior became the setting for regular Keith Waterhouse's play *Jeffrey Bernard is Unwell* in 1989. Peter O'Toole (once, of course, Lawrence of Arabia), another customer, was the star.

Serious drinkers and thinkers drank at 'the deep end' on the Romilly Street side, while the Greek Street 'shallow end' was said to be inhabited mainly by Italians, conmen, spivs and shoplifters. In between was poured a generous serving of students from the nearby St Martin's School of Art, (one of whom inspired a Jarvis Cocker song *Common People*).

Jeffrey Bernard also used the Coach, as it was known, as an office whence he produced the celebrated *Spectator* column, *Low Life* (or rather didn't when he was too drunk, in which case the unwell line would go in the magazine). His favourite Senior Service cigarettes (strong as they come) were kept in a special cupboard.

Balon wasn't really rude: he was adopting a persona that his clientele enjoyed, and the affection seemed mutual on the day he retired to go home to Golders Green (where he could run the Kosher Horses, presumably) in May 2006. *The Daily Telegraph* caught him sitting outside while the party went on and saying somewhat out of character:

I couldn't have wished for a better life.

Then he happily went back in the pub and returned to his role as London's rudest landlord.

Typical eccentric customers, besides painters Lucian Freud and Francis Bacon, were a man who invented cat racing and a deaf poet who spoke after a particularly noisy slanging match across the bar: 'Why's it so quiet today?'

One more Jeffrey Bernard story – he'd been drinking far too long and heavily with the comedian Tony Hancock, who had urinated in his trousers, as drunks sadly do. Bernard held Hancock up in the street while they persuaded a taxi driver to take them. In the cab Hancock slid to the floor and spent ages fumbling around trying to get something from all of his pockets. Eventually he retrieved his card, which he handed to Bernard:

Hancock: *'If you ever need my help, jusht call me.'*
Bernard: *'Why on earth should I want help from you?'*
Hancock: *'Becaushe...[seriously] 'becaushe I think you might have a drinking problem.'*

OLD DOCTOR BUTLER'S HEAD, MASON'S AVENUE, EC2

William Butler did for constipation what Vlad the Impaler did for human rights, and is rightly remembered in a London pub name. A medical quack and physician to James I, his legacy was for years known widely as Dr Butler's Purging Ale. This evil concoction was made by hanging a thin cloth bag containing senna, polypody of oak, very strong spices, agrimony, maidenhair and scurvy grass in a barrel of strong ale. It had a violently laxative effect likened by its victims to the largest cannon used in the Navy. Who knows, if the Richter scale had been invented, maybe it could have measured the arsequake involved. It was sold at pubs or shops with the sign, 'Butler's Head'. One survives, now known as **Old Doctor Butler's Head** in memory of this man. It also has a collection of politically incorrect Spitfire Beer ads (see page 28).

Dr Butler probably wouldn't have come to much had he not been approached by King James, who was suffering from an agonising bad back his doctors could not cure. Butler prescribed a barrel of his purging ale – as he did for most patients – and whatever happened to the king, he forgot entirely about his back. In gratitude he conferred a degree upon Butler and appointed him Court Physician, which went down with the other doctors like a dose of something very unpleasant.

His eccentric treatments were deeply unorthodox. For the relief of epilepsy, he would ask a patient to sit still and close his eyes, then fire a pair of pistols either side of his head, inches from his ears. For malaria or the ague, then common, he would throw patients into the Thames head first. For opium overdose he had a man inserted in the belly of a freshly killed cow. They loved it, and the rich queued up to be maltreated, as they still do.

To draught from overdraft

A lot of London banks have been converted into pubs, whatever that says about Londoners' priorities.

In the days when bank managers were respectable, disinterested professionals one was in awe of, the banks provided suitably impressive, confidence-building premises, many of them marbled halls that make rather atmospheric pubs or wine bars (better than being demolished or subdivided into offices). One such in Southwark is the **Barrowboy and Banker** in Borough High Street, the proximity of both the market and the City across the river giving the pub its name. But 'barrowboy' has a wider meaning now than merely one who works in a vegetable market shouting 'luvvly mush, luvvly caullies'. It means any cheeky chirpie cockney chappie who, nowadays, may even have his own TV or radio show and earn more than most of us. But he's still a barrowboy at heart and proud of it.

Across the river is another cavernous former bank, the **Hung, Drawn and Quartered** in Great Tower Street off Tower Hill. This particularly vile form of punishment would be suitable for certain classes of traitor or rebel. Samuel Pepys records this happening outside the Tower of London in 1660 but, of course, as a literary giant he should have said (well he did write in code) 'Hanged, drawn and quartered.' Being well hanged and well hung are completely different. As a heartless toff once remarked, one is for peasants, and the other's for pheasants.

The Banker, in Cousin Lane, EC4, wasn't a bank at all. It was, and is, a railway arch beneath Cannon Street Station, and there's no rhyming slang about the name. Another truly great bank-turned-into-boozer is the **Counting House** in the City's Cornhill.

LONDON'S MOST UNLIKELY BEASTS

This city hosts a strange collection of eccentric monsters, if you know where to look. Great griffins. Battling beasts. Ugly giants. Angry devils and Nazi butterflies. And why Wyverns?

The Dacre beasts

These fabulous four, seven-foot-high, carved creatures stood menacingly in Naworth Castle, Cumbria, for 485 years until 1999, when they were unceremoniously ousted by the castle's owner, Philip Howard, who declared financial necessity the reason for such a break with the building's heritage. They are now in the care of the **Victoria & Albert Museum**.

The creatures – a Red Bull, a Black Gryphon, a Crowned Salmon and a White Ram – look as if they had stepped out of Lewis Carroll's mad poem *Jabberwocky*. But they would be particularly menacing to Scots, given that their original job was to proudly hold aloft the battle standards captured in Lord Dacre's thrashing of the Scots at Flodden in 1513.

Thomas Dacre (1467–1525) was a formidable soldier who fought on the losing side at the Battle of Bosworth in 1485, at which Henry Tudor got rid of Richard III, and so became Henry VII. Richard, of course, was the king who died, according to Shakespeare, shouting: 'A horse, my kingdom for a horse.' He definitely wasn't yelling: 'My kingdom for a crowned salmon or a black gryphon!' What Dacre was yelling was his battle cry: 'A red bull, a red bull, a Dacre, a Dacre!' Pretty frightening, eh? Dacre was evidently forgiven for being on the wrong side, and went to be on the winning side in the Battle of Flodden Field against the Scots in 1513.

It turns out, like all apparent heraldic nonsense, that the Dacre Beasts mean something. The **Crowned Salmon** represents the crest of Elizabeth de Greystoke with whom Lord Dacre eloped as a randy young man; the **Black Gryphon** represents Dacre's ancestor Ranulph de Dacre who fortified Naworth Castle in 1335; the **White Ram** represents Ranulph's wife (charming); while the **Red Bull** was Dacre's family emblem. They were all carved from a single oak tree in 1520 and are splendidly unique. Worth a look.

BRITISH GALLERIES, Victoria and Albert Museum, South Kensington
☎ 020 7942 2000 ● South Kensington

Gog and Magog

Traditional guardians of the **City of London**, these giants have headed the Lord Mayor's Show procession since the 15th century. They are ugly and enormous but basically benevolent (a kind of wooden John Prescott, you may think). They are legendary pagan giants from so far back in British history that their origin is shrouded in the mists of deepest bulldung. In fact the story is so totally ludicrous it might just be true, because if you were inventing it, you'd want to make up something faintly credible, wouldn't you? Judge for yourself.

Diocletian – the Roman Emperor – had 33 wicked daughters, for whom he selected 33 strict husbands to curb their wilful and unruly ways. The daughters, ungrateful wretches, were not happy about this, and the eldest, Alba, hatched a wicked plot to slit the 33 throats of their husbands with 33 knives as they slept, presumably having 33 nightmares. For this vile crime they were set adrift in a boat with six months' food. So far so good.

Now comes the incredible bit – they chose Britain as their destination. I mean there you are, 33 gorgeous princesses, nothing to do, a good boat and six months' grub and where would you head? Nice? Monte Carlo? Capri? Nope. How about Gravesend? Yes, instead of Miami or Mustique they chose some rainswept island in the north, inhabited by miserable rude pagans with vile manners (probably Croydon, then). Mind you, it might just have been their map reading – let's not be sexist, but you know, lots of girls holding it up the wrong way and arguing. They renamed the island Albion after the eldest sister, which has remained the poetical name for this country ever since (hence the various football teams and pubs named Albion).

These 33 foxy ladies then chose not to move in with the Druids, too busy not building Stonehenge presumably, or the hunky woad-painted animal skin-wearing Mel-Gibsonesque ancient Brits, but shacked up instead with 33 of the ugliest giants they could find. This produced a race of the most evil giants in the history of the world. Two of them, however, came to London and befriended the City (was it the beer?). They were chained on the site of the **Guildhall** to guard the place. Hence Gog and Magog have remained giant guardians of the City since time immemorial.

Or there's another angle, version B, involving Brutus, son of Aeneas, escaping from Troy and his champion Corineus, another giant, slaying Gogmagog (just one giant in this version). As a reward, Corineus is given that end of England which he calls Cornwall after himself while Brutus sets up New Troy, or London.

OK audience, vote A or B now. No, there's not a 'none of the above, you credulous dipstick' button.

An outbreak of Wyverns

A wyvern, a sort of winged dragon, if you have never met one, is a mythical medieval heraldic beast of the sort that adorns the badge of every Vauxhall car, including the splendid Vauxhall Wyvern of the fifties, a car that looked to me more like a battleship. London, however, has a coven of wyverns at **St Pancras station**, for it was the adopted heraldic beast of the Midland Railway, which spent the equivalent of £300 million on building this insanely eccentric Gothic palace. The station itself has been imaginatively and lavishly recreated as the Eurostar terminus, and the former Midland Grand Hotel, a truly superb bit of Victorian fantasy, has been restored as the St Pancras Renaissance Hotel. Wyverns don't like to be confused with…

GRIFFINS

Please don't talk about the City of London *dragons*. It upsets them, apparently. Dragons are for the Welsh and Chinese. The City's beasts are *griffins*. There's a totally rampant, cosmic and fearsome version in **Fleet Street** to mark where the Temple Bar stood and a monarch visiting the City must stop (see Fleet Street walk, page 229).

DRAGONS

A nine-foot dragon (or is it a griffin?) surmounts Wren's huge spire at **St Mary-le-Bow** on Cheapside in the City of London. It wasn't on the cheap side, as it happened, the church in fact being the costliest of Wren's post-Great Fire reconstructions, the huge tower being, to my mind, a strange architectural mishmash, no doubt accounting for some of the huge cost, but this wonderful dragon is the icing on the cake. Cheapside the road, on the other hand, is well-named for a 'cheap' which was, quite logically, a market in medieval times, as in Eastcheap and those West Country towns such as Chipping Norton, Chipping Sodbury (don't ask) or whatever.

BEASTS UNDER YOUR FEET

One of the loveliest and simplest of London's churches is the round **Temple Church of St Mary**, a 12th-century gem of a building located in that lawyers' warren south of Fleet Street (see page 229) and a star of the novel *The Da Vinci Code*. The Purbeck marble effigies of crusading Knights Templar, or their supporters, show them often with their **sleeping dogs** curled up under their feet, a charming detail. Another interesting detail about crusaders and knights' tombs is that if their legs are crossed it indicates that they died in action (or possibly while waiting for the toilet). Romantic stuff of course – nowhere does it mention that the Crusades were usually a complete cock-up, with the armies diverted into attacking Christian Constantinople instead of the Muslims in the Holy Land, because there was more money in it for the Venetians.

LANDSEER LIONS AND DOGS

The most splendid lions in London sit proudly around Nelson's Column in **Trafalgar Square**; they were created by Sir Edwin Landseer (1802–73) in the 19th century. There's a painting by John Bollantyne of Landseer working on the enormous beasts in 1864. A little more homely are his **cast-iron dogs** on each side of the porch of **St George's Church, Hanover Square**. They would have been a little late to see the wedding of Emma Hart and Sir William Hamilton in that church in 1791, but there is a connection because the naughty Lady Hamilton later became the object of Nelson's affections, his greatest love. After the Navy, of course.

FOREST BEASTS

Lurking in the park at **Crystal Palace** is an unlikely set of **concrete dinosaurs**, which emerge from the undergrowth as one wanders round the park, terrifying generations of children. Some would emerge spookily from the lake as water levels changed. It's a kind of Victorian Jurassic Park (not to be confused with the railway restaurant car favourite, Jurassic Pork). The park adjoins Crystal Palace railway station and was home to Joseph Paxton's 1851 revolutionary glass and iron Great Exhibition building, brought to the site from Hyde Park but later destroyed.

THE COADE STONE LION

This lion at the south (County Hall) end of **Westminster Bridge** is the cause of more urban myths than most sculptures. It is made of Coade stone and many a London guide will tell you that the formula for this strangely indestructible artificial stone has been lost; no-one knows where the lion came from and why there are no similar statues elsewhere.

Its source is easy: it was one of a pair that adorned the Lion Brewery that was cleared away for the Festival of Britain in 1951 (like the Millennium Dome but much more successful); one was moved here, the other to **Twickenham**, home of the English rugby team. Far from being indestructible, the Westminster Bridge lion's male appendages were thought shockingly enormous now it was at ground level, so they were trimmed back.

The formula for the kind of cement that is Coade stone was invented by Mrs Eleanor Coade in the 1760s in Lambeth and a great many Coade stone statues decorate London houses, the Royal Opera House at Covent Garden, cemeteries and country estates too. The formula was not lost – some Coade stone was made in a university laboratory in recent years. And on the subject of the rubbish that bored guides spout, a colleague heard a coach PA system announce near here: 'And this is the world's oldest hole-in-the-wall cash machine; Henry VIII used this.' More than one of the tourists on the bus turned and took a picture of it.

CORNHILL DEVILS

These three devils that decorate the building at **54–55 Cornhill**, EC3, seem to be bearing a grudge against the adjacent St Peter's Church, as indeed they do. The architect of this 19th-century building had infringed the Church's land by a few inches and, on the insistance of the rector, building work was stopped and the plans redrawn. The Devils scowl at anyone entering the church, the one near the street particularly resembling the unfortunate cleric. Next door is the splendid Counting House pub.

THE NAZIS' FAVOURITE GIANT BUTTERFLY

The Camberwell beauty has long been an object of affection in southeast London. A 20-foot by 14-foot mural on **Wells Way Library**, SE5, honours the butterfly first recorded in Camberwell in 1748. Consisting of 231 tiles, the mural was assembled from separate ceramic tiles made in the 1920s at the Royal Doulton factory in Lambeth. During World War II, the Nazis' pet traitor Lord Haw-Haw, **William Joyce** (1906–46), said on his propaganda radio programme, *Germany Calling*, that the butterfly was aiding *Luftwaffe* navigation. Winston Churchill had it blacked out within hours, so when Lord Haw-Haw repeated his claim, Churchill replied: 'What butterfly?' Lord Haw-Haw was unable to go and check at the end of the war due to a prior appointment with a bit of rope.

THE STRANGEST LOOS OF LONDON

Loos, the middle classes call them – probably deriving from the French, 'lieu' or 'place'. However, nearly every other name for the bog is a euphemism that refers to cleaning: lavatory (*laver* or *lavare* – to wash or wash away), toilet (*faire la toilette* – to wash and dress), bathroom, washroom, etc, which isn't what you go there for. Ditto the euphemistic restroom. How on earth can you rest with people trumpeting all over the place? More honest is the French *pissoir*, the colonial long-drop, or the American outhouse (when it was). Other terms are comical: khazi, throne, great white trumpet, bogs, thunderbox or the Australian 'dunny', from a British dialect word, dunnekin, meaning dung house. Technically accurate (although absurdly used, as it is, in French) is WC for water closet, the wonderful invention that cleans everything away and shuts off the stink too.

Oddly, the WC was the cause of London's worst disease outbreaks because, until it became popular, it was illegal to deposit human manure into watercourses so it was, theoretically at least, emptied into cesspits and earth closets, or taken away by 'night soil men' for fertilising fields. Increasing wealth meant everyone wanted a WC, so the affluent society became the effluent society. The stuff was then flushed from those cesspits right into the same river from where many water companies drew their supplies.

Only the arrival of the great Victorian engineer **Joseph Bazalgette** (1819–91), who created sewerage systems separate from the rivers and drains, saved the situation.

The main early producer of the 'syphonic' bog that sucks the stuff through a U-bend, thus preventing the pongs returning into the house, was Victorian inventor **Thomas Crapper** (1836–1910). His grave may be inspected at **Elmers End** cemetery in South London. It was recently rededicated with several happy Crappers in attendance. (I expect the local paper had a headline *Flushed With Pride*.)

Thus we had the splendid spectacle of elaborate Victorian cast-iron and porcelain bogs proudly branded 'The Crapper'. Incidentally, I've heard many an intelligent person say that is the origin of the eponymous verb, but I have to pooh-pooh the idea, as the said verb appears in medieval literature. Nor did he invent the water-closet; he was just good at it: the vitreous virtuous. It's a fascinating subject; someone should open a London loo museum, because there'd be a lot to go on.

SOME OF LONDON'S FINEST BOGS

It may not have been a question that ever occurred to you – would a view of anteaters make your visits to the loo more interesting? The men's lavatories at **London Zoo** have a special porthole for such a purpose. Or maybe it's for the anteaters to watch what humans do...

The urinal in the **Warwick Arms** pub in Warwick Road, **Kensington**, has a daily paper framed dead ahead of men's gaze. Many bars have followed suit. Some North London wine bars have scenic views behind glass on their urinals, so you can pee on Austria or whatever.

The mind-boggling prospect of a **female urinal** came to pass in 2000 with the **Standolet**, a thing shaped like an upside-down racing bike saddle. One was installed in the Soho bar, Pop, but I gather they haven't taken off. Some people may try to wash their hands in them. Women tell me what they want is more bogs, not less privacy and wet shoes.

The **Roof Garden** in **Kensington High Street**, formerly Derry & Toms department store, features the most fabulous urinals, in a room whose brilliant lighting is typical of this, a most modern department store when it was built in the 1930s. The urinals are of the Adamsex Radio brand: I have a Radio ceramic hot water bottle from this era which could perhaps be explained in that it radiates heat, but what exactly does a urinal radiate? Don't answer that.

The splendid Victorian **Princess Louise** pub in **Holborn** has some splendid Victorian bogs. Time was – I'm told – when the glass cisterns had goldfish swimming about in them. They must have got swirled around a bit when flushed, and may have provided the odd flash in the pan if they were very unlucky. The thing is, can anyone remember this or is an old drunk pulling my leg? An urban myth, I'm assured, but one that got into two films – with goldfish specially introduced for the cameras.

The **Notting Hill Florist, Westbourne Grove** is a new building that contains a florist at one end and a public bog at the other, which has to be something of a challenge, fragrance-wise. It's hard to see any connection between florists and lavatories, their purposes being somewhat divergent. Of course, there's a fine plant called *Helleborus fetidus* (the much-maligned stinking hellebore) but a florist is unlikely to stock the humble dandelion, known to Shakespeare as the 'piss plant' and to the French as '*piss-en-lit*'. This is because of the severe diuretic qualities of the dandelion. The odd leaf in a salad is all very well but don't try serving all your dinner guests dandelion root coffee as I once did before attending a *Missa Solemnis* at St Albans Abbey. Everyone was bursting for relief by the end of the first part. And the second part? Well… back to Notting Hill, where this modern building serves two rather different necessities rather well. Why not?

London's most famous mayor, **Dick Whittington**, when he wasn't passing political motions, gave some thought to the need for public loos and came up with a typically practical solution. Every City ward (an administrative division) then had at least one public latrine (I think things were so much better run in the Middle Ages), but this wasn't always enough. In 1419 he had built, at his own expense, the most sociable super-bog in London, the **Long House**, roughly at the northern end of **Southwark Bridge**. There were places for 60 men and 60 women and the thing was purged twice a day by the tide. There were even almshouses for five pensioners above the stalls. Hopefully the oldsters' sense of smell had gone by the time they took up residence, but, sadly, this rather nice place for an afternoon chat was destroyed by the Great Fire of 1666.

Having laughed at the 'filthy froggies' for having hole-in-the-floor bogs for many years, we now face their revenge. Yes, they have out-bogged us while we weren't looking. *Voila!* The French-designed, self-cleaning, vandal-proof, fully automatic Gallic thunderbox, which I have dubbed **Robobog**. You enter these things, half sanitaryware, half machine, all bog, through a sliding door that hisses shut as if preparing you for a moon mission. After you leave, they go through some mysterious cleaning cycle whereby the thing is probably turned upside down and blasted with death rays or something. Has anyone ever been trapped in one during the cleaning cycle? Could this explain disappearances in London? These Schwarzeneggers of sanitaryware are all over London; some enlightened authorities (such as Hammersmith) have even made them free. *Formidable!*

The urethra! moment of invention

A BAR IN TOOTING, South London has installed in its men's toilets Britain's first urine-controlled computer game. The screen above the loos is controlled by the direction on the stream below. Talk about Nintendo Wee...

The games at the Exhibit pub include Off The Piste, where you are skiing down a mountain and have to try to hit penguins which pop up. And a general knowledge one called Clever Dick (with multiple choice).

Rather worryingly, the games are described as hands-free (no wonder men make such a mess). Ladies may, I'm afraid, feel left out but looking on the bright side, beer sales have soared as customers vie for the nightly title, Peer of the Realm.

Part Three

BIZARRE BITS OF INNER LONDON

EARL'S COURT

IRISH GIANTS AND
SPARROW'S KNEECAPS

Earl's Court – a great place for gunshot wounds, female nutcases, venereal disease and asylum seekers. Not today, when the place bustles round the clock, but in the 18th century, when it was still an isolated farm surrounded by market gardens. The farm is shown on a 1787 map, reached by a turning north from a crossroads on Brompton Lane, as you still can, if you don't mind being killed by one-way traffic hurtling south.

From early times it had been the **principal farm** in the area and thus a **manorial court**. A tenants' charter of 1610 says:

> *By custom any tenant may call a court, at his own charge, without suit unto his lord, the stewards and tenants to have their dinners provided and the steward to be pleased for his pains.*

How you pleased a steward in those days wasn't specified.

But by the 18th century, **Earl's Court House** was a substantial mansion. ('Barons Court', by the way, was just a bit of snobby, or possibly humorous, fiction to call the next stop on the District Line. It's just lucky they didn't carry on the line to Little Chalfont, which by my reckoning would have been 'Lord High Panjandrum Supreme Emperor of the Entire Galaxy's Cosmic Court'.)

Here at Earl's Court lived the strangely eccentric but pioneering anatomist **John Hunter** (1728–93), who was fascinated by the bodies of exotic species, and had first refusal on all the beasts that died in the 'London Zoo' of those days – the menagerie at the Tower of London. In fact he started a small zoo of exotic species at Earl's Court, where buffaloes, cattle, exotic goats, zebras, leopards, ostriches, eagle owls and snakes lived.

His oddest habit was wrestling with bulls, even odder when you find he was small in stature, so much so that the queen gave him a small one that

THE EXCELLENT HUNTERIAN COLLECTION at the Royal College of Surgeons at Lincoln's Inn Fields is open 10am–5pm Tuesday–Saturday and is free. Please bear in mind that this is a world-respected medical institution not a tourist destination. More info: ☎ 020 7869 6560 or email museums@rcseng.ac.uk ⊖ Holborn (Piccadilly Line), turn left (south) down Kingsway, turn left on Sardinia Street, keep going into Lincoln's Inn Fields and it's on the right. Or if in exploring mode, strike north from Temple (District and Circle lines). It's not for the squeamish. It's also just a femur's throw from the Soane Museum (see page 80).

The Hunterian Collection

was his favourite opponent. He was once trapped under a bull that had got the better of him and would have died if a manservant had not bullwhipped the beast.

Hunter made a name for himself by treating gunshot wounds and venereal diseases (separately, one sincerely hopes), although some said he was not properly qualified. He accumulated almost 14,000 stuffed animals or skeletons that added greatly to knowledge of comparative anatomy. He secretly bought the body of the then famous eight-foot-tall Irish giant, **Charles Byrne** (against the deceased's wishes he'd asked to be buried at sea because he feared anatomists taking his body apart), and, buying an especially huge pot for the gruesome purpose, boiled down the body and reassembled the bones into a remarkable skeleton that joined the other exhibits in his museum. What happened to the rest of this horrendous Irish stew is not recorded.

Eventually, after Hunter got rather angry at a meeting at St George's Hospital and dropped dead in 1793, his amazing collection was accepted by the Royal College of Surgeons of England. The Irish giant's skeleton still occupies pride of place in a glass case, and a portrait of Hunter hangs there too. The picture shows him at his desk with a book on skulls, a ghoulish specimen in a jar and part of a huge creature's skeleton hanging behind him. For details of how to visit, see the box above.

Following his death the house became a lunatic asylum for posh ladies who wanted to escape the public provision at Bedlam, and there was another one on Old Brompton Road at Cowper House, where Melton Court now stands.

I asked an eminent British surgeon and medical author whether he'd heard of John Hunter and received the following explosion worthy of James Robinson Justice in the *Doctor in the House* films:

Heard of him? John Hunter? Of course I've heard of John Hunter! He is one of the all-time British medical greats. Don't you know anything? His collection at the RCS was bombed in the war but a lot of it remains. I don't know whether the giant is still there. They would willingly let you in if you ask nicely – mention my name, I'm a Fellow. When he was investigating VD he courageously inoculated himself with infective material and may or may not have got syphilis as a result.

He had an only slightly less famous brother, William, who was also a physician and ran an anatomy school in Windmill Street near, or actually at, where the Windmill Theatre famous for dancing girls now stands, or stood. There's a joke in there somewhere about living and dead anatomy! Ha ha!

His name is held in the greatest reverence by us surgeons and there is a very old Hunterian Society. He had angina and knew that emotion was bad for him and said that any scoundrel who made him angry held his [Hunter's] life in his hands, but he persisted in fierce internecine politics at St George's and died therefrom. He was a genius.

Today there's a statue of Hunter at Leicester Square (where he later lived) and a massive one at St George's Hospital, Tooting (where that hospital ended up) plus a university in Australia named after him. And the giant's bones *are* still in the collection.

Earl's Court House was demolished in 1886 and Barkston Gardens built on the site.

The Victorian and earlier amateur anatomists, ornithologists, dinosaur hunters, etc, were often far from complete crackpots and their work led directly to the creation of the great museums we enjoy today, or to smaller personal museums such as the Horniman's, Pitt Rivers, or Soane's (see page 80). Nevertheless there is something odd about people who wrote letters to the Natural History Museum. One opened:

Dear Sir,

I am extremely interested in anatomy and – you must have plenty – will you please send me one horse's clavicle and a pair of sparrow's kneecaps.

EARL'S COURT TODAY

The unique character of Earl's Court – which, to overstate it a tad, gives it a seedy 24-hour rootlessness reminiscent of the film *Blade Runner* – is connected with the transience of its population and the multi-occupation of its large houses. It has been described as a reception centre for whatever ethnic group or desperate refugees are currently arriving at Heathrow, as the road and Tube from the airport lead to the capital through this district. This might be true now, but the neat explanation evaporates historically when you realise that the district featured cheap boarding houses from long before Heathrow and the refugee ghetto idea goes back at least to World War I when a million Belgian refugees fled the German invasion for fear of atrocities (very wisely, as it turned out) and several thousand ended up right here.

In the 1960s, the arrivals were largely **Australians** of the Rolf Harris or Clive James variety and the place was nicknamed 'Kangaroo Valley' or 'Dingo Gulch'. I can forgive Clive James anything for his brilliant description of the late Barbara Cartland's eye make-up: 'Like two crows that had collided with a chalk cliff.' But I'm not sure about Rolf Harris.

On the plus side, this makes the place constantly cosmopolitan, tolerant and interesting – didn't the then unknown Bob Dylan play at the Troubadour? Isn't there great jazz from time to time? Where else can you get Iranian groceries at 2am? Or a gay hang-out with no hang-ups? How much less boring than snooty Brompton just down the road, you may think.

You might imagine the great houses in the area have gone to seed in this process, but the truth is that the poshness that spread like golden syrup oozing through silver cutlery, from Mayfair's top-drawer sterling silver into Knightsbridge and Kensington's silver plate, never quite reached slightly tarnished Earl's Court, made of baser metals – and not entirely stainless.

Yes, the huge wedding-cake terraces of smarter bits of West London were ideal for well-to-do Victorian families of perhaps nine children and four servants, but how many people live like that nowadays? Even then there were many people who were neither servant nor master but just wanted temporary accommodation – a problem for snobs in the neighbouring upmarket wedding-cake terraces.

Even as close to Earl's Court as **Gloucester Road**, multi-occupancy of a building was often seen as lowering the tone. In Queen's Gate Gardens, near Gloucester Road, a woman who wanted to use one of these large houses as a boarding house in 1906 was reluctantly granted permission by the freeholder on the condition that no one called or whistled for a cab nearby and that windows were constantly curtained in such a way that no one in the street could see people seated inside.

Less snobbish Earl's Court itself – although part of that borough – has always been less worried about lowering the tone and has lustily embraced these changes. Houses have been divided up from the earliest times (that is, the 1870s) if not built as flats. Or just rooms for letting.

A GREAT CARRY ON, AND MORE IRISH ECCENTRICS

Thus generations of students and struggling actresses (struggling on the floor with MPs in Chelsea strip, in at least one case) have leavened the mix. The social change brought by the building of the Earl's Court area was rather sudden. The place was utterly re-invented in less than 20 years.

There is a charming photo in the borough archives of Earl's Court Farm in the 1860s, showing chaps sitting around in farm carts, wearing straw hats, with market-garden produce growing in the foreground. This was demolished in 1875 to make way for the railway station and associated housing. The coming of the District Railway changed everything.

Roads were laid out rapidly, some, such as Kempsford Gardens and Eardley Crescent, ingeniously cramming houses into the curve made by the railway junction, giving them the pleasing architectural unity they have today.

But Eardley Crescent, despite its orderly layout, has seen a few real characters. The great *Carry On* film star, **Hattie Jacques** (1922–80), who was also the matron in the above-mentioned *Doctor in the House* films, lived here.

Earlier, 58 Eardley Crescent was home to John Butler Yeats, an Irish painter, and his sons **William Butler Yeats** (1865–1939), and Jack B Yeats. The Yeats, particularly Mrs Lily Yeats, hated Earl's Court, or rather their cramped home, and later moved to leafy Bedford Park.

W B Yeats went on to become poet laureate, and not such a useless one as they often are. (Odd, when you think about it, how, when many of England's greatest heroes and intellectuals – such as Shaw, Yeats, Wilde, Swift and the Duke of Wellington – were in fact Irish by origin or connections, people used to tell jokes about Irish people being stupid. *That's* what I'd call really thick.)

Anyway, Jack B Yeats became a painter and died in 1957 having written a rather good epitaph for himself:

Under no stones
Nor slates
Lies Jack B
Yeats.
No heaped up rocks.
Just a collection box,
And we thought a Nation's Folly
Would like to be jolly
And bury in state
This singular Yeat.
But they were not so inclined
Therefore if you've a mind
To slide a copper in the slot
'Twill help to sod the plot.

So is this carved in the adjacent Brompton Cemetery? Not a bit of it. He's in Mount Jerome Cemetery, Dublin, and as for sods, they didn't even carve his bit of doggerel on the tombstone. Mind you, his poet brother's painting was bloody awful too. Which leads us neatly to perhaps the very best bit of Earl's Court across the road from the southern end of Eardley Crescent, on the south side of Old Brompton Road…

THE DEAD CENTRE OF EARL'S COURT

The most interesting residents of Earl's Court will definitely be in if you call round, for they are all dead. The massive **Brompton Cemetery** offers fascinating encounters, marvellous monuments, real heroes and villains, peaceful strolls and a surprising amount of greenery and wildlife.

London's church graveyards were literally bulging with the dead by 1800 and radical measures were needed (see pages 56–59). Great new cemeteries were opened with private capital behind them after the cholera outbreak of 1831. One of them was the **West London and Westminster Cemetery Company**, which opened these grounds, then outside London, in 1840. In fact, not enough people died (blame the new sewerage) – fewer than 100 customers in the first year, and London wasn't near enough. Soon, with the rapid spread of London up to and past the cemetery, more people were falling off their perches and the project became dead successful.

Not just quantity, it must be said, looking round this slumbering city of the dead, but quality too. The cemetery is positively brimming with artists, actors, singers, engineers and businessmen (two still familiar names among the last are **Samuel Sotheby**, who went for the last time in 1861, and **Sir Samuel Cunard**, who docked here in 1865). Yet another Irishman, the great journalist and *Times* correspondent in the Crimea, **W H Russell** (1820–1907), dubbed the world's first war correspondent, reached his final deadline here in 1907. The doctor who helped conquer cholera, **John Snow** (1813–58, see page 259), is without a healthy pulse here too. He also pioneered anaesthetics, using ether or chloroform, which must have been a great relief to those facing sawbones surgery (see page 73). It was certainly a relief to Queen Victoria, who took chloroform from Snow in 1853 at the birth of her son Prince Leopold – the first royal to use anaesthetic.

The founder of Chelsea Football Club, whose stand is next door, **Sir Henry Mears** (1873–1912), is here; his bones perhaps gently vibrate to the chants of 'Chelsea' on weekend afternoons. The great boxer **'Gentleman' John Jackson** (1769–1845), champion of England for many years, whose tomb is marked by a lion, once taught Lord Byron to box at his boxing academy. **Percy Lambert** (1881–1913) is here, first person to drive faster than 100mph, and who died… guess how. Plus the surveyor who named Mountt Everest, **Major General Sir Andrew Waugh** (1810–78) finally peaked here.

The great suffragette leader, **Emmeline Pankhurst** (1858–1928), was buried here, having won votes for women. Emmeline was force-fed in her hunger strikes before World War I, but once the war started put her energies into recruiting women for munitions work. Her rather beautiful grave records her, possibly rather oddly by modern feminist thinking, as simply 'Wife of R M Pankhurst'. She died after the aim of her life's work, the second Representation of the People Act, was passed.

Heroes are here too, such as Flight Sub-Lieutenant **Reggie Warneford**, VC (1891–1915), who, in 1915, brought down one of the much-feared Zeppelins over Ghent. This is particularly relevant here, as German bombers violently raised the dead in Brompton Cemetery in World War II, as the shrapnel marks on monuments near the north gate show. It was even suggested they blew up people previously blown up in World War I. If so, that's Teutonic thoroughness for you. On the other hand, perhaps they wanted to get old Warneford again, just to make sure.

DEAD ZEPPELIN'S GREATEST HITS

How long does it take nowadays for a courageous soldier, sailor or airman to be given a medal for bravery in battle? Months? Years?

Consider then this announcement from June 1915:

*His Majesty the King has sent the following telegram to Flight
Sub-Lieutenant Warneford:*

*I most heartily congratulate you upon your splendid achievement of
yesterday, in which you single-handed destroyed an enemy Zeppelin. I have
much pleasure in conferring upon you the Victoria Cross for this gallant act.*

GEORGE RI

This was from King George V, Rex Imperator (King Emperor) straight to
the ordinary airman and the speed of his recognition of Warneford's feat
indicates one thing: how desperate the British were to combat the **German
Zeppelin menace**.

Aircraft with wings were then primitive, made of wood and cloth with
puny, unreliable engines, difficult to control and likely to crash at any
time. The Zeppelin was a more reliable hydrogen-gas-filled cigar-shaped
balloon that enabled the Germans to go high above the reach of British
guns and bomb London with impunity. There was little that could be done
about these great silver menaces in the sky and even at this early stage there
was little pretence that military targets were being aimed at. The German
press published gleeful cartoons of men, women and children being blown
to pieces.

So although the number of bombs the Zeppelins were carrying was
small, the British were desperate for countermeasures. On that day in
1915 Flight Sub-Lieutenant Warneford – the RAF had yet to be formed,
so he was, in fact, a sailor – was flying a Morane aircraft over Belgium and
saw a Zeppelin, L37, returning from bombing Britain. Single-handed, he
flew to 6,000 feet and then manually tossed bombs on to the enemy while
trying to control the unstable aircraft at the limit of its altitude.

At least one of the bombs exploded, and those who have seen that amazing
film of the German civil airship the *Hindenberg* crashing, will know what
happened next – a huge unstoppable conflagration as the hydrogen inside
caught fire and escaped from the plunging Zeppelin.

Warneford's plane was caught by the blast, said the *Times* man in a
dispatch, and turned upside down so all his remaining petrol fell out of the
tank. Warneford calmly landed Biggles fashion on a Belgian road behind
German lines, filled up his tank from a spare can, restarted the engine and
took off for home.

The Dutch newspapers carried a different account that hints at civilian
casualties on the ground, but perhaps would have said explicitly if there

FAR MORE EXOTIC A TALE is that of Brompton's most extraordinary burial, that of a Red Indian brave, a chief in fact, whose life and death have proved equally dramatic and turbulent.

His bullet-scarred and sabre-slashed body lay here in Earl's Court for a century but has now gone. **Long Wolf** was undoubtedly a great warrior and the evidence suggests he took part in the Sioux people's greatest victory, the wiping out of Custer's 7th Cavalry at the **Battle of Little Big Horn** in 1876.

It was a last act of defiance on the part of a proud people standing in the way of the unstoppable juggernaut of history; the settlement of the Indian hunting grounds by millions of immigrants went ahead, ending their way of life. The humiliated American government could not let the Indian triumph stand (any more than the British felt the mutiny by real Indians in the same era could go unpunished).

The Red Indian culture was subjugated, its fighting prowess destroyed, historic freedoms lost – and replaced with different ones – and the proud chief could not bear it. He was told there was a great opportunity in London for a man of his romantic standing (to Londoners) and rather than exist in some reservation by permission of his former enemies as a second-class citizen, he came to London.

The Indian hero Long Wolf, and the falling Star

Here, in Colonel 'Buffalo Bill' Cody's **Wild West Show** at Earl's Court exhibition centre (see below), he was a huge success. He was no mere foreign curiosity put on display like a caged animal; he was respected and even a little feared by the awed crowds. He was the real thing, every inch a great chief.

were any, and has the action at a lower altitude. On 8 June 1915, *The Tyd* wrote:

> *Yesterday, at dawn, a Zeppelin appeared near Ghent, pursued by two Allied airmen. The German guns posted on the parade ground and at other points*

Sadly, as with Indian Princess Pocahontas (see page 189), such a proud Indian could defeat the white man's guns and swords, but could not cope with his common diseases. Long Wolf died of a cold that developed into pneumonia in 1892. A post-mortem examination at the West London Hospital described a body 'covered in gunshot wounds and sabre cuts'. So much for anyone who doubted Long Wolf's story.

Long Wolf's grieving wife and his daughter, Lizzie, could not afford to take his body back to America, although he expressed a wish to return to his homeland on his deathbed. They buried him in **Brompton Cemetery** (with a child performer, Star, who had fallen from a horse) and left for a lonely sea voyage home. For a century, that was the end of the story, the grave forgotten as wars, kings and queens came and went.

A dusty book about Long Wolf, written by explorer and MP Robert Cunningham Grahame, and an extraordinarily persistent Worcestershire housewife, **Elizabeth Knight**, who spent six years trying to track down Long Wolf's details and his people in America after reading it, resorting to advertisements in the American press, were instrumental in changing all that. Plus Lizzie's daughter, **Jessie Black Feather** (b 1910), who was not content to leave grandfather Long Wolf's grave forgotten 'somewhere in London'.

Eventually, in 1997, there followed an exhumation from West Brompton, a horse-drawn funeral procession through London, a flight to America and a combined Christian and Indian burial ceremony at Pine Ridge Reservation, South Dakota, near the site of the Wounded Knee massacre, the ancestral burial ground of the Oglala Sioux.

Jessie Black Feather, then aged 87, was quoted as saying that her grandfather's soul would not have been at peace until his body had come home. Perhaps Jessie, and that extraordinary woman from Worcestershire, both gained some kind of peace.

in the town opened a terrible fire on the aeroplanes, which were trying to cut off the Zeppelin's return. The airship was flying over St Amandsberg and attempting to escape the airmen by descending. The Zeppelin had already had a skirmish with its pursuers, as it was listing to the left side. Shots were exchanged with the pursuers, of whom one was daring enough to approach close to the dirigible in an attempt to fly over it. After a sudden bold swoop this airman was seen to drop some explosives on the Zeppelin, which was at once enveloped in flames. The balloon covering was fiercely burning, and, after some minor reports and one big explosion, the dirigible dropped on the convent school of St Amandsberg.

Not that this stopped the Zeppelin menace overnight. But the aircraft sent up to meet them were improving, and forward-firing machine-guns with incendiary bullets were not good news for Zeppelin owners. In September 1916, the first Zeppelin to be shot down over England fell at Cuffley, Hertfordshire, just north of the M25, after being attacked **by Lieutenant William Leefe Robinson** of the Royal Flying Corps. He, too, became an instant hero; he was awarded the Victoria Cross, a rather good monument was built by newspaper readers at Cuffley and a pub, the Leefe Robinson, was named in his honour, at **Harrow Weald**, Middlesex (northwest London).

And Warneford is far from the only **VC-holder** in this fascinating cemetery. There are five more, some of whom won the award during the Indian Mutiny of 1857–58. Another grave, intriguingly, is that of **Alice Mary Adams**, wife of a clergyman awarded the VC during the Afghan War; one of the others is **Private Parkes** of the 4th Hussars, decorated for his part in the Charge of the Light Brigade.

Other notables connected with this cemetery include:

JOHN WISDEN Cricket fans will need no introduction to this chap, for they will read Wisden's cricket almanac regularly, the bible of the sport. Here his grave is aptly marked with bat and ball. It was Wisden who said on seeing the mountainous waves of the Atlantic Ocean for the first time: 'What this pitch needs is ten minutes of the heavy roller.'

GEORGE GODWIN Local boy, born in Brompton, who contributed hugely to the area's architecture. A prodigy who won a medal for his treatise on concrete aged just 20, he campaigned for better housing for the poor and had an eccentric obsession with chairs. He collected those belonging to the famous – Shakespeare, Pope, Napoleon, Thackeray, Byron, etc. His memorial has two mourning maidens and a lamp of learning, as well as his portrait – but no chairs.

BEATRIX POTTER The legion of fans of the creator of Peter Rabbit, Jeremy Fisher *et al* will, having spotted her name on this page, be dashing to their old-fashioned typewriters to tell me she's not buried here, and they are right. Not that they know where she's buried either, for the eccentric Miss Potter desired her shepherd Tom Storey to scatter her ashes on her favourite spot on her Cumbrian farm after her death in 1943. He revealed its location to no one except his son, who died in 1989, so we shall never know.

However, she was raised in London around the corner from here and a fascinating bit of literary detective work in 2001 suggested she may have got the inspiration for naming her characters from Brompton graveyard rather than her beloved Lakeland. Her 23 animal stories with those lovely colour plates of her watercolours were published from 1902 onwards, and if you ever loved these books you will agree it is no coincidence that these names can be found in the cemetery: Peter Rabett, Jeremiah Fisher, Mr Tod, Mr Nutkins, Mr Brock and Mr McGregor.

Amateur sleuth **James Mackay** even found an early version of the Jeremy Fisher stories in which Potter had named her character Jeremiah, as on a headstone here. I'm convinced, Mr Mackay, although if you find a Flopsy, Mopsy and Cottontail I'll eat a row of soporific lettuce.

MAKING A COMPLETE EXHIBITION OF ITSELF

The main reason for Earl's Court being known to the outside world must be the huge **exhibition centre** that fronts Warwick Road. This vast building is a West London landmark and is visible from vantage points for miles around, the roof looking like the upturned hull of some gigantic ship that has somehow come to grief here.

You could say cathedral-like space for both buildings, but you'd be wrong. Cathedral builders didn't have steel and concrete and couldn't span these immense halls without interruption. Here one might see an entire fishing village, complete with harbour and boats floating in it, constructed for the Boat Show in January, or mini mountains of real snow at the annual ski show. The Royal Tournament (before it was banned for effectively being too British by New Labour) featured realistic battles with real cannon fired across the arena. Massive crowds greet the megastars of pop, rock and opera here too – Madonna and Pavarotti, for example.

Yet the siting of this extraordinary asset is entirely down to a side effect of Victorian technology. **Earl's Court station** is on a straight bit of track, perhaps half-a-mile long, between two triangular junctions. Being railway triangles, these are large with inwardly curved sides.

When the building boom followed the railway in the second half of the 19th century, at first the roads simply curved to fit in with the tracks behind (Eardley Crescent on one side and Philbeach Gardens on the other). The question arose for the Metropolitan District Railway Company of what to do with the vast triangle within the railway junction.

Enter entrepreneur **John Robinson Whitley** (1843–1922), who in 1886 was travelling in the United States and decided to bring a Wild West show to London. His instincts as to what Europeans wanted to see of America – sharp-shooting cowboys, wagon trains, bareback-riding, headdress-wearing whooping Indians, and feats of knife-throwing, archery, fire juggling, etc – were absolutely spot on. The massive site, located then, as now, between four railway stations that could rapidly deliver thousands of customers, was rapidly transformed by masses of labourers over that winter, many of them railway navvies, to include a large arena and stand, an exhibition building and extensive pleasure gardens, built with the aid of bridges over the tracks at all angles.

It opened in 1887 and was a rollicking success, and secured the future of this site for the more than a century that has passed since, although in 2012 there were threats of redevelopment.

Colonel 'Buffalo Bill' W F Cody was in charge of the acts that Whitley had encouraged to come from America, and the public loved them. It was the beginning of the fascination that continues today in Europe for Western films and novels, and Britons, led by Queen Victoria herself, flocked to see it. The crowned heads of Europe made visits while supposedly in London to pay their respects to the old Queen Empress who was, at Earl's Court at least, amused at last.

The theme of the shows changed over the years with varying success, but memorable hits were made with what we would today call theme park rides: the first 'Water Chute' (in which you rode down a railed track in a kind of boat and shot across an artificial lake with great sheets of water and much screaming from nervous passengers) and a Great Wheel at the end of the century which, several people have pointed out, was a more massive ancestor of the London Eye wheel on the South Bank erected 100 years later. London history repeated yet again.

FLEET STREET

FLEET STREET AND SMITHFIELD WALK

This is a circular walk of less than two miles, which will take you about three hours. You start and finish at Blackfriars, with an optional halt halfway at Farringdon station.

The **river Fleet**, one of London's seven lost rivers north of the Thames (see page 129), was once a pleasant rural stream, and at this end a river big enough to float a boat – hence 'Fleet' – in the lower reaches. But since the Middle Ages it has carried so much of London's filth and muck that people

THE REST OF THIS book includes walks around districts of London **A note about walks** that I love. Obviously, I have done all these walks (unlike some guide writers!) and thoroughly recommend them. However, they vary in length and are also just a convenient way of telling you some rollicking good yarns you would equally enjoy sitting in an armchair in Arkansas. Walking ain't compulsory! As you can't easily read while you walk, one approach would be to read them first and see what interests you and just visit those bits, or take breaks at the suggested watering holes and have a good read there. There are often escape routes at halfway points to help the less energetic. Just enjoy it and don't treat it as a Death March that must be endured while cursing the author...

who fell into it were sometimes found asphyxiated, legs in the air; on one occasion the by then covered-over river blew up from the accumulation of evil gases, destroying a few houses.

Today we will cross and recross it and never be far from it, yet will not see it. But it is silently slipping through the darkness under our feet towards Blackfriars Bridge, where it has an outfall you can really see only from a boat on the river. Its unseen presence explains the geography of the whole district.

Leaving Blackfriars Tube station, take the tunnel under the road, leaving by Exit 1, and take a look at the quite extraordinary decoration of the **Black Friar pub**, a rare gem of a place, and our first contact with the monastic heritage that once dominated this area (see page 274 for its history).

FLEET STREET AND SMITHFIELD WALK

We go on up the right-hand side of New Bridge Street, with tantalising glimpses of **St Paul's** to the right and **St Bride's** pretty spire, the model for the world's wedding cakes, on the left. When we pass **Apothecary Street** on the right, we are almost opposite the old **Bridewell Prison**, where people would pay to see semi-naked women flogged in a special chamber.

The major junction here is **Ludgate Circus** and I recommend crossing to the further corner (straight across) to get our bearings, and one of the finest views in the land. Standing on the corner and looking back towards Blackfriars and the river, it's worth realising that a dock as wide as the street reached up here from the Thames before the new road bridge (Blackfriars) was built. Ships and even river pirates lurked here. Looking in the opposite direction, this is the valley of the Fleet and the bridge over it in the distance is Holborn Viaduct, a road we'll encounter later. Holborn means 'hollow bourn' or 'valley of the stream'.

Looking east (that is to your left if you're facing back to Blackfriars) there's a **magnificent view of St Paul's** – actually, its best view. The contrasting slender black bulb of a spire in the foreground is almost too perfect a part of the composition to be a happy accident. In fact Sir Christopher Wren, the masterful architect of St Paul's – whose tomb inside the cathedral is marked *Si monumentum requiris, circumspice* or 'If you require a monument, look around you' – also had to fix a new spire on this church, **St Martin within Ludgate**, in the aftermath of the 1666 Great Fire. So he made it a perfect foil for his cathedral – without telling the parishioners why he chose the odd steeple.

Looking in the opposite direction up **Fleet Street** – and the hill on each side reveals that we are in a river valley and that Ludgate Circus was once a bridge over the Fleet – is the soaring Gothic majesty of **St Dunstan in the West**, and a glimpse of further splendours beyond.

Isn't this a fabulous perspective? If it's been so good for hundreds of years, why haven't more people painted it? Because the perspective *wasn't here*. From around 1672 until 20 years ago the perspective was obscured either in Fleet Street by the ugly Temple Bar, a massive arch that blocked the view and much of the traffic, or to the east by a railway bridge which carried trains from south of the river (crossing next to the Black Friar) heading for Smithfield Market and by tunnels to Farringdon and the north, which crossed over the road on a bridge not far from here. Or, for a short period, by both. The railway now goes under the road, using old tunnels to the market. We are, strangely, the first generation to enjoy this splendid view unhindered.

A word about the 'within' and 'without' names around here: they mark places inside and outside the old city walls that ran down near the Fleet

Britain's eccentric judiciary —

BRITISH JUDGES ABSOLUTELY reek of eccentricity. Many see them as ignorant of modern culture, completely out of touch, and having a flippant attitude to their powers. Their blindness to the feelings of female victims of crime is legendary. They are traditionally old, white, upper-class males (many have continued working until well into their 70s) who are insulated from real life in their chauffeured cars with police escorts and special houses with servants. This caricature may be unfair, but judges can't complain because they often play up to the legend.

Thus unbelievable questions – such as that of one judge who had to ask 'Who are The Beatles?' – receive unbelievable answers – 'a popular beat combo, m'lud.' There have been others: 'Who is Marilyn Monroe?', 'What are a woman's boobs?' When a judge asked from the bench, 'What does "humping" mean?', he had to order a young woman out of court for giggling.

Some play to the gallery. Particularly brilliant at this was High Court judge **Sir Jeremiah LeRoy Harman** (b 1930), an Old Etonian, who seemed to make a point of not knowing anything common people might know. He once asked: 'Who is Bruce Springsteen?' But his *tour de force* came during a case involving Paul Gascoigne, then Britain's best-known soccer star, known as Gazza and on every front page twice a week.

The upper classes from posh schools follow rugby football, and sneer at soccer or 'association football' as they would call it. Told that Gascoigne was a very well-known footballer, Harman asked:

Rugby or association football?

He was informed Gazza was a Tottenham Hotspur star, and had played in the World Cup. He replied:

Isn't there an operetta called La Gazza Ladra*?*

The Press fell off their bench. 'Batty old judge asks: is Gazza an opera?'

Mr Justice Melford Stevenson (1902–87) was the epitome of an eccentric British judge. He was once sitting in the Court of Appeal with the Lord Chief Justice, the most famous judge in the land, and another prominent legal figure.

He called the usher over and said:

a case to answer

Can you give me the names?
You've got them, m'lud, on your sheets.
No, no, not the counsel! The names of these other judges.

During another case he refused to believe the evidence of a witness because he chose to live in Manchester, 'a wholly incomprehensible choice for a free man'. He told an epileptic who had tried to kill himself in remand cells he should have done it with more efficiency 'to save us all the bother and expense', and said raped hitchhikers were asking for it.

During one high profile case at the Old Bailey, **Judge Leslie Boreham** (1918–2004) told the jury to learn from the statue of Justice on the roof.

She is blindfolded not because a jury should be blind when they are
looking at the evidence. She is blindfolded so she takes no account of
race, creed, colour, political parties or nationalities.

The jury who could see the statue was not blindfolded were left deeply puzzled.

Another judge told lager louts to try bitter and, when asked by a woman lawyer to explain why he told a criminal not to worry because 'it is a woman's function to upset men', retorted:

What lesbian group are you from?

In another case – obviously not in the Old Bailey or the High Court but priceless nevertheless – a judge said:

You leave the court without a stain on your character – except that you
were acquitted by a Welsh jury.

Such wit, if that's what it is, isn't confined to judges but affects barristers and solicitors in these courts. There was a terrific barrister, Caesar **James Crespi** (1928–92), who famously got blown up when the IRA attacked the Old Bailey. He was pictured covered in blood, but it wasn't long before he was back in El Vino's in Fleet Street, where he spent every evening, saying:

I thought I would put my person between the bomb and
the Old Bailey to protect it from the blast, but it didn't work.

(CONTINUED OVERLEAF)

Britain's eccentric judiciary — a case to answer

True, if anyone could protect the Old Bailey with his body, the portly Crespi was the man. He was so Falstaffian that he'd take a taxi to travel 200 yards to El Vino's; sadly he is no longer with us. One of his quips in court came when his chair collapsed under his enormous weight and a pathologist who was giving evidence rushed to help him. Crespi said:

My dear boy, thank you, thank you, but not just yet.

Neither is the public in British courts immune from eccentricity. There was a case in a magistrate's court – or so the story goes – where a German tourist was accused of shoplifting. The defendant made out he couldn't understand English, so the magistrate asked if anyone in court could speak German. A man in the public gallery volunteered, and came down to the well of the court.

Magistrate: *'Ask him his name.'*
Man: 'VOT IS YOUR NAME?'

They were both jailed.

And even cases that never come to court can go eccentrically. For instance, a motorist in a London suburb was snapped by a speed camera and police sent him the usual picture of his car speeding and a demand for £60. The motorist sent them a photograph of £60 in notes. However, he paid up pretty quick when police replied with a picture of handcuffs.

on the City side (unlike the present City boundary which includes Fleet Street). From Roman times the City of London was up on the hill where St Paul's is and the Romans' wall still exists in odd places. The Fleet ditch was the obvious defensive line.

The various gates such as Ludgate here and Newgate, which we shall encounter soon, were fortified entrances from the Middle Ages on. The road over the Fleet Bridge to the swampy thorn-infested island of Westminster and the west was where those who were not welcome within the City itself had to make their business as close to the City as possible – lawyers and writers, still Fleet Street's stock-in-trade.

Naturally, with this combination of people, the area boasted not only its share of eccentrics but a good number of drinking places for them to meet as well. Note the gilt sign of the **Punch Tavern** opposite, recalling the magazine of that name once based here. We go up Ludgate Hill towards St Paul's a few steps, passing **Seacoal Lane**, reminding us of the harbour once here, and left into Old Bailey.

SPIES, MURDERERS AND NOVELISTS

The **Old Bailey** – or rather the Central Criminal Court, which stands at that address – is globally famed. Entrance to the public galleries is free and it can either be the best, or the most boring, show in town. Spies such as **George Blake** (see page 47), gangland murderers such as **the Krays** (see page 277), and **Dr Crippen** (see page 31) and novelist **Jeffrey Archer** (b 1940) – have trodden through these courts whose history is soaked with blood, suffering and, of course, lawyers getting rich.

The old **Newgate Prison** was housed in another city gate at this point and was so overcrowded and vermin-infested that it was a death sentence for some just being admitted there. It was from here that the condemned walked to the gallows at Tyburn, at what is now Marble Arch, where the triple-sided gallows could dispatch up to 20 at a time. Later, they were instead held here in the broad space known as the Old Bailey, and Newgate Prison had by then been rebuilt (it was where the courts now are). The entire space was packed with people eager to see a good hanging. Quite often far more people were killed in the crush than on the gallows.

Moving on, notice on the opposite corner the **Viaduct Tavern**, a splendid Victorian gin palace with completely over-the-top interior, which had its own cells in the cellar for rowdy customers. This pub name serves to remind us that the main road to the left, **Holborn Viaduct**, is an artificial level and the road used to plunge down to Farringdon Road, with difficult access to Newgate.

We cross to the church of **St Sepulchre's**, actually an abbreviation of St Edward and the Holy Sepulchre, and a suitably gloomy church for one so associated with premature doom. The church still has a bell that would be rung outside the cell of the condemned at midnight before they were hanged (see page 43).

On the morning of the execution, prisoners were given a nosegay and blessed by the priest as they started their terrible journey to Tyburn. I fancy a fast horse and a pair of pistols would have been a lot more welcome.

It's far older than the Wren churches we pass (and therefore not as handsome), being a Saxon church from the three-figure dates and having been last rebuilt in 1450. It's interesting to Americans because of its connections with Captain John Smith and his saviour, Pocahontas (see page 189).

By the way, get a good look at the gilded **statue of Justice** on top of the Old Bailey from here. Yes, she carries a balance of justice and the sword of retribution (fat chance nowadays) in either hand, but she is not blindfolded, as nearly everyone seems to think.

SMITHFIELD: BEEF ENCOUNTER OR BOEUF OF A NATION

We turn right down **Snow Hill** beyond the church, past Snow Hill police station which was once the rowdy Saracen's Head pub. Drunken toffs used to roll down Snow Hill in barrels for sport in the 19th century, and the steepness of the road as an approach to the City explains why someone thought the Holborn Viaduct a good idea. It was here that, at the Duke of Wellington's funeral in 1852, the horses slipped on the wet cobbles and couldn't haul the enormous 12-ton funeral carriage manufactured out of the metal from French guns captured at the Battle of Waterloo, his greatest victory.

His escort of soldiers took hold of ropes and assisted the vast iron juggernaut, which may still be seen at the duke's country seat, Stratfield Saye in Hampshire, up the hill to St Paul's so he could be buried near Nelson, the other great hero of the Napoleonic Wars. The weather was suitably awful for a grief-stricken nation and Wellington's hearse had already overturned in the floods – the 'Wellington flood' it was known as locally – at Maidenhead on its way to St Paul's. It was the only maidenhead the duke had ever had much trouble getting past, the soldiers' joke went. The slippage on Snow Hill is why state funerals since, such as Winston Churchill's wonderful one in 1965, have included servicemen pulling the hearse on ropes. Thus are barmy British traditions made.

Turn right into **Smithfield Street** halfway down Snow Hill and we rapidly approach the giant Victorian meat market that dominates the area. Of all the great London wholesale markets, such as Covent Garden and Billingsgate, this is the only one that has stayed put in its splendid setting.

Just like those other markets, this one is at its busiest at about 6am. Pubs such as the **26 Smithfield** on the right, or the **Fox & Anchor** at the far corner, are thrumming in the early morning and don't follow normal licensing hours. In fact many a top-hatted heartless toff has ended up here after a night ravishing innocent chambermaids (or whatever they do) because you can get a damn good breakfast and a drink before dawn.

26 Smithfield serves a spanking breakfast indeed for around a fiver, a bloody marvellous one for a little more, and an insanely good one for about £30 for two including champagne (must be those heartless toffs again). Just don't be heard to ask for the vegetarian option unless you want 400 cleaver-carrying butchers to take offence.

Of course there are other pubs all round the market as we come into the open space known as **West Smithfield**, with glorious names such as **The Bishop's Finger** (don't ask, but the Shepherd Neame is a good pint) or **the Butcher's Hook & Cleaver** (ditto the Fuller's). I wonder if young women being eyed up by the blokes in these Smithfield pubs have ever said: 'This place is just a flaming meat market.'

West Smithfield is certainly worth a stroll round (and includes excellent public bogs). In the far right corner, next to the imposing and surprisingly original entrance to **Bart's Hospital**, is the half-timbered entrance to **St Bartholomew the Great** (as opposed to the nearby **St Bartholomew the Lesser**). Not only is the medieval entrance a gem, but the church itself is really special and well worth including, as the makers of the hit movies *Shakespeare in Love* and *Four Weddings and a Funeral* agreed, with crucial scenes set here.

The curve of the Romanesque arches is unusual and striking, and elsewhere I mention the rebus, or visual pun, in the overlooking oriel window, which has a crossbow *bolt* through a barrel, or *tun* as they were called in those days – a memorial to *Bolton*. William Bolton was the last prior of the order of monks here.

Other treasures in this wonderful building include the eccentric banner of the 'Worshipful Company of the Art or Mistery of Butchers of the City of London' (oh to be a member of such a grand organisation), which depicts their arms supported by a particularly well-endowed pair of bulls, a very unlikely angel-bull and a pig's head and a pair of cleavers. A vegetarian's nightmare, no doubt, but splendid too.

I'd also recommend the memorial to Edward Cooke, who died in 1652 aged just 37, for its fine bit of tombstone doggerel:

> *Unluce your briny floods, what can ye keepe*
> *Your eyes from teares, & see the marble weepe.*
> *Burst out for shame: or if yee find noe vent*
> *For teares, yet stay, and see the stones relent.*

MORE BLOOD AND GUTS

Back out into Smithfield, which the historians tell us was probably 'smooth field' originally. It was the biggest open space near the City and used for jousting, the famed Bartholomew Fair (banned in 1850 because of public rowdiness) and for public executions before Tyburn and Newgate took their turn. Monuments in the frontage of Bart's hospital tell of these bloody events.

Talking of blood, back to **Smithfield Market**. Before we plunge through the central Grand Avenue opposite, take a look at the fearsome **City griffins** perched high above the entrance. They guard the City as surely as nine invisible Chinese dragons guard Kowloon, but we prefer ours visibly terrifying – more fang showy than feng shui.

Unless you're here early in the morning, this vast Crystal Palace-like cathedral to carnage will be all quiet. A very different kind of slaughter is remembered on the fine war memorial to Smithfield men on the right.

Crossing Charterhouse Street at the bottom and passing the **Hope pub**, we move into **Cowcross Street** (they were driven through here to Smithfield on the hoof) and it's worth noting first the **Castle pub** on the right with its three different signs. One shows a cockfight, another the Tower of London, and the last depicts three golden balls signifying, unexpectedly, a pawnbrokers. There's a strange story behind this.

King George IV (1762–1830), the deeply unpleasant and greedy monarch whom we will meet in Hammersmith (see page 325), was enjoying a night out cockfighting (hence the cockfight sign) in a nearby cockpit when he ran out of money. So he went into the pub and asked the landlord to pawn his gold pocket-watch and give him some cash. The landlord, bold as brass, said he could do so only if he had a pawnbroker's licence. The king granted him one then and there (hence the golden balls) and the landlord claimed to be the only person licensed as a publican and a pawnbroker. The Tower sign refers to the pub's official name, the Castle.

Here is **Farringdon Station**, which we would have reached in two minutes if we'd taken the Thameslink train from Blackfriars under Smithfield. Oddly, if we'd taken the Circle Line between these two it would have been about as slow as walking with eight stops and, according to the misleading Tube map, we would have crossed London.

Here we cross Farringdon Road – the course of the Fleet River under our feet – and Holborn Viaduct is down to our left. We go straight up **Greville Street** (noting the sign of the **One Tun pub** on the right confirming my earlier remark about barrels and crossbow bolts).

You'd thought we'd left all the blood and gore behind, but on the left is the **Bleeding Heart Tavern** and down through the yard to the left, one of the hardest restaurants to find in London, the **Bleeding Heart** – scene of a gruesome 16th-century murder (see opposite and page 29).

Past the Narnian lamppost

Carrying on up Greville Street, we turn left into **Hatton Garden**. Along with Amsterdam, it's a world centre in diamond dealing and it's hard to find a shop that isn't flogging gems or gold.

But there's another gem of a pub tucked away near here, and you'll never find it on your own. You need a bit of Narnian magic, for in some ways it is in a different land. The wonderful *Narnia* stories of C S Lewis, you may recall, hinge on the strange fact that when the children pass a strange, wonky lamppost in the forest, they are crossing from one reality to another, from fir trees to fur coats in the wardrobe or back again. And what do we see on the pavement ahead of us near the end of Hatton Garden but a wonky lamppost? Plunge into the unpromising gloomy alleyway to the left and we find a pub, and a very singular pub, the **Old Mitre**.

Ignore the actually fascinating pub for a moment and come out at the other end of the path in **Ely Place**. This was the residence of the Bishops of Ely, and therefore part of Cambridgeshire. Hence the lodge and the gates at the end of the road to the right and, if you don't believe me, the lack of an EC1 district number on the street names, because they don't have district numbers in soggy Cambridgeshire.

Many a petty pickpocket has escaped the clutches of the law down these passageways because once behind these gates you were no longer in London.

The pub was built in 1546 by Bishop Goodrich, although it was completely rebuilt in 1772. In the small bar there is a fragment of cherry tree that formerly grew here which apparently has much significance.

For one thing, the tree formed the original boundary between the bishop's garden and the garden of Sir Christopher Hatton – yes, as in Hatton Garden and as in bleeding heart ripped out. As a young girl, Queen Elizabeth I danced around this tree while having an affair with Sir Christopher. Sir Christopher was still a favourite of hers when she became queen, so when he coveted the Bishop of Ely's house and gardens, and the bishop refused to sell, the queen intervened. She threatened to defrock him if he did not sell up, so a deal was done for ten quid, ten carts of hay and a red rose every year. Seems reasonable.

That the Mitre refers to a bishop's hat, not the diagonal groove thing for cutting nice wood joints (the eponymous chess piece has both, of course) can be shown by the hopelessly wonky corners in the woodwork here.

A relic of the former bishop's palace is the chapel and crypt of **St Ethelreda's**, now a Roman Catholic place of worship.

Leaving Ely Place at its only exit into **Holborn Circus**, we cross Charterhouse Street (again) and pause to look left along the top of Holborn

Viaduct (I only say this to help you get your bearings – St Sepulchre's is by the trees down on the left and we're heading south, back to Fleet Street). We cross the road, with the **statue of Prince Albert** to our right and pass the church, **St Andrew's**, on our left. This one didn't burn down in the Great Fire, which stopped near here but Wren did it up anyway (he was like that).

Note that the bottom of the church tower features a blue boy and blue girl in statues. These are surprisingly common all over London and denoted a school. I mean, if they needed to go to school there was no point sticking up a sign saying 'School', was there, because they couldn't read! These are far more charming and follow in the illiterate tradition that saw, for example, a wooden boot hanging outside a bootmakers.

This road, St Andrew's Street, rapidly becomes **Shoe Lane**. The road soon sloping off to the left is St Bride's Street and leads back to Ludgate Circus, but we go on down Shoe Lane noting the **Cartoonist pub** on the right and enter a kind of tunnel into what was, until around 15 years ago, the heart of newspaperland.

RATTED JOURNALISTS AND THEIR WATERING HOLES

As you come out into Fleet Street the *Daily Express* used to stand on your left with, bizarrely, the *Standard* upstairs somewhere even though it was owned for many years by the *Express's* greatest enemy, the *Daily Mail*. On your right was the *Daily Telegraph*. Opposite was Reuters and the Press Association, and on the other side of the road were narrow lanes hemming in the *Sun* and the *News of the World*, as well as the *Mail*. No wonder, as I describe in the box on newspapers, the place was seething with activity come late evening.

Luckily, someone has preserved the quite amazing lobby of the **Express building**, nicknamed the 'Black Lubyanka' after the Moscow prison, and you must take a few steps to your left to see this utterly extraordinary Art Deco black-and-chrome fest through the front windows. On reaching the end of the Express building, you will be able to see Wren's elaborate tower of the journalists' church, **St Bride's**.

Turn around and go back up this north side of Fleet Street, past Shoe Lane and under the extravagant Art Deco clock of the old *Daily Telegraph* (why some prat has taken the name of the paper out I don't know, it's obviously made for it).

We should pay our respects to the creator of the first English dictionary in 1775, **Dr Johnson** (1709–84), if only by popping into the legendary **Cheshire Cheese pub**, which is not, of course, up Cheshire Court but up Wine Office Court. This is a labyrinth of a building, with more bars and private dining rooms and more levels than you'd ever guess from the outside. Even after many visits and private dinners here, I still find new bits. Or maybe because of the visits, I've forgotten them.

There's always been a Dr Johnson legend based here, with his chair and even his chipped soup bowl available to the gullible to lap from. Actually there's no record of his ever having been here, but there is to his having visited nearly every other old pub within five miles.

One must assume that as this was his 'local', he didn't bother to mention it. Or it could be the old Fleet Street advice:

When the facts conflict with the legend, print the legend.

Johnson was the smart aleck who thought up the risible idea that if you didn't know how to spell a word, you could look it up in a book where you needed to know how to spell it to find it. Of course, it was easy for him as none of the spellings had been fixed yet – look at the Americans, for example. Then it is defined with other words which by definition mean something else.

He was scathingly funny about the Scottishness of his companion Boswell (and I write as part-Scot and not at all English by blood). For example:

The noblest prospect which a Scotchman ever sees,
is the high road which leads him to England.

Or:

Much may be made of a Scotsman, if caught young.

And an entry in his dictionary for the word 'oats' reads:

A grain, which in England is generally given to
horses, but in Scotland supports the people.

He wasn't vain about his work, as two further entries make clear:

Dull To make dictionaries is dull work.
Lexicographer A writer of dictionaries, a harmless drudge.

The most relevant quotation for this book is one I reluctantly drag out, because you must know it:

When a man is tired of London, he is tired of life.

I N FILMS, IT IS HOLLYWOOD. In food and fashion, it used to be Paris. In newspapers, the best place in the world to work is Fleet Street, meaning the London daily press, which used to occupy that road, but is now scattered around the city. Your Australian reporter, your Canadian photographer, your South African sub-editor all dream of working here – or they do if they're any good.

Nowhere else in the English-speaking world is there the cut-throat competition of a dozen or so dailies slogging it out. Newspaper editors and proprietors tend to become strange because they have absolute power. They can build up and destroy at a whim the lives of the hundreds of people who work for them, and can often do the same for the characters in national life. They can call on huge resources, spending – and losing – millions of pounds if they get it wrong.

The eccentric press barons of Fleet Street

In among the cut and thrust of Fleet Street, there was one proprietor who instantly sacked everyone on one side of the central newsroom carpet in order to make savings. He didn't care if they were any good or not.

There was the tyrannical *Express* owner, the Canadian, **Lord Beaverbrook** (1879–1964), who, when he was called by an editor who had displeased him, pretended not to know him. 'You know, I'm the Editor,' the confused man explained. To which Beaverbrook retorted: 'You **were**,' and slammed the phone down.

If Beaverbrook's Rolls-Royce was held up for a few moments, he would phone his editor on arrival and demand a hard-hitting leading article on the necessity for a new underpass on the A3, and it would be in the first edition. The underpasses are still there.

A newspaper boss's abuse of power can sometimes backfire, however. **Cap'n Bob Maxwell** (1923–91), tyrannical and crooked giant that he was, was apt to make the odd mistake while he controlled the *Daily Mirror*. He was once overheard in the Old Mitre pub (see page 239) making some arbitrary rule banning the wearing of jeans on one floor of the **Mirror** building.

One day, he was striding through the building smoking his fat cigar when he spotted an unfortunate who had not heard of this rule.

Hey, you! Didn't you hear I've banned jeans on this floor?

He peeled a bundle of £50 notes from the fat wad he always carried and gave a pile estimated at £5,000 to the humbled young man.

Now f*** off and don't come back!

The man left without a word. All very impressive and macho. Except the 'sacked' man could be seen dancing a jig in the street below. He didn't even work for the *Mirror* but was merely delivering a message.

Evelyn's Waugh's wonderful comedy about Fleet Street, *Scoop*, revolves around the story of two writers on the same paper with the same name – a gentle, nature-notes writer from a remote village and a hard-bitten war reporter – whose assignments become mixed up and the nature guy gets sent to some inexplicable war in Africa. Far-fetched?

Just a few years ago, a new editor was put in charge of the troubled *Daily Express* and in the ritual blood-letting that takes place on such occasions, one hapless hack was summoned to the managing editor's office, given a fat cheque and booted out of the door. In Fleet Street you know it might happen any day, so anyone remotely employable banks the cheque, takes a few days off and starts work elsewhere.

This individual was relaxing in his garden deck-chair the next day when the phone went. It was the normally mild-mannered *Express* editor who thundered:

'Where the hell are you?'
'At home, sunning myself, because you sacked me.'
'No I ****** didn't. Now get into the office right away, we need you.'

It transpired, as life imitates art, that there was someone else of the same name who should have been sacked. He kept the cheque.

Another colourful Fleet Street boss of the late 20th century was *Sun* editor **Kelvin MacKenzie** (b 1946), who, when judged by newspaper sales, was the greatest of his era. To journalists, the brilliant but eccentric MacKenzie was feared and revered equally in the great tradition of barmy but witty British press barons and editors. He sacked an astrologer with a letter beginning: 'As you already know…'; he also sacked the entire showbiz department, followed shortly by the replacements, as he was still cross.

People generally judge newspapers harshly. My favourite quotation is Adlai Stevenson:

An editor is one who separates the wheat from the chaff, and prints the chaff.

(CONTINUED OVERLEAF)

The eccentric press barons of Fleet Street

In the age before computers made lunchtime drinking impossible, boozing was *de rigueur*. You couldn't get a job, or your stories, without it, and Fleet Street hacks knew all the bars where after-hours drinking was rife.

The drink-related tales of old Fleet Street are endless. Veteran columnist **Keith Waterhouse** recalled taking the ashes of a departed colleague in a cardboard box for a last pub crawl – 'it's what he would have wanted' being the refrain on such occasions.

The rainy evening wore on, and on, as every watering hole was visited. Eventually, standing in Fleet Street in the rain, someone noticed that the bag and cardboard box containing the ashes was sodden, and the remains of the departed were swirling down the gutter. 'It's what he would have wanted,' they chorused.

Cue for two quotes, a century apart, about the gutter press:

Journalists belong in the gutter because that is where the ruling classes throw their guilty secrets.

Writer Gerald Priestland (1927–91)

We are all in the gutter, but some of us are looking at the stars.

Oscar Wilde, in *Lady Windermere's Fan* (1892)

Dr Johnson's House is accessible a few steps further up Fleet Street, through Hind Court to Gough Square, and here we see a statue to Dr Johnson's great companion – no, not Boswell, but **Hodge** his cat. Johnson's house, a museum to the great man, is opposite. Turning left in front of the house brings you through Johnson's Court back into Fleet Street, where we turn right.

You will have noticed that although the journalists have scattered from here, the lawyers – held in a similar regard by the public – are thick on the ground, the bundles of documents tied up with ribbon (how quaint) being hurried back and forth. The two breeds would meet at legendary venues such as **El Vino's**, which we'll cross to opposite, perhaps to discuss the day's events at the Old Bailey or the Royal Courts of Justice at the top of Fleet Street (The High Court). It wouldn't admit women at all until recent years and I remember coming a cropper of its 'no tie, no drink rule'. The barman lent me one – a tie, not a woman.

GIANTS, A SNARLING GRIFFIN AND THE WAY TO A DIFFERENT WORLD

Going on up Fleet Street, don't go too fast. Look left for the many picturesque courtyards of the legal profession whose patch this now is, such as Old Mitre Court, and upwards at the fascinating clutter on the buildings, which Londoners hurrying by will miss. For example, the golden bottle hung high as the sign of Hoare's Bank, or the plaque marking the site of the Devil's Tavern.

Across the road we get an excellent view of the tremendous tower of **St Dunstan's-in-the-West** and the two giants – Gog and Magog, I was told (see page 207) – bong their bells on the hour. To the right of them is a fine figure of **Mary Queen of Scots** (head not yet chopped off) and beyond them a reminder of Fleet Street's newspaper glory days with the mosaic titles of D C Thomson's newspapers, endowed with names such as *People's Friend*. But this Dundee-based publisher should include its frankly far more interesting publications, the *Beano* and the *Dandy* comics.

On the left, before the arch at the bottom of Chancery Lane and up some stairs, is an extraordinary little museum, **Prince Henry's room**. It is free, it's small (and therefore quick) and it tells some amazing stories. Prince Henry (1594–1612) was the eldest son of James I, hence the Prince of Wales feathers and Duchy of Cornwall crest in the stained-glass window, and the 'PH' in the plaster ceiling. This was the promising prince's London office, as it were, and, had he not died aged 18, the troublesome Charles I (1625–49), would not have come to the throne and there may have been no Civil War. The best king we never had, some say. But the interest is as much in the room itself, with its fine Jacobean plaster ceiling and original panelling, because the Great Fire of London didn't quite reach this far. Everything east of here is necessarily younger – a change of wind saved this house.

This quirky little museum is open only from 11am to 2pm and is actually used as part of a legal office the rest of the time. I was delighted to find the guide on duty was former Fleet Street printer, Len Hall. He told me how this ancient room had survived another conflagration and many other bizarre changes.

After Prince Henry's death the building was a pub and a coffee shop. Eventually, by the early 19th century, it was Mother Salmon's Waxworks.

THE ATMOSPHERE IN the old Fleet Street was unique, as was the atmosphere at the old Covent Garden market, and now the great newspapers have left the street, I'll have to conjure it up for you.

The newspapers were like massive warships. During the day, things were quiet as ammunition supplies – giant reels of paper – were hoisted aboard to fill the magazines for the coming battle. As day turned to night, things became increasingly frenetic as reporters and photographers rushed back aboard from their assignments. Sub-editors, the midshipmen of newspapers, who until now had had a fairly relaxed day, reported to their battle stations as things began to hum. The wire machines chattered relentlessly with intelligence from every corner of the globe. Pictures were coming in from all quarters, some by wire, some dripping wet from the darkroom.

Up on the bridge – as it were – the key officers planned the battle. Which way would the enemy – the other papers – go? Would they lead with so and so's story? Would they obey influential Mr X's pleas to hush up such-and-such an indiscretion? The spies in the enemy flagships were approached: did they have a whopper to blow the rest of Fleet Street out of the water? If so, a cunning paper would produce a dummy first edition with a boring story on the front, make sure the agents of all the other papers had got a paper, and then bring the big guns to bear, printing a massive scoop in the second edition. The hapless rivals would sink with all hands, trapped in this carefully sown minefield, befuddled by the enemy's smokescreen.

Down in the bowels of the building, the massive print works, shoe-horned into the ground floors and cellars of these medieval building plots, were the equivalent of the engineers and stokers – the blue-overalled print workers. They would be tending their massive, gleaming machines, oiling and inking, ready for the bell that indicated full steam ahead.

On another floor, the gun deck, as it were, hot metal typesetters would be working full tilt in the deafening row of the composing room. They produced metal lines on Linotype machines and these were rapidly clamped together by 'comps' with picture blocks and headlines.

The real atmosphere of old Fleet Street

A skilled sub-editor would read the text back-to-front, and possibly upside down, trying to catch any cock-ups. A story that was too short was 'leaded', not as today with a computer instantly spacing out the lines a bit more, but with a skilled compositor sliding ultra-thin bits of lead between the lines so fast you couldn't see his fingers move.

A bell sounded and, just as in the old black-and-white films, the mighty presses began to whirr, slowly at first, then gathering speed until the pages were just a blur. Upstairs, in the 'tween decks, where reporters and sub-editors worked, you could feel the whole building lurch when the presses started. A humming vibration grew as the machines ran faster and faster.

When a late story broke that really mattered, bells would ring, lights flash, the presses would be stopped, the whole place would lurch and hurrying crews of writers, sub-editors, comps and printers would rapidly make good the damage – as in a warship which has taken a hit. The top brass would pace the deck nervously until that reassuring hum of the engines meant the moment of sudden vulnerability had passed.

Outside in the tiny streets such as Bouverie Street, Tudor Street, and Shoe Lane, hundreds of vans in rival liveries would push and jostle for space, like sampans and lighters eager for trade round a great ship in Hong Kong Harbour. The presses disgorged thousands, nay millions, of bundled papers right on to the narrow pavement.

The van drivers, having cut up the rivals in their own queues as many times as possible with the usual cockney insults, would tear off up Farringdon Road, racing the other companies' vans at hell-for-leather speeds, to Euston, King's Cross and St Pancras and the other great railway stations where long trains of vans stood behind a simmering express engine. Tipsy lords and fur-coated ladies heading for the sleeping cars of the Scottish night trains after a night at a West End show would try to catch a glimpse of the next day's headlines.

Soon doors slammed, the platform-end signal clanged upwards, whistles blew and the monstrous snorting locomotives sprinted faster and faster into the night, towards thousands of darkened towns and villages where newsagents and paperboys slept soundly, ready for the final link in the chain.

At least, that was how it was supposed to work.

Dickens has Little Nell come here for work after the Old Curiosity Shop closes in the book.

The waxworks had huge advertising hoardings falsely claiming it to be a former royal palace, but also offering haircuts for 6d!

At length the London County Council bought the derelict building for £1,000, intending to demolish it. They pulled down the Waxworks frontage and were amazed – hey presto! – to find an entire Jacobean frontage behind. Len says:

> *I was a messenger boy during the 1940s Blitz, and three hundred tons of high explosive fell in this area. So much was flattened, Fleet Street workers used the bomb sites for car parks for years afterwards. Yet again this little room escaped, and the ceiling didn't fall in the huge shocks – I think the horsehair and plaster mix makes it so strong.*

On up Fleet Street just a little more to where the High Court's massive bulk becomes visible on the right and you see the snarling black griffin of the City of London in the centre of the road. This was the site of the **Temple Bar**, Wren's ceremonial entrance to the City. The **griffin**, guardian of the city, is spectacularly aggressive but don't miss the amazingly detailed frieze along the side of the monument facing this pavement (see box, opposite).

On the left, another gem not to be missed is the marvellous marbled foyer of Lloyds Bank – it's insane, frankly. What was the architect on? LSD? Ahead in the distance, in the middle of the road, lies **St Clement Danes** church with its fascinating oranges-and-lemons history (see page 100). There are public toilets in the middle of the road there too, if you need them.

But we go left down **Devereux Court**, a footpath, to visit the startlingly different world that is the **Middle Temple**, an ancient Inn of Court named after the Knights Templars who held sway round here until they were suppressed. We zigzag along the court past more pubs until the end where we turn left into the Middle Temple. Note the building on its left at the corner has anchors and SCD on it, to mark the boundaries of St Clement's parish – St Clement having been tied to an anchor and drowned. We enter the Temple on sufferance, it not being a public right of way, but as the notices explain if we don't bring dogs or make a noise the porters won't haul us out.

To the right is a scene a million miles from the hubbub of Fleet Street. A fountain restfully tinkles in a circular pool beneath beautiful trees, a scene marked by Dickens in *Martin Chuzzlewit*, perhaps his best work (I still can't decide on that). Rest on the curved benches or walk on to the left past the hall (note the lamb and flag, the temple's emblem, all over the place) and across the road into the arch, past another garden, up the steps and through some cloisters into a square. Here is the strange, circular **Temple**

WREN'S ARCH STOOD here in Fleet Street, where the snarling griffin sculpture now stands, from 1672 to 1878, a splendid entrance to the City, sometimes adorned with traitors' and murderers' rotting heads or other body parts on its spikes. This arch replaced an earlier wooden structure – a literal wooden bar at one point. As the Victorian City boomed, the narrow arch became hopelessly constricting for traffic.

Here's Dickens on the Temple Bar in *Bleak House*:

The raw afternoon is rawest, and the dense fog is densest, and the muddy streets are muddiest, near that leaden-headed old obstruction, appropriate ornament for the threshold of a leaden-headed old corporation: Temple Bar.

For him it perfectly symbolised the obstructiveness, sloth, greed and self-interest of the legal system. Nothing like today, then...

So in 1878 it was taken down, stored in pieces and later moved to Theobald's Park in Hertfordshire, where it served as a grand gate for a brewery magnate's country estate for a while, then was forgotten and left to moulder in woodland, neglected and vandalised.

Finally, in 2004, after more than a century in exile and a £3 million restoration, it was brought back to the City and rebuilt next to St Paul's Cathedral, where it can be seen. The statuary has been restored, although 95 per cent of the original stonework has been saved, so it is not a mere replica.

Temple bar: rotting heads and a snarling griffin

church (the original part; see page 209) of the medieval Knights Templars, and inside you will find their ancient burial effigies, glowing in the light from stained-glass windows as they have for so many centuries since they returned from the Crusades. Outside, a sculpture of a couple of knights is somewhat newer – it dates from 2000.

Monks, ghosts, skulls and the lawless Alsatia

Leaving the church door and going left we progress into the huge space that is **King's Bench Walk**, which feels more like a donnish old university or cathedral close than a part of Central London. Angle to the right somewhat to find the gap in the houses marked 'No Exit' (for cars) and proceed past the porter's lodge and through an arch into **Tudor Street**.

We are now nearing the end of this walk and back in the former newspaper territory, the 'Lost Valley of the Inkers'. **Bouverie Street**, next on the left, was the home of the *Sun* and the *News of the World*, and *Punch* before that. It is named after the family that owned all this land before it was built up. We go straight down Tudor Street (named because Henry VIII grabbed some of this land when he destroyed the monasteries) but pause at the corner of **Whitefriars Street**. There's just one more story, of monks and ghosts.

A few steps up Whitefriars Street (what with Carmelite Street, we are obviously in monastic territory once more) is the **Harrow pub**, haunted by the ghost of a tailor whose workshop was absorbed by the pub (his treadle machine can be heard running sometimes, I'm told).

Opposite, up some steps, is **Ashentree Court** where the only remaining part of the **medieval Whitefriars Monastery**, a vaulted cellar, remains in the basement of a modern office block. You can look at the outside by following the steps or go round to the front and demand to see the interior. (For how this vault once gave hardened Fleet Street hacks a shock, see page 147.)

The few stones relate a tale of sanctuary, for after the monastery disappeared in the 16th century the right of sanctuary from the law remained. It was much abused by criminals, and the area – called Alsatia, after the unruly borderland between France and Germany – became a lawless den of narrow streets, brothels and drinking dens where law officers would not dare enter. That the teeming refuge of criminals, prostitutes and other low life stood next to the Temple, citadel of the law, was ironic indeed, and fights ensued between the two communities, especially when the lawyers sought to brick up the arch at the end of Tudor Street we have just come through. After one particularly bad fight, the Alsatians' leader, **Captain Francis White**, was hanged here. So dense were the crowds watching, that you could walk across Fleet Street on the shoulders of onlookers. The sanctuaries were suppressed by Parliament in 1693, just as the monasteries had been a century-and-a-half earlier.

Well, all this blood and history is exhausting, so it's down to the end of Tudor Street and turn right for **Blackfriars** station, or a well-deserved drink at the Black Friar with its own unmissable interior (see page 274).

SOHO

FITZROVIA TO SOHO WALK

Just as the snobbish centre of London's wealthy classes has been gradually moving westwards over the centuries, to get away from proles and pollution and nearer to the Kensington Court, so the centre of vice and sleaze has been tracking northwest. From Elizabethan **Southwark** to 18th-century **Covent Garden** (which the upper classes had just left, going towards Mayfair) it had reached **Soho** by the 20th century and **King's Cross** by the 21st. At this rate, by the 25th century posh Radlett in Hertfordshire will be the home of all-night strip joints, transvestite dens and table dancing. Can't wait.

But of all these disreputable places it is Soho that has retained its agreeable, raffish quality. It has somehow maintained the cosy building height typical of scruffy poverty without imitating the massive tower blocks or pompous stuccoed terraces that surround it. Indeed, it is a refreshing antidote to those neighbouring districts. Intellectually, it is the closest thing London has to the Left Bank or Greenwich Village.

The vice and drugs are still here, but are not nearly as prominent as during the 1950s, when gangs were rampant. Instead of shootings, garish neon signs offering rip-off sex shows are about as threatening as it gets. And, of course, where Soho was once unique in offering such services (remember the famous *double entendre* cards in corner shops – 'French lessons', 'large chest for sale', 'young lady requires challenging position', 'stocks and bonds advisor' and no, I'm not going to decode them for you), today just about everywhere in Europe except frumpy Frinton has such sleaze.

So Soho has gone on its own unsavoury way, reinventing itself occasionally. Jazz clubs and restaurants come and go, but musically the area has always been at the leading edge.

Rock 'n' roll bands have, since the fifties, lived and died in venues such as the **Marquee Club** in Wardour Street, the **2is** in Old Compton Street, or the hot 'n' sweaty **100 Club** in Oxford Street. Jazz veteran George Melly (d 2007), remembering Soho in the atmosphere of post-war austerity, said:

> Soho was like another land, full of eccentric drunks. I discovered Soho when I was in the navy – sailors were very welcome.

The sixties saw an amazing flowering at the now-vanished **UFO Club** in nearby Tottenham Court Road, with Pink Floyd, Arthur Brown, Fairport

FITZROVIA TO
SOHO WALK

Convention and Procul Harem all appearing here within 12 months. Later the emergence of punk saw Poly Styrene strutting her stuff here. Doubtless today there's someone who's going to be huge playing somewhere in Soho, unknown to all but a few insiders.

The **film and TV industry** has taken root in Wardour Street, where many thriving independent production companies are based. Equally Soho has been a haunt for interesting literary types – the more Bohemian ones at any rate – for 100 years. Now you can hardly move without stepping on a publisher, independent film-maker or whatever. So although the area – named after a hunting call in what were wild woods – has a charm and a history well worth exploring, it is still alive, humming and free from the cloying clutches of the heritage industry.

ARIEL TO CALIBAN

The area is bounded by commercial Oxford Street to the north, elegant Regent Street to the west, theatreland's Shaftesbury Avenue to the south and bookish Charing Cross Road to the east. Ambling across this small patch need not be too organised, but here's a short walk with some highlights pointed out. I've bunged in a corner of Fitzrovia too for the mildly energetic. To keep just the Soho part, simply go to Tottenham Court Road Tube station and walk west on Oxford Street to pick up the walk at Wardour Street, soon on the left (and skip to page 255). Otherwise, start at Oxford Circus Tube. The walk ends at Piccadilly Circus, is about a mile (though it will feel like three) and will take about an hour-and-a-half.

If you walk north from Oxford Circus up **Regent Street**, preferably on the right-hand side, you soon come to the kink in the road where **Broadcasting House** faces you. On the right is the superbly sited **All Souls Langham Place**, positioned there by architect **John Nash** (1752–1835) who made such a brilliant job of the other end of Regent Street, where it sweeps into Piccadilly Circus.

Nash's simple genius in getting a spire into a classical setting was accomplished without the fiddly bits Wren would have used. Just a bloody great box for the church, a cylinder of pillars for the entrance hall with a cone walloped through the middle.

Broadcasting House is the centre of the BBC, and BBC radio in particular. It is a classic thirties building, with its Reithian high-mindedness and Art Deco motifs. Its symbol is Ariel, the girlie, wispy thing from Shakespeare's *Tempest*. Broadcasting House was built with massive sound-proofing so that a symphony orchestra could belt out Elgar next to a *Woman's Hour* studio. The BBC leans to the left, its critics say. It's hard to notice from this angle.

Of course, in the early days announcers would wear dinner jackets (on the radio!) and bow ties and speak in ludicrously plummy accents. Now if you see an apparent cockney oik or Liverpudlian lout in shabby old jeans shuffling past the steps of All Souls, he's probably a top BBC presenter. Nation Shall Speak Unto Nation, the old high-minded building says, and

Gaston, the perfect Gallic host

THE GREAT LANDLORD of Soho's **French House** pub, **Gaston Berlemont**, born upstairs in the pub to his French parents in 1914, and who died in 1999, had exaggerated Gallic charm. He would say to a customer who'd had too much to drink:

One of us has to leave, monsieur, and it cannot be me. Come back tomorrow morning and we'll drink a glass of champagne.

Or to a lady, with a raised-eyebrow *double entendre*:

Madam, I cannot wait to see more of you.

He would not serve pints, only the demi, not so much out of Frenchness but because there was more money to be made out of wine in those days. Plus he didn't fancy the beer-swilling types.

He would patiently indulge the Bohemian clientele, cashing cheques that were as bouncy as Barbara Windsor's frontage. Of one man who entertained a number of young women in the upstairs restaurant, he said:

I've never known anyone with so many nieces.

He was no snob and among the great writers and film-makers could be found prostitutes and tramps – one of his customers famously slept in a hollow tree on Hampstead Heath. A celebrated customer after the war was Pierre Labric, who had ridden a bicycle down all the stairs of the Eiffel Tower.

When Gaston retired in 1989, the pub was packed – as was the street outside – with hundreds of fans of this contradiction, a true British pub with a true French *patron* in charge.

that now includes yer actual efnics speaking wiv yer yoof, innit? Still good and ludicrous, then.

MORE SOULS AND I CAN'T BELIEVE... IT'S NOT BUDDHA?

Between All Souls and Oxford Circus take **Margaret Street** running east, and you will come to a completely contrasting church, called **All Saints** (see page 139). Instead of classical simplicity we get the most over-the-top Gothic revival decoration for decoration's sake. It's virtually psychedelic, as if you tried to decorate your home from hundreds of pages torn from wallpaper sample books. And it is amazing to stagger out of this rich sensation only to cross the road and find yourself in the **Fo Guang Temple** (see page 149), a Chinese Buddhist centre most unexpected in the heart of London (although we are not far north of Chinatown in Soho).

Going right and then left at the end of the street we come into **Eastcastle Street**, and then right into **Berners Street** we face Oxford Street and our entrance into Soho. **Fitzrovia** (see page 107), that unofficial patch of London, is up the other end of Berners Street and past the Telecom Tower. The best bit of it, if you're interested, is the beautiful Fitzroy Square, setting for Ian McEwan's brilliant novel, *Saturday*.

FRENCH CONNECTION, TOP MARX
AND GREAT LITERARY DRUNKS

Crossing Oxford Street, pickpocket centre of the universe, we enter **Wardour Street**, home to the independent film-makers, publishers and media hangers-on. The most interesting bit of Soho is really this and the parallel streets also running south to your left (that is, east) – **Dean Street**, **Frith Street** and **Greek Street** – so there's no harm in just blundering around, taking odd paths that suggest themselves to you. After all, it's a bohemian place so let's not be too organised.

But if you survive the raffish pubs and clubs with no ill effects (needless to say some of the sleazy red-lightish clubs are there to rip tourists off), there are some fascinating nooks and crannies to mention.

A literary landmark, or rather a set of literary landmarks, are the connections with Charles Dickens's *A Tale of Two Cities*, that evocative drama set between Paris and London during the French Revolution and for me perhaps his best book (I can't make my mind up). In **Greek Street**, the **Pillar of Hercules pub** features in the book as the Hercules Pillar and the nearby **House of St Barnabas**, a hostel, is said to be the model for the house of Dr Manette. In which case it's not surprising to find **Manette Street** nearby.

SOHO TODAY HAS a reputation for sleaze and sex, but the scale of the industry was once very much larger, and conducted more openly, in those days when one in eight London women worked in the sex industry. In 1796, for example, it was estimated there were 25,000 'ladies of the night' in London.

Nor were they all living in squalor and poverty. One survey said that in Marylebone alone, 1,700 houses, mainly elegant terraces, were inhabited by upmarket courtesans. Some charged phenomenal amounts of money and became rich property owners in their own right.

These sophisticated creatures made vast sums of money and helped account for the boom in property and building. There was even a printed directory of prostitutes, *Harris's Lists*, giving revealing descriptions.

There were specialist services on offer: what the French called the 'English perversion' was catered for at **Mrs Jenkins's Flogging Establishment**, on the spot where La Bohème Restaurant in Covent Garden now stands, where a sound thrashing with birch twigs would be applied to naked bodies.

Some brothels, as recorded in Hogarth's cartoons, were presented as Turkish baths or *bagnos* or *bagnios*. Couples would take hot and cold dips before retiring to discreet rooms. Society courtesans, royal mistresses and working-class prostitutes worked fairly openly up until the late 19th century

Soho and the sex industry: perversions and princes

Incidentally, there's a **French church** in Soho Square at the top (north end) of Greek and Frith streets, but this square, to be honest, is less interesting than it looks. I'm told the **statue of Charles II** appears to talk occasionally because the park-keepers in their pseudo-Tudor lodge hide a walkie-talkie in it, to play tricks on tourists, but I've never heard it. And dang, I've spoilt it for you now.

In **Dean Street**, the **French House** pub (see box, page 254) is legendary for literary connections, bohemian lifestyles and odd eccentricities. The Idiots' Club, which met here in recent years, was run by someone calling when Britain underwent a convulsion of morality which, despite the loosening of the bonds by the 1960s, has never entirely gone away.

For example, there's a blue plaque at 15 South Street, W1, honouring **Catherine Walters** (1839–1920), 'the last Victorian courtesan'. The word 'last' tells of the change in moral standards during that reign as much as it tells of the long life of this woman, known as Skittles, who survived well into the 20th century. She had a ravishing face, by all accounts, a stunning hour-glass figure that she displayed to great effect, tumbling tresses of red hair, and a Liverpudlian street-girl's way with words. The flame-haired temptress would put on her tightest corset with revealing decolletage, grab her riding crop, and go for a gallop along nearby Rotten Row in Hyde Park, where society men would be out riding. Once, when complimented by a gentleman on the pink flush on her cheeks after a gallop, she retorted: 'You should see my arse.'

Some of them did, but she was aiming higher. She became entangled with the heir to a dukedom and was soon provided with this house and a lavish income for life. In 1867 she befriended the Prince of Wales – before he met the actress Lily Langtry – and soon her civilised soirées were frequented by the great and the good of the age, such as Gladstone, Lord Kitchener, and leading artists and poets. She had reinvented herself as a society lady, but never disguised her past.

himself Baron Peter de Massenbach, who greeted potential members with 'An idiot, I presume'.

And the French House has countless theatrical and literary connections, from **Peter O'Toole** (b 1932) to **Keith Waterhouse** (1929–2009) to **Auberon Waugh** (1939–2001). As I was telling the Prince of Wales, it's not really on to name-drop, but I said to O'Toole (who seemed to me as a young film-goer in the 1960s the best actor in the world for *Lawrence of Arabia*) after the memorial service for Waterhouse (who seemed to me the funniest author in the world for *Billy Liar*), that the last named had been the most reliable columnist I'd ever dealt with, sending in his copy which didn't need a word changing, on time, with his own headlines written, twice a week for year after year. O'Toole replied how grateful he was to Waterhouse, because he'd reinvented him as an actor in old age when the world had forgotten about him, 'giving me a whole second career.'

Dylan Thomas (1914–53) once drunkenly left the manuscript for *Under Milk Wood* in the French House, to be rescued by the landlord. (Incidentally, he created the Welsh-sounding place name for that 'play for voices', Llareggub, perhaps to mock the English for taking Welshness so seriously, until they spelled it backwards.) When drunk, Dylan Thomas would play his rather puerile game called Cats and Dogs in which he would crawl round the pub on all fours biting the ladies' ankles, much to their surprise if they weren't regulars.

The pub was originally the York Minster and was in the control of Frenchman Victor Berlemont from 1910. It was a base for the French Resistance and Free French during World War II and their leader Charles de Gaulle came here for cloak-and-dagger wartime meetings. Or so they say… (Gallic shrug).

At **28 Dean Street** the father of communism, **Karl Marx** (1818–83), and his family took lodging rooms upstairs amidst dreadful poverty in 1850. They had no money, apart from what his bit of writing earned, and some hand outs from his friend and colleague, Friedrich Engels (1820–95). Eventually they inherited some money and moved to a more, er, bourgeois location in Hampstead. Eleanor Marx was born at this impoverished flat and went on to become a political firebrand in her own right. She was involved in the matchgirls' strike of 1888 and the dockers' of 1889.

While living at Soho, Marx liked nothing more than a stiff walk across Hampstead Heath and a stiff drink at the Jack Straw's Castle pub. See, he was almost human. Nothing on American humorist Groucho Marx, of course. He was a *real* revolutionary.

Which brings us neatly to **Groucho's**, a discreet club for media luvvies at 45 Dean Street. Here editors, writers, people from the nearby film centre of Wardour Street and others meet, launch books, raise funds and generally get sloshed. According to one member, everyone is constantly looking over the shoulder of whomever they're talking to, to see if there's someone more important to suck up to. They then cut the first person dead in mid-sentence as they go off to praise the big cheese and shout with laughter at his, or her, jokes. If you think that's cynical, I'm sorry, but I see it almost every day. However, anyone preferring Groucho to Karl can't be all bad. The club took its name from Groucho's famous dictum that he wouldn't join any club that would have him as a member. Just so long as they don't forget his other one:

I've got a good mind to join a club and beat you over the head with it.

MYSTIC PRAT, MEDICAL HERO, ECCENTRIC COMPOSER AND VAMPYRES

Now I'm suggesting carrying on south on Dean Street or Wardour Street to the end, but must first tell you about some great eccentrics who lived nearby (and you don't have to actually go to these streets). Soho's greatest eccentric was probably poet-artist and mystic **William Blake** (1757–1827), his birthplace being marked by a plaque in nearby **Marshall Street**. His poem *Jerusalem*, now set to music as an alternative national anthem and celebration of Englishness, was, in fact, a radical protest against what the industrial revolution was doing to the country and an attack on the system.

He and his wife used to sit naked in their garden, pretending to be Adam and Eve, and were frankly a complete puzzle to contemporaries. One suspects he was a combination of stocky cockney artisan, visionary and prat. His pictures and poems seem simple yet are easily made complex by English literature bods. (For example, the poem about the big cat, 'Tyger, tyger burning bright', is said to be about the French Revolution. Why doesn't he flaming well mention it then?)

Blake was naïvely direct about things, un-luvvie-like, and deeply attached to innocence. He once pointed to a group of children playing nearby and said with feeling: 'That is heaven.' His visionary poems live on in unpredictable ways. For example, he wrote:

If the doors of perception were cleansed, man
could see things as they truly are: infinite.

In the 1930s, Aldous Huxley borrowed the phrase for his book about drugs, *The Doors of Perception*. Then in the 1960s Jim Morrison took that for the title of his band, The Doors. You probably couldn't find a more different artist, but another one of Soho's finest was the Italian artist **Canaletto** (1697–1768), who lived at **41 Beak Street**, towards Regent Street, where he has a blue plaque.

In **Broadwick Street**, which is off Wardour Street to the west, **Dr John Snow** (1813–58), made a discovery that has since saved millions of lives. In 1854 there was an outbreak of cholera here, caused – contemporary thinking would have it – by air-borne vapours. He was convinced that pollution of the groundwater by sewage meant the disease was carried in drinking water. He persuaded the authorities to take the handle off the pump here at the centre of the outbreak and the epidemic suddenly stopped. You can find out more upstairs in the **John Snow** pub, Broadwick Street, said to be Soho's oldest.

Halfway down Wardour Street is the pub **The Intrepid Fox** at No 99. This refers not to the hunting background of the name Soho, but to the great radical politician **Charles Fox** (1749–1806) who once offered a kiss from a great society beauty to anyone who'd vote for him, and won by a landslide. The walls and ceiling look like a crack-crazed junk-merchant's yard, festooned with memorabilia and musical clutter, some connected with famous customers.

At the far end of **Wardour Street**, as you leave Soho, is the remarkable stone, brick and copper churchless tower of **St Anne's** with its strange bulbous shape. A Russian onion-dome in a foreign land. The church was destroyed by World War II bombing. Services are held in a building in the street to the rear.

The ashes of whodunnit writer **Dorothy L Sayers** (1893–1957), creator of Lord Peter Wimsey, are in the floor of the Sayers Room in the tower, where one can see her portrait. Sayers was a churchwarden here. There is also a dead deposed king here, **Theodore of Corsica** (1694–1756), a debt-ridden wastrel by all accounts (not like any of our royals, then). His epitaph read:

> *Fate poured its lessons on his living head,*
> *Bestowed a kingdom, but denied him bread.*

Another local who would have known St Anne's was the author of *The Vampyre* (1815), **John William Polidori** (1795–1821), who lived a few streets west at **Great Poultney Street**. He was Byron's doctor and would have been with the group in Italy when Mary Shelley wrote *Frankenstein*. Spooky.

Emerging from Soho proper onto **Shaftesbury Avenue**, London's Broadway in terms of theatreland, you can turn right towards **Piccadilly Circus**, beyond which on Piccadilly lies Fortnum & Mason's department store, where a great British eccentric of the 1930s, the conductor **Sir Thomas Beecham**, said to a woman he'd just greeted, and whose face he vaguely recognised but whose name escaped him (and, frankly, haven't we all done this?):

> *And what is your husband doing nowadays?*

The lady replied frostily:

> *He's still king.*

Beecham (heir to the Beecham's Powders fortune) was forthright as a conductor. He once brought his orchestra to a halt mid-score and bellowed at some poor woman cellist:

Madam, you have there between your legs that which could give pleasure to thousands, and all you do is sit there and scratch it.

This area simply fizzes in the early evening with bright-eyed crowds heading for the shows, and Leicester Square is where filmstars appear for premières on a regular basis, to be whooped at by adoring fans. Theatres have their 'nutty devotees' side too. Theatre groupies will hang around stage doors down side passages after the shows to catch a glimpse of the great stars, strangely ordinary out of the limelight and *sans* make-up, wigs and costume. Some people will attend these doors for all 14 nights of a show's run and are well known to the bemused actors.

Back to **Piccadilly Circus** and the Tube. As you look one way past the garish neon signs and back into Soho, don't forget to see how London completely changes character in a few yards by looking down **Lower Regent Street** to the frightfully restrained St James's area.

And if you have never seen the magnificent sweep of the bottom end of Regent Street proper (curving right away from Piccadilly opposite Shaftesbury Avenue), you *mustn't* miss it. This is the other end of the road from All Souls at the start of our walk and it is Nash's brilliance yet again. Look at the garret windows, and the magnificent way **Air Street** intercepts the grand sweep. Wonderful.

SOUTHWARK

BOROUGH TO BLACKFRIARS – HORRID HISTORY

Southwark, being just across the river from London, was home to every evil the medieval City could not tolerate within its walls but could not do without – brothels, bear-baiting, cock-fighting, gambling, theatres, fleeing criminals and unspeakably cruel jails. It was a medieval Soho or Vegas.

Some of this murky but fascinating history can be retraced by the inquisitive visitor today, as we shall see, and the atmosphere has been soaked up by dozens of film-makers precisely because it's not fake.

Dickens couldn't have created the insane, illogical world that he portrays in books like *Little Dorrit* without Southwark. It has never been anything like smart or fashionable, but today, with the Bankside's new Tate Modern and the wobbly Millennium Bridge, it's drawing some crowds across the river again, as it did for very different reasons for five centuries up to the Civil War.

The **Millennium Bridge** takes pedestrians across on a route many a lustful man used to take by boat from Stews Lane in the City (the 'stews' were the whorehouses) to the Bankside brothels that lined the stairs at the other side. The watermen who rowed you across were themselves often drunk and often as bloody-minded as the worst of today's cockney cabbies and were suitably lampooned in the hit film based in this area, *Shakespeare In Love*. London may seem odd in some regards today, but in previous centuries it was a seething mass of insane and eccentric contradictions like a Gormenghast made real.

For example, the **brothels at Bankside** were regulated by the government, owned by the Church (for much of their 400-year history), and the normal rule of law was set aside under the paradoxical term, the **Liberty of the Clink**. How the Clink – the very prison after which all others are nicknamed – could offer liberty was a typical eccentricity of medieval London.

Certain institutions around and near the City had their own jurisdiction, meaning normal law and regulations were suspended therein. The medieval manor of the Clink was one such, with its own manorial court (such as existed throughout rural England) and its own jail for wrong-doers, the Clink. Hence 'being in the Clink', British slang for being jailed, doesn't relate to the noise of the chains as I had assumed. Such an area of private jurisdiction was known as the Liberty. This particular one, a 70-acre patch along the South Bank, was owned by the **Bishops of Winchester** from 1107, and the operation of the stews was regulated by a law introduced by Henry II in 1161, although they had obviously been in existence for many years before that. Those who caught venereal disease from the Bankside brothels were said to have been 'bitten by the Winchester geese'.

Fair play for customers was ensured by a law from the 12th century ruling that 'no single woman to take money to lie with any man but she lie with him all night till the morrow'. We know little about the lives of the 'Winchester geese' beyond this, but they were not allowed to be buried in consecrated ground such as churchyards. There are masses of them buried a little way south of here at Cross Bones Ground near an old crossroads on Redcross Way.

Brothel-owning may seem a bizarre occupation for a bishop. The attitude of Catholic Church and king seemed to be that such things were better regulated than otherwise, but these were the only London brothels ever to be legalised. And, it has to be said, before the Reformation the Church was about big business, property and money as much as anything else.

It was not until the rise of Protestantism, partly in reaction to the Church's greedy commercialism, that Henry VIII – hardly a moral paragon – banned the Bankside stews in 1546. This forced the sex industry into backstreets and behind unmarked doors, where it has been ever since. It was not long after this that the City took over part of this area, making it the South Ward, or Southwark.

The area was by that time already booming as it serviced London's other pleasures and vices, with gambling, bear- and bull-baiting and theatres doing well by Shakespeare's time a few decades later. The **baiting of animals** involved setting vicious dogs upon other beasts for the amusement of the public who paid to get into a sort of theatre, and laughed as they watched enraged horses, bulls or bears being torn apart as they struggled with their tormentors. One show that made people laugh was a horse with a monkey on its back, the monkey trying to keep out of the way of the leaping dogs but eventually being killed when the horse was brought down.

Another factor in Southwark's notoriety is the existence of the small **sanctuaries** where fugitives could hide from justice. These generally had some kind of religious origin but became completely abused as they were used to evade the law or cheat people. One of these was known as the Mint, behind where Borough station now stands, and thousands of debtors lived here to escape imprisonment. Oddly, this sanctuary never had any legal status but it took several Acts of Parliament to close it down.

Another sanctuary was the **Paris Garden**, just upriver of Bankside, where bear-baiting and gambling thrived in the 16th century without the restriction of legal rules, despite the land being owned by a Church order in the first place.

The British who today collectively tut-tut bull-fighting seem to have conveniently forgotten that such 'sports' were enjoyed here by commoners and royalty alike – Elizabeth I loved to see such bloodsports (and Elizabeth II isn't averse to seeing the odd pheasant blown out of the skies). The greatest actor of Shakespeare's time, Southwark's **Edward Alleyn** (see page 294), was Master of the Royal Bears, Bulls and Mastiff Dogs, so close was the connection between theatre and bloodsports.

All these pleasures were banned by the rather boring Puritans who took control during the Civil War of the next century, but bull-baiting and dog-fighting returned with the Restoration of the monarchy in 1660. However, with theatres once more legalised and the growth of both pleasure gardens and theatres to the west of the City, Southwark was soon eclipsed by the emerging West End around the then new Covent Garden, and pleasure gardens elsewhere soon attracted crowds for pleasures both innocent and illicit.

The other aspect of Southwark's seedy past was the presence of several **prisons**. Not so much the visible evidence on the riverside of the already-mentioned Clink, which offers excellent visions of medieval hell-holes and grisly instruments of torture, but the **massive debtors' prisons** further south, around Borough High Street.

The **Marshalsea Prison** where Dickens's father was imprisoned for debt was one of these, and no wonder he felt angry about imprisoning people who could not pay bills and thereby making the situation worse. In *Little Dorrit* the heroine is born in the Marshalsea, which Dickens describes as:

… an oblong pile of barrack building, partitioned into squalid houses standing back to back, environed by a narrow paved yard hemmed in by high walls duly spiked on top.

As Dickens wrote, whole families lived and died in prison because one of them, not even a criminal, had once got into debt. The **King's Bench Prison** of earlier centuries stood nearby (and features in Dickens's *Nicholas Nickleby*), as did the **White Lion jail**, one of Surrey's main prisons for serious criminals. Further south, at Newington Gardens, stood yet another prison, **Horsemonger Lane jail**. Dickens's account of a gruesome husband-and-wife hanging there was instrumental in getting public executions stopped. The gloomy sombreness that this once massive and miserable population cast over this part of Southwark has never entirely dissipated. It's part of its charm.

Ancient inns, secret Bibles and bloody surgery

This walk will take about two hours and is about two miles in length. There are lots of opportunities to stop for refreshment along the way.

We start at **Borough station** on the Tube's Northern Line City branch. This section is the world's oldest Tube railway (see page 124). We'll stay above ground but it'll still be gloomy in places because that's what we've come to see: the simultaneously grim and cheerful Southwark, historical warts and all. It starts in Dickensian – even Chaucerian – picturesque grimness but ends with the most sublime views.

The sites of the many prisons (see page 265) are around here, and the name of the road on our sharp left, Marshalsea, is the most famous, thanks to Dickens.

Leaving the station and crossing Borough High Street, we're confronted with **St George the Martyr** church, one of Dickens's settings for *Little Dorrit*. The clock is lit on the three Borough sides but dark at night on the far Bermondsey side because, it's said, the parishioners in the latter district were too tight-pursed to fork out for the new church, so they can blunder around in their own time. This road junction is still where two great national roads meet – the A2 from Dover and the A3 from Portsmouth – transport being Southwark's other main role (beside plying pleasures and pandering to perversions).

Walk up the first bit of **Borough High Street**, the odd bit of fifties and sixties architecture hinting at bomb patterns of the 1940s. At one of these points, before the wacky blue spidermen sculptures on the front of Maya House on the left, note **Little Dorrit Court**, also on the left, which leads to a school. Southwark was riven, and still is, with hundreds of these little walkways through to the criminal sanctuaries and liberties of prisons. Evading the law through this network was all the easier.

We rapidly see on the right ancient names, many linked to inns and taverns: Chapel Court, Mermaid Court, St Christopher Inn, Mermaid Yard, Talbot Yard. The **St Christopher Inn**, still there in a rebuilt form, was where, until the railway age, travellers from London would gather to board the Dover stage. It was a good spot to catch those fleeing to France, and choice pickings for the highwaymen up on Blackheath. In an earlier era the famed **Tabard inn** was the assembly point for the Canterbury pilgrims walking the Pilgrims Way through Kent, recorded with such ribaldry and colour by Chaucer in the 14th century. (The Tabard was in **Talbot Yard** and is remembered by **Tabard Street** beside St George the Martyr church.)

Transport was Southwark's great *raison d'être*: where the stage routes from the south and abroad converged close to **London Bridge** – the only Thames crossing – which travellers could walk across, or take a sedan chair. We can see how close the City is from the tower blocks ahead, across the river – hence the stagecoach-sized entrances to many of these little lanes. One of the greatest of these old inns that really shows how things used to be is the **George**, again on the right. This is said to be London's last great galleried inn and is massive, yet is only a fraction of its previous size, this being one side of a huge rectangle of land it once occupied. It's owned by the National Trust and leased to a pub company. Shakespeare, Dickens, Pepys and Johnson would have known this place, as it dates from at least the 16th century (Stow's *Survay of London* of 1598 mentions it), although this rebuilding is a mere 330 years old, being of 1677. In its heyday this one pub received perhaps 80 coaches a week, and was just one of many great galleried inns in Southwark. They were the railway termini of their day, or the airport terminals and departure gates. And the fact that the City gates, including London Bridge, were locked at night meant there was a great deal of accommodation in demand from travellers arriving late.

Two easily missed details to see here: on the right a splendid shop front of **W H & H le May**, hop factors. You have to crane your neck or cross the road, but high up there's an ornamental front. Hops for beer brewing famously come from Kent so would have arrived in London on this road. To see just how important they were, go back ten paces and look across the street through a narrow walkway called Counter Alley. You will see a glimpse of the magnificent **Hop Exchange**. Counter Court, the narrow walkway you are looking through, is named after yet another prison, and it is soon apparent that the grand-looking HSBC Bank next to it is shaped like a slice of cake, perched on an odd bit of ground, a pattern we will see in a yet more extreme form in a truly splendid pub later in the walk. (You may wish to pop through to see better the splendidly ornamented frontage of the Hop Exchange, or the interior, which you may ask the chap on the left as you go in for permission to view. It is a cast-iron cathedral to hops, decorated with the white horse of Kent.)

Staying on the right of Borough High Street, you can appreciate that defining characteristic of this part of Southwark: a great convergence of roads, and a great convergence of railways overlaid on this medieval muddle giving a pleasing chaos to the geography as the lines, like the roads, twist and turn at different levels to make junctions and gain access to the bridges over the Thames. Ahead can be spotted through the railway bridge the golden ball of the **Monument** to the Great Fire in the City, from which Southwark was spared by the Thames. Conversely, we also have had dramatic glimpses of **the Gherkin** office block, ahead in the City, and the **Shard**, on the right and close-by in London Bridge – what a contrast!

Note the Borough Market front on the left, which we will soon enter.

There are yet more pubs or signs of them: **White Hart Yard** on the right was mentioned by Shakespeare in *Henry VI* and by Dickens in *Pickwick Papers*. Particularly atmospheric is **Old Kings Head Yard**, again on the right. Beyond it are the buildings of Guy's, one of the two great teaching hospitals historically based here.

We cross **St Thomas Street**, and on the right just before the massive railway bridge is a grey stone church-like building. This is the **old St Thomas's Hospital** – the other half of this area's great medical history. If we had turned right down St Thomas Street, we would have seen the church of **St Thomas Apostle**, where the hospital started in 1215. Today the **Old Operating Theatre Museum and Herb Garret** offer a fascinating glimpse of the bloody days when screaming patients endured saw-bones surgery in front of audiences (see page 73). Or perhaps they didn't endure it.

The old hospital building near the railway bridge on the main road is also the site where the first **English Bible** was printed in 1537. Until then it was heresy for Bibles to be in anything other than Latin, the exclusive medium of the monopolistic, then hopelessly corrupt Catholic Church, stopping ordinary people from understanding a word of it. As Protestantism spread in the 1520s, great pioneers such as **William Tyndale** (1494–1536) printed copies in English and smuggled them into England hidden among other cargoes. He was caught and executed for heresy by Catholic authorities in Europe in 1536, just one year before Bibles were printed here. Tyndale, as a student at Cambridge, had horrified a senior clergyman by vowing:

If God spare my life, I shall cause the boy that driveth
the plow to know more of the Bible than thou dost!

And so he did. St Thomas's Hospital is now further upriver, in Lambeth.

MURDER BY GASLIGHT AND A BISHOP'S BROTHEL

If we cross the main Borough High Street just by the railway bridge, we can plunge left through an archway in the bridge supports into the spooky and Dickensian atmosphere of **Green Dragon Court**, which rapidly takes us into **Borough Market**. This is murder-by-gaslight territory, and there's plenty more, often used for films, around London Bridge too, where entire streets are under the arches. It gets a lot more sinister after dark. Among recent films to use this setting are *Bridget Jones's Diary, Lock, Stock and Two Smoking Barrels, Keep the Aspidistra Flying, Wings of a Dove, Entrapment* and, of course, all kinds of 1950s British B movies. It's a black-and-white kind of place, really. Of course they are all slightly out-of-date with the 2011 new viaduct bolted on to the front of the old one. Does it spoil the charm of the chaotic Dickensian gloom – no not a bit of it, it adds to it.

The market – 'London's larder' it boasts – opens early, and so do the pubs. One of these pubs, the **Globe Tavern** on the left, is neatly dovetailed into the old and new railway viaducts either side – can you imagine sleeping upstairs there? – and the whole place seems designed to give the tidy-minded kind of town planner the screaming abdabs. I mean the ornamented pub, the chaotic market under the railway, the booming trains, yelling barrowboys, roaring traffic and **Southwark Cathedral** serene behind all that.

To the right of the market are two things which I'm not suggesting visiting, but might be interesting to read about. Firstly, the cathedral, which is set to the right of the market, somehow totally avoids the soaring inspiration of many such churches and squats low on the ground, girded by the railway viaduct and riverside buildings. It was, after all, just a large parish church until 1905; its low-key sombreness suits the place, and the poor neighbourhood it has served. It is not, architecturally, in the top ten or even top 100. There are a few fine monuments inside, including local stars **Shakespeare** and **John Harvard** (as in university; see page 192), and a strange one to a pill-merchant, John Lockyer. There is also a trendy exhibition/museum next to the shop but I didn't find it worth the admission fee.

Secondly, between the cathedral and the riverbank, is **St Mary Overie Dock** with its floating replica of the *Golden Hind* in which Francis Drake (1540–96) circumnavigated the world. Here, also, the legend is told of the miserly ferryman who used to control the crossing before the bridge was built. He was so tight with his money that one day he pretended to be dead so his family and servants would stop eating and save him a few pennies. Instead, however, they started celebrating with his best wine. As he rose angrily from his 'death bed', they assumed the Devil had got into the corpse and struck him really dead. His daughter's greedy fiancé, rushing over to claim the dead relative's property, fell off his horse and was killed. Not a good day for the daughter, Mary Overie. In disgust at the meanness and greed of them all she set up a monastery dedicated to aiding the poor; she eventually became a saint, while her monastery became St Thomas's Hospital.

Now, continuing along the line of Green Dragon Court through the market we reach **Stoney Street** (as you come out of the market) and turn right. The atmosphere here is definitely of riverside wharves and warehouses, and although Old Father Thames is not yet visible, you can already smell him. Looking higher, you can see we are amidst an aerial rail triangle. Also note Winchester Walk on the right (it's those naughty brothel-keeping bishops again).

If we go left at the far end we're in **Clink Street** and the high wall on the left is the only surviving part of that original. Nevertheless, there is a rather good Clink museum on the left (see page 79). There are similar grisly items nearby at the London Dungeon at London Bridge.

Soon we go under another railway and reach, on the riverbank, the **Anchor** pub. **Park Street** was the real site of Shakespeare's Globe Theatre, the re-creation of which is coming up. For 800 years a pub has stood here. But this is undoubtedly the site of the **Castle stewhouse**, one of the biggest brothels, and owned by the Bishop of Winchester. The diarist Samuel Pepys (1633–1703) sat here and watched the Great Fire of London rage across the river in September 1666. Sir Christopher Wren (1632–1723) sat here a few years later and watched his magnificent dome of St Paul's rising as a consequence. The river walls were not so high then, and there's a plate recording the highest flood level four feet up one of the walls of the pub to show why they are so high today. Now you have to go upstairs or cross to the riverside terrace to enjoy the view.

SUPERB VIEWS, HEROIC TALK AND AN ECCENTRIC RACE

The view along this riverbank, which we will follow left (westward), is superb. To the right, through the arches of the railway bridge, is London Bridge and Tower Bridge plus the 'museumified' World War II cruiser, HMS *Belfast*, Europe's largest surviving armoured ship of that conflict. In front is the City, with the best possible view of St Paul's coming up and other landmarks to admire – the steeple of St Bride's on Fleet Street being just one on the left, peeping over Southwark Bridge, and roughly where we are heading.

Following the riverside we approach **Southwark Bridge** – the office on the left is that of the *Financial Times* – and plunging under the arches there is a slate mural depicting the great Frost Fair of 1564. The building of the narrow-arched London Bridge in 1169 (the one with houses on) had enabled the Thames to freeze over, and in 1564 it froze so thoroughly that a fair was held here. Oxen were roasted on spits, newssheets were printed on the ice, sports and games were played and the river did not thaw for weeks.

Beyond the bridge the newest wonder on the Thames is the **Millennium Bridge**, a strange contraption making a footbridge from **St Paul's** to the Bankside and its new tourist honeypots, particularly the **Tate Modern**. The idea behind the bridge seems to have been to make it appear as thin as possible when viewed from the side, the result being that it swayed like one of those plank bridges over canyons. It has since been stiffened somewhat.

First on the left is Shakespeare's **Globe Theatre**, which is, of course, not Shakespeare's Globe but a complete and beautiful replica built thanks to the vision and drive of American actor and film-maker **Sam Wanamaker** (1919–93), who died during its construction, having fought for 25 years to get the project off the ground (or on to the ground). The thatched building is as faithful as possible a replica and one can tour the structure when no plays are showing. Before this, the only representation we knew was in films such as the wartime *Henry V*, starring Laurence Olivier. Shakespeare refers directly to the theatre building and to what literary types call the 'suspension of disbelief' – the way in which you let him take you out of the theatre into his imagined lands – in the prologue to that play:

Then should the warlike Harry, like himself,
Assume the port of Mars, and at his heels,
Leashed in like hounds, should Famine, Sword and Fire
Crouch for employment. But pardon, gentles all,
…Can this cockpit hold
The vasty fields of France? Or may we cram
Within this wooden O the very casques
That did affright the air at Agincourt?

And a little later:

Suppose within the girdle of these walls
Are now confined two mighty monarchies,
Whose high upreared and abutting fronts
The perilous narrow ocean parts asunder.

Shakespeare's talk here of the heroic few taking on the many must surely have been ringing in Churchill's ears when he spoke of the 'Few' in another such battle over the same narrow sea centuries later.

Leaping on (or, as Shakespeare put it so much better in that prologue, 'jumping o'er times, / Turning th'accomplishment of many years / Into an hour-glass'), we pass **Cardinal's Cap Alley** on our way to Tate Modern. The name commemorates an early 15th-century Bishop of Winchester who went to Rome to be made Cardinal Beaufort and it's said he landed here to parade his red cap of office through the Liberty of the Clink, which he owned. Others suggest it was where the cardinal's mistress lived and the road should be Cardinal's Tart Alley. Or Cardinal Sin Alley possibly.

And so to the **Tate Modern**, which is housed in the former Bankside Power Station, and judged a great achievement and, in some ways, recalling the French recycling of an old railway station, the Gare d'Orsay, on the banks of the Seine for a similar role. This one dwarfs the Parisian one for

SOUTHWARK

WHEN YOU WALK BY the obviously ancient, battered and unpretentious house at **49 Bankside**, opposite St Paul's and in the few original properties crammed between the reconstructed Globe Theatre and the Tate Modern, you will be astonished to see a plaque on the front wall boldly announcing its double claim to fame:

Here lived Sir Christopher Wren
During the building of St Paul's Cathedral
Here also, in 1502, Catherine
Infanta of Castile and Aragon
Afterwards first Queen
Of Henry VIII took shelter
On her first landing in
London

A house of mystery and history

Oddly, both claims are complete tosh. Having once been invited into this charming Queen Anne house (it is a home, not a museum, so don't knock), I could well imagine Wren relaxing in the upstairs sitting room with a first-class view of St Paul's going up across the river. Sadly, it's balderdash because when this house was finished, so was St Paul's, more or less. As for the Infanta, that notion should have been strangled at birth – infantacide – because the house is 200 years younger than her arrival. There was a tatty inn on the site, true, but Spanish princesses with their enormous retinue do not stay in tatty inns in an area known for brothels, gambling and bear-baiting. The plaque was a jape by an eccentric owner, who mockingly copied the idea from a nearby house, now long gone, where Wren *did* stay. Even odder, as I stood among the Mary Poppins-style chimney pots on the roof drinking in the quite marvellous view, I was to find out that the building could reasonably have two plaques to other events. One, as it was a Tudor tavern close to the Globe Theatre, it is inevitable that Shakespeare drank on this site and probably characters such as Marlowe too. The other – and this is a certainty – is that mid-20th-century silver-screen siren Anna Lee (1913–2004) lived there. There are pictures of the blonde bombshell reclining gracefully (frankly, she didn't do any other kind of reclining) where Wren and the Infanta certainly didn't in Gillian Tindall's fascinatingly detailed biography of this property, *The House Beside the Thames*.

scale, if not content, and much of the space is courageously left open. It's now the world's most visited modern art museum. It's well worth a visit, and is sometimes brilliant, sometimes rubbish.

Then past the **Founders Arms** pub (nice spot, dull building) to Blackfriars Bridge. We go under the railway bridge – properly called Alexandra Bridge but no one ever does – and up on to the road bridge. Across the road is one of London's odder pub names, **Doggett's Coat & Badge**, which refers to a prize offered in a strange annual Thames boat race. Comedian Thomas Doggett launched the race in 1716 to celebrate the accession of George I to the throne, and every July since (the precise date depends on tides) the race is held between London Bridge and Chelsea Bridge. Prizes, funded by Doggett's legacy, include a splendid full-length red coat with a tight waist and a silver badge. So the winner looks like a right ninny, giving comedian Doggett the last laugh.

Don't miss (almost opposite Doggett's Coat & Badge) the enormous colourful brackets marked with the arms of the London, Chatham and Dover Railway and featuring that Kentish White Horse and 'Invicta' the white horse we saw at the Hop Exchange. It splendidly holds nothing, as do a fine set of piers across the river. Oddly, when the railway bridge was recently widened, they did it by bringing in new arches on barges rather than using the empty ones, parts of which will be platforms in the new station. Maybe it was because the original bridge was abandoned for not being strong enough for modern trains. One of the architects, by the way, of that early bridge and the station on the north bank was one **Henry Marc Brunel** (1842–1903), son of Isambard Kingdom Brunel (see page 155).

Invicta, you may know from school Latin, means 'the undefeated ones', and the people of Kent who use this emblem insist they were never conquered by William the Conqueror, or the Norman bastard, in 1066, but met his army and agreed terms for his taking over from Harold. Yeah, right.

Crossing the bridge we might recall with a shudder that under one of these spans the body of 'God's banker' Roberto Calvi was found hanged in June 1982, his pockets stuffed, bizarrely, with cash and bricks. One of those Mafia things, it was suggested, but how the hell did they get poor Calvi up there? (Now some bankers just screw the entire world and get the bundles of cash *without* the rope, cynics may think.)

Another unpleasant thing under our feet is the outlet of the **Fleet**, once a freshwater river but for about 1,000 years a foul-smelling running sewer (see page 129). You can't see it except by craning out from the steps up to the bridge on the upstream side and I don't recommend that dangerous option, especially not if you've had a few pints. It's better seen from a boat if you must.

We go ahead, into the subway (pedestrian underpass) and up out of exit 1 to the **Black Friar** pub, small but perfectly formed. The name Black Friar comes from medieval monasteries and priories around here.

First regard carefully the outside, the tiny cheese-shaped wedge of land that it occupies. As I've noted elsewhere, the rebuilding of the City after the Great Fire of 1666 was so rapid that plans for a boring American-style gridiron pattern of roads were thrown aside and the daft medieval street pattern lived on – thankfully, in my view. Here the builders also had a railway line at first-floor height to contend with behind the pub, so the site was very restricted, and is only about four-feet wide at one end. Second, look at the rich ornamentation, the bronze signs and the mosaic detail.

Certainly, the architect did a good job in 1875, as can be seen by the interesting exterior, but the real treat is inside, and clearly dates from the early 20th century, with heavy Art Nouveau influences in its whimsical interpretation of the life of monks. I think that the interior is a national treasure, and the beer isn't bad either. I can't describe it fully, so see for yourself. It'll be crowded at City lunchtimes, but soon thins out at around 2.15pm so you can have a proper look round. Superb – and definitely eccentric.

Here you can sample what Brits call 'real ale', the living beer made with live yeast, water, hops and malted barley. If you are from a poor, benighted land where chilled lager is the only brew, I have to warn you that it's a bit of an acquired taste. Like sex and cigars (or both at once in former President Clinton's case), it gets better. The fourth pint is probably the best.

You can return to **Blackfriars** station, across the road, for a train home via the subway and don't miss a final detail in the station's booking hall. The ornate blocks, which formed part of the façade of this station before some blockhead removed it, were engraved with places the aforesaid London, Chatham and Dover Railway could take you to via its suburban lines but also via Channel ferries. These blocks were saved and put here. Thus we have prosaic Bromley ludicrously next to Bremen as alternative destinations, St Petersburg next to Westgate-on-Sea, and Beckenham next to Baden-Baden. I had hoped to see Penge next to Peking, but they seem to have lost that one.

WHITECHAPEL

Half the English-speaking world seems to watch a BBC TV soap opera called *EastEnders*. It would be called 'gritty' if it were about northerners, for all the characters are dysfunctional and constantly having affairs, abortions, fights, prison sentences, etc, and I can't remember the last 'normal' couple who merely brought up their own children and actually worked for a living. Perish the thought. And a 'gay outing' isn't a trip to Clacton.

But it's all far too tame compared to the real East End, which to judge by events around Whitechapel (the medieval White Chapel that gave this area its name was destroyed in the Blitz) is far more dramatic, murderous and violent than in the fictional Albert Square. For those who have a horrified fascination with Hannibal Lecter and such like, however, it's worth taking a look at the area which offers:

- Jack the Ripper's amazing killings
- A shoot-out involving mad anarchists and Winston Churchill
- The place where the bigots of the 20th century's worst 'isms' – communism and fascism – came to a bloody battle on British streets
- The Kray Brothers' merciless executions
- Layers of rapid cultural reinvention worthy of New York, as completely different waves of immigrants move in and out.

And that means there's fabulous and cheap Indian, or rather Bangladeshi, food. There are also the origins of America's greatest symbol of freedom and a radically different art gallery.

A SHORT WALK ABOUT WHITECHAPEL

This walk takes you down the Whitechapel Road, from the Tube at Whitechapel to the Tube at Aldgate, with a few diversions. It's about 1½ miles, and takes about 1½ hours with stops. Considering Whitechapel's horrible history, you will find today's Whitechapel both pleasantly fascinating and surprisingly unchanged from its poor East End origins despite being cheek by jowl with one of the world's richest financial centres. It's less dangerous than most inner cities. But then these busy pavements have had a lot of blood washed off them.

Coming out of the Tube, there's a great **street market** in front of you (except on Sundays). There are Asian stalls with saris and glittering cloths of all descriptions, the wonderful vegetables favoured by the sub-continent such as *brinjals* and *okra* (aubergines and ladies' fingers), plus stalls run by cockney costermongers selling tools or unbelievably cheap gadgets.

WHITECHAPEL WALK

The Krays, a Ripper victim and Elephant Man

In front of us as we leave the Tube is the London Hospital. Over the road, if you're interested in the social history of the East End with its communism and the Battle of Cable Street, is a good Lefty bookshop, **Eastside Books**.

Take a quick excursion to the left (east) to the **Blind Beggar** pub where **Ronnie Kray** (1933–2000), one of the merciless Kray Twin gangsters, protection racketeers and would-be Al Capones of London, killed **George Cornell** on 8 March 1966. Oddly, no one in the Blind Beggar had seen anyone at all. *We ain't seen nuffink, guv, 'onest.* Later, after the gang began to be rounded up, people's memory suddenly improved and the police put together what happened.

Cornell had made the mistake of calling Ronnie Kray a 'fat poof' ('poof' is British slang for 'homosexual'). This had the virtue of accuracy on both counts, but all the wisdom of Bambi's mum picking a pack of starving rottweilers as babysitters. He was doomed. Kray could not let such loss of face go unchallenged without his hold over the East End being weakened. Kray got away with this killing for a while but was jailed for life at the Old Bailey four years later. But not until Ronnie had spurred twin brother Reggie into shooting another minor criminal, Jack 'the hat' McVitie. That was the one that got the Krays into the dock.

Many years later, a Fleet Street newspaper printed a smuggled picture of Reggie Kray enjoying a cup of tea behind bars. Referring to a well-known British biscuit, the headline was: 'I could just murder a McVitie…' Brilliant.

There is a story that the name Blind Beggar comes from the great medieval warrior Simon de Montfort. Blinded in battle, and supposedly killed, he in fact returned incognito to London to beg on the streets, a broken man, and was found by his followers who had refused to believe he was dead. Or something like that. There's a 16th-century ballad entitled *The Blind Beggar of Bethnal Green*. It's a great yarn, but some people put it back a few more centuries and make it King Harold, he who got one in the eye from William the Conqueror.

At the major road crossing here, the road to the right (south) is **Sidney Street**, where the amazing events of the Siege of 1911 unfolded at **No 100** (see box, page 278) on the left, although the bullet-riddled house has been replaced at least twice, so I don't suggest going to look.

Turning back down **Whitechapel Road** towards the Tube, we are close to the spot where Jack the Ripper's second victim **Polly Nichols**'s body was found on 31 August 1888.

If you want to reach the actual spot, take a short deviation by turning right into Brady Street after the Sainsbury's entrance and go left into

WHITECHAPEL'S FIRST GREAT gun battle of the 20th century was the Siege of Sidney Street, involving the unlikely combination of Peter the Painter, Latvian anarchists and Winston Churchill (1874–1965) directing fire in his top hat. In fact, knowing Churchill's amazing subsequent life, perhaps it isn't all that surprising.

The gang of anarchists had come to Britain in the rush of immigration after the failed Russian revolution of 1905. Their leader was Peter Paiktow, who worked as a painter while in London.

In 1909 the authorities became aware of the dangers posed by these types when two Latvians staged an armed robbery in Tottenham and two people were killed and 27 people injured during the ensuing shoot-out and pursuit.

The siege of Sidney Street

In 1910, Peter the Painter's gang rented a Houndsditch shop with the aim of tunnelling into an adjacent jeweller's shop. Neighbours were made suspicious by the noise and when an unarmed constable entered the building, he was immediately shot dead. This was on 23 December 1910, the year after the 'Tottenham Outrage'. Three further policemen called to the scene were also killed. One of the gang was accidentally shot by a colleague as they escaped, and he was left to die with a nurse, who bizarrely was also a gang member (it's turning into a kind of Latvian Bonnie & Clyde). The police soon found the injured man and arrested various connected people.

By the New Year, the police learned that two of the gang were holed up at 100 Sidney Street in Whitechapel. On 3 January, as armed officers

Durward Street. Down here, on the left, you are soon faced with an old school, now converted into flats. At the nearest corner of this school's redbrick wall, there used to be a gate where a newer wall now stands. Here, half on the road and half on the pavement, cordoned off the street, a gun battle broke out and it soon became clear that the gang, with their machine-guns, could outshoot the police, who were armed just with revolvers.

The police asked the Home Office to call in the Army. The Home Secretary at the time was Winston Churchill, the larger-than-life figure who had already escaped from an armoured train in the Boer War, and who was later to lead the troops personally in the defence of Antwerp, introduce the tank in World War I, mount the daring but disastrous Gallipoli campaign, and then face down the might of Nazi Germany when Britain stood alone during World War II. Asking him if he'd mind summoning armed help was like asking Dawn French's Vicar of Dibley if she'd mind eating a cream cake.

Churchill arrived and took charge, sheltering behind a wall as the bullets flew. He called in the Scots Guards who were nearby. The Scots Guards riddled the building until it looked like a colander. It caught fire, but Churchill ordered the Fire Brigade to let it burn and let them die.

The two gunmen were indeed dead in the ruins, but neither turned out to be the leader, Peter the Painter. He was never traced. Neither was the criminal trial of the gang members who had been caught a great success. It couldn't be proved who had shot the policemen in Tottenham, and the case collapsed. The key members returned to Latvia and one of them, Jacob Peters, became a top Bolshevik and a high official in the communist government after the Russian Revolution. In the 1930s he, like hundreds of thousands of others, fell victim to one of Stalin's purges and was murdered. Better Latvian than never...

Polly's body was found at about 3am, severely chopped about.

She was a drunk and a prostitute, aged 42. That night she made three times the money needed to pay for her vermin-infested 'doss house' lodgings in Thrawl Street but drank the lot and was turned away, and was last seen looking for more custom in Whitechapel Road at 2.30am.

Return to Whitechapel Road, turn right and walk back past the Tube. Keep an eye out for **No 259** on this side of the road, now an ordinary shop but once home to **Joseph Merrick** (1862–90), the **Elephant Man** (see box, page 280).

THE ELEPHANT MAN, greatly deformed though he was, was perhaps a natural for Whitechapel Road in the 1880s. Then, as now, a market stretched along here and it included fun-fair elements trying to catch the attention of travellers using this artery eastwards – which in the Victorian way of thinking could mean paying to see the two-headed chicken, the amazingly fat naked girl, the world's ugliest dwarf, that kind of thing.

In November 1884 showman Tom Norman brought to a shop he had hired at **No 259** a number of attractions, including the professional freak **Joseph Merrick**, the Elephant Man. He was so called because his skin hung in folds like that of an elephant. His head and face were extremely disfigured so he didn't look human at all, with random growths akin to huge fungal bodies on a dead tree.

The humiliating circumstances in which Merrick performed are probably difficult to understand nowadays. He was kept in a darkened cage (for maximum shock value) and when punters paid their pennies he had to take off his hood and clothes and stand naked in front of them. He was ordered around like a dog, not because he couldn't speak, but because it made a better show. He had to stand naked in front of the appalled or jeering crowd.

The tragic truth about the Elephant Man

Sometimes the Elephant Man stood in the shop window, with his hood on, to entice passers-by, and there was a lurid representation of him on the outside of the building with sensational promises about the hideous ELEPHANT MAN prominently displayed.

MINARETS, BELLS, BRICKS AND ART

On a happier note, we soon see on the left the massive **East London Mosque**, heart of the Bangladeshi community round here, with its distinctive crescents where a church's crosses would be. And, of course, minarets wailing for Friday's prayer rather than bells tolling in steeples on Sundays.

The shop was opposite the London Hospital, and a surgeon-pathologist from there, **Dr Frederick Treves,** saw Merrick posing in the window one day and visited him. Dr Treves believed Merrick was suffering from Proteus Syndrome and, because of the way he was treated, expected him to be a simpleton. He was appalled, given Merrick's treatment, to find a highly intelligent and sensitive young man beneath the horrible appearance.

Merrick had learned to read using the only book he'd ever seen – a copy of the Bible. Treves had drawings and photographs taken to record his condition, but for a year or two Merrick remained in the freak show.

Merrick was then taken temporarily on show in Brussels, and on his return to Liverpool Street his sudden appearance caused a near riot. Dr Treves was called by the authorities and he 'bought' Merrick – paid off the showman Norman – and took him into the London Hospital. He spent the rest of his life there in an isolation room in the attic, at that time part of the nurses' accommodation.

Nurses who initially wanted to run shrieking from him found he was, underneath it all, a reasonable and even likeable young man. Many society figures, fascinated with what they had heard, came to visit him here, including the then Princess of Wales. He was famous, but for the wrong reasons.

His head was so deformed that he was told that to sleep on his back would be dangerous, although he expressed a longing to be able to sleep like other people. One night in 1890 he went to sleep on his back – whether with suicidal intentions, we shall never know – and died aged 28.

A movie, *Elephant Man*, was made of his story in 1980. Anthony Hopkins played Dr Treves and John Hurt was Merrick. His key-line was: 'I am not an animal... I am a human being... I am... a man!'

That's ironic, for the world's oldest bell foundry is on the left. The **Whitechapel Bell Foundry** is Britain's oldest manufacturing business and must be one of the world's oldest. There are records of Richard Chamberlain, 'bell founder of Aldgate', in 1420, and the business may be a lot older than that.

It's well worth popping into the office at **34 Whitechapel Road** and looking at the display in the foyer of the offices. Opening the door rings a bell, of course, like an old-fashioned sweet shop, and as you enter you step through the bell-frame (the stencil-like thing that gives the contours) of possibly the world's most famous bell, **Big Ben**.

This nine-foot-high, seven-foot six-inch-wide, 13½-ton job cost £572 2s 0d – you can see the bill – and rings the hours at Parliament's clock tower. It's heard from one end of the earth to the other on the BBC radio news.

If it's a business day you can probably get a glimpse into the workshops from the side street and no doubt there will be several bells on the ground, the church names chalked upon them: St Mary the Virgin, St Botolph's, etc.

Of course Americans would disagree that Big Ben is the most famous bell in the world, as they've got their own candidate, the Liberty Bell of Philadelphia, made right here in Whitechapel in 1751. Tours of the foundry are possible by arrangement, and there is sometimes an annual open day on the first Saturday in September (for enquiries ☎ *020 7247 2599*).

We go on down Whitechapel Road and it's worth recalling that on the British version of the Monopoly board, this is the poorest (brown) end of the game while Mayfair (royal blue) is the richest. Some things never change.

At **Brick Lane** (or Osborn Street) we turn right, although the constantly radical **Whitechapel Gallery**, with a rather cool frontage, if that's an object of your visit, is just a few yards further straight ahead, on the right-hand side.

Let's wander up fascinating Brick Lane, where Whitechapel's ethnic tidal waves came ashore over the centuries, bringing Huguenots, Jews, then Bangladeshis. This road, named after a brickworks here, has a great market on Sundays and an annual festival (see page 16).

The rest of the Ripper story

As you turn the corner here, and head down **Brick Lane**, you're near the murder site of the Ripper's first victim, **Martha Tabram**, who was killed at George Yard tenements, Gunthorpe Street on 7 August 1888. If you're interested, turn left down Wentworth Street and it's an alley on the left, leading back to Whitechapel Road.

But scurrying on up Brick Lane, enjoying the rich sweets and colourful garments, and noting a small outbreak of trendy 'loft living', we soon reach **Fournier Street** on the left. The building on the right as we enter has had several religious incarnations (Huguenot, Jewish and Muslim, none of which believes in reincarnation, but never mind) and halfway down on the right there's a chance to see another Ripper murder spot. If you wish, take a right along Wilkes Street to Hanbury Street at the end and find where **No 29** was, opposite Nos 28 and 30. Here, in the backyard, was found the third victim of the Ripper, **Annie Chapman**, on 8 September 1888.

Tides of immigration in the East End

FOR OVER 100 years, the East End has meant the 'rag trade' – tailoring at its posh end, sweat shops at its cheap end. In adjacent Spitalfields, near Petticoat Lane, there's Fashion Street, and nearby Weaver Street and Vallance Road. The thriving clothing trade – carried on by French Huguenots, then Jews, and now Bangladeshis – has given the street names real resonance. French, Yiddish, Bengali, Sylheti (a related language), and of course cockney have been the weft and warp of this place. Eventually each robustly working-class group did well and moved to middle-class suburbs, making room for the next wave of immigrants.

In Fournier Street, Spitalfields, there's a religious building which has seen these tides of people come and go. Built for the French Huguenots in 1743 it has been a Methodist church, a synagogue and is now a mosque. Like the mosque in Whitechapel Road, it is packed to overcrowding for Friday prayers.

Around here not only has halal food become more common than kosher, with the delicious sweets well worth a try, you can see the traditional dress, the bilingual shop and street signs, the books, CDs and videos and newspapers in Bengali. The culture is alive.

But then, like the Jews before them, the Bangladeshi community is hardly a minority. In Spitalfields it's said to make up 60 per cent of the population; in London as a whole one estimate is 123,000, mostly in the borough of Tower Hamlets. Like their Huguenot and Jewish predecessors, these people are tight-knit and hard-working. Will they, too, move on into the more comfortable strata of British society to make room for another wave of the dispossessed?

Meanwhile, a joke to cheer things up. A Jewish seamstress is walking home late at night in Whitechapel. She meets a 'flasher' – a man who is naked except for his overcoat, which he opens wide, facing her. She looks him up and down contemptuously and snorts: 'Call that a proper lining?'

BACK IN THE 1930s, while the Nazis were trying to blame the Jews for the economic troubles in Germany, the East End came the closest Britain has ever got to embracing this intolerant politically organised race hatred, this blind worship of political '-isms', that ruined hundreds of millions of lives in the 20th century.

In those days, just as fascism had not yet been exposed to the wider public as the evil it was, so communism was held up by British intellectuals such as George Orwell and the working class of the East End as an ideal way of life. No one would have believed that what was going on in Stalin's Russia was as terrible as in Nazi Germany. There were communist MPs and councils in the East End. Times were hard and the great -isms seemed to offer a simple answer.

On Sunday, 4 October 1936 would-be fascist demagogue, Sir Oswald Mosley, and around 3,500 would-be fascist Blackshirts tried to march into the East End, shouting: 'Get rid of the Yids.' They had put up stickers saying that Jews were taking jobs

The Battle of Cable Street

that 'white workers' should have, trying to drive a wedge between the two economically hard-pressed groups. The event had been well publicised among the Left, and thousands of communists, socialists and Spanish Civil War veterans converged on the scene, as did the fascists.

The police tried to clear the way and used baton charges on horseback when the going got rough. And it *did* get rough. The battle was almost entirely between the police – who in upholding the Blackshirts' right to march seemed to be on their side – and the Left, who adopted the Spanish Civil War slogan '*No Pasarán*' (they shall not pass). There was huge support in East London for the Left – far stronger than for the fascists, in fact. On this day, perhaps 300,000 communists, Jews, socialists and anti-fascists gathered to block the Blackshirts in what became the **Battle of Cable Street**.

The police started using baton charges and the whole mounted division to clear the crowds from Leman Street, but at Aldgate they came up against a tram immobilised by an anti-fascist driver. More trams joined, forming a massive road block surrounded by tens of thousands of people – some papers said half a million, some 100,000. Plans for the Blackshirts to march down Commercial Road, going east from the City, were scuppered.

The Blackshirts could have pressed eastwards down The Highway, further south, but there were no Jews there to intimidate and attack, which was the whole point of the operation, so the only route left to the east was Cable Street. The police tried to force their way through.

The Left had a plan ready. A lorry was turned over and a builders' yard ransacked to make a barricade. All the way along the road the inhabitants pelted the police – rather than the Blackshirts who never really got going from their start in Royal Mint Street – with bottles, fruit, bricks and the contents of chamber pots. Every time the police cleared a barricade a new one sprang up. A witness quoted in *The Battle of Cable Street 1936* (Five Leaves Publications) described the women throwing down everything they had – beds, chairs, tables – to build the barricades. 'I can remember the old girls with their aprons and shawls on... and glory on their faces.'

A whistle blew and someone shouted: 'The dockers are coming' and they swarmed from a side street in their hundreds, carrying pick handles. They prised up the cobblestones to use as missiles. Another eyewitness said: 'The most amazing thing was to see a silk-coated Orthodox Jew standing next to an Irish docker with a grappling iron. This was unbelievable.'

Police – the unfortunate meat in this political sandwich – were getting seriously hurt and getting nowhere. After three hours battling, the police advised the fascists that they could not march through and, humiliated, they dispersed westwards, never to pose a major threat in British politics again. Whether the dreaded political -isms would ever have taken hold in Britain as a whole is doubtful. But to treat the Battle of Cable Street as some kind of exaggerated silly scuffle is to under-estimate the volatile rip-tide of history flowing through here at the time. Many of those on either side at Cable Street were also volunteers in the Spanish Civil War where Left and Right fought to the death. Those people, if not yet the wider public, understood what fascism meant.

By the way, No 3 Fournier Street was the location for the 1992 film *The Crying Game*, starring Miranda Richardson.

Continuing along Fournier Street, whose architecture is much the same as in the Ripper's time (and indeed long before, to judge by the French Huguenot-style window shutters) we find at the end Hawksmoor's spectacular masterpiece – in some eyes – of **Christ Church**, Spitalfields.

On the opposite corner of Fournier Street, the **Ten Bells** was where Annie Chapman had her last drink before leaving with a man, presumably the Ripper. It was also a regular drinking place for the customers of most of the victims, so here we are closer to the Ripper and his victims than anywhere.

He, whoever he was, and his victims would have stood here occasionally and looked up at this spire just as you do. It was built in 1714–29 and, unlike Wren, **Nicholas Hawksmoor** made no bones about adding a 225-foot Gothic-based spire to a classical temple-shaped barn of a church. Wallop, like sticking a giant ice-cream cone on a shoe box. But then Hawksmoor, associated with great classical churches such as this and St Alfege's, Greenwich (see page 309) – both built under the Fifty New Churches Act of 1711 and both paid for partly by Coal Dues (see page 182) – was also a master of Gothic style. Probably the first bit of flamboyant Gothic people think of in London, the west front of Westminster Abbey, is also by Hawksmoor, and is not medieval at all.

There's a difficult-to-read inscription on the corner stating 'In Case of Fire, apply for the key of the engine house at No 1 Church Passage Cottages etc' and I think dated 1843. In which case it was understandable, as the tower had burned down in 1836, on Ash Wednesday, appropriately, so the parish had to pay for it to be rebuilt. The original tower had more Gothic detail than the rebuilt one, incidentally. Even so, it's an amazing structure, starting with four absolutely massive Tuscan columns and then going through various stages to the top.

Across the road is **Spitalfields Market**, which like Smithfield shows direct lineage from gardener Joseph Paxton's glass-and-iron Crystal Palace of 1851. They're just overgrown cucumber frames, really, these Victorian markets, railway stations and glasshouses. There's food, drink and toilets in here, plus an indoor market. This place was a Fruit Exchange and Wool Exchange. Go up **Brushfield Street**, beside the market, more or less straight on from Fournier Street, and as you start up here, the site of the Ripper's most gruesome murder, that of his last victim, 25-year-old Irish prostitute **Mary Jane Kelly**, in her room on 9 November 1888, is a few yards on your left, the actual building having disappeared.

We want **Gun Street**, at an angle on the left. Go down here to the end, and take a look at **Artillery Passage** on the right, truly an ancient bit of the East End. There were warrens of such passages and streets in the East End where the law dared not enter – the so-called rookeries where characters like Dickens's Fagin held power.

Going not right but left into Artillery Lane we come down to **Crispin Street**, where on the left is the **Providence Night Refuge and Convent**, still a home for the poorest and most desperate but also where Ripper victim Annie Chapman spent her last night alive.

Crossing Crispin Street, and going down White's Row, we come to the place where Mary Jane Kelly was killed on the left.

We emerge back on to **Commercial Street** and cross over. We don't go down Fashion Street (ahead) but have a look before turning right.

Again not much has changed from 100 years ago, although the use of the houses and their interiors certainly has, from lodgings for the poor to posher homes and businesses. Fashion, and the rag trade, is still in evidence here with almost every shop in Commercial Street connected with it in some way. The other striking thing about this area is how we are next door to the millions of billions of pounds the City handles, yet we have the once poorest and meanest streets in the capital.

We go on down Commercial Street going south (away from Christ Church, that is). At the corner of Whitechapel High Street, as Whitechapel Road has become, you have a chance to escape down Aldgate East Tube, and why not? I'd recommend it, frankly, but read the rest in case you want more, or rather so you feel you know the whole Ripper story.

If you turn right (west) down Whitechapel High Street, you can soon reach another Ripper murder site. You go past Aldgate Station (the road becomes Aldgate High Street) and about the same distance again (across Houndsditch) you'll find Mitre Street on the right, leading to **Mitre Square**, where his fifth victim, **Cathy Eddowes**, was killed. She was found still warm by a policeman shining his lamp into dark corners of the square, just 20 minutes after she'd been seen alive, yet she had been expertly butchered like the others. The policeman blew his whistle to summon help (there were always police within earshot, unlike today) and a crowd of appalled onlookers gathered. Even today, locals say, a ghostly woman is seen late at night sometimes lying across the cobblestones.

If we go through Mitre Square and out the other end into Duke's Place, we have the choice of looking at **Britain's oldest synagogue** in Bevis Marks to the left, or going right and back to Aldgate High Street and left to the Tube.

And what, you may ask, of fourth victim, **Lizzy Stride**, the Ripper victim whose murder site we have missed? This is in another direction, south of the rest, but can easily be reached by an energetic walker. You go back down to Aldgate East (not Aldgate) Tube and turn right down the main road, Leman Street, then the third left into **Cable Street** where the eponymous battle took place. The fascists wanted to come from Royal Mint Street on your right at the junction.

Go down Cable Street, left up Christian Street a couple of blocks down, left into Fairclough Street and right into **Henriques Street**. At this end of the street on the opposite side there's a gateway, almost opposite Baron Bernard House. This is where Lizzy Stride was killed. Then go to the top of the road and turn left on Commercial Road, which quickly brings us back to the major junction with Aldgate East Tube on it, to the north (the right).

Well that's it. Actually there were at least two more gruesome murders on this walk, but we don't want to give the area a bad name...

Part Four

VILLAGE LONDON

DULWICH

A CRAZY MIXED-UP PLACE

Dulwich, picturesque and peculiar, is geographically rather confused – fittingly, for the home of so many eccentrics. East Dulwich is north, not east, of West Dulwich, while North Dulwich is southeast, not northwest, of East Dulwich. South Dulwich is called Sydenham, as far as I can make out, but Upper Sydenham is mostly known as Crystal Palace after a palace that wasn't crystal, or a palace, wasn't here in the first place and certainly isn't here now.

Dulwich also contains what should be the National Gallery of Poland. Borough-wise, some smart aleck leftie put Dulwich under the control of Southwark, which made about as much sense as putting the posh bits of Long Island in the hands of the Bronx.

None of this geographical nonsense matters, but being England, the social divisions certainly do. **Dulwich Village** (as if a city of millions can have a real village in it) is the prettiest, oldest, poshest and most interesting part. **West Dulwich** retains some of this cachet and is a hang-out for professionals.

East Dulwich, on the other hand, used to be rather good for other kinds of activity: murders, rapes, police stabbings, that kind of thing. I thought this was mere West Dulwich snobbery until I analysed newspaper files for the past 20 years and found a horrendous litany of crime in East Dulwich.

The records of crime in the area go back a fair way. In 1334, one Richard Rolf at the old manor court (where Court Lane now runs) alleged that William Hosewood 'at Dylwysh had carried off Edith, his wife, together with one cow worth ten shillings, clothes, jewels and other goods'. No change there then, apart from the value of the cow.

But East Dulwich has outgrown its rough past, and is now said (by estate agents, mainly) to be becoming gentrified – trendy among the chattering classes with not quite enough money to live in Fulham; and indeed some lovely people and posh celebs (not always the same thing) already live, with their upwardly mobile lifestyles, Volvo estates, nannies, whatever, in East Dulwich.

This guide will, however, concentrate on Dulwich Village and its environs, because it is far more interesting. To put it another way, East Dulwich may have had crooks and nannies, but Dulwich Village has nooks and crannies.

VILLAGE PEOPLE AND THE CRYSTAL PALACE

The 'village' tag for Dulwich isn't such a joke. With its pond, archaic 'finger' signposts, pubs, toll gate giving prices per pig, and leafy green roads without formal edges, you could think you were somewhere in the Chilterns. Well, you could if it were five o'clock on a June morning, with no one around.

In medieval times the place was Dilwihs, the meadow where dill grows; being surrounded by wooded hills it must have seemed a rural paradise, if less than half-a-dozen miles from Charing Cross.

Even in Victorian times this isolated bliss was still to be found. The essayist and philosopher John Ruskin who lived at nearby Herne Hill, wrote affectionately:

> The crowning glory of Herne Hill was that, after walking along its ridge southward from London, through a mile of chestnut, lilac and apple trees, hanging over the wooden palings on each side – suddenly the trees stopped on the left, and out one came on the top of a field sloping down to the south into Dulwich valley – open fields animate with cow and buttercup and below the beautiful meadows and high avenues of Dulwich, and beyond, all that crescent of the Norwood hills; a footpath, entered by a turnstile, going down to the left…

Something of that remains, making Dulwich special.

On the other hand, things were changing. The **Crystal Palace**, that famous conservatory-like shed built by **Joseph Paxton** (hence the pub named after him) for the **1851 exhibition** in Hyde Park, was relocated here after that show and burned down in the 1930s. I can remember from childhood West Dulwich old folk saying: 'Oo yes, dearie, I can remember molten glass flowing down the hill as if it was yesterday.' This I didn't believe, for how anything made of iron and glass could burn was a puzzle. Anyway, we were expecting a nuclear attack on London at any moment so it didn't seem too important at the time.

However, today there's such nostalgia over Paxton's creation, the forerunner of the great railway station arches around the country, that nothing less than a replica would seem to satisfy some campaigners.

So have the people always loved the Crystal Palace?

Well, let's hear what Ruskin had to say in the 1880s about the newly arrived Crystal Palace, which stood on the hill across Dulwich's wooded valley, opposite his vantage point:

- One of the characters livening up the sometimes tedious race to be the first Mayor of London in 2000 was Dulwich chemist **Ashwinkumar Tanna** (his shop is in Lordship Lane), who wanted to run as an independent. His best quote was: 'There are too many chiefs and not enough Indians.' He said, 'I am the only Indian left.' He managed a creditable 51,000 votes despite being virtually ignored by the mainstream media.
- Among Dulwich's plethora of schools is one for butlers, set up by **Ivor Spencer**, president of the Guild of International Toastmasters and head of his International School for Butler Administrators. Some 750 of these gentleman's gentlemen have been turned out from Alleyn Park, appropriately just a stone's throw from the alma mater of P G Wodehouse, creator of Jeeves, butler *par excellence*.
- Another alumnus of Alleyn's School is the great tabloid newspaper editor **Kelvin MacKenzie** (b. 1946), who famously left with not many O-levels (one) and went straight into reporting as a teenager (the best way). His reign at the *Sun* was famed for (naked) Page 3 girls, provocative headlines such as 'Gotcha!' over the sinking of the Argentine cruiser the *Belgrano*, and on the French banning British lamb: 'Hop Off You Frogs' (see page 229 for more on Fleet Street).

Some of Dulwich's more eccentric celebs

...the Crystal Palace, without ever itself attaining any true aspect of its size, and possessing no more sublimity than a cucumber frame between two chimneys, yet by the stupidity of its hollow bulk, dwarfs the hills at once; so one thinks of them as three long lumps of clay, on lease for building.

- In late 2000, Dulwich pensioner **Bob Talley** read his 100th-birthday telegram from the Queen, proudly announced 'I've made it', then dropped dead. The party planned for him went ahead as a wake.
- Boxer and bemonocled and caned dandy (I didn't say that, Chris, honest) **Chris Eubank** (b 1966) was born in Dulwich. Comedienne **Jo Brand** (b 1957) lived here. British actor **Jude Law** (b 1972) went to Dulwich's Alleyn's School. Mrs, later Baroness, **Thatcher** (b 1925) had a house here. **Charles Dickens** lived in Dulwich, and in a great number of other places. Actor **Tim Roth** (b 1961) of *Reservoir Dogs* film fame grew up in West Dulwich. Not enough killings, presumably. A large number of great authors attended Dulwich College (see box, page 302).
- Quintessential castaway and great eccentric, **Gerald Kingsland** who repeatedly set himself up in remote desert islands in the Pacific, Indian Ocean and anywhere hot and empty, usually with a young lady in tow, came home to less exotic Dulwich to die in 2000. He had famously advertised for a Girl Friday in *Time Out* magazine and secured the young and naïve **Lucy Irvine**, half his age, who in the event beat him to a publisher when their ordeal ended. The book *Castaway* and the film of the same name starring Oliver Reed and Amanda Donohoe, made Lucy Irvine a celebrity, but Kingsland carried on with his experiments, fathering the odd child. When he became seriously ill in Samoa with his fifth wife and seventh child, he returned to his London family who were surprisingly forgiving. Irvine was quoted as saying he had lived the life of four men, but he had already written his epitaph:

In memory of Gerald Kingsland. He caused a lot of damage.

He didn't really prove his thesis that a man and a woman could live most happily in a Garden of Eden state of paradise, merely what a lot of women already knew: that some men walk away from their responsibilities and find the grass greener on the other side of the hill, no matter how old they are.

And later in the same essay (from *Praeterita*, 1890), he goes on:

> *Then the Crystal Palace came, for ever spoiling the view through all its compass, and bringing every show-day, from London, a flood of pedestrians down the footpath, who left it filthy with cigar ashes for the rest of the week: then the railroads came, and expiating roughs by every excursion train, who knocked the palings about, roared at the cows...*

As it turned out, the palace didn't spoil the view for ever (not as much as the two Eiffel Tower-like transmitters that now crown this, London's highest point, do).

Ruskin was a bit strange. He was appalled to discover on his wedding night that his bride Effie Gray had, unlike sculptures of women, pubic hair. The marriage went unconsummated.

A WALK AROUND PICTURESQUE DULWICH

This walk starts at West Dulwich station and finishes at Sydenham Hill station (both on the same line and about ten minutes from Victoria), taking in places to eat and drink, with an opt-out to cut the walk short, and with an optional extension to take in Horniman's Museum. It will take about two hours, plus stops. The car- or bike-borne can trace the same route.

West Dulwich station bestraddles **Thurlow Park Road**, also the South Circular A205 (a rather eccentric road for a national trunk route, with its total lack of main roadness at some points). Cross the road on the pedestrian crossing, noticing the monogram 'EA' high up on the bridge, and the first of many archaic wooden fingerposts beneath pointing vaguely to Norwood. The monogram is that of **Edward Alleyn**, a 16th-century chum of Shakespeare, who dominates the Dulwich story (his monogram, name or coat of arms is just about everywhere. We are near Alleyn Park, one of three roads named after him).

Going east a little from the station (that is, turn right out of the entrance) you soon take a turning to the left, **Gallery Road**. Or you can cut through the small gate across the road from the station into the grounds of **Belair House**, an elegant 18th-century (1785) white mansion which you should aim for. On the right through the trees (if it is winter and the branches are bare), you may glimpse the spires and the backside of **Dulwich College** public school, where many famous backsides (see page 302) have been tanned over the years, plus mine. Brits will know that, eccentrically, 'public'

DULWICH WALK

means definitely not public, but private, and that 'college' means not college but school. More on the school, (sorry college), and its extraordinary old boys (sorry, Old Alleynians) when we come to it.

Walking down this leafy Gallery Road, we reach on the right **Dulwich Picture Gallery** (☎ *020 8693 5254* 💻 *www.dulwichpicture gallery.org.uk*).

THE STRANGE STORY OF DULWICH PICTURE GALLERY

This surprising, world-class gallery located in a sleepy London suburb, is stuffed with works by Poussin, Rubens, Watteau and Canaletto, and has a bizarre history. In fact, it should have been the National Gallery of Poland.

In the 18th century, the Dulwich collection was greatly enhanced by art dealer **Noel Desenfans** (1745–1807), who had been collecting by order of the King of Poland, **Stanislas Augustus**. When Poland was partitioned in 1795 (as, sadly, it often has been), that was the end of Stanislas's dreams and Desenfans was left with dozens of Old Masters and nowhere to hang them. To his credit, he suggested they should become the nucleus of Britain's own national gallery, a concept novel at the time.

Desenfans and his wife Margaret lived with a painter called **Sir Francis Bourgeois** (1753–1811), and when Desenfans died, the odd couple inherited the collection and passed them on to create, in effect, Britain's first national gallery at Dulwich. The three in that unlikely *ménage-à-trois* are buried in a mausoleum right here at the gallery. Actually they're not buried but are in sarcophagi in an odd little hall, dimly lit by amber glazing. Restful and not at all spooky.

But why did Bourgeois and the widow Desenfans choose the unlikely village of Dulwich, then some miles from the edge of London, to be the recipient of their hugely valuable collection?

Re-enter the great actor manager, **Edward Alleyn** (1556–1626), a friend of Shakespeare, of fellow playwright Marlowe, and an even bigger friend of Dulwich. He and another actor called Cartwright had gathered several hundred pictures in the 17th century, which were bequeathed to Alleyn's other great legacy, Dulwich College.

These early pictures are valuable sources of information on the life of the stage in Shakespeare's time (before the Puritans closed the theatres) and the Dulwich gallery contains the only picture of the great actor **Richard Burbage** (1567–1619), the greatest of his age, for whom Shakespeare wrote the parts of Hamlet and Richard III. To the left, just beyond the gallery, after Christ's Chapel on the right, is **Burbage Road**, named in memory of this giant of the original Globe Theatre.

In 1811, Bourgeois was contemplating the gallery that the college would need to house Britain's first national collection, and commissioned the great eccentric collector **Sir John Soane** (see page 80) to build a combined gallery, mausoleum and set of almshouses for poor widows.

Soane, architect of the Bank of England, considered it such a noble project that he refused to be paid for this work. He designed a radical yet brilliant scheme.

Soane knew that the governors of the college were hardly awash with cash, so he eschewed the fancy Portland stone porticoes and pillars that were at that time *de rigueur*. He opted instead for plain but strong London brick in starkly modern and simple outlines – daring even by today's standards. In those days, the exterior severity was shocking to many, but in the late 20th century taste caught up with Soane and his work was widely praised and imitated.

Instead of spending money on outside grandeur, Soane concentrated on making the galleries inside work. He did this brilliantly by using ingenious natural-light-gathering rooflights that threw masses of light on to white supporting walls, which then diffused this light over the paintings. This meant there was no need for any side windows, which create too much reflection and damage the paint colours with direct sunlight, and also little need for artificial lighting even today.

The only hint of grandeur comes in the antechamber of that mausoleum constructed for the munificent dead. Here is the portentous atmosphere that Soane assiduously avoided in the rest of the gallery, yet it avoids total gloom with the aid of amber lighting.

Much extended, and restored after a World War II German 'doodlebug' landed nearby and caused severe damage, the Dulwich Picture Gallery lives on, a testament to these three's eccentric vision.

Dulwich's 'takeaway Rembrandt'

DULWICH GALLERY HAS OFTEN been in the headlines, the 'takeaway Rembrandt' of the late 20th century being the centre of Pink Pantheresque shenanigans. This small portrait of the engraver Jacob de Gheyn, worth an estimated £5 million, was stolen no fewer than four times in 20 years.

Raiders entered through skylights, drilled through reinforced doors or simply stuffed it under a macintosh, and the painting ended up in the oddest places: in the back of a black cab, under a tree on Streatham Common, tied to a bicycle in Dulwich and in a left luggage locker at a German railway station. They get around, these Rembrandts.

Yet again in 2001 a Polish aristocrat who claimed descent or connection with Stanislas Augustus (see opposite) turned up to say: 'Can we have our paintings back, please?' The gallery authorities politely asked him to come to Dulwich and view the pictures, but I suspect the words 'chance', 'snowflake' and 'hell' may have been privately constructed into a well-known phrase.

And the odd story goes on. Around ten years ago, a mysterious stranger, acting like someone out of a John le Carré spy novel, turned up with something for the gallery.

With his Panama hat pulled down so he could not be recognised, a coat and scarf covering him, the mystery man walked up to the reception desk and gave the puzzled staff a package, which he said had been found on a bus. He disappeared without giving his name and has not been seen again.

When the parcel was unwrapped, the astonished experts at the gallery found three valuable English 17th- and 18th-century miniatures, worth tens of thousands of pounds. A letter accompanying the gift said:

I am dying and have asked a dear friend to deliver the enclosed three miniature portraits to the trustees of Dulwich Art Gallery as my anonymous gift, because I have lived in obscurity into old age and wish to remain so in death.

If they are unsuitable for display at Dulwich, it is my wish that they be given to a gallery where they blend in. May God be with you. Anon.

A poignant note indeed, but why if the deliverer was the 'friend' described in the note did the man in the Panama hat come up with the story about the package 'being found on a bus'? Staff at the gallery suspect the man in the overcoat was the anonymous dying benefactor. Yet again Dulwich had benefited from a very strange circumstance.

THE VILLAGE HEART AND A PUB WITH A DICKENSIAN HISTORY

Continuing down the road, into what is now known as Dulwich Village, notice **Pickwick Road** on the left for a Dickens connection. Soon we reach a number of rather olde worlde shops, many Victorian or Georgian.

On the right is the imposing **Crown and Greyhound**, a splendidly convivial meeting place. But what have crowns and greyhounds got to do with each other? These were once two ancient Dulwich taverns. The Crown, on this site, was a very unpretentious alehouse, popular for thirsty farmworkers. The Greyhound, then across the road, was a much posher inn, and banquets and balls were held here. Here, too, **Charles Dickens** (1812–70) attended the snooty Dulwich Club. Eventually the businesses were merged in today's grand establishment.

There is a strange old bench inside marked 'When you bee wearie reste', which is nice, if a little obvious. Why not reste before getting wearie?

There are several grand 18th-century houses here, but a particularly charmingly tiny one on the left at the crossroads ahead, where more quaint fingerposts point all over the place. Turn right at the junction and take just a few steps up **Calton Avenue** and on the left before the car dealer is a stone marked: 'It is a sport to a Fool to do Mischief to Thine Own Wickedness shall correct thee.'

This marks the site of the **village stocks** where wrongdoers would be chained up and pelted with dung, etc, but does that engraving make a lot of sense, if you read it again? Are you doing mischief to Thine Own, or is Thine Own Wickedness correcting thee? It's bad enough being chained up and having chamberpots poured over thy head without this kind of grammatical inexactitude facing thee. I just hope the poor criminals couldn't read. The Calton family, recalled in the road name, bought the land from Henry VIII after he dissolved the monasteries in 1536, and the Caltons sold it to Alleyn.

Retracing our steps, we cross **Court Lane**, a reminder that in the old manorial system the main landowner, here Court Farm, dispensed justice as well as collecting the rent. Hence several London names, such as Earl's Court. On the corner of Court Lane and the high street – Dulwich Village, as it is called – lie many of the inhabitants of those fine 18th-century houses in the old **cemetery**.

(If you are 'wearie' after visiting the Greyhound, you could continue through Dulwich Village for a few hundred yards, across a road junction and reach North Dulwich station, with frequent trains to London Bridge. If so, note the eccentric ornamentation in the old station master's house just before the station and the totally over-the-top coats-of-arms on the bridge opposite.)

But if we turn back through the village towards the gallery, there is much more to see.

CYCLE LOGICAL PROFILES AND PICKWICKIAN TYPES

On the same side as the Greyhound there are some particularly fine 18th-century houses at Nos 103 and 105. Taking the left fork, **College Road**, and leaving the gallery to the right, you pass the Old College Gate of **Dulwich Park** on the left. This rambling park, where the lines of old oaks show the old field shapes, has four impressive gates, a lake and an aviary, and also offers the oddest bicycling in the form of **London Recumbents** (☎ *020 8299 6636*), a literally laid-back version of cycling that its fans believe should be more widespread. It looks odd but it's really cycle logical.

The man at the heart of it is cycling crusader, not to say fanatic, Nigel Frost, who has even bought a fantastic £8,000 machine called an Octos which bizarrely seats seven and on which one can have civilised face-to-

299

face conversations. Mr Frost believes they should become widespread to combat the evils of pollution, noise, unfitness, etc.

That's if you can handle maintaining 14 pedals, three brakes and nine chains and can always find half-a-dozen people wanting to go in the same direction. The latter question isn't a great problem, Mr Frost believes. He enthuses:

> It's the most sociable vehicle around – you set off alone but begin to pick up onlookers within 100 yards. Everyone can have a face-to-face conversation, except of course the driver… [And] as well as being pollution-free, it carries more passengers than most cars and can be used by people with special needs, including the blind, as it requires only one person to steer.

I'm beginning to think I want one. I just need to get six blind cyclists.

Staying on College Road, past the park gates, is the impossibly pretty **Bell Cottage** on the left, looking a bit like a New England clapboard house, with a fire mark above the door. These marks date from before proper fire brigades, when insurance companies operated horse-drawn fire engines but would put your fire out only if you had a fire mark showing your house was insured. Otherwise it was: 'Tough, burn to death, suckers!' Mind you, being about the only wooden house around here, I expect Bell Cottage's owners were more nervous than most.

Then there's the very pretty **Pickwick Cottage** on the left. Charles Dickens liked Dulwich and used to stay in the village. His most affectionately drawn hero, Mr Pickwick, retired to live here. He writes of him:

> 'Somewhat infirm now', he 'may still frequently be seen, contemplating the pictures in the Dulwich Gallery, or enjoying a walk about the pleasant neighbourhood'.

Soon we cross the road called **Dulwich Common**, the busy South Circular again. This is a point of decision. The feeble-hearted or weak of body could go right and quickly return to West Dulwich station, but it's not much further to continue on my route. The very strong of heart, or bike- or car-borne, could go left (and then right at Lordship Lane) to take in the extraordinary tea magnate **Horniman's Museum** (see page 76), but that is perhaps a mile away and worthy of a day out on its own.

The best option is to go straight on, up College Road, as we are now more than two-thirds through our walk. Dulwich College hoves into view on the right, its three massive Victorian-Italianate blocks by **Charles Barry Jnr** (1823–1900) layered like massive gateaux and set off by the landmark clock tower. The gates, of course, are larded with Alleyn's arms.

DULWICH COLLEGE, GREAT IMPRESSIONISTS AND TUNNEL VISION

Dulwich College is the grand replacement for Alleyn's original school down in the village. By the mid 19th century the governors, who could hardly afford to host the picture gallery a few years before, were rolling in cash thanks to the incursions of railway companies, who were snapping up land as suburban London spread, and for some reason running all over the Dulwich estate in various fairly random directions. But the college landowners insisted on the railway companies putting posher bridges than elsewhere, including Edward Alleyn's monogram and sometimes, as at North Dulwich station, the whole caboodle of Alleyn's arms and those of the railway companies not just once but three times over.

The style of the college is Italianate, but the **Great Hall** in the centre block is completely different in style, obviously influenced by ancient Westminster Hall (see page 166), hardly surprising as Charles Barry supervised the restoration of that medieval building.

The college grounds are massive and, what with the park, various sports grounds, the golf course and ancient woodland nearby, contribute to the remarkably rural feel of this otherwise town-locked area. That and the charming row of old cottages facing the **Mill Pond** on the left.

The view from the pond was immortalised by **Camille Pissarro** (1830–1903), the French Impressionist who fled the 1870 Franco-Prussian War to live in nearby Norwood and painted many local scenes. A letter from him to English Impressionist painter Wynford Dewhurst (1864–1941) backs up the notion that Turner (see page 156) was an influence on this French movement:

> In 1870 I found myself in London with Monet. Monet worked in the parks, whilst I, living at Lower Norwood, at that time a charming suburb, studied the effects of fog, snow and springtime… The water-colours and paintings of Turner and Constable certainly had influence on us.

Contemporaries, not yet up with the play about Impressionism, assumed his painting was unfinished, poor French chappie.

Dulwich College has certainly had far more than its share of characters (see box, page 302) but the survival of Dulwich's special village feel has been largely down to the school too, or rather the landlords of the Dulwich Estate, properly the Estates Governors of Alleyn's College of God's Gift.

Certainly one of the oddest survivals in their control lies ahead on College Road: the **toll gate**.

T HE 20TH CENTURY saw an amazing flowering of literary talent in Dulwich College's old boys, or Old Alleynians as they are correctly called.

Where else could two authors as different as **P G Wodehouse** (1881–1975) and **Raymond Chandler** (1888–1959) have rubbed shoulders, for instance? Did **C S Forester** (1899–1966) and **Michael Ondaatje** (b 1943), who wrote about the same war from such different angles, ever meet? Dulwich also contains fascinating clues to the origins of several of these writers' heroes.

Actually, I was disappointed to learn on investigation that Wodehouse the prefect couldn't have thrashed pipsqueak Chandler for running in the North Block ('contravention of the Block Rules, Chandler you oik') because their time at Dulwich was separated by a summer holiday.

If **Wodehouse**, creator of the ever-funny Bertie Wooster, Jeeves, Lord Emsworth and his pig, seems a bit comfortable, even smug, for some tastes, the answer lies right here.

As the relentlessly cheerful Wodehouse wrote:

The three essentials for an autobiography are that its compiler shall have had an eccentric father, a miserable, misunderstood childhood and a hell of a time at his public school, and I enjoyed none of these advantages. My father was as normal as rice pudding, my childhood went like a breeze... while, as for my schooldays at Dulwich, they were just six years of unbroken bliss.

Wodehouse is immortalised at the **College Library** by a display of his typewriter, desk, pipe and manuscripts. He worked for a while at some indescribably boring job at the Bank of England (where another employee was Kenneth Grahame, author of *Wind in the Willows*, the children's classic).

As for **Chandler**, the great crime thriller writer and creator of the quintessentially American gumshoe, Philip Marlowe, his completely contrasting life was far from charmed.

He was always on the move, never putting down roots. By the time he joined Dulwich in the autumn term (sorry, Michaelmas term at Dulwich)

The extraordinary old boys of Dulwich College

in 1900, the 12-year-old Chandler had already lived in Waterford, Nebraska and Chicago, Illinois. After he left Dulwich in 1905, he moved on average once a year, owning barely any furniture, his restlessness always driving him on to another rented address. In this case a disturbed life did produce great writing.

One bit of Dulwich may have stayed with Chandler. At the college new boys are put into houses for sporting purposes which they stay in throughout the school. They are named after Elizabethan heroes: Spencer, Sydney, Drake, Grenville... and Marlowe. I wonder which house Chandler was in.

More literary detective work can be enjoyed with **C S Forester**, creator of the eponymous swashbuckling hero Hornblower (and the book *African Queen*, which made a great film). When at Alleyn's School, which he attended before Dulwich College, Forester would have attended St Barnabas Church in the village. In that church there's still a war memorial a possibly bored young Forester may have gazed upon during the sermon; it has the name 'Hornblower' carved upon it. It can't be a coincidence, can it?

Other authors include **A E W Mason** (1865–1948), author of *The Four Feathers*, plus **Dennis Wheatley** (1897–1977), thriller writer, expelled after a short stay. And much-missed comedian **Bob Monkhouse** (1928–2003), who said:

> When I was young they laughed at me for saying I wanted to be a comedian. Well they're not laughing now!

Not that all Dulwich's success stories have been literary. For many years a small open boat called the *James Caird* has lain here almost unnoticed by the boys straggling back from choir for double Latin. Had they but investigated they would have found that it was in this boat that the greatest of Antarctic heroes, **Ernest Shackleton** (1874–1922), made his almost unbelievable escape across hundreds of miles of terrible seas to get help for his men after his ship, the *Endurance*, was crushed by ice.

It was heroism of the highest order, and all the *Endurance*'s men were saved, although by the time they got back to Britain, years later, World War I was in full spate and no one was interested in live heroes any more. For by far the best account of his journey – and I've read the lot – read *Shackleton's Boat Journey* by F A Worsley.

(CONTINUED OVERLEAF)

The extraordinary old boys of Dulwich College

Before that last terrible journey, Sir Ernest had taken part in Scott's first expedition. After returning a hero, Shackleton gave a talk to Dulwich schoolboys. He put up a slide of frozen wastes and snow and left it without commentary. After a while the boys began to fidget, and Sir Ernest said:

Well boys, you've stuck it for 45 seconds, we stuck it for five weeks.

Sir Ernest had been particularly bad at his lessons at Dulwich and was said to have been thrown out of the place for climbing the clock tower, from the outside. If so, it was just a rehearsal for far, far greater feats of daring.

If Wodehouse and Chandler didn't meet, Wodehouse and Shackleton certainly did. Wodehouse was made a German prisoner-of-war in World War II and famously and unwisely made radio broadcasts from his camp which were seen as collaboration with the enemy, although they were perhaps more his being typically and naively genial. His reputation never quite recovered from this so he spent much of the remainder of his life in America.

While a German prisoner, Wodehouse wrote:

Under certain conditions, the mind is bound to dwell on food. Shackleton once told me that when he was on the Polar high seas, he used to dream every night he was running about a field chasing those three-cornered jam tarts which were such a feature of our life at our mutual school. And if that is how Shackleton felt, I am not ashamed of having felt that way myself.

London was once surrounded with roads that became impassable morasses in the winter and, given the rain, at other times too. (They say the Devil, tossing the damned to the eternal fires, chucks some aside in a heap. These, he explains to those waiting to be judged, are the English, too wet to burn.)

The solution to the road problem was turnpike roads, properly drained, with macadam stone dressing on top, which sped the booming stagecoaches of 1750–1840. In many parts of London if you look carefully you can spot the old toll-houses, sometimes octagonal single-storey lodges too close to the road for modern comfort, sometimes not much more than a shed. This toll gate is the only one surviving in use in London, and the road it's on is still in the hands of the Estates Governors. Prices for hogs, donkeys, sheep or whatever are still listed.

Passing through the toll gate and up the hill, we reach on the right, just before the handsome spire of **St Stephen's**, Sydenham Hill station, the end of our walk. If you fancy another pub, you can instead go left here at Low Cross Wood Lane, and climb steeply to the **Dulwich Wood House**, a tavern which reminds us that the woods on the hillside are ancient and still full of wildlife such as foxes, badgers, bats, etc, coming out at night.

The sylvan setting of **Sydenham Hill station** was once described by the architect Ian Nairn as the 'quintessence of true suburbia due to its rural nature'. The deep cutting contains a nature reserve.

The platforms are way down, at the mouth of the south's longest railway tunnel which burrows right under Crystal Palace hill to Penge East, and (since they built the Channel Tunnel) Warsaw, Moscow and Vladivostok. You need the further platform for your return to London.

You can see right through the straight tunnel today, which you rarely could in the days of steam. It is a good example of recycling. The clay extracted from the boring of the tunnel was dragged out at either end and baked into the millions of bricks that line the tunnel.

As you ride back past the college grounds on the right after the bridge, your train may be ignored by boys playing cricket or rugby down below.

But many a catch may have been dropped here 50 years ago when a steam whistle sounded and the glorious *Golden Arrow* London–Paris train hoved into view just once a day. It had a French tricolour and a Union Jack fluttering on its front buffer beam. A massive golden arrow attached to the side of the loco bore the proud legend '*Golden Arrow*' or '*La Flèche D'Or*'. It towed a rake of immaculate brown and gold Pullman carriages, all named, and manned with uniformed flunkies who greeted you as you joined the train at Victoria station and polished the brass handrails as you climbed into the interior of marquetry woodwork, deep pile carpet, starched tablecloths and heavy silver, and diplomats, spies and filmstars resting in the deep red armchairs. Your train won't be quite like that.

GREENWICH

That Greenwich is truly special is undeniable. The place is a World Heritage Site for its fabulous maritime history on show. Architecturally, it is rightly famed too. The atmosphere of the place is unique, with its back alleys and strange little shops, its creaking pubs soaked in history, its sweeping views dominated by Old Father Thames sliding past in a superb bend in its millennia-old meanders. The tides and fogs have brought heroes, pirates, murderers and kings and queens to this little place.

But it's not all history – there are modern follies such as the **Millennium Dome**, now housing the **O2 Arena**, and **new transport links** such as the Docklands Light Railway and the Jubilee Line extension, the latter provided with fabulous stations in innovative styles, trendy shops and a buzzing craft market, plus some strange sculptures very much of the 21st century.

Now we have the thrilling new cable car – the latest in the deeply eccentric river crossings downstream of Tower Bridge – to link the peninsula near the O2 to the Royal Docks. This thrilling ride adds to the panoply of daft Thames crossings including used and disused foot tunnels, three road tunnels, a trunk road (the North–South Circular, no less) that inexplicably becomes a ferry at Woolwich, and loads of railway tunnels but not one proper bridge till you get to Dartford.

Not that Greenwich is isolated (except by car across the river). There was a myth put about in 2000 that the Dome would fail because transport to its North Greenwich peninsula site was impossible. Balderdash! Greenwich had tunnels under the Thames galore – foot and road nearby – two new rail routes to East London; good bus links; new rail links to South London, and good rail links to Central London. Plus the traditional route along the river from Charing Cross pier, fun but far from quick.

Nor is the line from Central London, which links Greenwich in around 15 minutes to four London termini (London Bridge, Waterloo East and Charing Cross or Cannon Street), anything new. Far from it; it is the oldest mainline in the capital, dating from very early in the railway age.

The first part of this, the **London & Greenwich Railway**, was opened astonishingly early in the railway age in 1836; it was finished in time for Christmas 1838. The world's first purpose-built commuter railway, it was also the world's longest viaduct, because the whole route was, bizarrely, built on arches – 978 of them – not so much anticipating the car dealers who would rent out the noisy caverns in the arches beneath, but to cross the numerous roads and creeks *en route*.

Many a strange business is located within the cave-like arches of London's railways: a lobster breeding farm for gourmets in Battersea, a golf range for top City types beneath Cannon Street, a garden centre, wine cellars, a shooting gallery, sound-insulated offices and a security vault, to name a few. Later railways into the capital resorted to the much cheaper method of using earth embankments.

So if you come to Greenwich by mainline train, the route you ride on is a lot older than some of the relics, such as the *Cutty Sark*, that you are coming to see. And if you are visiting Greenwich via this route for the first time, look left soon after leaving London Bridge station for an unusual longways view of Tower Bridge.

A WALK AROUND THE BEST AND ODDEST BITS

This walk is about 2½ miles long, which takes about two hours. But with stops and add-ons, not to mention visiting to the National Maritime Museum, *Cutty Sark* or the former Royal Naval College, all well worth several hours, I recommend dedicating a day to the area or doing the walk on one fine day, then visiting a selection of the indoor treasures on another, perhaps less fine one.

Emerging from Greenwich station, we are confronted with the strange mixture that is Greenwich's real charm. Here you can see working-class London's shabbiness in the unpretentious row of shops opposite which, however, include an excellent secondhand bookshop (first of many), Halcyon Books, and a fascinating junk shop that sells the oddest architectural details to the Greenwich yuppie incomers; an ancient almshouse is to the right of this, while to the left is the staggering shaft of the Modernist–Art Deco town hall, beyond which a classical church and some ship masts.

The **almshouses** opposite have a pretty courtyard, which blows with a snowstorm of cherry blossom in May. Called The College of Queen Elizabeth, they were set up by philanthropist William Lambard in 1576,

Isle of Dogs

GREENWICH
WALK

Island
Gardens

MANCHESTER
GROVE
MANCHESTER ROAD
SAUNDERS NESS RD
FERRY ST
FERRY ST

↗ Millennium Dome

BALLAST
QUAY

Thames

Cutty Sark Pub

River

Trafalgar
Tavern

HIGH BRIDGE
HOSKINS
LASSEL
WOOLWICH
STREET
TRAFALGAR ROAD
OLD

Trinity
Hospital

CRANE
EASTNEY ST

Greenwich foot
tunnel

Water Gate

PARK ROW

GREENWICH PARK RD

MAZE
HILL

PARK VISTA

FEATHERS
PL

Cutty Sark

Royal Naval
College

ROMNEY ROAD

Cutty Sark
Charter
Market

CROSS AVENUE

Queen's House

CREEK ROAD
Second-hand shops
BARDSLEY LA

Nevada st
well st
nelson rd

GREENWICH HIGH RD
KING WILLIAM WALK
GREENWICH CHURCH ST

National
Maritme Museum

One Tree Hill

St Alfege's †

ROAN STREET

STRAIGHTSMOUTH

Greenwich Park

START
FINISH
★
Greenwich

STOCK-
WELL ST
NEVADA ST
BURNEY ST

Fan
Museum

CROOMS HILL

THE AVENUE

Royal
Observatory

Wolfe Statue

NORMAN ROAD

GREENWICH HIGH ROAD
Library
Town Hall

ROYAL HILL

PETTON PL
CIRCUS ST

KING GEORGE STREET

BLACKHEATH AVENUE
GREAT CROSS AVE

BOWER AVENUE

The
Gardens

LANSDALE

Queen
Elizabeth
almshouses

GREENWICH SOUTH STREET

EGERTON DRIVE

POINT HILL

N

Bradt

0   100m

CROOMS HILL

Blackheath

Tennis
Courts

Ranger's
House

Princess
Caroline's Bath

GENERAL WOLFE RD

CHESTERFIELD WALK

Blackheath
Gate

CHARLTON WAY

SHOOTERS HILL
SHOOTERS HILL

early in the popular Virgin Queen's reign. However, the neat row of homes you are looking at is an 1819 rebuild.

Walking left towards the town centre and waterfront, we pass evidence of another remarkable philanthropist; a Carnegie library is marked as such on its weather-worn front. This **West Greenwich library** is one of dozens of Carnegie libraries that have enriched the lives of Britons for more than 100 years thanks to the Scots-born billionaire (1835–1918) who became America's greatest steel magnate. The human face of capitalism.

The inhuman face of socialism, some may think, is evident in the massive **Town Hall** block jammed up against the Carnegie and extending round the corner into Royal Hill. Severe, bereft of all adornment, it would in fact sit well with a massive red star and portrait of Joe Stalin on top, or Nazi banners unfurled, for a film backdrop, or would do well as Orwell's faceless Ministry of Truth in *Nineteen Eighty-Four*. It is architectural high drama.

Yet in its way this 1939 building by **Clifford Culpin** is brilliant and daring. That it works is thanks to its crowning glory – the superb and improbable clock tower that looks as though it stabs down from the sky, much as if God had angrily thunked down a carving knife into a bread board. Don't miss – it is easy to do so – the underside of the entrance canopy near the corner, which makes up for its lack of colour with an elaborate mural (well, whatever you call a ceiling mural). Onwards down the High Road, past the oddly named road called Straightsmouth, we reach the rather extraordinary **St Alfege's church** (▨ *www.st-alfege.org*), which despite its elegant classical exterior contains more dramatic history than a dozen normal churches.

GREENWICH PILLAGE: SAINTS, HEROES AND BRILLIANT CREATORS

St Alfege's is a wonderful church, but built on spilt blood. **Alfege** was a medieval churchman, greatly loved and more Christian than most. When he was Bishop of Winchester there were no beggars in that city, the histories say. From 954 to 1012 he was Archbishop of Canterbury at a time when rampaging Danes were raping and pillaging their heathen way across country. The Danes landed here at Greenwich several times in their longboats and struck inland in search of riches (had there been newspapers at the time, doubtless an editor would have yelled: 'Hold the front pagan').

Alfege was urged to leave and save himself but he sat in his cathedral calmly awaiting the battle's outcome. He was seized by the Danes who demanded:

Give us gold.

He replied: *The gold I give you is the Word of God.*

The Danes dragged Alfege back to their landing place at Greenwich and pelted him to death with stones, meat and bones.

Moving on a few centuries – all these great characters are remembered with monuments and stained-glass panels in this church – we come across the extraordinary composer and musician **Thomas Tallis** (1505–85). He was organist here, something to do with the proximity of Greenwich's royal palace, no doubt. Nothing more beautifully haunting had then yet been devised – nor has since, some would argue – in church music than his complex harmonies rooted in the chants of medieval monks. His 40-part motet *Spem in Alium* is emotionally overpowering.

His amazingly long career spanned an astonishing range of religious policy, from Henry VIII, so loyal a Roman Catholic at first that the pope called him Defender of the Faith (hence FD on our coins), and later an aggressive Protestant who suppressed the monasteries, through Edward VI (1537–53), who clobbered Catholics, 'Bloody' Mary (1553–58) who burned hundreds of Protestants at the stake; and finally, Elizabeth I (1558–1603), who persecuted Catholics once again, but not quite as much.

Few people in high position could weather such violent storms, yet Tallis the survivor lived through the lot as a royal musician and composer, adjusting his music to the times. He is the Wren of church music, the Shakespeare of sound.

But Christopher Wren isn't the architect who comes to mind as you look round this elegant creation, for it was one of his followers, **Nicholas Hawksmoor** (1680–1740), who rebuilt this church as part of the Fifty New Churches campaign of the government of the day (of which around a dozen were actually built).

Another notable parishioner was **John Flamsteed** (1646–1719), Astronomer Royal at the nearby **Greenwich Observatory** (see page 322). He said his mapping of the heavens was a way of understanding the mind of God.

Back on earth we meet one of Greenwich's greatest heroes, **General James Wolfe** (1727–59). You can see his home at **Macartney's House** at the top of Croom's Hill on the west side of Greenwich Park later in the walk. Wolfe not only squashed the ambitions of the French in Canada, making that huge country British for many years, but also had the great merit of dying heroically at the moment of victory (as did Nelson), thus cementing himself in the public's affection. (If only Wellington had had the sense to get cannon-balled at Waterloo.)

Aged only 32, Wolfe captured Quebec, the French-held city in Canada, in 1759 in a surprise attack by storming the Heights of Abraham up steep cliffs. He was killed in action and was buried here at St Alfege's.

Back to Victorian times, when **Dickens** knew and loved Greenwich. In *Our Mutual Friend*, perhaps my favourite Dickens novel, he goes all sentimental at the end, as ever, when Bella is married in this church to John Rokesmith:

> *…the church porch, having swallowed up Bella Wilfer for ever and ever, had it not in its power to relinquish that young woman but slid into the happy sunlight Mrs John Rokesmith instead.*

A real Victorian hero from Greenwich is remembered here too: **General Gordon** (1833–85), he who was slain at Khartoum in the Sudan and was portrayed in the film *Khartoum* (1966) by Charlton Heston. Oddly Gordon of Khartoum was known as Chinese Gordon at the time, more famed for putting down a rebellion in China than his work suppressing slavery in the Sudan.

Then in 1941 Nazi bombers blew in the roof of St Alfege's, possibly aiming for London Docks. It was not until 1954 that the building was fully restored.

There you are: exactly 1,000 sweeping years of dramatic history, blood, war, love, art, bigotry, heroism all within one building. Amazing.

SHOPPING AND CHANGING

Now, thank God, the arrival of the Danish means delicious pastries. Tourists from all the countries mentioned in this turbulent history are welcomed in peace to poke around Greenwich and find its historical nutty bits, the architectural icing on the cake and perhaps in a junk shop, the occasional cherry.

Going on down **Greenwich Church Street** one can glimpse through an archway to the right an intriguing view of pubs and treasures beyond. Leave it for a moment and turn the corner left into **Creek Road** to check out a couple of rather strange shops. The first is **Emporium**, dedicated to the clothes of the 1950s, 1960s, 1970s and 1980s. It's well known by film companies who come here for period costumes; some of today's big-name designers have even been seen browsing the shelves, according to proprietor Jonathan Hale, who set up here in 1986.

Is it nostalgia? He says:

> *No, not really. For one thing, a lot of the people who come in here don't remember those times because they were too young. It's about style and originality – being different from the designer pack.*

Further down a shop called **Flying Duck** has a huge range of 1950s, 1960s and 1970s design and kitsch objects. Spindly metal chairs with pastel-coloured plastic seats. Elliptical cane chairs. Chopper bikes. Squeezy tomato-shaped tomato sauce bottles, like you used to get in Wimpy bars.

Back on Church Street, a step or two further towards the masts of the *Cutty Sark*, there's a cockney cultural checkpoint, a pie and mash shop (complete with liquor and eels, the sign reassures us). **Goddard's Pie House** has been run by the same family since 1890, so they must be doing something right. Every possible type of pie *except* eel pie – apple, steak, cheese –

seemed to be being eaten when I popped in, but I expect someone eats eels. (Hence, perhaps, the cockney song: 'Eel meat again, don't know where, don't know when.')

Over the road is another gem of a shop, **Unique Collections**, which on my visit is stuffed with strange firemen's helmets, a Rochdale County Borough Police badge, a Memphis police captain's regalia, plus more model cars than I've ever seen in one place. Matchbox, Dinky, Corgi – you had to have grown up in those days to really love them. And model Thunderbirds and Thunderbird dolls. Heaven for some people, and immensely collectable.

Now, if you like this kind of thing you could peek into **Greenwich Charter Market** by walking a little way up College Approach. It's a colourful place and my only hesitation in recommending it is that if you like shopping and browsing in old bookshops, you may never complete the walk. That's up to you – there's always another day.

The market runs on Wednesday, Friday and Saturday until 5pm selling arts and crafts and on Thursday selling antiques and collectables. Note over the College Approach colonnaded entrance the cast-iron proclamation:

> A FALSE BALANCE IS ABOMINATION TO THE LORD
> BUT A JUST WEIGHT IS HIS DELIGHT

The market is still worth a look on non-market days, all the better to examine the interesting surrounding arts, craft, antiques (we're too posh for mere junk by now) and bookshops and the cobbled lanes connecting it to the rest of the town, which is hemmed in against the lush grounds of the former Royal Palace rather in the way that many a crammed medieval village huddles against spacious castle walls.

Back to the waterfront and the ***Cutty Sark*** (☎ *020 8858 3445* 🖥 *www.cuttysark.org.uk*), a beautiful, fascinating ship whose name lives in the hearts of any Briton with salt in their blood as surely as that of the *Victory* at Portsmouth. Actually a better comparison is with the *Flying Scotsman* or the *Mallard* steam engines, for this is a sleek racer, the fastest of the clippers. Aptly, given Greenwich's interest today in fashion, the ship is named after a girl's garment (it was a short petticoat). This was a truly beautiful, historic ship but in 2007 some numbskull left a machine on over a weekend and the hull was burnt out in a fire. The security guards, police said, had put their feet up, so the fire was not stopped early enough. I'm not impressed, and further not impressed by the appeal to restore it, now done. It will be a very expensive useless replica. Why not restore it as a beautiful working clipper then?

THE TUNNEL OF FLATULENCE AND THE BEST VIEW IN LONDON

Over to the left of the *Cutty Sark*, there lies another Greenwich dome. Across the river you'll see a matching one, joined by the **Greenwich foot tunnel**, a fun and free experience I recommend to all except claustrophobes.

It was created to help workers reach the then-booming London Docks in 1902. You can take the lift or be a big kid and race down the steps as I always did as a child living in Greenwich. Racing up is a bit harder. At the bottom you appreciate its 1,217-foot length and the 200,000 glazed tiles that line it. We are told it is 33 feet under water at low tide and 53 feet at high tide. They must mean the top of the water, which doesn't worry me. How close is the *bottom* of the water?

Well this isn't entirely academic, as when **Marc Brunel** (see page 155) pioneered the first tunnel under the Thames at Rotherhithe, the water burst through several times before they could get the lining up, drowning the workers within. And they say you can hear the beat of ships' propellers above you in that tunnel, so it's quite a thin riverbed.

However, this tunnel is quite safe (it's a century old) and I've always enjoyed the walk down to the dip in the middle and up the other side. What they don't tell you is that the reinforced and therefore narrowed bit on the far side, just before you leave the tunnel, is like this because a German bomb landed on the foreshore, damaging the tunnel, in the 1940s.

And they also don't tell you about the opening day's big embarrassment. When top-hatted mayors and officials emerged from the champagne banquet held in the tunnel below they forgot about the slight decompression effect, exaggerated by champagne, and they all began to fart and burp uncontrollably. If you merely walk through, such effects are unlikely. But stay off the fizz while you're down there. On the other side we're on the **Isle of Dogs**, so called because hounds for the Greenwich hunt used to live here.

GREENWICH PALACE, THE HOSPITAL AND LONDON'S FINEST VIEW

The trip under the river is well worth it for the utterly splendid view it gives you – London's finest, many say – of Greenwich from the waterfront on the other side, which gives you a good chance to place everything in your mind. The pair of buildings in front of us directly on the waterfront opposite is the **Old Royal Naval College**, built by **Sir Christopher Wren** as a naval hospital from 1694. It was not finished until the middle of the next century by Wren's successors, **Nicholas Hawksmoor** and **John Vanbrugh**.

It replaced Greenwich Palace, which stood here in Tudor times, but the architects cleverly not only kept the elegant Queen's House behind but also preserved views between there and the water.

The **Queen's House** by **Inigo Jones** (1573–1652) is a gem of a building and now forms the centrepiece of the National Maritime Museum. This was the first mathematically disciplined classical building in England. At first glance it looks to be 18th century, by which time every architect was copying Jones. In fact it was built between 1616 and 1635 and was revolutionary at the time.

Looking beyond up the hill is the **Royal Observatory**, start of all the world's longitudes and birthplace of modern timekeeping. If you have very good eyes you will see at the top of this hill a **black statue of General Wolfe** (see page 310).

You can return via the foot tunnel but more fun and less tiring is to stroll a couple of hundred yards inland to the **Docklands Light Railway** station (it's signposted) and catch one of the frequent tram-like trains back to the *Cutty Sark*. If you choose to do this, sit near the front for a view of how this rail tunnel dips under the river, like the foot tunnel.

Back on the **South Bank**, go past the *Cutty Sark* and along the waterfront footpath outside the grounds of the former Royal Naval College. This building, now turning into colleges plus a major heritage site, is worthy of several hours; you can find out more about it at the tourist information at the nearest corner to the *Cutty Sark*. I don't propose to describe it, or the National Maritime Museum, or the Royal Observatory in full detail here, where we are supposed to be looking for eccentric bits ordinary tourists would miss. But the interior of the Naval College is amazing. Most astounding is the **Painted Hall**, the ceiling of which took **Sir James Thornhill** (1676–1734) nearly 20 years to paint.

It was here that Nelson's body was brought following the Battle of Trafalgar in 1805 when his fleet destroyed a much larger Spanish–French fleet after he hoisted his famous signal: 'England expects every man to do his duty.'

The national grief that followed was immense. This quotation from *The Times* about that day his body lay in state in the Painted Hall captures the nation's overwhelming grief and gratitude:

Before eight in the morning, every avenue from the metropolis to Greenwich was crowded with vehicles of every description... the approach to Greenwich Hospital Gate a little before that hour must baffle the conception of those who did not witness it. When the gate was thrown open, above ten thousand persons pressed forward for admittance.

Passing along the front of the college on the riverside path we see two fine **obelisks**, wonderfully useless things except in one regard – they remind us of things we would otherwise forget, making a point in every sense.

The one nearest the *Cutty Sark*, within the grounds of the Naval College, is by Hardwicke and remembers sailors from here who died in the New Zealand war of the 19th century. The rights and wrongs of that war are another story but suffice it to say that, as with the Boers in the Boer War, if the British thought the Maori would be a push-over they were sorely disappointed. The military were so impressed by the Maori fortifications that they sent experts to study them at the end of the war. As with the Gurkhas and the Fijians, the Brits made sure they were on the same side in future.

The second obelisk recalls one M Bellot, a heroic Frenchman whose efforts to find Sir John Franklin (1786–1847), the British explorer who went missing in the Arctic, ended up with his sharing the same fate in the frozen wastes of the north. You can read the story on the landward side.

Next is the **Water Gate**, the elaborate entrance where monarchs would have landed to enter the previous palace, and to visit the later buildings. Notice how one of the great domes – you can't get away from that word round here – tells the time while the other tells wind direction, both then vital for mariners.

The **statue of George II** was put up by some fawning creep so the monarch would see it first when he arrived at Greenwich and grant the man some vast amount of money. The grovelling git got his dosh, as cockneys might have it.

THE MOST FAMOUS PUB, WORST HANGOVER AND WISEST LITTLE FISH

At the end of the riverside path walk we come to the **Trafalgar Tavern**. This pub has a special memory for me because in the late 1950s, my father took a lease on a flat upstairs. I remember how up-and-down the floor was, as well as running along the riverside walk to the *Cutty Sark* and the foot tunnel under the Thames but, do you know, I didn't once stop to look at the river view or even appreciate the architectural splendour around me. The only issue then was if they would have pink ice cream across the water.

Today, at these same windows, one sees a fascinating, inspiring sweep of ever-changing view that could keep me mesmerised for hours (and that's even before having a pint). Funny things, children…

This graceful building dates from the 1830s, a tribute to Lord Nelson's then recent victory giving it its alliterative name. Famed for its whitebait suppers (those tiny fish that you get fried by the hundred, eyes and tail and all), which were a big hit with Dickens and his chums. Didn't Dickens say there is no hangover like that following a Greenwich supper? Many Victorian politicians such as Gladstone dined here. Perhaps the best advice came from Lord Palmerston during one such whitebait supper:

Let us all imitate this wise little fish, and drink a lot and say nothing.

The Ballast Quay extension
and a question of philosophy

After the Trafalgar Tavern (or tshlaugar tashern if you've enjoyed too many drinks), we strike inland straight up **Park Row**. But if you're a good walker, and haven't drunk too much, dive down **Crane Street** first for an interesting half-mile there-and-back extension. (Otherwise skip to *A ghost on the stairs*, see opposite)

You pass the **Yacht** pub, again with splendid riverside views, and a couple of rowing clubs before coming to a beautiful little almshouse, **Trinity Hospital**, built in 1616. This place – really quite exquisite if you look through the gates at the courtyard fountain – is 'for retired Greenwich gentlemen'. Well, I hope to qualify on one of those counts eventually.

Don't miss on the river wall behind you the high tide marks from certain Thames floods. London is now protected from the North Sea tides and winds by the 1982 Thames Barrier at Woolwich around the corner of the river – you can take boat trips from Greenwich. Nicknamed the 'drowning nuns' because of their cowl-like appearance, a set of massive gates shaped like gas taps lie in the river bed ready to be swivelled upright when needed.

Next to the Jacobean almshouses, which sit on the meridian line, by the way, stands a massive **power station** that dwarfs the place. The juxtaposition is astounding, like that of the Carnegie Library and the neo-Nazi Town Hall mentioned earlier. No one would dream of allowing it today, which makes it all the more delicious. It's insane. Surreal. Walk past the slumbering giant – it was built to power trams and is now a stand-in for tube power – and its old loading jetty built with Doric columns and we're in industrial docks mode. Keep straight on a few more yards and there's yet another gem of a riverside pub, the **Cutty Sark**. This was used as a location for the film *Original Sin*, a P D James detective story featuring Roy Marsden as Adam Dalgliesh.

It stands on **Ballast Quay**, so-called because those clipper ship crew, poor beggars, had to load the empty hulls of their vessels after their cargo had been landed, with hundreds of tons of gravel or stones – by hand – to make them stable enough for the long sea voyages back to China or Australia. If your ballast shifted in a typhoon, you'd had it.

A GHOST ON THE STAIRS, MAD TUNNELS, AND TUMBLING LADIES

Heading away from the river up **Park Row**, over the pedestrian crossing on the main road that slices between the Naval College and the **National Maritime Museum** (☎ *020 8858 4422* 🖥 *www.nmm.ac.uk*), the latter building becomes obvious by the parade of anchors on our right. The first of them, a rather modern, black and evil-looking job, is from a nuclear submarine. It's funny to think these sinister, unseen high-tech Darth Vader machines which could end the world (or prevent it being ended, arguably) could need anything as prosaic as an anchor, but they do; this one's odd shape is so that it can be retracted exactly flush with the hull of the submarine, so no undue swirling of water is created that might be detected when the vessel is in motion.

The museum, superb for content and container alike, cannot be detailed here. The elegant **Queen's House** (1637), which forms the centrepiece, is a perfect gem of its time, with its splendid hall, a perfect cube, and haunted **Tulip Staircase**. It was here that, on 19 June 1966, retired Canadian clergyman the Reverend R W Hardy took an extraordinary picture. With witnesses watching, he waited until the staircase was entirely clear of people and, with his Zeiss camera, the best there was, took a photo. When the picture was developed and printed, a shadowy hooded, monklike figure could be seen climbing the stairs, his white left hand clearly grasping the banister. The film was examined by Kodak and the museum authorities but no hint of any fraud was detected.

We enter **Greenwich Park** – a royal park like those in Central London and Richmond – through the gate ahead. Entering the park, you can check the time on a massive sundial on the left. This sundial is slap bang on the Greenwich meridian, so it should be right.

Up the hill from the boating lake there is a small feature that looks like a bricked-up tunnel. There are extensive **tunnels**, medieval in origin, throughout Greenwich, for which no plausible explanation has ever been devised. They are far too large to have been water supply conduits for the

The Dome – perfect storage for the Eiffel Tower

FURTHER ALONG THE river, nestling in the crook of the next bend in the river, the **Dome** was a kind of Millennium exhibitiony circusy thingy; it was widely derided, regarded as pointless and inaccessible by those who had never been there and, compared to the 1851 Great Exhibition and the 1951 Festival of Britain, came a poor third in terms of success. The government's 'Dome Secretary' Peter Mandelson (no, I'm not still on about spooky aliens) was the grandson of Herbert Morrison, the brains behind the 1951 show.

I'm not entirely sure what all the moaning was about. The doomed Dome, now a great venue for rock concerts, tennis, etc, cost the taxpayer not a penny (it was all funded by National Lottery loot). To be positive, its coming regenerated a polluted, poisonous peninsula, gained Greenwich two 21st-century rail links that wouldn't otherwise have been built and gave possibly six million people a good time (instead of the 12 million expected). Any other country on earth would think six million visitors to a millennium attraction a resounding triumph. I can recall a similar event in Wellington, New Zealand, where as far as I could see, four people and a chihuahua had turned up.

The Dome was supposed to be a good thing just because it was big. Big enough to accommodate the Eiffel Tower laid down on its side. They like figures like that round here. Another one is that Canary Wharf, the highest office block you can see across the river, the one with the pyramid top, could be accommodated within the new Tube station underneath it. In fact, if the people who messed up Heathrow's new underground railway (which fell in at one point) were in charge, it probably soon *will* be accommodated within the station. Anyway, if anyone needs to store the Eiffel Tower sideways under cover in London for 25 years, the Dome will be seen as a brilliant piece of foresight. You never know.

former royal Greenwich Palace, as has often been suggested. There are repair bills for these tunnels dated 918 and 1268.

Joseph Conrad's gripping 1907 story *The Secret Agent* has a man blown to pieces in a botched revolutionary bomb attack before World War I here. It's not so far-fetched, as there was an attempt to blow up the Royal Observatory in 1894 and in Whitechapel there was a gun-battle with anarchists in 1911 (see page 284). Incidentally, in this book Conrad talks of Greenwich Park station, which sounded like fiction. But it turns out there was one on Royal Hill on a line long vanished, which means yet another abandoned tunnel, under Blackheath on the way to Lewisham.

We go up the hill to the old **Royal Observatory**, a hill that, with its superb view, has for centuries been a great place for Londoners to stroll. Dickens records in his *Sketches*:

> *The chief place of resort in the day-time... is the Park, in which the principal amusement is to drag young ladies up the steep hill which leads to the Observatory, and then drag them down again, at the very top of their speed, greatly to the derangement of their curls and bonnet-caps, much to the edification of the lookers-on from below.*

MORE WOLFE, HALF OF THE WORLD AND MERIDIAN MADNESS

Heading on, we reach **General Wolfe's statue** (see page 310), the man who denied France Canada and single-handedly reduced one of those great nations to also-ran status for ever. I refer, of course, to Canada's cuisine… what else?

Talking about status, the meridian line that passes through the observatory – if you go through the little iron gate and along the path on the downhill side of the observatory a few steps there's a **brass meridian line** in the ground where children can stand with one foot in either hemisphere – provides evidence of Britain's pre-eminence in navigation at the time. Britain got ownership of the Prime Meridian, 0 degrees, and Greenwich Mean Time, just as in the 20th century, when the US which had taken over the role of super-power, got 1 as their international telephone country calling code. Come to think of it, Britain's reward for inventing post boxes and stamps is that we are the only country that doesn't have to put its name on our stamps, just as Americans don't have to put .usa on the end of their websites. Don't worry, people of Burkina Faso – your time will come.

The **Royal Observatory** (☎ *020 8312 6565* 🖥 *www.rog.nmm.ac.uk*; see box page 322, for history) has long since moved its HQ to Sussex and now conducts its serious stargazing from better-suited viewpoints overseas. The old observatory is now a museum that gives an insight into matters such as the search for means of fixing longitude – upon which thousands of sailors' lives depended and led to the surprise literary hit of 1995, *Longitude* by Dava Sobel.

Between the brass meridian line and General Wolfe stands a monument to what could in some regards be seen as a final crushing victory for the French. Here there's a set of brass imperial measures pegged out to be

LOOKING BEHIND THE Wolfe statue, you see that the line of Greenwich's great view carries on down Blackheath Avenue to the park gates, beyond which can be seen Blackheath and the church of All Saints perfectly aligned. Cosmic. This would be your route to Blackheath station if you fancied striking out – it's perhaps a mile-and-a-half.

In the park itself there's a rather indifferent café on the left of this avenue. On the right of the avenue, about halfway down, there's a path through an ornamental rose garden to the **Ranger's House**, now home to the Wernher Collection of rare treasures (see page 80). On my visit I turned left in front of the Ranger's House which brings you to some unremarkable paving slabs that, unknown to most local people and unsigned in the park, tell the astounding story of a Caroline, Princess of Wales (1768–1821), spurned by her husband George IV, who preferred his mistress, and who was mourned by all London at her emotional funeral. Yes, this is **Princess Caroline's sunken bath**, marked only with a small plaque on the wall, a last relic of this strangest of royal stories (see page 338).

Leaving Greenwich Park and heading for that spire of All Saints across Blackheath, you can see why this great open space was used by Londoners for welcoming victorious kings home from European wars, such as Henry V in 1415 after Agincourt.

As the route from London to Europe in the days of stagecoaches, Blackheath was a notorious spot for highwaymen, who were often strung up on gibbets to deter others. Samuel Pepys records seeing one such decayed corpse swaying in the wind with the flesh falling from its bones: 'A filthy sight.' The road east from here, **Shooters Hill**, gave people their

The Blackheath extension

used as universal references. It was a long way uphill to come to measure something, which had to fit between the pegs *exactly*.

Today it's as if Wolfe, Nelson, Trafalgar and Waterloo had never happened. Everyone must use the aforementioned metric system, which is based on some French madman's idea of the distance from the Equator to the North Pole (he was wrong); it's a more logical, but, sadly, less eccentric one than the imperial one it replaced. There was a human side to the imperial system – a foot was a foot (that tired thing on the end of your leg),

first or last view of London and is recalled at the start of Dickens's possibly greatest work (sorry, I can't make my mind up), *A Tale of Two Cities*, and in Byron's poem *Don Juan*.

Hidden under Blackheath are vast networks of **underground tunnels** for which no known purpose or date exists. There is a similar set at Chiselhurst, Kent, not too far from here. They say you can cross Blackheath from one side to the other without ever coming up on the surface.

Oddly, then, Blackheath has several ponds (you'd think they'd drain away down all those tunnels); and if it is midwinter, youths sometimes skate on them. I wouldn't recommend skating on thin ice at all; I happen to know that the pond a couple of hundred yards to the left of All Saints church – in the angle between Prince of Wales Road and South Row – is at least in part shallow. I fell through the ice here one Boxing Day myself.

Just around the corner from the pond, along South Row a little, is the most exquisite and perfect crescent of houses in London, the **Paragon**, well worth a look.

The way down to the village is behind All Saints, down **Montpelier Row** and Montpelier Vale. If you had heaps of energy, or were car- or bike-borne, there is one more fascinating link with Princess Caroline, in **Pagoda Gardens**, reached by following the railway on this north side of the tracks to the right (west) up Collins Street, Blazdon Road and Eliot Vale (not down Heath Lane).

This is the eccentric building, **The Pagoda**, built around 1775 for the Duke of Buccleuch; it has a dramatic Chinese-style roof with almost ludicrously upturned corners. This is part of that era's fascination with Chinoiserie which also gave us the much higher pagoda at Kew Gardens, but is of more interest because Princess Caroline came to stay here in 1799 after separating from her husband and before going to live in Greenwich Park.

CHARLES II, WHO put Greenwich on the map with its Royal Observatory in 1675 – in fact on every map on this planet, as all longitudes, and indeed time, are measured from Greenwich – was less than generous to his first Astronomer Royal, **John Flamsteed** (1646–1719).

He paid him just £100 a year and insisted he pay his staff and buy his own telescopes from this amount. He also insisted that architect **Christopher Wren** (him again) used stones, brick and lead from part of Tilbury Fort further down the river (you could call this recycling). But he did agree that the hill above Greenwich was the very spot for the observatory. This allowed it in the coming centuries to help the mariners in the nearby London Docks, by observing the time precisely and dropping a ball down a flagstaff at exactly 1pm. Then sea captains could set their chronometers to the same precisely measured time, essential for navigation. A gun signal, as at Edinburgh, would have made the signal too inaccurate for this

Skinflint Charles puts the place on the map

and a yard was the distance from the king's nose to his outstretched thumb, but there was also a pleasing insanity about what we called imperial measures. I mean if you defend them, can you work out the cost of one stone nine pounds and 7½ ounces of kippers at four shillings and eightpence farthing a pound? Go on, if you like old measures, just try it. It's near impossible. *Mon dieu, alors*, thank God for the French! And if they always put a dozen bottles, not ten, into a case of wine, who's complaining?

purpose given the relatively slow speed of sound. They weren't too bothered about the faster speed of light then, however, not knowing it had any speed at all. You can still witness the falling of the ball each day.

But is the **Prime Meridian**, 0 degrees, actually right here? A big deal was made of the fact that the Millennium Dome (see box, page 318) had to be in its absurd location on an allegedly inaccessible peninsula because it was on the line (it passes up the reach of the river next to the Dome and just clips a corner of the site). But a yachtsman passing the site on the Thames will find that his navigation equipment, based on references from global positioning satellites, says he is on the meridian 336 feet further *east*. And students of the first Astronomer Royal, John Flamsteed, will find that the first meridian he laid down in 1675 by simply lowering his telescope, is 61 feet three inches *west* of the one used for the millennium celebrations.

The Curator of Astronomy at the Old Royal Observatory at the time of writing, Maria Blyzinsky, told me:

> In fact we have four meridians recorded here, each a little further east as new astronomers built bigger and better telescopes. Halley's, for example, was set up in 1725.

It's the fault of Flamsteed for putting his telescope on the edge of the hill. Later ones had to be behind this.

The meridian line used by the satellite system referred to above was established in 1984 and moves slightly as satellites, wobbling as they orbit the Earth, try to compensate for the globe's imperfections and movements. But for the millennium celebrations, the 1851 Official Greenwich Meridian established by **Sir George Airy** was the one that counted.

The observatory is the highpoint of the walk, so it's all downhill from here with a relatively short stroll through pleasant parts to the station. There's an optional Blackheath extension (see page 320), ending at that rather charming village. You could sit here on one of the benches and read about it while resting your weary feet rather than actually do it. Or you could save it for another time.

BACK TO THE STATION AND THE CREAM OF SOCIETY

Assuming you intend to visit Blackheath another time, let's return from the observatory over the meridian line and go downhill to the left and then straight across, crossing the road descending through the park, the Avenue, and leaving by one of the gates beyond into **Crooms Hill**. Here you might see some fine 17th-, 18th- and 19th-century houses, Wolfe's home at **Macartney's House** (not open to the public), plus an unusual and splendid **belvedere**, an isolated room set to command a fine view over the wall that had made a garden more private but had cut off the house's view. This room is built on an oblique angle and has a fine moulded ceiling. Have a good gawp – that's what the thing is there for, gawping at you.

There's also a blue plaque to a great philanthropist who lived here, **Benjamin Waugh** (1839–1908), who founded the National Society for the Prevention of Cruelty to Children.

Here, too, further down Crooms Hill, is one of London's most eccentric museums, the **London Fan Museum**. A good place to stop on a hot day (see page 76).

Coming out by the theatre, there is a former fine old coaching inn opposite; glancing right up the oddly named Nevada Street you can see a statue of William IV, looking like the total prat that he really was.

Our quickest way to the station is to go left down **Burney Street**, on the far corner of which we come across one of London's more eccentric little parks. This tiny scrap of earth has more monuments than many a large park; there's a marble obelisk-thingy saying 'Built by Greenwich People 1981–82', a plaque saying the Duke of Edinburgh planted an oak tree here in 1982, and yet another plaque raving about a milkman, Dougie Mullins, who was born here. I asked some local people what all the fuss was about, but they didn't know. Please write to me and put me out of my misery.

Rounding the corner we're back marvelling again at that staggering Stalinist-fascist Town Hall clock tower and behind it, across the High Road, is Greenwich railway station. Phew!

HAMMERSMITH

A JEWEL WITHIN A TOAD

For too many, Hammersmith is a place you pass through. On the Tube, by river, in the air and, of course, by the trunk roads that have converged here from the four points of the compass since time immemorial. Today, the A4 flyover leading to the M4 and M3 slices through this former village and, motorists on them might reasonably assume, totally ruins the place.

That assumption couldn't be more wrong and it's utterly typical of London that within a stone's throw of this thundering road – virtually beneath it even – you can find delights ranging from bizarre architectural oddities, some of the most wonderful views in London, tales of love, courage, daring, devotion and creation involving death and a princess, numerous fascinating nooks and crannies, and some of the world's best pubs.

Come on a walk around Hammersmith and you'll be convinced. But allow yourself plenty of time – it's too good to hurry.

A WALK AROUND HAMMERSMITH

You could do this walk in about 45 minutes flat out, but allow at least a couple of hours to include fascinating pubs, churches and shops. Start at **Hammersmith Tube station**; by going anticlockwise we'll save the best stuff till last. When I say start at the Tube, it's daft in itself that the Tubes just fail to connect by about 100 yards. The Hammersmith and City line station is nicer and, of course, is the one that *doesn't* head towards the City, and it's also on the Circle Line but not, of course, on that circle.

Starting between the two, at the northwest corner of the race track that runs round the Piccadilly and District Line Tube station roundabout (it's so large and incorporates so many roads that we'll call it the Megabout), you'll notice at the corner of King Street and Beadon Road the splendid

HAMMERSMITH ROAD

SHORTLANDS

GREAT CHURCH LA

TALGARTH ROAD

• The Ark

GARDENS

BUTE

HAMMERSMITH ROAD

ST DUNSTAN'S ROAD

Charing Cross Hospital

START FINISH

HAMMERSMITH BROADWAY

Shopping Centre

FULHAM PALACE ROAD

Hammersmith Apollo

CHANCELLORS ROAD

SHEPHERD'S BUSH ROAD

Brach

N

The Swan Hammersmith

St Paul's

Snail-like surgery

CRISP ROAD

Riverside Studios

HAMMERSMITH GROVE

BEADON ROAD

KING STREET

Hop Poles

Lyric Theatre

ANGEL WALK

BRIDGE AVE

ASPEN GDNS

SUSSEX ST

WORLIDGE ST

QUEEN CAROLINE STREET

HAMMERSMITH BRIDGE ROAD

BRIDGE VIEW

MALL

LOWER MALL

Blue Anchor

HAMMERSMITH BRIDGE

CASTELNAU

OVERSTONE ROAD

LEAMORE STREET

GROVE

DOWN PLACE

RUT. LAND GRO

MALL ROAD

Rutland Arms

CAMBRIDGE

GLENTHORNE ROAD

0   100m

Salutation Inn

MACBETH ST

HOLCOMBE ST

RIVERSIDE GARDENS

Furnivall Gardens

The Dove

STUDLAND ST

Town Hall

WEST ROAD

GREAT WEST ROAD

UPPER MALL

Kelmscott House

River Thames

DALLING ROAD

RAVENSCOURT PLACE

CROMWELL AVE

RIVERCOURT ROAD

KING STREET

Ravenscourt Park

RAVENSCOURT AVE

WELTJE ROAD

Ravenscourt Park

RAVENSCOURT ROAD

Gate

RAVENSCOURT PARK

Queen Charlotte's Hospital

HAMLET GARDENS

BEAVOR LANE

OIL MILL ROAD

The Old Ship

Black Lion

ST PETER'S ROAD

STANDISH ROAD

St Peter's

BLACK LION LA

GOLDHAWK ROAD

RAVENSCOURT GARDENS

WESTCROFT SQUARE

KING STREET

BLACK LION LANE

ST PETER'S VILLAS

ST PETER'S SQUARE

GREAT WEST ROAD

HAMMERSMITH TERRACE

CHISWICK

Chiswick Eyot

Stamford Brook

BRITISH GROVE

ST PETER'S SQUARE

EYOT GARDENS

HAMMERSMITH WALK

Swan pub with its mosaic sign and over-the-top brickwork; ignore what a pig's ear they have made of the ground floor – there are more splendid pubs on this walk than even the late Oliver Reed could have got round in one session. But not as many as in 1873, when Hammersmith was recorded as having 139 pubs.

Turning down King Street we venture, very briefly, into multiple-chainstore-land and ghastly concrete shopping centreville, but don't despair – it doesn't last long; notice as we head west how the shops become more and more fascinating. But historic pubs start straight away.

The **Hop Poles** on the left, for example, is where punk pioneer **Ian Dury** of Blockheads fame used to prop up the bar. If he were here, he would no doubt point out that the bar would have to prop him up now as he died in 2000, but the point of such blockhead remarks is that Hammersmith was, and is, riddled with rock and pop stars who quietly sup pints in the most unassuming places.

On the right here, invisible amidst the charmless concrete, is an amazing architectural survivor. Suspended within all this seventies stuff is the quite beautiful gilt and chandelier and red velvet interior of an entire Victorian theatre moved from nearby. The **Lyric** was designed in 1895 by celebrated theatre designer Frank Matcham. When the theatre was demolished in the 1970s, the lavish interior was carefully taken down, stored for a few years then somehow saved intact within the dull concrete King's Mall shopping centre. It's like cutting open a toad and finding a jewel in it. Plus it's got rather a good caff upstairs.

The old Lyric had enjoyed a boom under the manager Nigel Playfair in the 1920s, which put Hammersmith on the map for the theatre-going classes, so much so that the humorous magazine *Punch* remarked:

> *No greater name than Nigel Playfair*
> *Occurs in Thespian lore or myth*
> *'Twas he who first revealed to Mayfair*
> *The whereabouts of Hammersmith.*

Soon on the right (after a plaque announcing bizarrely 'Investor in People: Co-operative Funeral Service') is the **Salutation Inn**, which dates from 1750 when this was the main road west from the capital. The late Queen Mother, partial to the odd tincture or three herself, gamely pulled a few majestic pints here in 1989. The fabulous early 20th-century tilework is a gem, and the beer is local, from Fuller's brewery just half a mile west on the A4 Great West Road, a place of pilgrimage for real ale fans from around the globe (tours can be arranged).

It was at around this point in King Street where the Salutation stands that a creek came all the way up from the river and, difficult though it is to imagine today, those massive spritsail Thames barges could unload right here. Now the creek has been enclosed, although its outlet may be seen from the river. **Furnivall Gardens**, between here and the river, is laid out where the factories and warehouses were clustered round the wharves of this lost harbour.

On the left, opposite the Salutation, we pass one end of the somewhat Stalinist Hammersmith **Town Hall** (by Stalinist, I mean the architecture, not the politics; they're *far* more left-wing than that, silly). Then there's the UGC cinema, which, although being a thirties building, stands on

YOU MAY BE SURPRISED at the amount of Polish you hear spoken or the number of Polish goods in shops. But this is not surprising as this area was virtually the capital of free Poland from the time the post-war victors of World War II carved up Europe in 1945 (no jokes about Stalinists this time; is it not a matter of deep regret, if not shame, that having gone to war supposedly to save Poland from a mad dictator in 1939, we, or perhaps history, reluctantly handed it over to another one just a few years later?) to when Lech Walesa and Solidarity reclaimed the place for its people.

Not far from here by car on the A40 is the superb Polish war memorial that commemorates the Polish Air Force heroes who fought and died in sorties from these islands in the desperate days of 1940. I went to school near a wartime air base and there were kids there with names which looked to me (in my ignorance) like opticians' test cards, evidence that some of these heroes thrived. In the 1990s a new wave of young Poles came to work in London, renewing the ties.

Here there's Polish food aplenty, Polish arts a-thriving, and much info about Poland today. The Poles are just one of many nationalities who exist and thrive together in this polyglot borough. Here, too, at the Polish Arts Centre there is the **Joseph Conrad Library**, a tribute to a Polish master who could write better in his third language than most people, myself included, can write in their first.

Polish Hammersmith

the site of one of the earliest cinemas in Britain, dating from 1912. (Hammersmith has been for centuries a place of large-scale entertainment for West London – the Palais, the Apollo, the Riverside Studios, and Olympia.) Further down on the right is **POSK**, the centre for Polish Arts and Culture, where a kind of government-in-exile kept the flame of freedom burning through the years of communism post-World War II (see box opposite).

Massive Testicles, Strange Leanings and a Shot Ghost

Soon, tucked away on the left, is possibly the strangest tribute to an MP that I can recall. A large bull with massive testicles stands with a wordy tribute to former Hammersmith big cheese **Sir William Bull** (1863– 1931). Unless he spent all his time making love to actresses in local flats while wearing a Chelsea strip here in Hammersmith, like a modern MP we could mention, then I suppose the massive testicles are irrelevant. The thing is merely a rebus, a visual pun on the old chap's name.

If that's not enough bull about Bull, on the right here are some totally over-the-top gates also dedicated to Sir William. They lead to **Ravenscourt Park**.

On just a little more, if you can force yourself past the curious curio shops you'll find here, and on the corner of Goldhawk Road at the traffic lights (opposite British Grove) stands an unassuming shop. But look at the brickwork above, a fantasy in terracotta well worth a second glance.

We go no further west lest we venture into Chiswick, but instead turn left down to **St Peter's Square** (the turning before British Grove). At this point, a magic wand has been waved, for here, just a few feet from the cosmopolitan hubbub of King Street, and a few feet short of the thundering A4 beyond, is an elegant island of total tranquillity, **one of London's nicest squares**, unknown by those who speed so closely by. Unlike many a Central London square of similar elegance, these gardens are open to the public, so one may stroll through them, noting a fine central sculpture, then proceeding to the far end and turning left towards the church of the same name, where a strangely provocative sculpture of a woman resting upon nothing sits half-forgotten to the right.

The church, **St Peter's**, a large 1829 classical job, was too early for the Gothic revival and thus contrasts nicely with St Paul's later in the walk. I wouldn't tarry here unless you love religious wall paintings, of which it offers splendid examples.

Dive through the subway beneath the A4 and we pop up in **Black Lion Lane** (of which we saw the other end in King Street).

Soon we reach the **Black Lion** pub on the left, which tells the melancholy tale of the St Peter's haunting. From 1804 onwards, the old St Peter's graveyard was haunted by a frightening **ghost** on dark nights. One Francis Smith, fed up with his ghoulish next-door neighbour, 'loaded his blunderbuss with shot and himself with ale' and blasted the thing. Sadly, it was not the ghost that the inebriated Smith shot but the white-clothed bricklayer Thomas Millwood, whose body the shocked residents carried to the Black Lion pub.

CRAFTY MORRIS AND THE FIRST WORLDWIDE WEB

Now we are entering an area with some quite wonderful 18th-century houses – the tall **Hammersmith Terrace** between the pub and the river was built in 1750. Here, at the Black Lion steps, before Hammersmith Bridge was built, people needing a boat would shout 'Oars!' Out of the dark and swirling fog a waterman, often half-drunk, would come, water dripping from his oars, to ferry you expertly through the swirling eddies across the Thames to Barnes, or maybe, if he was too far gone, across the river Styx into the underworld.

But cheer up: around the corner are the finest river views you could ask for. Turn left into the **Upper Mall** walkway and head east along the river front.

Looking back along the river westwards there is a view of the island, Chiswick Eyot, not far west and of the sweep of Corney Reach beyond as the loop of the river turns due south. Ahead, to the east, is the elegant **Hammersmith Bridge**, a picturesque scene that thousands of artists have tried to capture on canvas.

Here, at No 26 Upper Mall, **Kelmscott House** is, where **William Morris** (1834–96), thinker, socialist (but not Stalinist), fabric and wallpaper designer *par excellence* and all-round Arts and Crafts revolutionary, lived and worked from 1878 to 1896, when he died. What a spot to contemplate the world from, with its view of the sweep of the river both ways! You could be envious – particularly when you learn his country house, Kelmscott Manor, much further upriver near Oxford, looked out across the same Thames from where Morris, as he himself remarked, might have contemplated the very same gallons of water he could have seen later at his London house downriver.

Actually, if you delve into the William Morris Society's little museum (open 2pm–5pm, Thursday and Saturday afternoons), you'll find he was much too busy to do that much sitting around. He ran the Kelmscott Press, turning out socialist tracts but with the most wonderful typography.

He would have meetings of the angry young men of the day, with people crowding into the coach house of Kelmscott – chaps such as George Bernard Shaw, Sidney Webb and W B Yeats were regulars. Failing that, Morris would march down to Hammersmith Bridge and harangue passers-by. (For more on this William Morris and the car-maker of the same name, see my book *Eccentric Oxford*.)

Several arty printers operated from here at the end of the 19th century and one of them, after a horrendous row over a printing contract, took all the carefully engraved printing plates he'd been commissioned to make to Hammersmith Bridge and threw them off. Now that'd be a find for the metal detectors. Morris's energy was prodigious and his artistic vision rare; his influence in so many fields changed the course of British art.

When it was his, Morris's house was only a century old (built 1780s) but was already famous for two previous creative geniuses. **Sir Francis Ronalds** (1788–1873) made the first electric telegraph here in 1816; it was eight miles long. His invention soon transformed the railways, the empire, news-gathering, trade, in fact almost everything. Clocks and time zones had to be sorted out. Bristol time was about 12 minutes behind London, for example, before all this. A global wiring up of the very first worldwide web rapidly took hold and started right here. The house's other illustrious inhabitant was popular children's author **George Macdonald** (1824–1905).

A PERFECT PUB, INSPIRATION FOR GREAT MINDS

Perhaps these great minds gained inspiration from being across the pathway from **the Dove**, one of the most perfect pubs imaginable. Although crowded on summer Saturdays, the pub had just four people in it (including a certain ageing rock star) when I visited on a November morning when the fire was cheerful in the snug, and the river views from the bar at the back just as good. Don't miss, as I nearly did, the reputed smallest public bar in the world on the right as you come in – it's easy to assume it's a broom cupboard. In there a brass plate marks the high point of a particularly high tide in 1928. No wonder there's not a level floor or straight beam in the place. And have a close look; in the first bar by the entrance, at the drawings of Hammersmith Bridge, for reference later on the walk.

It was originally the Dove Coffee House – they were all the rage in the 18th century; famous ones such as Lloyd's in the City became institutions – and was bought by the aforementioned local brewery Fuller's in 1796. That was more than a century after Charles II and his saucy mistress Nell Gwyn supped here. You can prop up the bar and watch Old Father Thames go by, musing that for more than 200 years – since well before New

Zealand was founded and when the United States was just a smattering of East Coast settlements – this same, splendid Fuller's beer has cheered many a Londoner at this very same spot. Not that it's been called the Dove ever since. A careless painter painted two doves on the sign in the 1850s and so it became the Doves until 1948 when a new sign corrected this error.

The Dove also cheered the novelist **A P Herbert** (1890–1971) who loved this spot and thinly disguised the Dove as The Pigeons in his novel *The Water Gipsies*. He lived in Hammersmith Terrace, which we have just walked past, and his portrait is in the Black Lion, another of his favourite pubs.

The poet **James Thomson** (1700–48) took enough inspiration in the Dove to write the rumbustious *Rule Britannia* in one of its upper rooms. Britannia may have ruled the waves, but the waves ended up ruling Thomson. After a row down the river to Kew, he took a chill and died not knowing half the country and thousands more round the world would bellow his words with gusto on the Last Night of the Proms for centuries to come. Talking of great music, local composer **Gustav Holst** (1874–1934), whose house can be seen at Barnes on the opposite bank and who wrote *The Planets* suite while music master at St Paul's School, composed the *Hammersmith Suite* in an upstairs room at the Dove.

Dragging ourselves away from this tavern, and continuing along the riverside, there are three more pubs, all good in their own way and superbly situated, along the waterfront, which soon becomes the Lower Mall, before Hammersmith Bridge: the **Old Ship**, the **Rutland** and the **Blue Anchor**, the last-named cosy hostelry having been licensed since at least 1722.

Here, the rowing clubs come thick and fast and give drinkers who linger in the pubs by the riverfront something to watch. One of them, Furnivall Sculling Club, is named after local doctor and rowing enthusiast Dr F J Furnivall who outraged some in 1896 by setting up this club for women only initially, although decorum required they had to row their skiffs somehow in long skirts without an ankle being revealed to onlookers!

All along here are beautiful, mainly 18th-century buildings. Now we reach the splendidly over-the-top **Hammersmith Bridge**, a fabulous confection nothing like the one we saw in the Dove (see box, page 334). It's a pleasant stroll across the bridge and back (if it hasn't been blown up again) and under it at the Hammersmith end.

Beyond you will see the **Riverside Studios**, where prince of ginger geeks, Chris Evans, made his fortune with *TFI Friday*, a cult post-pub TV show. Further beyond, one of the football grounds thick on the ground round here is visible. This one is Fulham's, being not in Fulham but Hammersmith, whereas Chelsea's *is* in Fulham, not Chelsea. I think I've got that right. Same with hospitals: Charing Cross Hospital is not at Charing Cross but here at Hammersmith, but the Hammersmith Hospital is at Wormwood Scrubs. Simples.

SYDNEY OPERA COMES TO LONDON AND A RIPPED-OUT HEART

One more thing before we leave the river on the road going left from the bridge. This stretch immediately downstream of the bridge was, it is difficult now to believe, once one of London's airports. In 1925 a French company got permission to use the Thames here as an aerodrome and elegant seaplanes would swoop between the towers of Bazalgette's bridge and splash down in the river. Charming, and why not revive it? After all, most great European cities have suitable rivers right in their centre.

Go left up Hammersmith Bridge Road, where there are yet more pubs, and soon on the right we find a remarkable small new building – the sail-like, **shell-like surgery** of Dr Fernandes and partners. Sydney Opera House comes to Hammersmith. It is denying the existence of the thundering adjacent flyover and it somehow contrives to arrange matters so that every one of its rooms has an outside view that doesn't include the flyover. Brilliant (by Guy Greenfield) and, when I saw it, unblemished with graffiti – may it stay that way.

Now walk towards the Gothic 1882 church ahead, **St Paul's**, that provides a contrast to the giant shoe box of St Peter's, which had not a pointed arch or a spire in sight. Both churches are 19th century but the Gothic revival style of St Paul's couldn't be more different – strange to see how completely styles had changed in only 53 years. The church houses a great organ and offers tremendous recitals from time to time. But St Paul's itself is remarkable more for its astounding contents than for its architecture. A clue is in two street names behind the church: **Crispe Road** and **Caroline Street**.

BIZARRELY, THE UNUSUALLY ELEGANT Hammersmith Bridge has, four times in the past century, come within an ace of being blown to smithereens.

Once in the 1930s an IRA bomb was fizzing and spluttering when a passer-by threw it in the river; once when a wartime Nazi bomb fell in the river near the bridge; and once in 1996 when enough IRA Semtex explosive to blow shreds of the bridge all over West London – the largest such bomb yet planted in Britain – failed to detonate properly. A few months later an IRA man was shot dead in a hideout a few hundred yards away.

Finally, it was controversially closed in 1998 for drawn-out repairs. At last the bridge was nearly ready. Then Irish terrorists blew up a bit of it again, delaying its re-opening until late 2000. Notices said the closure was due to 'unforeseen circumstances'. Totally predictable circumstances, I'd say.

In the unlikely event that the bridge is still there when you read this, it's well worth the walk across. If you look very carefully on the west side handrail, you can see

The bizarre story of Hammersmith Bridge

a plaque marking where a hero, **Charles Wood**, plunged in to save a dying woman, presumably a would-be suicide, and lost his own life in the process.

Now to the extraordinary bridge itself. It is pretty, or pretty ghastly, depending on your view of Victoriana and twiddly bits. The finials on the towers look as if they should turn around while the rest of the contraption does something else (like the breakfast machine in the film *Chitty Chitty Bang Bang*), and it has more outrageous abutments than Dawn French.

Splendid, in its way, the bridge would seem to have granted its designer a kind of immortality (IRA permitting), and indeed in **Hammersmith church (St Paul's**, which we pass later on the walk) there is a fancy memorial tablet on the wall to bridge builder **W Tierney Clark**, who died in 1852. It bears a detailed picture of Hammersmith Suspension Bridge and the fine words:

> The great suspension bridge at Pesth in Hungary, those at Hammersmith and Shoreham, and many other works attest to his talent, perseverance and skill and are lasting monuments to his fame.

A close look at his bridge carved on his tomb shows that it is not the current elegant Hammersmith Suspension Bridge, clearly dated in its arches 1887, but an earlier one that it replaced. This is the same design you may have seen on the Dove pub's wall earlier in the walk round Hammersmith. W Tierney Clark's fame is all but extinguished – so much water under the bridge.

He may have joined Buda and Pest (and the bridge there today indeed *does* directly resemble the drawings of the old Hammersmith Bridge), but only temporarily did the same for Hammersmith and Barnes. 'Lasting monuments' indeed, although at least Budapest is kinder in naming a street and a hotel after him.

The creator of the bridge we see today was the great Victorian engineer **Sir Joseph Bazalgette** (1819–91), who arguably did more for London and left more positive impact on the city than anyone in its history. Victorian London was riddled with disease, much of it, such as cholera, caused by the lack of proper sewage-disposal systems and the consequent pollution of drinking water supplies. The poor drew their water only yards from where others threw their filth. The 'Great Stink' of London's summers was intolerable.

Bazalgette had the vision to build great intercepting sewers going west–east and installed powerful steam-driven pump houses, which allowed water and sewage distribution systems to be completely separated. He was the mastermind behind the simultaneous creation of the great embankments, such as the Victoria Embankment at what is now called Embankment, and the Albert Embankment at Vauxhall. He tamed the river (as his monument on the Victoria Embankment says: '*Flumini Vincula Posuit*' – he put chains upon the river) and created not only charming walks along the previously impenetrable riverside, but also useful through routes for the burgeoning traffic and even space for the Tube lines.

Some say by eliminating diseases such as cholera, caused by drinking water contaminated with sewage, Bazalgette saved more lives than any other Victorian, including Florence Nightingale.

So Bazalgette's rebuilding of Tierney Clark's bridge is the one we see today. It's not as wedding-cakey as the prettier Albert Bridge, but like so many Victorian things, it makes a virtue out of necessity in a way we find hard to do today.

And just in case the IRA feel honour-bound to blow the thing up properly, get a good look at it now. Perhaps the Mayor of Hammersmith should just fix it with them so that no one gets hurt. ('How about next Tuesday at 10am?'). Then it could be rebuilt properly.

At the back of the nave stands an urn in which Hammersmith bigwig **Sir Nicholas Crispe** requested his heart be put on his death in 1665. The urn is below a bronze bust of 'that glorious martyr Kinge Charles the first of blessed memory' and symbolises Crispe's role as a 'loyall sharer in the sufferings of his late and present majesty'.

Just how loyal can be understood by Crispe's request that on his death his heart be cut out and put in an **urn** at the foot of a statue of Charles I. He wanted to be for ever at the feet of the king whose head was chopped off by those republican types in 1649. Crispe left money in his will so that someone would take his heart out every year and 'refresh' it with wine to stop it becoming too, well, crisp.

Curiously, the urn is empty. In 1898 the Royalist knight's body was moved to Hammersmith from St Mildred's, Bread Street (in the City of London); someone with a strong stomach took the two-centuries-old heart (now thoroughly crisp as the yearly marination ritual had lapsed) from the urn and reunited it with its body in the churchyard where it lies today beneath the thundering A4 flyover. Also in the church, don't miss the telling memorial to the builder of Hammersmith Bridge.

Even more remarkable is the story of **Queen Caroline** and the gravestone in the corner nearest the Hammersmith Megabout which tells of the amazing goings-on at her funeral – more dramatic than that more recent one of the Princess of Wales, but in almost exactly the same circumstances (see box, page 338).

Leaving the church, don't cross the hurtling traffic of the Megabout itself but note amidst the cliff-like offices in the middle of it an ancient Georgian brick frontage facing the church. This 1709 Baroque front was saved as a mere skin while everything behind it was ripped down for the Centre West reconstruction of 1992.

Pressing on, you'll walk past a huge thirties picture palace, now one of London's leading live stage and music venues, since 1992 named the **Apollo**, having previously (since 1936) used up most of Britain's cinema names. Formerly it was (in turn) the Gaumont Palace, Gaumont and the Odeon.

Cross busy **Fulham Palace Road**, which leads south from the swirling Megabout, using the underpass unless you wish to join Sir Nicholas and the others in their graveyard.

When you surface on the far side there is a stunning view of the **Ark**, one of London's most imaginative and dramatic modern buildings, which avoids the boring cigarette-pack shape of so many glass and steel towers nowadays. The building does indeed loom like a large ship, moored in the city, but the brilliance of its design can perhaps be fully appreciated from many different angles. From the air, its oval shape fits perfectly the hole left by the road flyover on one side and the Tube railway tracks on the south, which curve tightly around it like this: (0). From the ground, pleasing details such as the drain near the front and the rusticated brick texture on the vertical pillars add a little lightening detail to the looming mass. Inside, it has a massive atrium with dramatic suspended walkways and a strange meeting-room, globe-like thing that apparently hovers in mid-air.

Built in 1992, it was designed by **Ralph Erskine** (1914–2005), a British-born Swedish architect, and constructed by Ake Larson, a Swedish developer – which just goes to show that there's a lot more to Swedes than flatpack furniture, sensible cars and root vegetables.

This, your weary feet will be pleased to hear, is the limit of our walk. We return under the Megabout (or over it) to the Centre West thingy that houses one of the Tube stations and a shopping centre. Its architecture is inoffensively bland (is it post-modern and does that make us post-post-modern and does modern therefore mean ancient?). A fitting location, perhaps, for Coca-Cola's HQ. The Centre West project, including the hugely busy transport interchange costing £20 million, may have been an unremarkable way to spend £85 million, but it was at least finished on time and to budget.

If you leave via the Tube station underneath, there's one more detail to note: the station itself was to have been the architect's answer to the DeLorean car – a sweeping gullwing canopy with no visible supports. Difficult and brilliant, so the last thing you'd do would be to clutter up the platforms with buildings that look as if they support the canopy, right? Wrong. They have completely spoilt the effect with waiting rooms that almost reach the roof. Personally, I'd rather shiver a little. Another thing – the canopy is designed so that an out-of-control Tube train driven by a psychopath trying to get to Cuba can smash down one prop without the whole thing coming down. Well, I'd still rather not be there when it's tried out.

So that was Hammersmith with all its fascinating quirks and oddities. If you've got this far, the chances are that you haven't been a victim of violent crime, which at earlier times would have been a strong possibility here.

Hammersmith, as with anywhere close to London straddling a main road out of town, has always been good for highwaymen and robbers. Dick Turpin was a regular at the Queen's Head on Brook Green.

In the 18th century, before the inception of an organised metropolitan police force, we hear of a fund being collected here to give a 'proper reward for the apprehending and convicting of housebreakers, murderers, footpads, robbers of gardens, orchards, poultry, etc, as so many daring and atrocious offences have of late been committed'. Even as recently as 1818, local

Clues to the Royal Family's weirdest story

A T ST PAUL'S CHURCHYARD (see page 336) lies a fascinating gravestone you must not miss. It has a poignant, tragic story to tell.

It is the tale of a spurned **Princess of Wales** whose husband, the Prince of Wales, preferred the company of his mistress, a previously married woman, and whose eventual funeral through Kensington, which the authorities tried to downplay, moved the entire population of London to unprecedented public demonstrations of mass emotion.

She was subjected by the Royal Family and the media to constant calumny about her private life, but was, in part, the authoress of her own downfall, becoming an adulterer, as her husband certainly was. Towards the end of her life she frequently appeared in public, often scantily clad, with her most unsuitable playboy lover.

When I add that her story explains the presence of Britain's most eccentric building, the oriental fantasy that is the Royal Pavilion at Brighton, it should become clear that we are talking not about the late 20th-century Princess of Wales, Diana, but her early 19th-century counterpart, Caroline, whose name, although totally forgotten by the average Londoner, is at least marked by Queen Caroline Street at this spot in Hammersmith.

In 1795 **Caroline of Brunswick** married the unpleasantly priggish 'Prinny', the deeply unpopular Prince Regent who was to become **George IV**. They soon became estranged as the prince spent more and more of his time at a farmhouse near Brighton with a previously married (scandal) Catholic (more scandal) commoner (yet more scandal) woman (well, no scandal about that bit) called Mrs Maria Fitzherbert. In fact Prinny had secretly married Mrs Fitzherbert in 1785, ten years before his therefore bigamous marriage to Caroline. The earlier marriage was declared invalid.

After the prince's official marriage in 1795, the court put it about that the new Princess of Wales was unfaithful and unhygienic, never changing her undergarments and eating mainly raw onions and garlic. She had consequently the most monstrous breath and bad teeth, one courtier complained.

The unfaithfulness was true but only after she had been shabbily treated by the prince's shameless flaunting of his mistress (is this at all familiar?). Actually she really did go a bit scatty later, travelling with an unsuitable lover to Jerusalem, appearing topless at an Italian ball, that kind of thing.

The prince's claims about her personal hygiene can be seen to be a complete falsehood by travelling to Greenwich Park today where you'll find Princess Caroline's sunken bath (see page 320)

She had moved here to Montague House in 1801, only a few years after arriving in Britain, and when she left to live overseas in 1814, the prince, who loathed the sight of her, had the house flattened. His minions forgot, however, to remove the sunken bath, which gave the lie to the story about her personal filth. It was rediscovered in 1909.

The prince, meanwhile, was indulging in the ultimate barn conversion with his Brighton bit on the side (the Royal Pavilion in that city).

When he was being crowned **George IV** on 19 July 1820, Prinny had Caroline shut out of Westminster Abbey. This led to the amazing scene of a legal Queen of England being shut out of her own Coronation. The mob outside were clearly behind Caroline; it was no wonder the doors were barred.

Caroline's popularity with Londoners increased in proportion to Prinny's attempts to sideline her. When she died in the following year, on 7 August, said to be heartbroken at being so thoroughly rejected, the government tried to downplay her **funeral** and stop the procession going up through Kensington. The people wanted her to have a proper funeral, and they marched past Kensington Palace behind the coffin – yes, on the same route taken by the funeral of the recent Princess of Wales.

(CONTINUED OVERLEAF)

Clues to the Royal Family's weirdest story

When troops tried to stop the cortège at Hyde Park Corner, shots rang out and two working men were killed, but the crowd refused to flee and took her coffin through the middle of London to give her due honour, bearing it all the way to a ship, which took her to her homeland for interment. You can still see the gravestone of the two men who were killed – carpenter Richard Honey, 36, and bricklayer George Francis, 43 – at St Paul's Church in Hammersmith. It's certainly worth a look for its bitter wording.

The royal row continued even to her grave. The princess had requested her coffin bear the inscription 'Caroline of Brunswick, the injured Queen of England'. King George IV tried to prevent this being done as 'offensive' but the crowd of supporters insisted the inscription was added. The troops dared not interfere. Again there were fights between her supporters and her detractors at Harwich over the inscription.

Perhaps the oddest thing was that that sorry saga was so soon forgotten. George IV died in 1830 after a few more years of disgusting greed, alcoholism and sloth, slightly bonkers like his father but still wearing a locket with a picture of Mrs Fitzherbert inside it.

One last quotation that is attributed to George IV. On Napoleon's death in 1821, a courtier came to the king and said:

Great news, Sire, your greatest enemy is dead.

The king replied:

Is she, by God?

people had to pay for a watch patrol for the village where several murders, robberies and other crimes had recently been committed by gangs of young people completely out of control. Not at all like today, then.

KENSINGTON

STRANGE SECRETS BEHIND ALL THE BOLLARDS

It may be an odd thing to say in a guidebook, but here goes. Kensington High Street is a right bore. It's full of international shopping saddos who could be at the same tedious chain stores and burger bars in their home towns, rich Arabs, snobs in their 'Ringe Ravers' trying to be above the throng, and show-offs jogging or rollerblading with great difficulty through the crowds rather than making use of the acres of great parkland at both ends of the street. Harmless, but boring. Forget it.

But within yards of this street, if you plunge through the bollards and away from the crowd, are untold treasures and unique gems, wonderful pubs, eccentric buildings, quiet mews, strange towers, palatial mansions, secret gardens and a seriously cool Arab hall with a tinkling fountain. No crowds, all fascinating, all free, utterly unforgettable. It's there waiting for the in-the-know visitor to discover…

DARK SATANIC MILLS AND THE MOUTH OF HELL

This starts and finishes at High Street Kensington Tube, covers about 2½ miles and will take at least two hours with Campden Hill as an optional extension.

Leave **High Street Kensington** Tube station and turn right, past a few shops and turn right down **Derry Street**. On the left as we walk down this short street is the former **Barkers** department store, a fine Art Deco pile, which we can see the front of later, and whose upstairs accommodates the *Daily Mail, Mail on Sunday, Independent, the I, Metro* and *Evening Standard*,

---

Kensington Walk

part of the Fleet Street diaspora. On the right is the former **Derry & Toms** department store, which, besides having wonderful ornamentation at the top (we will see this more clearly later from the other side of the road), also has an almost incredible Spanish-style **roof garden** whose trees you can see poking over the parapet. For a free visit to these gardens of the sky, sign in at **99 Kensington High Street**, entrance in Derry Street.

We go through the bollards at the end of the road into **Kensington Square**, illustrating again how the atmosphere of London can utterly change in a few yards: here all is peace, historic charm and leafy gardens. This is one of the oldest squares in London, with some buildings dating back to the 1660 Restoration of the monarchy, and the remainder mostly from the 18th century. You're not allowed into the gardens. This square was laid out in open countryside, south of the country road linking Kensington Palace, as it now is, to the village of Hammersmith where one

could take a ferryboat across the Thames. There were no buildings at all to the south, east or west, except farms.

On the right as we enter the square is an old **brown plaque** – from before the oval, blue ones – to **Mrs Patrick Campbell**, the great actress and Bernard Shaw's star performer. Indeed, houses throughout the square bear one or more plaques to the great characters who have lived here.

Walking ahead to the right-hand corner of the square we see a **convent**, in full working order despite Henry VIII's best efforts to stamp the things out, and not (as local author William Makepeace Thackeray invented at this spot) a pub. The **Maria Assumpta Convent** is more massive than its frontage here suggests, with gardens going back a long way and including a grotto with a statue of the Virgin Mary. Unfortunately the gardens are just above a cutting holding the world's noisiest underground railway junction, as the trains on the Circle and District lines clatter and bong as they cross each other's tracks and make desperately for their respective tunnel mouths. It's not exactly the mouth of Hell, as Tennyson put it on another occasion, but in the days when steam engines belched smoke into pea-soup fogs, it might have seemed it. You can visit the relative paradise of the convent gardens on **London Garden Squares Day** (when you may also visit the remarkably uninteresting interior of Kensington Square outside the convent, with people playing lutes or weird Indonesian instruments or similar).

Going left along the far side of the square, past the first of many diplomatic buildings on the right, and the home of **John Stuart Mill** (1806–73), the heavyweight philosopher-economist who was one of the 'dark satanic Mills', I was going to jest, but whom should we find next door – taraa, taraa! – the composer who put those very words to music. Here at **No 17** lived **Sir Charles Parry** (1848–1918), whose setting of William Blake's *Jerusalem* to music has produced England's splendid non-royalist alternative national anthem.

I recall a story about one of John Stuart Mill's servants here accepting a manuscript from **Thomas Carlyle** (1795–1881), the somewhat boring Chelsea historian/philosopher, and assuming it to be a supply of fire-lighting paper, gradually burned the lot. I hope she was rewarded with a tip and a day off; pity she didn't burn more of his tedious stuff.

343

THACKERAY PLAQUERY

Reaching the far corner of the square and glancing left up **Young Street**, which runs back to the High Street up the other side of Barkers, we can see the other pub Thackeray mentions, the **Greyhound**. Not the one he knew, as that was blown to pieces, not by Irish terrorists but by equally deadly English gas fitters. Look out for his yellowbrick house on the left just before Barkers. (There's a story about Thackeray and this house. Some time after he'd left it, he was passing here with his American publisher friend J T Fields. Thackeray remarked to Fields: 'Down on your knees, you rogue, for here *Vanity Fair* was penned, and I will go down with you, for I have a high opinion of that little production myself.' Not vain, then.)

We're going straight ahead into **Thackeray Street**, a quiet street justly celebrated for having no connection with Thackeray, and about the only place round here where he didn't live or work. It harbours poky little odd shops of the kind the High Street once accommodated before chain stores took over. Here is an excellent little café, where I am astonished to be addressed in French by the staff.

The road has a few arty shops including one at the end of the road selling, apparently, obelisks. Eccentrically useless things, really, although the Obelisk Society, based in this area but not this shop, would not agree; they have an obelisk newsletter, sell obelisk mugs, meet at obscure obsolete obelisks to be obsequious. (*That's enough obfuscation, Ed.*) Bizarre.

KENSINGTON COURT, PALACE AND GARDENS

Going left at the end of the street, we encounter in **Kensington Court** the Black Forest gateau school of architecture – layered buildings with what looks like icing every few floors, an 1880 building speculation by Albert Grant MP. You can see why Hitler's bombers had such a hard job denting Kensington – they're massive and look difficult to demolish.

Continue right past the massive mansion blocks, and bear right at the end. Now we are in foreign territory, with the interesting combination of Antigua, Mongolia, Belarus and Azerbaijan **diplomatic missions** all in a row. I hope they have social evenings together; it's possible they aren't *that* diplomatic. The characters engraved in the brass plate of the Mongol horde (well, there are only a few really) are particularly elegant but you have to get close to see them. At the Kensington High Street end of the road, on the right at the corner, four massive black dragons hang on the building for no particular reason. Perhaps it makes the Mongolians feel at home. Isn't Heilong Jiang (Black Dragon River) on their border with China?

The building they are attached to is called the **Milestone Hotel**, and if you pop round the corner you can see why. An ancient milestone (not *that* ancient, in fact, as it is iron) says Hounslow $8^1/_2$, London $1^1/_2$. But surely we are in the heart of London – why does the milestone record it as being far away? As mentioned above, less than 300 years ago, the few houses of Kensington were isolated from London and reached only by crossing muddy wastes infested with highwaymen.

We go not towards London but left, back across Kensington Court's entrance and down to the pedestrian traffic lights. Ahead of us is a pub, the **Goat**, that has a tale of some of the most gruesome murders in living memory attached to it – the acid bath killings (see page 37).

But we cross over by the traffic lights and, going left on the far side, pause by the entrance to **Kensington Gardens** (spiritual home of Peter Pan, to whom there's a memorial here). Look into the quadrangle of grass between the High Street and Kensington Palace beyond the gilt gates at the far side. This was the scene of the mass mourning of Princess Diana (see page 356).

Carrying on past the entrance to the gardens, there's a gate with a long road down to the palace. The gate posts are adorned with a lion and unicorn holding the royal arms – the unicorn holding the motto of the Order of the Garter, the eccentric and ancient high order of chivalry based on a female undergarment. Real gas lights add to the atmosphere at night.

Don't go up this narrow road but carry on past the Royal Garden Hotel, with an excellent view of the Art Deco towers of **Barkers** store ahead. Turn right at the unmarked cobbled road, where there's a watchman in a green box. This is the discreet entrance to London's most exclusive road, Palace Green or **Kensington Palace Gardens** as it becomes. If you haven't got £50 million or so, don't bother house-hunting round here. In fact don't bother anyway, because the powers that be ensure that only sultans or kings (of other countries) or ambassadors get a toehold in this lovely road.

As you pass the gate, note the robo-bollards that protect the road from unauthorised vehicles, rising and falling as required to keep out suicide bombers. The first building on the left is the **Israeli embassy** and this serves as a reminder of how necessary such precautions are. It was blown up in 1994 and I remember, being in the Barkers building at the time, that the place shook as if hit with a massive demolition ball.

It would be better not to dwell on the security around this embassy today, but it is clearly formidable. The gentleman with a bulge in his pocket isn't necessarily pleased to see you, as Mae West pointed out. Don't make a sudden lunge for the Mars bar inside your jacket. It's a strange thought but by walking the length of this road, you will be on the security video footage of a dozen countries.

345

On the right, **Kensington Palace** comes into view through the railings. If you don't see bicycles chained to these railings, it is because this practice is thought unseemly for a royal palace. Militant gay activist Peter Tatchell, who likes to be a pain in the thingy to the establishment, was, for once, not seeking confrontation when he chained his bike up here in 2001. However, when he returned he found it even more padlocked. He had to seek out the palace staff, and I'm told this surreal conversation ensued:

Palace staff: *Her Majesty does not want bicycles chained up to her palaces.*

Peter Tatchell: *There's no notice saying that.*

Palace staff: *Her Majesty does not want notices on her palaces' railings.*

Posh shops and pubs

At the far end of this road, with its gorgeous plane trees and huge mansions, is Notting Hill Gate and Bayswater, but we go left opposite the solar-powered parking meter into the passageway with the two wooden bollards.

At the end we reach **Kensington Church Street** and a good view of **St Mary Abbot's** spire, said to be the tallest on a London parish church.

We cross over by the lights and turn left down the far side, noting the name of **Holland Street**. The many references to Holland around here are connections not with the country but with the place in Norfolk, where the family based at Holland House stately home have their roots. Going down to the corner of Kensington High Street, don't miss an intriguing detail on the opposite corner – the sign of a long disappeared pub, the Civet Cat.

Turning right on to the High Street we can at last get a good view of the superb 1930s detail on the frieze on the front of **Barkers** across the road, showing the latest steam engines, aeroplanes and similar symbols of modernity, now charmingly dated. Plus the whole building looks like a 1930s radio set. You half expect these vertical windows to light up with forgotten station names such as Hilversum and Daventry.

Walking a bit further down, one can see the equally marvellous but totally different detail on the old **Derry & Toms** building, the other side of Derry Street, showing similar scenes of industry plus, high up, signs of the zodiac. From here you can also see a glimpse of the astounding roof gardens mentioned when we passed this on the other side earlier.

We go right up **Kensington Church Walk** and, passing some peaceful gardens, do a right and then a left by the church's west front. As you turn left on the path the building on our right is a school – don't miss the charming figures of a blue-coated boy and girl, which appear further along the frontage and were typical of a London school of 200 years ago.

We go on up a Dickensian lane past some odd shops and go left at the end. We are now on Holland Street again. Soon we pass the low-key cottages of Gordon Place – we could be 100 miles from the High Street bustle, couldn't we? On the right is the excellent **Elephant and Castle** pub. Unspoiled, good ales, good food, no carpet or jukebox, this presses all the right buttons – for me, at any rate.

Plus, if you like this kind of thing, on the walls in the snug at the far left there's a great collection of *Evening Standard* front pages of the past, including of course Diana's funeral. More fun is the 'exclusive' engraving of the Queen's Coronation dress, and a particularly professional piece of journalism about the first dog in orbit. Clearly the hacks had no idea what the spacecraft looked like – the drawing was hopeless – and only about three facts to go on, but they filed a whole hysterically excited page nonetheless. Brilliant.

We follow Holland Street, past Drayton Mews, which were once where the horses and servants for the great houses lived and now are most sought-after and respectable, but retain their original, cobbled and unpretentious appearance.

On the right, as we approach the ghastly red-brick **town hall** at the end, don't miss the medallion to the Virgin Mary (I think) high up on a gable. It's positioned at exactly the height where a fire insurance mark would have been in the old days (gaining the protection of the private fire brigades) but I suspect this one was invoking a higher authority.

At the end as we come out on the right, is musician **Sir Charles Stanford's house**, a rare survivor of old, low-rise Kensington before the march of the monstrous mansion blocks which now dominate.

At the five-way junction ahead, we are, ultimately, going straight ahead, down the **Duchess of Bedford's Walk**. If you wish to do this straight away, skip the next section; do have a look, however, because you may fancy a drink in the pub, and the eccentrics who have lived here are intriguing.

CAMPDEN HILL: STRANGE OLD COWS, A MAHARAJAH, A REAL PAINE

This now extremely well-to-do area has in recent centuries contained some very odd properties and strange characters. Indeed, it still does. It also boasts a little gem of a pub. A brief and rewarding stroll up this hill to take a peek at this odd district will take only 15 minutes there and back, excluding however many hours you stop in the pub.

So going right, up **Campden Hill Road** on its left side, we can see on the right the space known as Observatory Gardens, opposite the college on the left. The view of trees and mansion blocks from this pavement is frequently painted by artists, and frame it with your outstretched arms to imagine why.

Going on up Campden Hill Road, we find the **Windsor Castle**, a completely un-messed-up 200-year-old pub without moronic jukeboxes, one-armed bandits, taped music, carpet or any of that nonsense, but original wood interior and a roaring open fire in the winter, and cool ale in the summer. Excellent. The pub's name comes from the fact that you could see Windsor Castle from the upstairs windows before other buildings got in the way. Allegedly. After seven pints you can see the Statue of Liberty. The area is thick with celebs: Madonna and John Cleese have been seen here, for example.

Another strange story is that a beer drinker once traded a human skeleton here to settle his booze bill. The skeleton was that of **Thomas Paine** (1737–1809), the philosopher and author of *Rights of Man* who died in America. The beer drinker was the son of William Cobbett, the outspoken MP and social reformer who wrote *Rural Rides* in the early 19th century. It seems Cobbett had earlier had Paine's bones shipped back to England but his wayward son had little respect for them. It is probably

true, for there's another record of Paine's stuffed head turning up in various places. Bit of a Paine really, but now we've got used to London beer costing an arm and a leg.

Whether you go into the pub or not, take a peek down **Peel Street** just past it and to the right. There's a surprisingly long view across London with the Telecom Tower showing how high we are here.

If you took the next left at **Aubrey Walk** – and I'm instead proposing turning back to the Duchess of Bedford's Walk here – you could walk the length of that to discover a house with a fascinating history. **Aubrey House** is a relic of the days when Campden Hill was an isolated hamlet well outside London. This was a country estate.

Lady Mary Coke, the highly eccentric courtier, diarist and author, lived here from 1767 to 1788, this being her country house (she had another in what she considered London). Her cow, Miss Pelham, escaped one day.

She wrote:

Miss Pelham took a frisk this morning, got out of my grounds and went nearly as far as London before I heard of her. I believe she thinks my place too retired, for she was found among a great herd of cattle.

She was furious when one day the hunt streamed across her garden and disappeared over the fence into Holland House's grounds. Foxes, however, as we shall see, have a great connection with Holland House.

Lady Mary Coke was for a time a frequent visitor to nearby Kensington Palace where she would play cards with Princess Amelia, but the splendour of the court faded with the death of George II; royalty moved away, leaving it a dusty shell for many years. Lady Mary attended Kensington Church where she frequently and fiercely criticised the sermons.

Daughter of John, Duke of Argyll, she was described in one history as 'this termagent lady'. She had travelled Europe causing ructions wherever she went for no apparent reason.

She claimed to have been driven out of Austria by Empress Maria Theresa and out of France by Queen Marie Antoinette. She started a quarrel with Prime Minister Horace Walpole, who said she 'had a hundred distresses abroad which did not weight a penny together'.

She claimed the Duke of York, brother of George III, was in love with her, but as Walpole said:

She is like Don Quixote who went in search of adventures, and when she found none, imagined them.

In 1807 she moved to Chiswick, where she had bought the now vanished Manor House, and died four years later 'in a wonderfully uncomfortable manner' half stuck in a recess, surrounded by 'many decrepit pets' and vast heaps of rubbish.

Just to the east of Aubrey House stood **Moray Lodge**, built in 1817, where great men and strange goings-on coincided.

In the 1860s wealthy, art-loving bachelor Arthur J Lewis used to hold entertainments here, plying his male friends with oysters and beer, with theatricals and music all evening. The calibre of guests was such that they included Thackeray (who as we have seen lived nearby), Dickens, Trollope, Arthur Sullivan, George du Maurier, Tattersall (as in horses) and John Millais, the painter who ran off with Mrs Ruskin. The conversation and wit of such illustrious company must have been sparkling: in fact they mostly spent the afternoons drinking beer, and playing billiards and croquet.

The house comes to notice again at the time of the coronation of Edward VII at the beginning of the 20th century. With nearly all the princes and potentates of the world coming to London, finding somewhere to put them all was difficult. The Maharajah of Jaipur was more difficult than most to accommodate, as he had a retinue of 200, and as a devout Hindu needed his own cow and could drink no water that had come through a pipe. Moray Lodge, now empty, was ideal, possessing its own well and gardens big enough to hold a cow and sheds for the staff. Later, in 1940, the balloon literally went up for the Blitz, as some of the barrage balloons were launched from its grounds. Moray Lodge was demolished in 1955. We return down Campden Hill Road to Duchess of Bedford's Walk, now on your right.

Across Holland Park to artistic heights

Going down **Duchess of Bedford's Walk**, there are more massive mansion blocks on the right, and not very attractive ones either. Very Kensington, they look more like government ministries than homes.

At the end of this walk we go straight ahead through the bollards (the emblem of Kensington, really, a load of old bollards) across a path (watch out for whizzing cyclists) and into **Holland Park**. The stately home job on the right is only a part of what was once there, the remainder having been bombed to hell in World War II. Built in 1605 for a courtier of James I, it became **Holland House** in 1768 when Baron Holland bought it. Under his famous son, **Charles James Fox** (1749–1806), it became the social centre of Whig Party intrigue with many a great statesman coming here.

Holland House was bombed severely in 1940 and only the east wing and the arcades remind us of what a splendid Jacobean pile this must have been. Fox was the family surname, not the title, and when Charles James Fox was offered a peerage in later life he said:

> I will not close my politics in that foolish way.

At the white arch ahead we go left and downhill fast into the artistic world of **Melbury Road**. We come out on to a bit of road called Ilchester Place, but go straight on down to Melbury Road and turn sharp right into what was once a rather fascinating artistic colony.

A mad Gothic fantasy and the upper crust

Here in **Melbury Road** are a pair of extraordinary houses, the weirder being the **Tower House**, on the bend ahead, a six-bedroomed Gothic fantasy which Led Zeppelin's Jimmy Page bought in 1974 (beating, it is said, David Bowie). It has a conical tower, gargoyle, fabulous stained glass and a dark, castle-like interior. The vendor was hell-raising actor Richard

Harris, and the buyer had a great interest – academic, no doubt – in black magic, etc. And I don't mean the chocolates.

It was built by outrageous Victorian architect/designer **William Burges** (1827–81) for himself. He was the father of mad Gothic revival extravagances, and reshaped Cardiff Castle for the third Marquess of Bute with quite incredible embellishments, and built the Bavarian fantasy of Castell Coch nearby. He loved high Gothic but didn't want it to be taken too seriously. Gothic could be fun as well as 'churchy', he argued:

> *There are some people who … consider medieval art as eminently ecclesiastical, and therefore profoundly serious to be approached with caution, forgetting that mankind has been very much the same in every age, and that our ancestors joked and laughed as much as we do.*

Next door (before the Tower House on the same side) was at the time of writing the home of flamboyant film maker, **Michael Winner** (b 1935), a deeply eccentric man (praised elsewhere for his memorials to policemen who were killed on duty) who has lived here since 1947.

The director and producer has said he has 87 telephones in this building. He has a Rolls-Royce, is probably worth many millions, and owns quite a few works of art, yet he cheerfully confesses to opening toothpaste tubes at the wrong end, when almost empty, to get a bit more out. He came in for some stick from the *Daily Mail*, at the other end of Kensington High Street, for having a girlfriend in 2000 who was claiming state benefits; in other ways, however, he can be extraordinarily generous, helping out young actors behind the scenes. He once said he doesn't want to live in a tolerant country but an intolerant one, vociferously backing the Tories while they were on top in the 1980s and then switching to Labour just in time for their landslide.

Mr Winner, maker of such successes as *Death Wish* (along with a few not quite so successful movies), gets credited, bizarrely, in certain productions as Arnold Crust Jr. Or just Arnold Crust. No doubt he's the toast of the film industry.

This is not to trivialise the rich heritage of Melbury Road, centre of an area of rich Victorian artists from a time when artists were not poor and struggling but had the mega-rich beating a path to their doors and were heaped with honours – even a peerage for one of the 'Melbury Road set' – by the art-loving establishment. Thus you will see wonderful studio buildings all around this area, with vast acres of glass facing the necessary north (no direct sun, but bags of light).

Winner's own house was built by Victorian painter **Sir Luke Fildes**, who included an immodestly monogrammed weathervane. Mr Winner suggested to one interviewer that this was 'a little vane', a rather good pun that evidently passed over the interviewer's head, who wrote it as 'vain'. The dates on the blue plaque are a little awry; they should read 1877 to 1924. Edward VII sat in the studio here for a formal portrait, such was Fildes's standing, and described it as 'one of the finest rooms in London' – and he had, after all, seen a few rather fine ones. More recent sitters – in Mr Winner's cinema – have included Lauren Bacall, Marlon Brando, Michael Caine, Charles Bronson, Jeremy Irons and Anthony Hopkins.

Going on down Melbury Road there are more studios and plaques to artists on the left, and reaching the busy **Addison Road** there's a fine studio house on the opposite side, but avoid crossing the busy road and go left and left again into Holland Park Road, doubling back east into peaceful territory once more.

A MOORISH PARADISE AND SENSUAL WOMEN

Here, on the left, is **Leighton House**, the ultimate in fantasy studio-homes in the artists' colony around here. A half-forgotten gem in London from the same era as exotic arabists like Richard Burton (whose strange Arab tent tomb is featured on page 70), this was the home of the great Victorian artist **Frederic, Lord Leighton** (1830–96). The creator of the familiar *Flaming June* picture lived at this quite extraordinary house, such an unexpected find in this quiet road. Note the Islamic crescent moon on the dome. Here one can experience the heady incense in the exotic, bejewelled Arab hall where Leighton's unique collection of Moorish tilework is brilliantly employed, complete with tinkling fountain and the lofty dome once described as the eighth wonder of the world.

Lord Lloyd-Webber and Lady Lucinda Lambton have been among great fans of what the latter rightly calls 'the secret heart of Kensington'. Leighton, whose career received a huge boost when Queen Victoria bought one of his pictures, was made a peer – the only artist so honoured – shortly before his death in 1896. I sometimes wonder what separates his lifelike nudes, sensually clad in soft fabrics, from soft porn, and of course the answer is his skill. But would he have received as much interest at the time if he had painted sunflowers? As it was, he was the darling of the establishment, although surely not rated among the top ten artists of history today.

Continuing up Holland Park Road, turn right into Melbury Road and cross Kensington High Street by the traffic lights on your right, turning right at the other side and then left into **Edwardes Square** (or rather the approach road to it). Before plunging down here, take a look at the grand sweep of **Earl's Terrace** to your left with its lodges at each end. This terrace, recently restored to provide *bijou* homes with underground parking for the mega-rich, is inextricably linked to the strange story of Edwardes Square.

THE FRENCH INVADERS AND THE BATTLE OF EDWARDES SQUARE

One of the most enduring urban myths about Kensington, still circulating almost 200 years after local word of mouth started it, is the story of how Edwardes Square, a rather charming backwater off the High Street, was built by a Frenchman with an eye to housing the French army after they had invaded during the Napoleonic Wars. Of course, dreams of invasion were sunk during the Battle of Trafalgar (1805) and the Battle of Waterloo (1815), but the story never was true, as the plaque screwed to the charming garden lodge on the far south side of this agreeably low-rise square records.

A French trader from Hammersmith, **Louis Changeur**, *was* involved in around 1811 in a speculative development, Earl's Terrace, which was the first part of Edwardes Square to be built, opposite the gate to Holland House. With the French – Boney's men – being the bogey men of the era, that was enough to start the rumour mill. But he soon went bankrupt and was out of the picture. Not that it stopped the pub at the southeast corner, the rather good **Scarsdale** (great *cappuccini* and recommended food, good beer but not over-generous with the ginger beer shandies) from going along with the Battle of Waterloo yarn for many years.

In fact, if you had stood on the north side of Edwardes Square very late at night on 5 November 1805, you would have heard the sounds of hooves and the rattling wheels of a carriage being driven as fast as was possible through the swirling fog eastwards along Kensington High Street. This sound was the death knell for Napoleon's invasion hopes, and ultimately the end of his empire.

The post chaise contained one **Royal Navy Lieutenant John Lepenotière** who had ridden non-stop for nearly 37 hours from the fast schooner *Pickle* in which he had landed at Falmouth after a nine-day, 1,000-mile dash by sea. He carried the momentous news that the Royal

Navy had smashed the combined French/Spanish fleets at Trafalgar, and that Admiral Lord Nelson was dead. Lieutenant Lepenotière had changed horses 21 times on his journey – the last time at Hounslow, a few miles west of here. True, the Napoleonic Wars were to carry on for another ten years, but as with Hitler and the Battle of Britain over a century later, the continental despot had failed to deal with Britain (and then stupidly attacked Russia), and had thus signed his own regime's death warrant. The hooves in the fog were beating out the rhythm:

Europe will be free again, Europe will be free again.

Oddly there *was*, though totally forgotten today, a **Battle of Edwardes Square**, but it took place 100 years later, in 1908.

The square itself, finished by 1819, had its own Act of Parliament and its own laws, which included penalties for the beating of carpets outside the house and for the exercising of horses. Residents also had to clean the footpaths outside their houses by 9am; failure to do so could result in a fine or three months' hard labour. Not unreasonable when you think about it.

In 1910 the leases on the houses were due to expire and a speculative firm, Allen Bros, bought the freehold with the aim of flattening Earl's Terrace and building over the garden in the centre of Edwardes Square, thus increasing the rent, and pushing out the remaining tenants.

The residents waited until the firm tried to shut off the gates into the gardens, which they sneakily did while the chairman of the gardens committee was away. He was told and telegraphed back:

Keep possession of remaining gate; take gate off hinges if necessary; employ watchmen day and night to guard.

Every day Allen Bros put up barricades to shut off the gardens. Every day the residents pulled them down. The matter went to the courts and the residents won. It went to appeal and they won again. It went to the House of Lords in January 1912 and they won a third and final time.

This was Edwardes Square's finest hour. A 50-foot-high bonfire was made with 40 cartloads of timber, soaked in flammable oil. Decorative lamps were strung all around and some of the residents proceeded round the square with a pipe band, everyone else leaning out of their windows banging gongs, saucepans, baking trays and celebrating their success in saving the square.

After that atypical display of noisy emotion, Edwardes Square returned to its respectable diffidence. Yes, the people of Kensington had rushed to the barricades, but only to make their point politely and firmly with good humour. No bayonets, blazing braziers or republican bare-breasted women here. Or beating carpets outside the house.

A CANNON-BALL FROM HELL AND GOD'S JEWELLERY BOX

Talking about battles, there's a link with one of the worst British military disasters ever (and by God we've had a few of them) in the centre of the square. If you come here on London Garden Squares Day (see page 11), when there'll be access to the rather lovely private gardens in the square, with teas and musicians playing amidst the shrubbery, you'll find a **cannon-ball from Balaclava**. It was brought here as part of the Victorian fascination with the Charge of the Light Brigade, a monstrous cock-up which – involving as it did, massive heroic and completely pointless sacrifice – was just the sort of thing the British love, or loved. Due to bungled orders, on 25 October 1854 the Light Brigade charged straight into the Russian guns, knowing they would be massacred. As the cannon-balls cut through the ranks, the horses and men re-formed time and time again.

It made a rather good poem and a film. You probably recall the lines:

Their's not to reason why
Their's but to do and die
Into the valley of death
Rode the six hundred...
Into the jaws of Death
Into the mouth of Hell.

Precisely the sort of mawkish morbid melodrama Victorians adored (look at the pleasure they took in the deaths of children in their literature). A more dispassionate judgement came from a French general, who said:

C'est magnifique, mais ce n'est pas la guerre.

– It's magnificent, but it's not war.

The Edwardes in Edwardes Square came, like a lot of Edwardes still do, from Wales. **William Edwardes** (1712–1801), MP for Haverfordwest, owned farmland stretching from what is now Kensington High Street south to Earl's Court and nearly to Fulham Road. He, the first Baron Kensington (an Irish title, oddly), along with the second baron, attempted to make money by property speculation, such as Edwardes Square.

One more thing about Edwardes Square: its blue plaques tell us a lot about the shortcomings of blue plaques. See page 151 for that story.

Having noted the studios and superb brickwork opposite the lodge, on the south side (some completed in 2006), leave Edwardes Square by the southeast (far left) corner and turn left immediately after the Scarsdale into a path known as **Earl's Walk**. Along here a couple of Indian bean trees flower spectacularly at certain times, even though one is positioned inconveniently a few inches in front of someone's door. At the end of the road, desist from illegal carpet-beating, as Kensington police station is on our left.

We cross the road to **Abingdon Villas** opposite and plug on down here, passing the Abingdon restaurant on the right at one crossroads and the **Britannia** pub (recommended) up on the left at the next. We go straight on, however, and then left up **Iverna Gardens** where the gorgeous London plane trees grow at a slight slant as if they were growing in a canyon, which indeed they are. Here in the quiet square at the end is a charming building – **St Arkis Armenian Church**. This is like a perfect little jewellery box. God's hand, one feels, might come down at any minute, seize the stubby spire of this perfectly symmetrical building and lift off the lid to reveal all kinds of treasures. Quite superb, built in 1922 by Mews & Davis architects; don't miss the Armenian inscription on one of the entrances (in English over another).

Going to the end of Iverna Court, as the road becomes beyond the little square, we're in **Wright's Lane**. Turn left back into the High Street, turn right and the Tube home is just on the right.

COMPLEX DIANA AND THE UNPALATABLE TRUTH

Sadly, we have been deprived of Kensington's most intriguing resident – Princess Diana (1961–97). She was more complex than her billions of adoring fans – worshippers, frankly, at some points – ever wanted to believe.

I recall her sitting at the traffic lights here in the crowded High Street in her open-top Mercedes preening herself around the time she claimed she wanted less media attention, then turning around and coming back down the busy street. Or taking her sons to McDonald's (it burgers belief, one might say – can you think of a more calculated insult to Prince Charles and all his organic talk-to-vegetables stuff than feeding his sons a Big Mac with fries and Coke?). Or phoning one of the newspapers where I worked to guarantee publicity for one of her 'anonymous' midnight visits to a hospital. Or steering reporters to the friends who would give her side of the story in her marital battles.

On one typically bizarre occasion she was pursuing her vendetta against the nanny of her sons, Tiggy Legge-Bourke. She instructed her staff to provide a quote for a certain newspaper calling Tiggy (are these people grown-ups with names like this?) 'thoughtless, foolish and idiotic' because she had been seen drinking champagne with Prince William, then just 14. Diana was fiercely criticised by the other Press for making such a bitchy attack, so Diana's aides phoned the first newspaper editor back.

They complained: *How could you do that? It's totally untrue.*

The bemused editor replied: *But you know it's true. You told me yourself two days ago!*

Diana had forgotten, or chosen to forget, and was furious. The aides had to follow orders, however insane.

Of course she was also a force for great good in making concern about AIDS respectable, hugging the victims and not treating them like lepers (and the same with lepers), and taking the landmines issue to the world's sitting-rooms via TV as nobody else could have done. Her sincerity shone through on so many occasions. But it just wasn't that simple.

People wanted her to be a sexy version of Mother Teresa – who died five days later and received a fraction of the publicity. But she wasn't a saint; she was a modern, mixed-up woman. She died not rushing to some child's surgery or to a landmine or AIDS victim but on yet another huge freebie holiday (the sixth or seventh of that year) with a rich and unsuitable playboy, and because their stupid, irresponsible response to people taking pictures was to drive through a concrete tunnel at perhaps 90mph while not wearing seatbelts. The bodyguard who did put one on survived. Typically, Diana had let it be known that she'd arrived in Paris and yet was outraged when the paparazzi – I wouldn't defend their low-life actions for a minute – followed her.

She hated the pressure of the publicity yet could not do without it, for she was as addicted to adoration as the world seemed addicted to her. Do you remember the time she said she would be dropping out of the public eye to lead a reclusive life, with all that head-tilted-on-one-side and doe-eyed sadness? It was a good speech, which attracted much sympathy, and she was probably sincere at the time. How long did it last? Years? Months? No, it was just a few *weeks* before her aides were phoning the Press and tipping them off about her next action.

The Press used her and she used them. The public despised the media yet at the same time lapped up the coverage, buying magazines with her image on the front by the millions and reading every word they could find about her in the newspapers. Woe betide any paper that ignored the latest Diana story: its sales would fall through the floor. Who was using whom?

Like many people, I despised the paparazzi at the lower end of the business and as a working journalist I'm deeply ashamed of those who printed sneaky pictures. (Remember the shots in the gym, from a secret camera above Diana's exercise machine? Why stop there, why not have a toilet cam, for God's sake? I hope I would have walked out rather than handle those gym pictures.)

But who was buying millions of papers when an exclusive picture was announced, or reading every word of an exclusive interview with someone who betrayed her confidence – the same hypocritical people who condemned it all. Thanks to global TV and Press picture transmission, more people knew more of Diana's face and her life than *anyone before in history*, and I'm not exaggerating. It was like the adoration of Eva Peron but involving nearly the whole globe, not just one small nation.

True, parts of the Western world were obsessed with Jackie Kennedy just before her husband was killed in 1963, but look how unsophisticated the media were then. One picture a month in most papers, with just a few respectful words. No one would have dared suggest JFK was a lying philanderer, which we now know he was, and no one publicly took apart his marriage as they did Diana's, albeit with her help.

The Diana phenomenon was totally different. Many papers had pictures of Diana *every day*, and features thousands of words long analysing her relationships. Her picture was familiar on TV news in China, Fiji, Arkansas, New Zealand, Japan, Peru, everywhere. It was an inexplicable phenomenon, a kind of global insanity where everyone wanted to believe in a saintly, beautiful superperson who didn't really exist. It couldn't have gone on.

As I prepare this edition of this book, another attractive, slim young royal slips out of a side gate at Kensington Palace and I spot her popping into the same shops the woman who should have been her mother-in-law visited only 15 years before. One doesn't have to be a royalist to wish her much better luck...

A SCENE THAT MUST BAFFLE CONCEPTION OF THOSE WHO DID NOT WITNESS IT

Let me describe the scene in the square of grass between Kensington Palace and the High Street at midnight, in the days between Diana's death and her funeral.

It was quite amazing, an experience I'll never, ever forget, and recalling it, writing this book, put me in mind of the day Nelson was mourned at Greenwich nearly 200 years ago. I quote *The Times* man in that case saying the scene '*must baffle conception of those who did not witness it*' and this is truly how it seemed that warm September night, but I'll try to unbaffle you.

The reason I went to see the scene at midnight (twice) was because I was working at a nearby newspaper and my shift ended thereabouts. We knew from the words on the pages before us that something truly extraordinary was happening, so we walked up the road to have a look.

The sight that greeted us was something out of the Middle Ages, or out of a great religious film with tens of thousands of extras. Hundreds upon hundreds of people were filing slowly up the road from the Tube and bus stops bearing flowers, cards, messages, and pictures of Diana. No one was talking. Some were, or clearly had been, crying.

The scene in that great grass quadrangle was astonishing. It was packed with tens of thousands of people silently queueing to pay homage to their dead princess: old people, young parents with small children, teenagers.

They shuffled forward in a silent throng, a great line of people five or six deep moving down one path, and leaving in a similar column that must have held many hundreds more. Everywhere there were candles, cards and messages tied to trees, railings, or anything people could find. Oddly, many of the trees had small teddy bears tied to them, I remember, as if a child had been lost. Posters of Diana with heartfelt messages, amateurish poems of obviously strong emotions.

But most amazing was the sea of flowers you could not possibly cross near the great gilt railings of the palace that was her home. In itself this sea of bouquets, messages, candles burning in jars, and tributes seemed to cover hundreds of feet, although my memory may be wrong – the emotion was so over-powering, you could not help but be moved. The far gates were still in the distance when your feet lapped this floral sea of welling emotion.

This outpouring of silent love and mass devotion was perhaps like a pilgrimage to a great medieval saint's shrine, one where touching the relics would lead to miracles; more accurately, however, it was a moment of unquestioning love and devotion by thousands of pilgrims. Amid those thousands of people, the intense feeling was magnified until it was a tangible, irresistible force sweeping around you. It was amazing. You could *not* be neutral.

If at times I comment on Diana's life and death negatively in this book – because I'm trying to tell it how it was, not how we wanted it to be – I don't in any way doubt or belittle the strength of many good people's feelings at that moment. It was an emotional flood-tide that rose to an awful point when the funeral bier left these gates, turning left along the bottom of Hyde Park and proceeding to Westminster Abbey amid quite incredible scenes as thousands of people howled and wept with sorrow.

There was the awe-inspiring moment when her brave sons, her brother, her former husband and her father-in-law fell in behind the coffin. There was that peak of the surging, irresistible tide when Earl Spencer gave his emotional outburst in Westminster Abbey and we had a frightening glimpse, for a second, of what a revolutionary uprising would be like. If he had called the angry crowd listening outside the Abbey to burst in and lynch the Windsors, it is impossible to say where it would all have ended. Such was the anger and grief, and love and hatred in that one explosive moment in history.

I felt a little of that anger directed against myself on a bus in Kensington High Street that week when a colleague unwisely referred to something about our work on a newspaper and one of the bus passengers turned to us and said 'You killed her, you bastards', referring to the paparazzi who chased Diana to her death in that Paris tunnel. 'Get off the bloody bus.' As we did so, shame-faced and frankly a little scared, the bus seethed with the collective fury of the lynch mob.

Then, thankfully, the moment had gone. The cathartic effect of the beautiful funeral did its magic, the tide turned, and the anger ebbed away as powerfully as it had flooded in, laying bare deeper, more lasting emotions. It was quite, quite amazing and people said that nothing like this had ever happened before.

But, astoundingly, it had – almost *exactly the same story,* here in this very same Kensington High Street, with another tragic Princess of Wales, another scene at the Abbey, another angry funeral, less than two centuries before and then totally forgotten about, as I recount in the Hammersmith section (see page 338).

But that's London for you. One amazing story after another, in layers going back thousands of years, waiting to be rediscovered. What a city!

INDEX

INDEX

INDEX

INDEX